D0792652

WEST'S LAW SCHOOL
ADVISORY BOARD

JESSE H. CHOPER
Professor of Law,
University of California, Berkeley

JOSHUA DRESSLER
Professor of Law, Michael E. Moritz College of Law,
The Ohio State University

YALE KAMISAR
Professor of Law, University of San Diego
Professor of Law, University of Michigan

MARY KAY KANE
Professor of Law, Chancellor and Dean Emeritus,
University of California,
Hastings College of the Law

LARRY D. KRAMER
Dean and Professor of Law, Stanford Law School

JONATHAN R. MACEY
Professor of Law, Yale Law School

ARTHUR R. MILLER
University Professor, New York University
Professor of Law Emeritus, Harvard University

GRANT S. NELSON
Professor of Law, Pepperdine University
Professor of Law Emeritus, University of California, Los Angeles

A. BENJAMIN SPENCER
Associate Professor of Law,
Washington & Lee University School of Law

JAMES J. WHITE
Professor of Law, University of Michigan

INVESTMENT ADVISER REGULATION

IN A NUTSHELL

By

JEFFREY J. HAAS
Professor of Law
New York Law School

STEVEN R. HOWARD
Adjunct Professor of Law
New York Law School

THOMSON
—★— ™
WEST

Mat #40537616

© 2008 Thomson/West
      610 Opperman Drive
      St. Paul, MN 55123
      1–800–313–9378

Printed in the United States of America

ISBN: 978–0–314–17265–5

TEXT IS PRINTED ON 10% POST CONSUMER RECYCLED PAPER

*To Peter, who reteaches me about the world
each day. Happy 5th birthday, buddy!*

J.J.H.

*For Margaux and Monique Howard,
Mom and Dad*

S.R.H.

*

PREFACE

This book is designed for those interested in learning the fundamentals of investment adviser regulation as set forth primarily in the Investment Advisers Act of 1940 and the rules and regulations promulgated by the Securities and Exchange Commission thereunder. In particular, it is targeted towards investment advisers and their chief compliance officers. However, those associated with mutual funds, hedge funds, private equity funds and collateralized debt obligation (CDO) funds will likely find it useful as well.

Investment adviser regulation has changed significantly over the last few years, and it is likely to be a moving target going forward. In particular, the Securities and Exchange Commission has attempted to regulate advisers to hedge funds and other private investment funds, but has had only limited success. This effort likely will continue, as Congress and the various states, in addition to the SEC, become involved to varying degrees.

We endeavor to put the most current and accurate information available in this book. Accordingly, we welcome any suggestions and comments that could improve on its contents. Please feel free to e-mail us at the addresses below with those suggestions or comments.

Many provided assistance with this book. We gratefully acknowledge New York Law School's support through Summer research stipends and the encouragement provided by Dean Rick Matasar and Associate Dean Stephen Ellmann. We would like to thank Tom Majewski, Jonathan Goldstein, Curtis Stefanak, Fred Schmidt, David Dami, Brent Friedman, Alicja Biskupska and Won Kyung Chang for their substantive comments and support. Finally, we would like to thank our Summer research assistants, Joe Masi, Matt Baum, Sara Lustig and Bobbie Semkova, for their assistance and dedication.

JEFFREY J. HAAS
New York, New York
E-mail: jhaas@nyls.edu

STEVEN R. HOWARD
New York, New York
E-mail: steven.howard@hotmail.com

OUTLINE

Page

PREFACE --- V
TABLE OF AUTHORITIES -------------------------------- XXV
TABLE OF STATUTES AND RULES --------------------- XXXIII
ABBREVIATIONS --------------------------------------- LIII

I. INTRODUCTION

Sec.
1. Historical Overview ----------------------------- 1
   A. Legislative Response to Crash of 1929 ------------------------------------ 1
   B. Evolution of the Advisers Act ------------ 3

II. WHO IS AN INVESTMENT ADVISER?

2. Introduction ------------------------------------- 9
3. Definition of "Investment Adviser" --------- 10
   A. Three Elements ------------------------------ 10
      (1) Advice Concerning Securities ------- 11
      (2) "In the Business" --------------------- 13
      (3) Compensation -------------------------- 15
   B. Definitional Exclusions ------------------- 16
      (1) Banks, Bank Holding Companies and Savings Associations ---------- 17
      (2) Lawyers, Accountants, Engineers and Teachers ------------------------ 19

Sec.
3. Definition of "Investment Adviser"—Continued
   - (3) Certain Brokers and Dealers 21
     - a. Generally................................ 21
       - 1. Exchange Act Registration.. 22
       - 2. "Solely Incidental"............ 23
       - 3. "Special Compensation"..... 26
     - b. Foreign Broker–Dealers 29
     - c. Registered Representatives of a Broker–Dealer 30
     - d. Availability of Other Exclusions 32
   - (4) Publishers of Bona Fide Publications of General and Regular Circulation 35
   - (5) Government Securities Advisers ... 42
   - (6) Nationally Recognized Statistical Rating Organizations 42
   - (7) Other Persons Excluded by the SEC Pursuant to Statutory Authority 43
   - C. Governmental Entities.................... 44
4. Exemption From Registration 44
   - A. Intrastate Advisers....................... 45
   - B. Advisers to Insurance Companies Only...................................... 46
   - C. Private Investment Advisers............. 46
     - (1) "Fewer than 15 Clients" 47
       - a. General Rules on Counting Clients 47
       - b. Special Rules on Counting Clients 49

Sec.
4. Exemption From Registration—Continued
    (2) "Holding Itself Out" Generally to
        the Public ---------------------------- 50
    (3) Registered Investment Companies
        and Business Development
        Companies ---------------------------- 51
  D. Charitable Organizations ----------------- 52
  E. Church Plans ------------------------------- 53
  F. Commodity Trading Advisers ------------ 53

III. FEDERAL AND STATE AUTHORITY OVER INVESTMENT ADVISERS

5. Regulatory Scheme ------------------------------- 55
  A. Dual Regulatory Scheme (Pre–1997) --- 55
  B. Bifurcated Regulatory Scheme (1997
    to Present) ----------------------------- 55
    (1) Federal Registration and Regula-
        tion ----------------------------------- 56
      a. Mandatory Federal Registra-
         tion----------------------------------- 56
      b. Optional Federal Registration-- 58
      c. "Assets Under Management" -- 60
      d. State Authority Over SEC–
         Registered Investment Ad-
         visers ------------------------------ 61
    (2) State Registration and Regula-
        tion ----------------------------------- 62
      a. Registration ------------------------- 62
      b. SEC Authority Over State–
         Registered Investment Ad-
         visers ------------------------------ 64

Page

Sec.

5. Regulatory Scheme—Continued
  (3) Transitioning From State Regis-
      tration to SEC Registration 66
  (4) Transitioning From SEC Registra-
      tion to State Registration 66
6. Registration of Hedge Fund and Collateralized Debt Obligation (CDO)
   Advisers -- 67
7. ERISA Considerations --------------------------- 67
   A. Generally -------------------------------------- 67
   B. Registration and Qualification ----------- 68
   C. Bonding--------------------------------------- 69
   D. Other Potentially Applicable ERISA/
      DOL Regulations ------------------------- 70
8. CFTC Considerations ---------------------------- 71
   A. Generally -------------------------------------- 71
   B. Exemption From Registering as a
      Commodity Trading Adviser ----------- 71
   C. Exemption From Registering as a
      Commodity Pool Operator (CPO) 73

IV. HEDGE FUND AND COLLATERAL-
IZED DEBT OBLIGATION (CDO)
ADVISERS

9. Current Registration Environment --------- 75
   A. Overview ------------------------------------- 75
   B. Exemptions and Exclusions for Hedge
      Funds and Their Advisers ------------- 77
      (1) What Is a Hedge Fund? -------------- 77
      (2) Registration Exemptions Under
          the Company Act-------------------- 78

X

Page

Sec.

9. Current Registration Environment—Continued
   - a. Section 3(c)(1) Fund 78
   - b. Section 3(c)(7) Fund 80
   - (3) Registration Exemption Under the Advisers Act 82
   - C. Conditions That Led to the Implementation of the Former Hedge Fund Registration Provisions 83
   - D. The *Former* Hedge Fund Registration Provisions 85
     - (1) The Starting Point: Definition of a "Private Fund" 85
     - (2) Counting "Clients" Under the Former Hedge Fund Registration Provisions 86
     - (3) Amendments to Advisers Act Rule 205–3 88
   - E. The Demise of the Former Hedge Fund Registration Provisions 89
     - (1) *Goldstein v. SEC* 89
     - (2) Where Do We Go From Here? 92
       - a. Advisers Act Rule 206(4)–8 92
       - b. Proposed Securities Act Rule 509 95
       - c. Other Initiatives 98
     - (3) Withdrawing Registration 98
10. Applicability of Advisers Act to Unregistered Hedge Fund and CDO Advisers 101
    - A. Registration Exemption 101
    - B. Antifraud Provisions 102
    - C. Principal Transactions 103

V. REGISTRATION AND FORM ADV

Sec.   **Page**

11. Generally --- 104
12. Form ADV -- 105
    A. Part 1A of Form ADV ---------------------- 105
    B. Part 1B of Form ADV ---------------------- 109
    C. Part II of Form ADV ----------------------- 111
13. Filing Form ADV ---------------------------------- 117
14. Amending Form ADV ----------------------------- 119
15. Adviser Qualification, Disqualification and Withdrawal --- 122
    A. Qualification of Advisers ------------------ 122
    B. Disqualification of Advisers -------------- 124
    C. Adviser Withdrawal ------------------------ 125
16. State Notice Filings ----------------------------- 126

VI. ADVERTISING BY INVESTMENT ADVISERS

17. Introduction ------------------------------------- 128
18. What Is an "Advertisement"? ----------------- 129
19. Prohibitions and Restrictions Under the Advertising Rule----------------------------------- 130
    A. Specific Prohibitions and Restrictions--- 131
        (1) Testimonials----------------------------- 131
        (2) Past Specific Recommendations---- 132
        (3) Charts, Graphs and Formulae ------ 135
        (4) Free Services --------------------------- 136
    B. General Prohibition------------------------- 136
20. Advertising Performance Information------- 138
    A. Generally--- 138

Page

Sec.

20. Advertising Performance Information— Continued
  B. Actual or Model Performance Information... 139
    (1) Advertising Actual Performance Information to the Public 140
      a. Net of Fees 141
      b. Mandatory Disclosure............... 142
    (2) Advertising Model Performance Information to the Public 143
      a. Net of Fees 144
      b. Mandatory Disclosure............... 144
    (3) "One–On–One" Presentations 146
  C. AIMR Performance Presentation Standards 147
21. Portability of Performance Information 147

VII. THE ADVISORY RELATIONSHIP

22. Solicitation and Referral Arrangements 152
  A. "Solicitors" Generally.......................... 152
  B. Cash Compensation 153
    (1) Background of the Cash Solicitation Rule....................................... 153
    (2) Requirements of the Cash Solicitation Rule 154
      a. Investment Adviser Requirements.................................... 156
      b. Solicitor Requirements 157
      c. Requirement of a Written Solicitation Agreement............... 158
        1. Affiliated Solicitors............... 158
        2. Unaffiliated Solicitors 159

Page

Sec.

22. Solicitation and Referral Arrangements—
Continued

    (a)   Promotion of *Imper-sonal* Advisory Ser-vices 159

    (b)   Promotion of *Person-alized* Advisory Ser-vices 159

  d. Disclosure Requirements 160

    1. Affiliated Solicitors 161

    2. Unaffiliated Solicitors 161

    (a)   Promotion of *Imper-sonal* Advisory Ser-vices 161

    (b)   Promotion of *Person-alized* Advisory Ser-vices 162

  e. Supervisory Requirements 164

C. Non–Cash Compensation 164

D. Registration Status of Solicitors 165

  (1) Solicitor for an SEC–Registered Investment Adviser 165

    a. Registration Under the Advis-ers Act 165

    b. Registration Under State Law 167

  (2) Solicitor for a State–Registered Investment Adviser 168

23. Disclosure Requirements Relating to Clients and Prospective Clients 169

A. Introduction 169

B. The "Brochure Rule" 170

  (1) General Provision 170

Page

Sec.

23. Disclosure Requirements Relating to Clients and Prospective Clients—Continued
    (2) Timing of Delivery 171
    (3) Contents of Brochure 172
    (4) Wrap Fee Program Disclosure 173
    (5) Hedge Fund Advisers 173
    (6) Solicitors 174
  C. Adverse Financial Conditions and Certain Disciplinary Events 174
    (1) Generally 174
    (2) Legal or Disciplinary Events Presumptively Subject to Disclosure 177
    (3) Timing and Delivery of Disclosure 178
24. Advisory Agreements 180
  A. Necessity of a Writing? 180
  B. General Contractual Provisions 181
  C. Contract Prohibitions 182
    (1) Performance Fees 183
      a. Fee Arrangements Generally ... 183
      b. Regulation of Potentially Abusive Fee Arrangements 184
      c. Performance Fee Prohibition ... 187
        1. General Restriction 187
        2. Exceptions to the Performance Fee Prohibition 187
          (a) Asset–Based Fees 188
          (b) Fulcrum Fees 188
            (I) Generally 188
            (II) Choosing an Appropriate Index 190

Sec.

24. Advisory Agreements—Continued
                    (III) Making the
                        Comparison ----- 191
                (c) Business Develop-
                    ment Companies ---- 192
                (d) Section 3(c)(7)
                    Funds ----------------- 193
                (e) Non–U.S. Resident
                    Clients ---------------- 193
                (f) "Qualified Clients" ---- 194
            d. Hedge Fund Advisers ------------ 195
            e. NASD Conduct Rule 2330(f) ---- 196
        (2) Assignment of Advisory Con-
            tracts --------------------------------- 196
        (3) Notification of Change in Partner-
            ship ---------------------------------- 198
    D. Other Notable Provisions in Advisory
        Contracts --------------------------------- 198
        (1) Disclaimer of Liability/Indemnifi-
            cation Provisions --------------------- 198
        (2) Arbitration Provisions ---------------- 201
        (3) Termination Provisions -------------- 202
25. Reports Provided to Clients -------------------- 203
26. Privacy of Consumer Financial Informa-
    tion -- 203
    A. Generally ------------------------------------- 203
    B. Information Covered by Regulation
        S–P --- 205
    C. Clients Covered by Regulation S–P ----- 206
    D. Investment Advisers Covered by Regu-
        lation S–P --------------------------------- 207
    E. Notice Requirements ----------------------- 207
    F. Opt Out Options --------------------------- 210

Page

Sec.

26. Privacy of Consumer Financial Informa-
tion—Continued
  G. Exceptions 212
    (1) Generally 212
    (2) Service Providers and Joint Mar-
        keting 213
    (3) Processing and Servicing Transac-
        tions 214
    (4) Other Exceptions to Notice and
        Opt Out Requirements 214
  H. Establishing Procedural Safeguards 215
  I. Relationship to State Laws 216

VIII. PERFORMANCE OF DUTIES

27. Introduction 217
28. General Fiduciary Obligations of Invest-
ment Advisers 218
  A. Concept of Fiduciary Duty 218
  B. General Application 220
  C. Specific Fiduciary Responsibilities 220
    (1) Disclosure 220
    (2) Loyalty and Fairness 221
    (3) Care 222
        a. Implied Duty 222
        b. Informed Basis 222
    (4) D & O/E & O Insurance 222
  D. Custody and Possession 223
    (1) The Custody Rule 223
    (2) Exceptions to the Custody Rule 227
  E. Proxies 228

Page

Sec.

28. General Fiduciary Obligations of Investment Advisers—Continued
    (1) Proxy Voting Under the Advisers Act 229
    (2) Proxy Voting Under the Company Act 231
  F. Pursuing Claims Against Third Parties 231
29. Suitability 232
  A. Generally 232
  B. Proposed Advisers Act Suitability Rule Abandoned 232
  C. Dual Registrants 233
30. Best Execution 234
  A. Generally 234
  B. What Constitutes Best Execution? 235
  C. Conflicts of Interest 236
  D. Continuing Duties 236
31. Principal and Cross Transactions 237
  A. Generally 237
  B. Types of Transactions and Their Regulation 238
    (1) Principal Transactions 238
    (2) Agency Cross Transactions 240
    (3) Internal Cross Transactions 242
32. Investments in Investment Companies 244
33. Allocation and Aggregation Issues 245
  A. Allocation of Securities Among Clients 245
    (1) Generally 245
    (2) "Hot IPOs" and NASD Conduct Rule 2790 247

Page

Sec.

33. Allocation and Aggregation Issues—Continued

   B. Aggregation of Client Orders 248

34. Soft Dollars 251

   A. Historical Background 251

   B. Exchange Act Section 28(e) Safe Harbor 252

   C. Complying With Exchange Act Section 28(e) 254

      (1) "Research Services" Under Section 28(e) 256

         a. Guidance on Specific Products and Services 258

            1. Mass–Marketed Publications 258

            2. Inherently Tangible Products and Services 259

            3. Market Research 260

            4. Third–Party Research 261

            5. Data 262

            6. Proxy Services 263

         b. "Lawful and Appropriate Assistance" 263

      (2) Eligibility Criteria for "Brokerage" Under Section 28(e).......... 264

         a. Temporal Standard 265

         b. Ineligible Overhead 267

         c. Custody 268

      (3) "Mixed–Use" Items 269

      (4) An Adviser's Good Faith Determination as to Reasonableness Under Section 28(e) 270

Page

Sec.

34. Soft Dollars—Continued
    (5) Linkage Between "Provided by" and "Effecting" Under Section 28(e) 271
        a. Separation of Execution and Research 272
        b. "Provided by" in the Context of Third–Party Research Arrangements 273
35. Client Directed Brokerage 274
36. Adviser Benefitting From Brokerage 276
    A. Generally 276
    B. Investment Company Clients 277
       (1) Adviser Liability 277
       (2) Broker–Dealer Liability 278
37. Affiliated Brokerage 280
38. Trading Errors 282
39. Key Man Life Insurance 283

IX. WRAP FEE PROGRAMS

40. Generally 284
    A. Wrap Fees Are Negotiable 285
    B. Wrap Fee Program Structures 286
41. Registration Requirements 287
    A. Generally 287
    B. Broker–Dealer Exclusion Not Available 287
    C. Company Act and Securities Act Concerns 288
42. Disclosure Requirements 290
    A. Wrap Fee Brochure 290

Page

Sec.

42. Disclosure Requirements—Continued
    B. Contents 292
    C. Delivery of the Brochure 293
    D. Updating 293

X. PROPRIETARY AND INSIDER TRADING

43. Generally 295
44. Code of Ethics 296
    A. Generally 296
    B. Distinction Between a "Supervised Person" and an "Access Person" 298
    C. Reporting Requirements Under the Ethics Code Rule 300
       (1) Holdings Reports 301
       (2) Transaction Reports 303
    D. Pre–Approval of Certain Investments .. 304
    E. Analogous Rules for Advisers With Mutual Fund Clients 306

XI. RECORDKEEPING REQUIREMENTS

45. Advisers Act Section 204 308
46. Required Books and Records 308
    A. Adviser Formation, Governance and Ownership Documents 310
    B. Accounting and Related Records 310
    C. Client Relationship Records 311
    D. Marketing and Performance Information 313
    E. Solicitor Records 315

Page

Sec.

46. Required Books and Records—Continued
    F. Code of Ethics and Personal and Pro-
        prietary Trading Information............ 316
    G. Portfolio Management and Trading
        Records 317
    H. Custody Records 320
    I. Proxy Related Records 321
47. Means of Storage............................ 322
48. Foreign Advisers 323

XII.   CHIEF COMPLIANCE OFFICERS (CCOs) AND ISSUES RELATING TO THEM

49. Necessity of a Chief Compliance Officer 325
50. Role of the Chief Compliance Officer 326
    A. On-going CCO Responsibilities.......... 328
    B. CCO Responsibilities During On-site
        SEC Visit or Review of Proce-
        dures................................... 332
        (1) Initial Interview 333
        (2) Walk Through of Operations........ 334
    C. NASAA Best Practices 336
51. Compliance Manual 338

XIII.   COMPLIANCE, INSPECTION AND ENFORCEMENT UNDER THE ADVISERS ACT

52. Generally 340
53. SEC Inspections 341
    A. Routine Inspections.................... 342
        (1) Inspection Process 344
        (2) Examination Results............... 346

Page

Sec.

53. SEC Inspections—Continued
   B. Cause Inspections 347
   C. Sweep Inspections 347
54. Inspection Phases 347
   A. Pre–Inspection Phase 348
   B. On–Site Inspection Phase 350
   C. Post–Inspection Phase 351
55. Enforcement 353
   A. Advisers Act Sections 203(e) and (f) 353
   B. Failure to Supervise 355
   C. Adviser "Cooperation" 356
56. Penalties 360
   A. Non–Monetary Sanctions 360
   B. Monetary Sanctions 361
   C. Criminal Penalties 364
57. Achieving Prohibited Goals Through Indirect Means 364
58. Consultation With Federal Banking Authorities 367

XIV.   LIMITED PRIVATE RIGHT OF ACTION

59. No Express Provision 368
60. Limited Private Right of Action 368
61. Other Actions Possible 370

XV.   PURCHASE AND SALE OF INVESTMENT ADVISERS

62. Generally 371
63. Assignment of Advisory Contracts 372

Page

Sec.

64. Employment Contracts and Non–Compete/Non-Solicit Agreements --------------- 375

XVI. SPECIAL ISSUES RELATING TO THE ADVISORY BUSINESS

65. Holding Companies of Investment Advisers --- 377
66. Taking an Investment Adviser Public ------- 378
67. "Pay–To–Play" Rules Relating to Political Contributions ----------------------------------- 379
68. Payments to Labor Organizations ----------- 381

Annex A. Investment Advisers Act of 1940 ---- 383
Annex B. General Rules and Regulations Under the Investment Advisers Act of 1940 -- 445

INDEX -- 541

TABLE OF AUTHORITIES

References are to Pages

A

ABN AMRO–NSM Int'l Funds Mgt., B.V., In re, Advisers Act Rel. No. 1767, 1988 WL 668122 (Sept. 30, 1998), *239*

Account Mgt. Corp., In re, Advisers Act Rel. No. 1529, 1995 WL 579449 (Sept. 29, 1995), *246*

Applied Financial Group, Inc. and Dennis Holcombe, Matter of, Advisers Act Rel. No. 2436, 2005 WL 2413652 (Sept. 30, 2005), *355*

A.R. Schmeidler & Co., SEC No–Action Letter, 1976 WL 12236 (avail. June 1, 1976), *139*

Association for Investment Mgt. & Research, SEC No–Action Letter, 1996 WL 729385 (avail. Dec. 18, 1996), *141, 142*

Auchincloss & Lawrence Inc., SEC No–Action Letter, 1974 WL 10979 (avail. Feb. 8, 1974), *200*

B

Barclays PLC, SEC No–Action Letter, 1991 WL 176731 (avail. Feb. 14, 1991), *30*

Basic, Inc. v. Levinson, 485 U.S. 224, 108 S.Ct. 978, 99 L.Ed.2d 194 (1988), *93*

Bell Capital Mgt., Inc., In re, Advisers Act Rel. No. 1813, 1999 WL 641795 (Aug. 6, 1999), *137*

Boston Investment Counsel, Inc. and Robert E. Campanella, In re, Advisers Act Rel. No. 1801, 1999 WL 373782 (June 10, 1999), *137, 179*

Bramwell Growth Fund, SEC No–Action Letter, 1996 WL 450346 (avail. Aug. 7, 1996), *148*

TABLE OF AUTHORITIES

Bypass Wall Street, Inc., SEC No–Action Letter, 1992 WL 19987 (avail. Jan. 7, 1992), *137*

C.

Cambiar Investors, Inc., SEC No–Action Letter, 1997 WL 528245 (avail. Aug. 28, 1997), *132*

Capital Gains Research Bureau, Inc., S.E.C. v., 375 U.S. 180, 84 S.Ct. 275, 11 L.Ed.2d 237 (1963), *218, 219, 222, 295*

Charterhouse Tilney, SEC No–Action Letter, 1993 WL 277798 (avail. July 15, 1993), *30*

Clover Capital Mgt., Inc., SEC No–Action Letter, 1986 WL 67379 (avail. Oct. 28, 1986), *139, 141, 144, 149*

Contingent Advisory Compensation Arrangements, Advisers Act Rel. No. 721, 1980 WL 19231 (May 16, 1980), *184*

D

DALBAR, SEC No–Action Letter, 1998 WL 136415 (avail. Mar. 24, 1998), *132*

Dean Witter, Discover & Co., SEC No–Action Letter, 1997 WL 192125 (avail. Apr. 18, 1997), *373*

Denver Investment Advisors, SEC No–Action Letter, 1993 WL 313090 (avail. July 30, 1993), *132*

Dougherty & Co. LLC, SEC No–Action Letter, 2003 WL 22204509 (avail. July 3, 2003), *158*

Douglas Capital Management, Inc., SEC No–Action Letter, 1988 WL 233565 (avail. Jan. 11, 1988), *176*

E

Edward D. Jones & Co., L.P., Exchange Act Rel. No. 50910, 2004 WL 31777119 (Dec. 22, 2004), *280*

Equitable Life Assurance Society, SEC No–Action Letter, 1984 WL 47223 (avail. Jan. 11, 1984), *373*

F

Financial Planning Assoc. v. S.E.C., 482 F.3d 481, 375 U.S.App. D.C. 389 (D.C.Cir.2007), *26, 29, 32, 33, 44*

FinArc, LLC, In re, Advisers Act Rel. No. 1763, 1998 WL 667628 (Sept. 29, 1998), *123*

Forty Four Mgt., Ltd., SEC No–Action Letter, 1983 WL 30741 (avail. Jan. 31, 1983), *367*

Franklin Mgt., Inc., SEC No–Action Letter, 1998 WL 853257 (avail. Dec. 10, 1998), *135*

G

Gallagher and Assoc., Ltd., SEC No–Action Letter, 1995 WL 447626 (avail. July 10, 1995), *131*

Gartenberg v. Merrill Lynch Asset Mgt., Inc., 694 F.2d 923 (2d Cir.1982), *186*

Goldman, Sachs & Co., SEC No–Action Letter, 2007 WL 516135 (avail. Jan. 30, 2007), *274*

Goldman, Sachs & Co., SEC No–Action Letter, 1999 WL 123998 (avail. Feb. 22, 1999), *238*

Goldstein v. S.E.C., 451 F.3d 873, 371 U.S.App.D.C. 358 (D.C.Cir. 2006), *7, 49, 77, 83, 85, 89, 92, 98, 99, 101, 102, 173*

Great Lake Advisors, SEC No–Action Letter, 1992 WL 105179 (avail. Apr. 3, 1992), *148, 151*

Gun Soo Oh Park, S.E.C. v., 99 F.Supp.2d 889 (N.D.Ill.2000), *40*

H

Horizon Asset Mgt., SEC No–Action Letter, 1996 WL 554956 (avail. Sept. 13, 1996), *149, 150*

I

In re (see name of party)

Investment Company Institute, SEC No–Action Letter, 2001 WL 436249 (avail. Apr. 10, 2001), *210*

Investment Company Institute, SEC No–Action Letter, 1998 WL 235405 (avail. Sept. 23, 1998), *130, 146, 147*

Investment Company Institute, SEC No–Action Letter, 1987 WL 108086 (avail. Aug. 24, 1987), *141, 144*

Investment Counsel Assoc. of Amer., Inc., SEC No–Action Letter, 2004 WL 892243 (avail. Mar. 1, 2004), *134*

Investor Intelligence (John Anthony), SEC No–Action Letter, 1975 WL 8971 (avail. Apr. 18, 1975), *136*

J

James R. Waters, SEC No–Action Letter, 1995 WL 498690 (June 1, 1995), *187, 191*

Jennison Associates Capital Corp., SEC No–Action Letter, 1985 WL 55687 (avail. Dec. 2, 1985), *198, 374*

J.P. Morgan Investment Mgt., Inc., SEC No–Action Letter, 1996 WL 282573 (avail. May 7, 1996), *142*

K

Kaufman v. Merrill Lynch, Pierce, Fenner & Smith, Inc., 464 F.Supp. 528 (D.Md.1978), *27*

Kemper Financial Services, Inc., In re, Advisers Act Rel. No. 1387, 1993 WL 431535 (Oct. 20, 1993), *246*

Kenton Capital, S.E.C. v., 69 F.Supp.2d 1 (D.D.C.1998), *27*

L

LBS Capital Mgt., Inc., Matter of, Advisers Act Rel. No. 1644, 1997 WL 401055 (July 18, 1997), *138*

Lowe v. S.E.C., 472 U.S. 181, 105 S.Ct. 2557, 86 L.Ed.2d 130 (1985), *36, 40, 41*

M

Mandell Fin. Group, In re, SEC No–Action Letter, 1997 WL 274828 (avail. May 21, 1997), *123*

Mark Bailey & Co., In re, Advisers Act Rel. No. 1105, 1998 WL 901756 (Feb. 24, 1988), *275*

Matter of (see name of party)

McEldowney Fin. Services, SEC No–Action Letter, 1986 WL 67330 (avail. Oct. 17, 1986), *201*

McKenzie Walker Investment Mgt., Inc., In re, Advisers Act Rel. No. 1571, 1996 WL 396091 (July 16, 1996), *247*

M & I Investment Mgt. Corp., Matter of, Advisers Act Rel. No. 1318, 1992 WL 160038 (June 30, 1992), *283*

TABLE OF AUTHORITIES

N

Nathan and Lewis Securities, SEC No–Action Letter, 1990 WL 286885 (avail. July 19, 1990), *112, 170*

National Football League Players Assoc., SEC No–Action Letter, 2002 WL 100675 (avail. Jan. 25, 2002), *155*

New York Investors Group, Inc., SEC No–Action Letter, 1982 WL 29455 (avail. Sept. 7, 1982), *131*

Nicholas Applegate Mutual Funds, SEC No–Action Letter, 1996 WL 450350 (avail. Aug. 6, 1996), *140*

Nikko Int'l Capital Mgt. Co., SEC No–Action Letter, 1987 WL 108059 (avail. June 1, 1987), *373*

O

Owen T. Wilkinson & Assoc., Inc., SEC No–Action Letter, 1987 WL 108842 (avail. Feb. 3, 1988), *250*

P

Pretzel and Stouffer, SEC No–Action Letter, 1995 WL 737153 (avail. Dec. 1, 1995), *245, 251*

Putnam Investment Mgt., LLC, Advisers Act Rel. No. 2370, 2005 WL 673295 (Mar. 23, 2005), *278*

R

Reservoir Capital Mgt., Inc., In re, Advisers Act Rel. No. 1717, 1998 WL 193159 (Apr. 24, 1998), *132, 137*

Richard Ellis, SEC No–Action Letter, 1981 WL 25241 (avail. Sept. 17, 1981), *365, 366*

Richard Silverman, SEC No–Action Letter, 1985 WL 54061 (avail. Mar. 27, 1985), *131*

Rodriguez de Quijas v. Shearson/American Express, Inc., 490 U.S. 477, 109 S.Ct. 1917, 104 L.Ed.2d 526 (1989), *201*

S

Salomon Brothers Asset Mgt. Inc. and Salomon Brothers Asset Mgt. Asia Pacific Ltd., SEC No–Action Letter, 1999 WL 528854 (avail. July 23, 1999), *151*

Schield Mgt. Co., Matter of, Advisers Act Rel. No. 1872, 2000 WL 694288 (May 31, 2000), *147*

Scudder, Stevens & Clark, SEC No–Action Letter, 1985 WL 54004 (avail. Mar. 18, 1985), *198, 374*

S.E.C. v. _____ (see opposing party)

Securities Industry Assoc., SEC No–Action Letter, 2005 WL 3526529 (avail. Dec. 16, 2005), *24*

Shearson/American Express, Inc. v. McMahon, 483 U.S. 1056, 108 S.Ct. 31, 97 L.Ed.2d 819 (1987), *201*

SMC Capital, Inc., SEC No–Action Letter, 1995 WL 529274 (avail. Sept. 5, 1995), *245, 251*

Starr and Kuehl, Inc., SEC No–Action Letter, 1976 WL 9116 (avail. Apr. 17, 1976), *134*

Subcommittee on Private Investment Entities of the Amer. Bar Assoc., SEC No–Action Letter, 2005 WL 3334980 (avail. Dec. 8, 2005), *88, 228*

T

Templeton Inv. Counsel Ltd., SEC No–Action Letter, 1986 WL 67662 (avail. Jan. 2, 1986), *198, 374*

Thomson Advisory Group, SEC No–Action Letter, 1995 WL 611553 (avail. Sept. 26, 1995), *366*

Transamerica Mortgage Advisors, Inc. v. Lewis, 444 U.S. 11, 100 S.Ct. 242, 62 L.Ed.2d 146 (1979), *368*

TSC Indus. v. Northway, Inc., 426 U.S. 438, 96 S.Ct. 2126, 48 L.Ed.2d 757 (1976), *93*

V

Valicenti Advisory Services and Vincent R. Valicenti, In re, Advisers Act Rel. No. 1774, 1998 WL 798699 (Nov. 18, 1998), *180*

Valicenti Advisory Services, Inc. v. S.E.C., 198 F.3d 62 (2d Cir.1999), *180*

W

Washington Investment Network, S.E.C. v., 475 F.3d 392, 374 U.S.App.D.C. 383 (D.C.Cir.2007), *125, 221*

TABLE OF AUTHORITIES

Z

Zinn v. Parrish, 644 F.2d 360 (7th Cir.1981), *15*

*

TABLE OF STATUTES AND RULES

INVESTMENT ADVISERS ACT OF 1940
15 U.S.C. § 80b et seq.

Sec.	This Work Page
201	45
202(a)(1)	197
	373
202(a)(2)	7
	18
202(a)(11)	6
	8
	9
	10
	16
	17
	32
	43
	46
	50
	62
	63
	156
202(a)(11)(A)	8
	17
202(a)(11)(B)	6
	19
	20
202(a)(11)(C)	21
	32
	287
202(a)(11)(D)	35
202(a)(11)(E)	32

INVESTMENT ADVISERS ACT OF 1940
15 U.S.C. § 80b et seq.

Sec.	This Work Page
202(a)(11)(E) (Cont'd)	
	42
202(a)(11)(F)	8
	32
	42
	57
202(a)(11)(G)	26
	29
	32
	33
	43
	44
202(a)(13)	115
	319
202(a)(16)	11
202(a)(17)	62
	64
	166
	296
202(a)(18)	12
	301
202(a)(22)	52
	95
	192
202(a)(25)	61
	63
	168
	299
	325
202(a)(28)	8
202(b)	44
203	62
	111
	123
	130
	154
	156
	157
	170
	296
	309

TABLE OF STATUTES AND RULES

INVESTMENT ADVISERS ACT OF 1940
15 U.S.C. § 80b et seq.

Sec.	This Work Page
203 (Cont'd)	
	316
	353
203(a)	37
203(b)	10
	44
	75
	104
	157
	167
	182
	187
	195
	197
	198
	366
	372
203(b)(1)	45
203(b)(2)	46
203(b)(3)	46
	51
	72
	82
	85
	86
	98
	101
	183
	195
	207
	220
	365
203(b)(4)	52
203(b)(5)	50
	53
203(b)(6)	53
203(c)(2)	123
	124
203(e)	124
	157
	158

TABLE OF STATUTES AND RULES

INVESTMENT ADVISERS ACT OF 1940
15 U.S.C. § 80b et seq.

Sec.	This Work Page
203(e) (Cont'd)	
	354
	355
	360
203(e)(1)	361
203(e)(2)	361
	364
203(e)(2)(A)—(D)	157
203(e)(2)(B)	8
203(e)(3)	157
203(e)(4)	8
203(e)(5)	361
203(e)(6)	327
	355
	361
	362
203(e)(6)(A)	356
203(e)(6)(B)	356
203(e)(8)	361
203(e)(9)	354
203(f)	125
	157
	158
	354
	360
203(g)	125
	372
203(h)	126
203(i)	361
203(i)(1)	362
203(i)(2)	363
203(i)(3)	364
203A	10
	56
	123
203A(a)(1)	56
203A(a)(2)	60
203A(b)(1)	9
	17
	167
203A(b)(1)(A)	61

INVESTMENT ADVISERS ACT OF 1940
15 U.S.C. § 80b et seq.

Sec.	This Work Page
203A(b)(1)(A) (Cont'd)	
	63
	126
	127
	167
203A(b)(2)	61
	64
	65
204	121
	126
	295
	308
	341
204A	66
	295
	296
205	65
205(a)	180
	182
	183
	373
205(a)(1)	89
	183
	187
	366
	367
205(a)(2)	197
	372
205(a)(3)	198
205(b)	183
205(b)(1)	187
	188
205(b)(2)	189
	191
	193
205(b)(3)	192
205(b)(4)	193
205(b)(5)	193
205(c)	190
205(e)	183
	194

TABLE OF STATUTES AND RULES

INVESTMENT ADVISERS ACT OF 1940
15 U.S.C. § 80b et seq.

Sec.	This Work Page
206	10
	16
	44
	65
	91
	102
	130
	152
	153
	164
	165
	169
	170
	201
	202
	218
	219
	220
	221
	222
	232
	244
	276
	281
	295
	369
	370
	378
206(1)	217
	219
	242
206(2)	217
	219
	220
	242
	246
	277
206(3)	35
	65
	103

TABLE OF STATUTES AND RULES

INVESTMENT ADVISERS ACT OF 1940
15 U.S.C. § 80b et seq.

Sec.	This Work Page
206(3) (Cont'd)	
	217
	237
	238
	239
	240
	241
	242
	243
	281
206(4)	128
	132
	153
	174
	224
	230
207	105
	118
	119
	121
	126
208(a)	123
208(b)	123
208(c)	124
208(d)	364
	365
	366
	367
209(b)	353
210A	8
	367
211(a)	32
	43
215	369
	370
215(a)	200
215(b)	183
217	364
222(d)	63

TABLE OF STATUTES AND RULES

INVESTMENT COMPANY ACT OF 1940
15 U.S.C. § 80a et seq.

Sec.	This Work Page
2(a)(19)	244
	282
2(a)(20)	300
2(a)(51)(A)	96
	195
3(c)(1)	78
	79
	81
	82
	85
	91
	93
	95
	97
	195
	207
	211
3(c)(1)(A)	79
3(c)(7)	78
	79
	81
	82
	85
	93
	95
	97
	187
	193
	195
	207
3(c)(10)(D)	52
	53
3(c)(14)	53
12(d)(1)	245
15(a)	180
15(a)(3)	202
15(a)(4)	197
	372
	374

TABLE OF STATUTES AND RULES

INVESTMENT COMPANY ACT OF 1940
15 U.S.C. § 80a et seq.

Sec.	This Work Page
15(c)	172
15(f)	374
17(d)	249
17(e)(2)	281
17(f)	228
17(g)	70
17(h)	200
17(j)	306
34(b)	278
36(b)	185
	186

SECURITIES ACT OF 1933
15 U.S.C. § 77a et seq.

Sec.	This Work Page
2(a)(1)	12
3(b)	80
4(2)	79
	80
	84
	305
4(6)	305
5	288

SECURITIES EXCHANGE ACT OF 1934
15 U.S.C. 78a et seq.

Sec.	This Work Page
3(a)(10)	12
3(a)(18)	31
3(a)(25)	25
3(a)(62)	42
6(e)(1)	26
	251
	252
10(b)	295

TABLE OF STATUTES AND RULES

SECURITIES EXCHANGE ACT OF 1934
15 U.S.C. 78a et seq.

Sec.	This Work Page
10(b) (Cont'd)	
	370
12(g)	81
15	22
21(a)	357
28(e)	217
	239
	252
	253
	254
	255
	256
	257
	258
	259
	261
	262
	263
	265
	266
	270
	271
	272
	273
	274
	275
28(e)(1)	253
28(e)(3)(A)	254
	256
	257
	263
28(e)(3)(B)	254
	256
	257
	262
	263
28(e)(3)(C)	254
	264
	266
	268

TABLE OF STATUTES AND RULES

INVESTMENT ADVISERS ACT RULES
17 C.F.R. § 275.–

Rule	This Work Page
0–2(b)(2)	323
0–7	108
202(a)(1)–1	197
	373
202(a)(11)–1 (judicially vacated in 2007)	23
	26
	43
	44
203–1(b)(2)	119
203–1(c)	118
203–1(d)	118
	119
203–2	98
	126
203–3	118
203–3(a)(2)(i)	119
203–3(b)(2)	119
203(b)(3)–1	48
	72
	85
203(b)(3)–1(a)(1)	87
203(b)(3)–1(a)(2)(i)	48
	49
	83
	85
203(b)(3)–1(a)(2)(ii)	48
203(b)(3)–1(b)	49
203(b)(3)–1(b)(1)	49
	50
203(b)(3)–1(b)(2)	50
203(b)(3)–1(b)(3)	50
203(b)(3)–1(b)(4)	50
203(b)(3)–1(b)(5)	50
203(b)(3)–1(c)	51
203(b)(3)–1(d)	49
203(b)(3)–2 (judicially vacated in 2006)	49
	85
	86
	87

INVESTMENT ADVISERS ACT RULES
17 C.F.R. § 275.–

Rule	This Work Page
203(b)(3)–2 (Cont'd)	
	88
	90
	91
203A–1	56
203A–1(a)(1)	56
203A–1(a)(2)	58
203A–1(b)(1)	66
203A–1(b)(2)	67
203A–2	56
203A–2(a)	57
203A–2(b)	57
203A–2(c)	57
203A–2(d)	58
203A–2(e)	59
203A–2(f)	60
203A–3(a)(1)	63
	167
203A–3(a)(2)	64
	168
203A–3(c)	58
203A–4	62
204–1	121
204–1(a)(1)	119
204–1(a)(2)	120
204–1(b)	122
204–1(c)	119
204–1(d)	122
204–1(e)	121
204–2	308
	331
204–2(a)(1)	311
204–2(a)(2)	311
204–2(a)(3)	320
204–2(a)(4)—(6)	311
204–2(a)(7)	320
204–2(a)(7)—(10)	313
204–2(a)(10)	158
	316
	320
204–2(a)(11)	130

TABLE OF STATUTES AND RULES

INVESTMENT ADVISERS ACT RULES
17 C.F.R. § 275.–

Rule	This Work Page
204–2(a)(11) (Cont'd)	
	315
204–2(a)(12)	317
204–2(a)(12)(i)	298
204–2(a)(12)(ii)	298
204–2(a)(13)	317
204–2(a)(13)(i)	302
	303
204–2(a)(13)(ii)	300
204–2(a)(13)(iii)	306
204–2(a)(14)	170
204–2(a)(15)	164
	316
204–2(a)(16)	100
	139
	150
	151
	315
204–2(b)	226
204–2(b)(1)—(4)	321
204–2(c)(1)	320
204–2(c)(2)	230
204–2(c)(2)(i)—(v)	322
204–2(e)	126
204–2(e)(1)	311
	312
	315
	317
	318
	320
	321
204–2(e)(2)	310
204–2(e)(3)(i)	314
204–2(g)(1)	322
204–2(g)(2)(ii)(A)—(C)	310
204–2(g)(3)	323
204–2(j)(1)	323
204–2(j)(3)	323
204–3	111
	163
	169

TABLE OF STATUTES AND RULES

INVESTMENT ADVISERS ACT RULES
17 C.F.R. § 275.–

Rule	This Work Page
204–3 (Cont'd)	
	180
	290
	313
	315
	328
204–3(a)	104
	170
	291
204–3(a)(2)(iii)(B)	163
204–3(b)	163
204–3(b)(1)	171
204–3(b)(2)	171
204–3(c)	203
204–3(c)(1)	171
204–3(c)(2)	171
204–3(c)(3)	172
204–3(d)	117
	173
204–3(e)	117
	169
	172
204–3(f)(1)	285
	291
204–3(f)(2)	291
204–3(f)(3)	291
204–3(g)(1)	172
204–3(g)(2)	171
204–3(g)(4)	284
204A–1	296
	316
204A–1(a)(1)	298
204A–1(a)(3)	299
204A–1(b)(1)	301
204A–1(b)(1)(i)(A)—(C)	301
204A–1(b)(1)(ii)	302
204A–1(b)(2)	303
204A–1(b)(2)(i)(A)—(E)	303
204A–1(b)(2)(ii)	304
204A–1(b)(3)	304
204A–1(b)(3)(i)	303

TABLE OF STATUTES AND RULES

INVESTMENT ADVISERS ACT RULES
17 C.F.R. § 275.–

Rule	This Work Page
204A–1(c)	305
204A–1(d)	304
204A–1(e)(1)	299
204A–1(e)(3)	301
204A–1(e)(5)	300
204A–1(e)(6)	305
204A–1(e)(8)	300
204A–1(e)(10)	301
205–1	191
205–2	191
205–3	64
	65
	89
	168
	196
205–3(a)	88
	194
205–3(c)	100
205–3(d)(1)	89
	194
205–3(d)(1)(iii)	87
205–3(d)(2)	195
206(3)–2	65
	241
	242
	281
206(3)–2(a)	241
206(3)–2(b)	240
206(3)–2(c)	242
206(3)–3T	34
206(4)–1	65
	129
	130
	221
206(4)–1(a)	130
206(4)–1(a)(1)	131
206(4)–1(a)(2)	133
206(4)–1(a)(3)	135
206(4)–1(a)(4)	136
206(4)–1(a)(5)	137

TABLE OF STATUTES AND RULES

INVESTMENT ADVISERS ACT RULES
17 C.F.R. § 275.–

Rule	This Work Page
206(4)–1(a)(5) (Cont'd)	
	138
	148
206(4)–2	203
	217
	223
206(4)–2(a)(1)	224
206(4)–2(a)(2)	225
206(4)–2(a)(3)	225
206(4)–2(a)(3)(i)	226
206(4)–2(a)(3)(ii)(A)—(C)	226
206(4)–2(a)(4)	225
	226
206(4)–2(b)(1)	227
206(4)–2(b)(2)	227
206(4)–2(b)(3)	228
206(4)–2(b)(4)	228
206(4)–2(c)(1)	223
	320
206(4)–2(c)(2)	225
	226
206(4)–2(c)(3)	225
206(4)–2(c)(4)	228
206(4)–3	153
	221
	276
	315
206(4)–3(a)(1)	316
206(4)–3(a)(1)(i)	156
206(4)–3(a)(1)(ii)	157
206(4)–3(a)(1)(iii)	158
206(4)–3(a)(2)(i)	159
	162
206(4)–3(a)(2)(ii)	159
	161
206(4)–3(a)(2)(iii)(A)	160
	163
206(4)–3(a)(2)(iii)(B)	163
206(4)–3(a)(2)(iii)(C)	164
206(4)–3(b)	163
206(4)–3(c)	155

INVESTMENT ADVISERS ACT RULES
17 C.F.R. § 275.–

Rule	This Work Page
206(4)–3(d)(1)	154
206(4)–3(d)(2)	154
206(4)–3(d)(3)	159
	162
206(4)–4	117
	169
	173
	174
	176
	179
	180
206(4)–4(a)(1)	175
206(4)–4(a)(2)	175
206(4)–4(b)	176
	177
206(4)–4(c)	179
206(4)–4(d)(1)	176
206(4)–4(d)(3)	178
206(4)–4(d)(4)	178
206(4)–4(f)	177
206(4)–6	230
	321
206(4)–6(a)	230
206(4)–6(b)	230
206(4)–6(c)	231
206(4)–(7)(a)	326
206(4)–8	92
	94
206(4)–8(a)(1)	93
206(4)–8(a)(2)	93
206(4)–8(b)	93

INVESTMENT COMPANY ACT RULES
17 C.F.R. § 270.–

Rule	This Work Page
2a51–1	96
3a–4	288
3c–1	79

TABLE OF STATUTES AND RULES

INVESTMENT COMPANY ACT RULES
17 C.F.R. § 270.–

Rule	This Work Page
3c–5(a)(4)	73
12b–1(h)	271
	277
17a–7	243
17d–1	223
	249
17e–1	282
17f–1—7	228
17g–1	70
17j–1	306
17j–1(b)	306
17j–1(c)—(f)	307
30b1–4	231

SECURITIES ACT RULES

17 C.F.R. § 230.–

Rule	This Work Page
501(a)	20
	73
	79
	96
	97
501(a)(5)	80
	81
	95
501(a)(6)	80
	81
	95
501(h)	20
502(c)	80
502(h)	20
504	80
505	80
506	20
	79
509 (proposed)	95
Regulation A	80

TABLE OF STATUTES AND RULES

SECURITIES ACT RULES
17 C.F.R. § 230.–

Rule	This Work Page
Regulation D	79
	80
	95
	97
	305
Regulation S	93

SECURITIES EXCHANGE ACT RULES
17 C.F.R. § 240.–

Rule	This Work Page
10b–5	9
	295
	369
	370
10b–10	35
12g–1	81
15a–6	30
15g–9	234
16a–1(2)(a)	301

EMPLOYEE RETIREMENT INCOME SECURITY ACT OF 1974
29 U.S.C. § 1001 et seq.

Sec.	This Work Page
3(38)	181
403	68
404	68
406	68
	69
412	69

*

ABBREVIATIONS

ADV	Adviser (Form ADV)
Advertising Rule	Advisers Act Rule 206(4)–1
Advisers Act	Investment Advisers Act of 1940, as amended
AIMR	Association for Investment Management and Research
Brochure Rule	Advisers Act Rule 204–3
Broker-Dealer Safe Harbor	Former Advisers Act Rule 202(a)(11)–1 (judicially vacated in 2007)
Cash Solicitation Rule	Advisers Act Rule 206(4)–3
CCO	Chief compliance officer
CDO	Collateralized debt obligation
Company Act	Investment Company Act of 1940, as amended
Custody Rule	Advisers Act Rule 206(4)–2
D & O/E & O	Directors and officers/errors and omissions (insurance)
DOL	U.S. Department of Labor

Dual Registrant	An investment adviser which is registered under the Advisers Act as an investment adviser and is also registered under the Exchange Act as a broker-dealer
EDGAR	SEC's Electronic, Data, Gathering, Analysis, and Retrieval system
ERISA	Employee Retirement Income Security Act of 1974, as amended
Ethics Code Rule	Advisers Act Rule 204A–1
Exchange Act	Securities Exchange Act of 1934, as amended
FINRA	Financial Industry Regulatory Authority
GAAP	U.S. generally accepted accounting principles
GLBA	Gramm-Leach-Bliley Financial Modernization Act of 1999
GSA	Glass-Steagall Banking Act of 1933
IAR	Investment adviser representative
IARD	Investment Adviser Registration Depository
IPO	Initial public offering

ABBREVIATIONS

IRC	Internal Revenue Code of 1986, as amended
NASD	National Association of Securities Dealers, Inc.
NASAA	North American Securities Administrators Association
NRSRO	Nationally Recognized Statistical Rating Organization
NYSE	New York Stock Exchange, Inc.
OCIE	SEC's Office of Compliance Inspections and Examinations
Performance Fee Prohibition	Advisers Act Section 205(a)(1)
Private Adviser Registration Exemption	Advisers Act Section 203(b)(3)
Proxy Voting Rule	Advisers Act Rule 206(4)–6
Recordkeeping Rule	Advisers Act Rule 204–2
Rel.	SEC Release
SEC	Securities and Exchange Commission
Securities Act	Securities Act of 1933, as amended
SOX	Sarbanes-Oxley Act of 2002
SRO	Self-regulatory organization

*

INVESTMENT ADVISER REGULATION

IN A NUTSHELL

*

I. INTRODUCTION

§ 1. HISTORICAL OVERVIEW

A. Legislative Response to Crash of 1929

Following the stock market crash of 1929, the Roosevelt administration valiantly fought to reestablish the trust of the American people in the U.S. securities markets. Over the next decade, Congress passed, and the President signed, multiple bodies of Federal securities laws that were designed to accomplish this goal: the Securities Act of 1933 (the "Securities Act"); the Securities Exchange Act of 1934 (the "Exchange Act"); the Public Utility Holding Company Act of 1935 ("PUHCA"); and the Trust Indenture Act of 1939 (the "TIA").

With respect to investment companies (commonly referred to as mutual funds) and those advising them, Congress was concerned that the disclosure and antifraud provisions of the Securities Act and the Exchange Act did not provide sufficient protection to purchasers of investment company securities. This stemmed from the unique corporate structure of mutual funds that gave rise to conflicts of interest between the interests of fund advisers and those of fund shareholders. Although fund advisers are separate and distinct legal entities from the funds they manage, they typically create those funds. As a result, fund advisers retain a tremendous influence over the internal management of the funds they advise usually for the life of the fund. Unless this influence is kept in check, fund advisers could easily exploit the funds to the detriment of fund shareholders.

Under the authority of Section 30 of the PUHCA, Congress directed the Securities and Exchange Commission ("SEC") to conduct an in-depth investigation into the nature and practices of investment companies, particularly the conflicts of interest inherent in their structures. After four years of work, the SEC published its findings in the Investment Trust Study, which revealed a great deal of abuse by advisers to investment companies. Based on this study, Senator Robert F. Wagner of New York introduced a Senate bill containing two Titles. Title I ultimately became the Investment Company Act of 1940 (the "Company Act"), while Title II became the Investment Advisers Act of 1940 (the "Advisers Act").

Congress enacted the Company Act in order to curtail the conflicts of interest between investment advisers and the funds they manage. Among other things, the Company Act requires the presence of independent directors or trustees on the board of a fund. These independent directors are to serve as "watchdogs" for the interests of fund shareholders. Also, the Company Act gives the SEC broad authority over the business practices of mutual funds in order to correct abusive self-dealings between investment advisers and the funds they manage.

The Advisers Act, by contrast, centers around the delicate fiduciary nature of the investment advisory relationship. Its primary purpose is to provide the investing public with disclosure about persons who are paid for advice concerning the desirability of investing in securities. Like all other Federal securities acts, the Advisers Act rejects the notion of caveat emptor and instead embraces a philosophy of full disclosure in order to help achieve a high standard of business ethics in the securities industry. Moreover, the Advisers Act is designed to prevent investment advisers from engaging in fraudulent practices that could potentially injure the investing public. In particular, the Advisers Act eliminates, or at least exposes, all conflicts of interest which might preclude an investment adviser from rendering disinterested investment advice to its clients.

B. Evolution of the Advisers Act

Congress' weariness with New Deal legislation discouraged it from creating a sweeping investment adviser statute. Thus, the Advisers Act was originally modest in scope, containing only 21 sections (it now has 26). In large part, it was originally designed only to facilitate a census of the investment adviser industry.

The Advisers Act remained virtually unchanged for the first 20 years following its passage. However, further studies by the SEC, which were undertaken as a result of several major market scandals, exposed numerous deficiencies in the Advisers Act. In particular, the SEC believed it did not afford advisory clients and other members of the investing public sufficient protection. After many investment advisers exploited the Advisers Act's shortcomings, Congress passed amendments to it in 1960, 1970, 1997, 1999 and 2006.

The 1960 Amendments added the word "manipulative" to the list of acts that are proscribed by the Act. More importantly, the amendments authorized the SEC "by rules and regulations [to] define, and prescribe means reasonably designed to prevent, such acts, practices, and courses of business as are fraudulent, deceptive, or manipulative." Changes to Section 204 of the Advisers Act granted the SEC the authority to require investment advisers to keep appropriate books and records. It also granted the SEC inspection authority over investment advisers, similar to the authority that the SEC has over broker-dealers under the Exchange Act. The 1960 Amendments further gave the SEC the power to suspend or deny Advisers Act registration to any person who violated other Federal securities laws or engaged in certain specified offenses. Finally, the antifraud provisions of the Advisers Act were extended to apply to all investment advisers including advisers of hedge funds and private equity funds, not just advisers which were registered with the SEC.

Most of the 1970 Amendments, by contrast, were geared towards the Company Act as opposed to the Advisers Act. The 1970 Amendments, which were in large part a political compromise, left it to independent directors, rather than the courts, to decide in the first instance whether an investment adviser's fee charged to an investment company was reasonable in light of the costs incurred and services rendered by the adviser. These Amendments also provided that at least 40% of the directors or trustees of an investment company must not be "interested persons" of that investment company, a standard viewed as more stringent than the former "unaffiliated" standard required under the Company Act.

Significantly, the 1970 Amendments imposed liability on investment advisers for their failure to supervise their employees and other persons under their supervision with a view towards preventing violations of securities and other financial laws. This provision is similar to the provision imposing supervisory responsibility on broker-dealers under the Exchange Act. See Nutshell Section 55B.

The 1997 Amendments resulted from the passage of the National Securities Markets Improvement Act of 1996 ("NSMIA"). Among other things, NSMIA divided regulatory authority between the Federal Government and the individual states. By eliminating unnecessary regulatory duplication, NSMIA promoted efficiency and capital formation in the financial markets. Importantly, the bulk of the authority to regulate investment advisers was left to the SEC, with state regulatory authority primarily restricted to investment advisers with relatively small dollar amounts of assets under management. See Nutshell Section 5.

The 1999 Amendments resulted from the passage of the Gramm–Leach–Bliley Financial Modernization Act of 1999 ("GLBA"). The most significant change to the Advisers Act was a revision made to the definition of "investment adviser" found in Advisers Act Section 202(a)(11). Prior to the 1999 Amendments, banks and bank holding companies were entirely exempted from regulation under the Advisers Act. This directly reflected the Glass–Steagall Banking Act of 1933's ("GSA") limitation on banks' ability to engage in securities activities, such as advising and distributing mutual funds. The GLBA, however, repealed the GSA; therefore, the 1999 Amendments were designed to fill a perceived regulatory gap. Pursuant to those Amendments, as of May 12, 2001, banks and bank holding companies providing investment advisory services to mutual funds and other registered investment companies would be subject to SEC jurisdiction and the requirements of the Advisers Act. See Advisers Act 202(a)(11)(B) and Nutshell Section 3B(1).

In 2002, the SEC requested that its staff conduct a study on hedge funds, which are essentially "private" mutual funds. The insolvency of the Long Term Capital Fund, a multibillion dollar hedge fund that threaten the stability of the U.S. and global securities markets, was the precipitating event for the hedge fund study. Hedge funds and many of their investment advisers are exempt from Company Act registration and Advisers Act registration, respectively. The SEC became concerned about the exponential growth in the number of hedge funds and the dollar amount of assets they had under management, especially in light of the increasing participation by retail investors in hedge funds and the lack of information and other regulatory constraints on hedge funds and their advisers.

In 2003, the staff produced a study entitled the "Implications of the Growth of Hedge Funds." This study, in turn, provided the catalyst for the development and subsequent implementation of several rule changes. These rule changes (referred to collectively as the former "Hedge Fund Registration Provisions") had the effect of requiring most hedge fund advisers to register with the SEC under the Advisers Act as of February 2006. They also subjected these advisers to the recordkeeping and disclosure requirements of the Advisers Act, as well as SEC inspection.

In June 2006, just four months after the Hedge Fund Registration Provisions went into effect, the U.S. Court of Appeals for the District of Columbia, in a unanimous decision, vacated them. The Court deemed the provisions "arbitrary" and labeled the SEC's justifications for promulgating them "unreasonable." See *Goldstein v. SEC*, 451 F.3d 873 (D.C. Cir. 2006). For a thorough discussion of the former Hedge Fund Registration Provisions, the *Goldstein* decision and that decision's aftermath, see Nutshell Section 9.

In 2006, several provisions of the Advisers Act were amended while others were added. Section 202(a)(2), which sets forth the definition of a "bank" for purposes of the Act, was amended to include savings associations. As a result, most savings associations are now excluded from the definition of "investment adviser." See Advisers Act Section 202(a)(11)(A) and Nutshell Section 3B(1). Section 202(a)(11) itself was amended to exclude most nationally recognized statistical rating agencies ("NRSROs") from the definition of "investment adviser." See Advisers Act Section 202(a)(11)(F) and Nutshell Section 3B(6). Sections 203(e)(2)(B) and (e)(4) were amended to make clear that misconduct by an investment adviser in its capacity as a credit rating agency could lead to the suspension or even revocation of the adviser's registration as an investment adviser. Section 202(a)(28) was added to provide a definition of "credit rating agency." Finally, Section 210A was added to require consultation between the SEC and appropriate Federal banking authorities with respect to the investment advisory activities of banks, bank holding companies and savings associations. See Nutshell Section 58.

II. WHO IS AN INVESTMENT ADVISER?

§ 2. INTRODUCTION

Because the requirements of the Advisers Act apply only to those persons who meet the definition of "investment adviser," the question of who is an investment adviser and who is not is fundamental. Persons who do not meet the definition need not comply with any provision of the Advisers Act. However, depending on their activities, they may still be subject to other provisions of the Federal securities laws, most notably the antifraud provisions contained in Exchange Act Rule 10b–5.

As described in Nutshell Section 3B below, the definition of "investment adviser" found in Advisers Act Section 202(a)(11) contains *six exclusions*. An excluded adviser need not comply with any of the provisions of the Advisers Act, including the antifraud provisions of Section 206. Moreover, Advisers Act Section 203A(b)(1) prohibits the states from applying their laws requiring the registration, license or qualification of an investment adviser to any person excluded from the definition of "investment adviser" under Advisers Act Section 202(a)(11).

A person that falls within the "investment adviser" definition and is not excluded may, nevertheless, still be exempt from *registration* under the Advisers Act. Indeed, the Advisers Act and the rules promulgated thereunder contain a number of specific registration exemptions. See Advisers Act Section 203(b). An "exempt" adviser is not required to register with the SEC and is not subject to most provisions of the Act. This includes the Act's record-keeping requirements and performance fee restrictions. Notably, exempt advisers are still subject to the antifraud provisions of Advisers Act Section 206, as well as the antifraud provisions of the other Federal securities laws.

Finally, persons who fall within the "investment adviser" definition and do not qualify for either a definitional exclusion or a registration exemption must register as investment advisers. However, some may be required to register with one or more states rather than with the SEC depending on their particular facts and circumstances. See Advisers Act Section 203A and Nutshell Section 5B(2).

§ 3. DEFINITION OF "INVESTMENT ADVISER"

A. Three Elements

The definition of "investment adviser" has three main elements and six exclusions. Under Advisers Act Section 202(a)(11), an "investment adviser" is defined as:

any person who, for compensation, engages in the business of advising others, either directly or through publications or writings, as to the value of securities or as to the advisability of investing in, purchasing, or selling securities, or who, for compensation and as part of a regular business, issues or promulgates analyses or reports concerning securities. . . .

A "person" falling within the definition can be either a natural person or an entity. See Advisers Act Section 202(a)(16).

Unless one of six exclusions applies, a person is definitionally considered an "investment adviser" under the Advisers Act if each of the following three elements is met:

(i) The person provides advice or issues reports or analyses to others concerning securities;

(ii) The person is in the business of providing those services; and

(iii) The person provides those services for compensation.

Each of these three elements is discussed below.

(1) Advice Concerning Securities

The "advice" requirement contained in the first element generally covers persons who give advice or make recommendations or issue reports or analyses with respect to securities. The specific information that the person conveys must, as a matter of common sense, reflect that person's judgment, deduction or selectivity. Otherwise, the information does not constitute "advice" for purposes of the first element. Importantly, a person who has not been given investment discretion by a client may be, and typically is, an investment adviser, depending upon the nature of the "recommendations," "reports" and "advice" that the person provides to the client.

The advice can be about specific securities or about securities generally. Moreover, recommendations as to (1) when to purchase or sell securities, (2) when to switch between different investment alternatives (at least one of which must involve securities), (3) whether investing in securities is or is not preferable to investing in some other type of non-security investment, (4) how securities are valued or appraised, and (5) how to select or evaluate investment advisers all constitute "advice" for purposes of the first element.

Of course, the advice in question must, in fact, concern "securities." Advisers Act Section 202(a)(18) broadly defines what a "security" is for Advisers Act purposes. Not surprisingly, that definition is substantially similar to the ones contained in Securities Act Section 2(a)(1) and Exchange Act Section 3(a)(10). Thus, the term "security" includes, among other things:

· debt instruments, such as notes, bonds, debentures and other evidences of indebtedness;

· traditional stock, both common and preferred;

· certain derivative instruments such as options (including puts, calls and straddles) on any security or on any group or index of securities;

· an investment contract; and

· any interest or instrument commonly known as a "security."

Importantly, the definition of "security" does not cover many things about which people provide advice for compensation. For example, certain hard assets (*e.g.,* coins, artwork, rock 'n roll and sports memorabilia and other collectibles), real estate (but not real estate investment trust ("REIT") interests), futures contracts relating to commodities (but not futures contracts relating to securities), and business opportunities not involving securities are not covered. Accordingly, the Advisers Act does not regulate those providing advice regarding these investments.

(2) "In the Business"

The second element of the "investment adviser" definition concerns whether a person is in the "business" of providing investment advice. While the statutory definition of "investment adviser" contains two potentially different "business" standards ("engages in the business" versus "part of a regular business"), the SEC interprets both in the same manner yet very broadly. See Advisers Act Rel. No. 1092, 1987 WL 112702 (Oct. 8, 1987) ("Release 1092").

The giving of advice need not constitute the principal business activity or any particular portion of the business activities of a person in order for that person to be "in the business." The key inquiry revolves around the frequency and regularity with which a person provides advice: Does the person give advice on such a basis that it constitutes a business activity occurring with some regularity? Frequency, while obviously important, is not the only factor.

The SEC, in Release No. 1092, stated that it considers a person to be "in the business" of providing advice if one or more of the following three conditions is met:

(i) The person holds himself out as an investment adviser or as one who provides investment advice;

(ii) The person receives any separate or additional compensation that represents a clearly definable charge for providing advice about securities, regardless of whether the compensation is separate from or included within any overall compensation, or receives transaction-based compensation if the client implements the investment advice; or

(iii) The person provides specific investment advice other than in rare, isolated and non-periodic instances.

The first condition of "holding oneself out" as an adviser is an advertising/publicity-oriented notion. Thus, business cards, business stationery, a business listing in a telephone or building directory, a business website, and/or advertisements that indicate a person is an investment adviser or is seeking clients to advise satisfies this condition. Even encouraging existing clients to refer other potential clients ("word-of-mouth" advertising) is enough. The SEC has also indicated that seeking out a specific class of prospective clients, such as utility company pension plans, as opposed to the public at large *does not* change the analysis.

The second condition relating to compensation can become complicated when there is no direct connection between the advice rendered and the compensation received. If a client is paying for a "package of services" that includes investment advice, particularly in the context of a broker-dealer arrangement, then it is not always clear whether additional compensation is being paid for the advice. Determining whether a similar package of services that excludes the investment advice is available at a lower cost to the client is one possible way to tell.

The third condition concerns the regularity of investment advice. The SEC has indicated that the provision of investment advice done only occasionally as an accommodation to a client does not satisfy the "regularity" requirement of the third condition. The courts have generally agreed. In *Zinn v. Parrish*, 644 F.2d 360 (7th Cir. 1981), the Seventh Circuit held that the agent of a professional football player was not engaged in the "business" of being an investment adviser. The agent had performed investment activities irregularly and in a manner incidental to his contract negotiations and other non-investment related functions.

(3) Compensation

The third element of the "investment adviser" definition requires the person in question to provide services for "compensation." *If the person receives no compensation, he cannot be an "investment adviser" under the Advisers Act.* This effectively spares a great many persons from being regulated under the Advisers Act.

Having said that, the SEC has construed the compensation element very broadly. According to Release 1092 (emphasis added), "the receipt of *any economic benefit*, whether in the form of an advisory fee or some other fee relating to the total services rendered, commissions or some combination of the foregoing" satisfies the compensation element. The actual amount of the compensation is irrelevant to the analysis. Moreover, the compensation need not come directly from the client, but instead can come indirectly from a third party.

Compensation does not have to come in the form of a separate fee. Instead, the compensation can be part of a single fee charged for a package of different services. However, the fact that no separate fee is charged for the investment advisory portion of the services could be relevant in determining whether the person is "in the business" of giving investment advice. See Nutshell Section 3A(2).

B.   Definitional Exclusions

The definition of "investment adviser" found in Advisers Act Section 202(a)(11) contains six exclusions. An "excluded" adviser, like persons not covered by the definition in the first instance, need not comply with any of the provisions of the Advisers Act. This, of course, includes the antifraud provisions of Section 206. Moreover, states are prohibited from applying their laws requiring the registration, license or qualification of an investment adviser to any person that is an excluded adviser. See Advisers Act Section 203A(b)(1).

Section 202(a)(11) of the Advisers Act generally excludes the following six categories of persons from the definition of "investment adviser," subject to certain limitations set forth in the exclusions themselves:

- · Banks, bank holding companies and savings associations;
- · Lawyers, accountants, engineers and teachers;
- · Certain brokers and dealers;
- · Publishers of bona fide publications of general and regular circulation;
- · Government securities advisers;
- · Nationally Recognized Statistical Rating Organizations ("NRSROs"); and
- · Other persons excluded by the SEC pursuant to statutory authority.

Each of these exclusions is discussed below.

(1) Banks, Bank Holding Companies and Savings Associations

Advisers Act Section 202(a)(11)(A) excludes most bank holding companies, banks and savings associations from the definition of "investment adviser." The definition of "bank holding company" is the same as that found in the Bank Holding Company Act of 1956. The definition of "bank" generally includes Federally chartered banks and savings associations, member banks of the Federal Reserve System, and, so long as a substantial portion of their business consists of receiving deposits or exercising fiduciary powers similar to those permitted to national banks, certain other banking institutions, savings associations or trust companies doing business under the laws of any state or the United States and regulated by state or Federal bank regulators. See Advisers Act Section 202(a)(2). *Not included in the definition of "bank" are foreign banks.* Savings associations, while included, were only recently added as part of the Financial Services Regulatory Relief Act of 2006.

The bank and bank holding company exclusion has two important exceptions. First, subsidiaries of a bank or bank holding company are not entitled to the exclusion. Therefore, subsidiaries generally must register as investment advisers unless another exclusion or registration exemption applies. In this regard, the SEC has granted exemptive relief to bank subsidiaries that provided advice only to affiliated entities rather than to the public at large.

Second, any bank or bank holding company that serves as the investment adviser to a registered investment company is not entitled to the exclusion. However, if, in the context of a given bank, the investment advisory services are performed through a separately identifiable department or division of that bank, then that department or division, rather than the entire bank, is deemed the "investment adviser" and is required to register.

(2) Lawyers, Accountants, Engineers and Teachers

Advisers Act Section 202(a)(11)(B) excludes from the definition of "investment adviser" any lawyer, accountant, engineer or teacher who performs investment advisory services "solely incidental" to the practice of her profession. Congress recognized that these professionals sometimes provide investment advice to clients in connection with the performance of their professional duties. So long as their advisory activities do not constitute a separate business activity, they will not have to comply with the Advisers Act. If and when their activities rise to the level of a separate business activity, professional firms, particularly accounting firms, typically establish registered advisers to provide personal financial planning services.

The "solely incidental" language in the exclusion is the key to determining whether a professional's provision of investment advisory services constitutes a separate business activity. The SEC looks at the following three factors when determining whether a particular professional has crossed the line in this context:

(i) Whether the professional holds himself out to the public as providing investment advisory services;

(ii) Whether the advisory services rendered are in connection with and reasonably related to the professional's contract to provide professional services; and

(iii) Whether the compensation for those services is based on the same factors looked at when determining the professional's usual compensation for providing professional services.

A vivid example of when the provision of investment advisory services is not "solely incidental" to a professional's practice arises in the context of a private placement of securities conducted pursuant to Securities Act Rule 506. That rule requires that each purchaser of securities who is not an "accredited investor" (as defined in Securities Act Rule 501(a)) have, either alone or together with her "purchaser representative" (as defined in Securities Act Rule 501(h)) such knowledge and experience in financial and business matters that she is capable of evaluating the merits and risks of the prospective investment. Often, an accountant or lawyer assisting with the private placement in a professional capacity will agree to serve as the "purchaser representative" for the offering. The main function of a purchaser representative, however, is to advise prospective offerees about the merits and risks of the prospective investment. See Securities Act Rule 502(h). Because the provision of these advisory services is not "solely incidental" to the accountant's or lawyer's provision of professional services, it falls outside the exclusion provided by Advisers Act Section 202(a)(11)(B).

The "teacher" component of the professional exclusion is particularly important to one of your coauthors. Whether a particular "teacher" can take advantage of this exclusion depends on whether the alleged teacher is really a teacher or simply someone who provides investment advice under the guise of being a teacher. Thus, those that teach at accredited educational institutions as part of a regular curriculum may take full advantage of the professional exclusion. Those who do not will have the burden of showing that the primary purpose behind their "instruction" is truly educational.

(3) Certain Brokers and Dealers

a. Generally

Most broker-dealers routinely give investment advice as part of their regular business and, as a consequence, must register as investment advisers. However, the broker-dealer exclusion to the definition of "investment adviser" found in Advisers Act Section 202(a)(11)(C) explicitly recognizes that broker-dealers are already extensively regulated under the Exchange Act, state law, and FINRA rules (which will be replacing those of the NASD and the NYSE).

To take advantage of the broker-dealer exclusion, a broker-dealer must satisfy the following three requirements:

(i) It must be registered as a broker-dealer under the Exchange Act;

(ii) Its provision of investment advisory services to clients must be solely incidental to its broker-dealer business; and

(iii) It must not receive any special compensation for providing investment advisory services.

Each of these requirements is explored below.

1.   Exchange Act Registration

In order to take advantage of the broker-dealer exclusion, a broker-dealer must be registered as a broker-dealer under Section 15 of the Exchange Act. This requirement is not explicit within the Advisers Act itself. The SEC staff, however, has historically (and logically) taken this position and even codified it in subsection (a) of former Advisers Act Rule 202(a)(11)–1, the broker-dealer safe harbor ("Broker–Dealer Safe Harbor"). Unregistered broker-dealers, of course, have substantial regulatory headaches to deal with under the Exchange Act in addition to any issues arising under the Advisers Act.

Exchange Act registration also has an additional benefit in the context of the Advisers Act. Under subsection (c) of the former Broker–Dealer Safe Harbor, an Exchange Act registered broker-dealer would be deemed an "investment adviser" solely with respect to those accounts for which it provided services or received compensation that subjected it to the Advisers Act in the first place. This meant that neither the holders of all other accounts nor the SEC could pursue Advisers Act allegations against the broker-dealer with respect to those other accounts. While the Broker–Dealer Safe Harbor was judicially vacated in 2007, presumably the SEC would continue to take this position.

2. "Solely Incidental"

The second requirement of the broker-dealer exclusion is that the broker-dealer's provision of investment advisory services to clients be *solely incidental* to its *broker-dealer business*. Logically, the same considerations that arose in a context of the professionals' exclusion to the definition of "investment adviser" should be applicable in the broker-dealer context. See Nutshell Section 3B(2). Thus, a broker-dealer who renders advice incidentally rather than as a part of a regular and separate business should satisfy the "solely incidental" element.

Nevertheless, because broker-dealers generally provide more investment advice, and do so more frequently, than professionals, significant confusion arose with respect to the "solely incidental" requirement of the broker-dealer exclusion. In 2005, the SEC provided some guidance with respect to the "solely incidental" requirement by adopting former Advisers Act Rule 202(a)(11)–1, the Broker–Dealer Safe Harbor, which was judicially vacated in 2007. According to the SEC staff, the former Rule "except[ed] from the definition of investment adviser certain broker-dealers that provide[d] non-discretionary advice, solely incidental to their brokerage services, regardless of the form of compensation." Advisers Act Rel. No. 2376, 2005 WL 849053 (Apr. 12, 2005) ("Release No. 2376").

Pursuant to subsection (b) of that former Rule, a broker-dealer would *not* have satisfied the "solely incidental" element in three *nonexclusive* situations:

(i) Where it charged a separate fee, or separately contracted, for advisory services;

(ii) Where it provided advice as part of a financial plan or in connection with the provision of financial planning services, *and* it either (A) held itself out generally to the public as a financial planner or as providing financial planning services, (B) delivered a financial plan to the customer, or (C) represented to the customer that the advice was provided as part of the financial plan or in connection with financial planning services; or

(iii) Where it exercised investment discretion over any customer accounts (excluding any temporary or limited grants of discretion).

With respect to situation (ii) above, the staff of the SEC had provided significant guidance. See, e.g., Securities Industry Assoc., SEC No–Action Letter, 2005 WL 3526529 (avail. Dec. 16, 2005). On the issue of whether a particular document or financial tool constituted a "financial plan," the staff had stated that a "financial plan" generally seeks to address a wide spectrum of the client's long-term financial needs. Indeed, "what [typically] distinguishes financial planning from other types of advisory services is the breadth and scope of the advisory services provided." Release No. 2376. Thus, a financial plan could include recommendations about insurance, savings, tax and estate planning, as well as about investments.

The SEC had also distinguished a financial plan from a "financial tool." A financial tool could include questionnaires, financial calculators, asset allocation and analysis and cash flow analysis. See Release No. 2376. It could also be used to provide guidance to a customer with respect to a particular transaction or an allocation of customer funds and securities based upon the long-term needs of the client. However, it could not be applied in the context of a more comprehensive plan of the type discussed in the preceding paragraph. When a financial tool was used in this limited way, it ordinarily would have been viewed as part of a broker-dealer's brokerage relationship with its customer.

With respect to situation (iii) above, the SEC stated that the term "investment discretion" had the same meaning as that ascribed to it in Exchange Act Section 3(a)(25). Thus, as a general matter, a broker-dealer would have investment discretion with respect to a particular account if it *were authorized* to determine what securities or other property were purchased or sold by or for the account or *actually made* decisions as to what securities or other property were purchased or sold by or for the account even though some other person may have had responsibility for those investment decisions.

The Broker–Dealer Safe Harbor, particularly subparagraph (a)'s perceived liberal treatment of "special compensation," caused a great deal of consternation in the financial planner community. In an attempt to protect its turf, the Financial Planning

Association sued the SEC challenging its authority to adopt that Safe Harbor under subparagraph (G) of Advisers Act Section 202(a)(11). The U.S. District Court for the District of Columbia sided with the Financial Planning Association and vacated Advisers Act Rule 202(a)(11)–1. See *Financial Planning Assoc. v. SEC*, 482 F.3d 481 (D.C. Cir. 2007) and Nutshell Section 3B(3)d.

3. "Special Compensation"

Pursuant to the third requirement of the broker-dealer exclusion, a broker-dealer must not receive any *special compensation* for providing investment advisory services. This is true even if the advice provided is "incidental" to the broker-dealer's business. Factual determinations as to what is "special," however, have become less clear since Congress passed legislation deregulating commission rates as part of the Securities Acts Amendments of 1975. Among other things, those Amendments added Exchange Act Section 6(e)(1). This Section prohibits national securities exchanges from imposing any schedule, or fixing rates, of commissions, allowances, discounts, or other fees charged by its members.

Over the years since 1975, brokerage firms developed different ways to charge for commission services, with some "unbundling" their brokerage commissions from their research and advisory service charges. Moreover, no-frills "discount" brokerage firms gained substantial popularity thus posing a significant competitive threat to more traditional "full-service" brokerage firms. Therefore, the key questions to ask in this regard are: Was the broker specifically compensated for investment advice itself? Or was the compensation the broker received merely incidental to the brokerage or other services he provided?

In making these determinations, the SEC will not consider any differential between the fee individually negotiated with one client as opposed to that negotiated with another client or clients. "Special consideration" will not be found merely because a broker-dealer receives a large amount of brokerage commissions unless additional evidence indicates that the broker-dealer received the revenue "specifically" for the rendering of investment advice. See *Kaufman v. Merrill Lynch, Pierce, Fenner & Smith, Inc.*, 464 F.Supp. 528 (D. Md. 1978). However, even if a broker's large share of profits is not designated for any specific purpose, it may nevertheless be deemed "special consideration" if it does not constitute a broker's commission earned in the ordinary course of business. See *SEC v. Kenton Capital, Ltd.*, 69 F. Supp. 2d 1 (D.D.C. 1998).

In 2005, the SEC attempted to provide some guidance with respect to the "special compensation" requirement by adopting former Advisers Act Rule 202(a)(11)–1, the Broker–Dealer Safe Harbor, which was judicially vacated in 2007. According to the SEC staff, the former Rule "except[ed] from the definition of investment adviser certain broker-dealers that provide[d] non-discretionary advice, solely incidental to their brokerage services, *regardless of the form of compensation.*" Advisers Act Rel. No. 2376 (Apr. 12, 2005) (emphasis added).

Pursuant to subsection (a)(2) of that former Rule, the SEC would not deem a registered broker-dealer to have received special compensation solely because it charged a commission, mark-up, markdown or similar fee for brokerage services that was greater than or less than one it charged another customer. This was consistent with the position the SEC had historically taken on this issue.

Moreover, pursuant to subsection (a)(1) of that former Rule, even if a registered broker-dealer received special compensation, the SEC would still not deem it to be an investment adviser provided that the following three conditions were met:

(i) It must not have charged a separate fee, or separately contracted, for advisory services with a customer;

(ii) Any investment advice it had provided with respect to accounts from which it received special compensation must have been solely incidental to the brokerage services provided to those accounts (in particular it must not have exercised investment discretion over those accounts); and

(iii) Advertisements for, and contracts, agreements, applications and other forms governing, accounts for which it was to receive special compensation must have included the following statement prominently displayed:

"Your account is a brokerage account and not an advisory account. Our interests may not always be the same as yours. Please ask us questions to make sure you understand your rights and our obligations to you, including the extent of our obligations to disclose conflicts of interest and act in your best interest. We are paid by both you and, sometimes, by people who compensate us based on what you buy. Therefore, our profits, and our salespersons' compensation, may vary by product and over time." [Note: this statement must also have identified an appropriate person at the broker-dealer with whom a customer could discuss the aforementioned differences.]

The Broker–Dealer Safe Harbor, particularly subparagraph (a)'s perceived liberal treatment of "special compensation," caused a great deal of consternation in the financial planner community. In an attempt to protect its turf, the Financial Planning Association sued the SEC challenging its authority to adopt that Safe Harbor under subparagraph (G) of Advisers Act Section 202(a)(11). The U.S. District Court for the District of Columbia sided with the Financial Planning Association and vacated Advisers Act Rule 202(a)(11)–1. See *Financial Planning Assoc. v. SEC*, 482 F.3d 481 (D.C. Cir. 2007) and Nutshell Section 3B(3)d.

b. *Foreign Broker–Dealers*

Generally, a foreign broker-dealer, like a domestic broker-dealer, must register as a broker-dealer under the Exchange Act if it wants to avail itself of the broker-dealer exclusion under the Advisers Act. See Nutshell Section 3B(3)a1. However, many foreign broker-dealers actively seek to legally avoid broker-dealer registration under the Exchange Act. The question thus arises as to whether an *unregistered* foreign broker-dealer should nonetheless be able to avail itself of the broker-dealer exclusion under the Advisers Act with respect to its investment advisory services.

In a series of no-action letters, the SEC has indicated that broker-dealer registration under the Exchange Act is not necessary when a foreign broker-dealer meets certain of the conditions specified in Exchange Act Rule 15a–6 (*i.e.,* those found in paragraphs (a)(2), (a)(3) or (a)(4) of that Rule *and* limits its advisory activities to those described in the broker-dealer exclusion under the Advisers Act. See, e.g., Charterhouse Tilney, SEC No–Action Letter, 1993 WL 277798 (avail. July 15, 1993); Barclays PLC, SEC No–Action Letter, 1991 WL 176731 (avail. Feb. 14, 1991). Exchange Act Rule 15a–6 provides a foreign broker-dealer with an exemption to Exchange Act broker-dealer registration when its activities in the U.S. are limited to those prescribed in the Rule.

c. Registered Representatives of a Broker–Dealer

A registered representative of a broker-dealer is covered by the broker-dealer exclusion if his advisory activities are subject to the control of a broker-dealer. The control exercised by the broker-dealer must satisfy the test for control provided in Section 3(a)(18) of the Exchange Act. That Section defines the term "person associated with a broker or dealer" or "associated person of a broker or dealer."

A key factor in determining the availability of the broker-dealer exclusion is the capacity in which a registered representative provides investment advice. If the registered representative gives the advice apart from his employment with the broker-dealer (such as by him establishing a separate financial planning practice), or is given without the approval of the broker-dealer, then the exclusion is not available. Thus, in these cases, the registered representative must register under the Advisers Act unless another definitional exclusion or a registration exemption is available.

Traditionally, a registered representative who held himself out personally to the public as a financial planner could not rely on the exclusion. The staff of the SEC has indicated that a representative's use of an educational or specialized training credential or degree such as "Certified Financial Planner" on his business card or letterhead would constitute "holding out." In 2005, pursuant to former Advisers Act Rule 202(a)(11)–1(b)(2), the Broker–Dealer Safe Harbor, the SEC required a representative to not only hold himself out to the public but also to provide a customer with advice as part of a financial plan or in connection with providing financial planning services before losing the availability of the broker-dealer exclusion. In 2007, the

Broker–Dealer Safe Harbor was judicially vacated. See *Financial Planning Assoc. v. SEC*, 482 F.3d 481 (D.C. Cir. 2007) and Nutshell Section 3B(3)d.

d. Availability of Other Exclusions

Given that Congress provided a specific definitional exclusion for broker-dealers in Advisers Act Section 202(a)(11)(C), should a broker-dealer which does not qualify for that exclusion nevertheless be able to take advantage of another definitional exclusion assuming it satisfies the requirements of that exclusion? If yes, the obvious exclusions would be subparagraphs (E) and (G) of Advisers Act Section 202(a)(11).

Subparagraph (E) excludes a person who provides advice *solely* with respect to U.S. government securities. A broker-dealer, therefore, who satisfied this requirement would qualify for an exclusion under subparagraph (E). See Nutshell Section 3B(5). Subparagraph (G), by contrast, allows the SEC to exclude other persons from the definition of "investment adviser" by rule, regulation or order if they do not fall within the Congressional intent of Section 202(a)(11). See Nutshell Section 3B(7).

The SEC pointed to subparagraph (G) (formerly subparagraph (F)), as well as Advisers Act Section 211(a) (its general Congressional grant of authority to make, amend and rescind rules and regulations under the Advisers Act), as providing it with the authority to adopt Advisers Act Rule 202(a)(11)–1, the former Broker–Dealer Safe Harbor. See Advisers Act Rel. No. 2376, 2005 WL 849053 (Apr. 15,

2005). In a classic battle over turf between financial planners and broker-dealers, the Financial Planning Association ("FPA") sued the SEC challenging its authority to adopt the Broker–Dealer Safe Harbor. See *Financial Planning Assoc. v. SEC*, 482 F.3d 481 (D.C. Cir. 2007). In its brief, the FPA argued that, despite the SEC's assertions to the contrary, subparagraph (G) of Advisers Act Section 202(a)(11) did not allow the SEC to rewrite the terms of the existing broker-dealer exclusion found in subparagraph (C). In the FPA's view, the Broker–Dealer Safe Harbor interpreted the "solely incidental" prong of subparagraph (C) out of existence and essentially eliminated Congress' "special compensation" requirement. Furthermore, the Broker–Dealer Safe Harbor allowed a class of broker-dealers calling themselves "financial advisers" and "financial consultants" to operate outside the fiduciary obligations of the Advisers Act. Indeed, the fact that brokers were providing more investment advisory services, according to the FPA, could not be a good reason for exempting them from the Advisers Act. The FPA asserted that the Broker–Dealer Safe Harbor injured the reputations of its members, lowered those members' apparent professional standards and injured their competitive interests.

In response, the SEC stated that it "reasonably concluded, under subparagraph [(G)], that: (a) broker-dealers offering fee-based brokerage accounts covered by the [Broker–Dealer Safe Harbor]—who indisputably could not have existed in 1940—were 'other persons' than the subgroup of broker-dealers already excepted from the [Advisers] Act; and (b) it would be inconsistent with congressional intent to subject them to [Advisers Act] regulation." Furthermore, the SEC contended that the FPA's "inflammatory and baseless argument" that it "distorted the [Advisers Act's] legislative history to 'protect broker-dealers' misconstrue[d]'" the agency's findings "and the relevant history."

The U.S. Court of Appeals for the District of Columbia ruled in favor of the FPA, holding that the SEC exceeded its authority under subsection (G) and vacated the Broker–Dealer Safe Harbor. Specifically, the Court found that an exemption for broker-dealers that was broader than that described in subsection (C) was not supported by legislative intent due to the fact that broker-dealers were expressly addressed in subsection (C). The Court found that the Broker–Dealer Safe Harbor did not meet the statutory requirement that exemptions under subsection (G) be consistent with the "intent" of Section 202(a)(11). Accordingly, broker-dealers were not "other persons" under subsection (G), as "other persons" were only those persons not explicitly addressed by Congress.

The SEC chose not to appeal the adverse decision, although most observers had expected the SEC to seek an en banc rehearing by the full Court. According to the SEC, the Court's ruling affected an estimated one million brokerage accounts, holding an estimated $300 billion in assets.

The SEC, however, has adopted Advisers Act Rule 206(3)–3T, a temporary rule that provides investment advisers who are Dual Registrants with limited relief from the trade-by-trade prior written consent requirement under Advisers Act Section 206(3) for principal trades executed with clients on a nondiscretionary basis. See Nutshell Section 30B(1) for a discussion of principal trades. The temporary Rule, which expires on December 31, 2009, requires a Dual Registrant to provide written notice to and obtain a blanket written consent to principal trades from a nondiscretionary investment advisory client. The written notice and consent requirements are required on a one-time basis, and the written notice must inform the client that the client can revoke his consent at any time without penalty. Once the Dual Registrant has satisfied the written notice and consent requirements, it need only inform the client orally at the time of each trade that the firm may trade with the client on a principal basis in the transaction. The client must agree to the principal trade, and the trade confirmation required by Exchange Act Rule 10b–10 must indicate that the client authorized the principal trade.

The temporary Rule does not provide relief if the principal trade involves (a) a security issued by the Dual Registrant (or its affiliates) or (b) a transaction in which the Dual Registrant (or its affiliates) acts as an underwriter, other than offerings involving investment grade debt securities.

(4) Publishers of Bona Fide Publications of General and Regular Circulation

Under Advisers Act Section 202(a)(11)(D), any "publisher of any bona fide newspaper, news magazine or business or financial publication of general and regular circulation" is excluded from the definition of "investment adviser." Historically, the SEC narrowly interpreted this exclusion by making it available only to a newsletter that was not primarily a vehicle for distributing investment advice. In *Lowe v. SEC*, 472 U.S. 181 (1985), however, the U.S. Supreme Court construed the exclusion much more broadly. As explained below, the Court held that an alleged publisher's publication must meet three requirements before the publisher can avail itself of the bona fide publisher exclusion:

(i) The publication must be *"bona fide,"* meaning that it must contain disinterested commentary and analysis as opposed to promotional material disseminated by a "tout";

(ii) The publication must be of *"regular and general circulation,"* meaning that its issuance must not be timed to activity in the securities market; and

(iii) The publication must offer only *"impersonalized advice,"* which is advice not tailored to the special needs of a specific client or group of clients.

Lowe involved Christopher Lowe, the president and principal shareholder of Lowe Management Corporation. His corporation had been a registered investment adviser under the Advisers Act, but the SEC revoked its registration due to fraud and other malfeasance. The SEC also prohibited Lowe himself from associating with any investment adviser there-after.

Despite this, Lowe began issuing *impersonalized* investment advice and commentary in securities newsletters published by him and certain of his affiliated companies. He also established some in-vestment "hotlines" that disseminated updated in-formation in between publications.

Upon learning of Lowe's activities, the SEC brought suit against him alleging that he and his affiliated companies were unregistered investment advisers in violation of Advisers Act Section 203(a). The SEC sought a permanent injunction restraining Lowe from distributing any further newsletters. The District Court enjoined Lowe from giving in-vestment advice to subscribers through his tele-phone hotline, by individual letter or in person, but it refused to enjoin him from continuing his publi-cation activities believing that they fell within the bona fide publisher exclusion. The Court of Appeals, however, reversed the District Court, holding that Lowe was an unregistered investment adviser and his publications did not fall within the exclusion.

The U.S. Supreme Court ultimately agreed to hear Lowe's appeal in order to determine whether the injunction against Lowe violated his rights un-der the *First Amendment* to the U.S. Constitution. The SEC argued that the restraint on investment advisers' free speech was warranted due to the history of abuse in the securities industry relating to unregistered and unqualified persons giving out investment advice. Lowe countered that "person-to-person" communication in a commercial setting may be subjected to regulation, but that the term "investment adviser" could not be so broadly defined as to encompass the distribution of "impersonal investment advice and commentary in a public market."

Although the Supreme Court believed that Lowe fell within the definition of "investment adviser" based on his activities, the Court also noted that the definition was "far from absolute." It then turned to an analysis of the bona fide publisher exclusion. According to the Court, two points were "tolerably clear." First, Congress did not intend to exclude publications that are distributed by investment advisers as a normal part of the business of servicing their clients. Indeed, Congress was primarily interested in "regulating the business of rendering personalized investment advice...." Second, regulating the press through the licensing of impersonalized publishing activities clearly raised First Amendment concerns.

The Court pointed out that the bona fide publisher exclusion itself imposed two requirements on those who wished to use it. First, the publication in question must be "bona fide." To be "bona fide," the publication must contain "disinterested commentary and analysis" as opposed to promotional material disseminated by a "tout." Second, the publication must be "of regular and general circulation." While the Court did not elaborate on this second requirement, it did state that "people who

send out bulletins from time to time on the advisability of buying and selling stocks" or the "hit and
run tipsters" would not satisfy it. In a footnote, the
Court described a tipster as a person "who through
newspaper advertisements offers to send, for a nom-
inal price, a list of stocks that are sure to go up."

The Court then held that Lowe's publications met
the two requirements contained within the bona
fide publisher exclusion, as those publications contained disinterested material and were offered to
the public on a regular schedule. However, the
Court then created a third requirement to the use
of the bona fide publisher exclusion that was not in
the exclusion itself. That third requirement is that
the publications must not be personalized communications directed at "clients." Indeed, the Court underscored that the dangers of "fraud, deception, or
overreaching that motivated the enactment of the
[Advisers Act] are present in personalized communications but are not replicated in publications that
are advertised and sold in an open market." Lowe's
publications satisfied this third requirement.

In response to the SEC's argument that the publications made suggestions about specific securities,
the Court stated that a publication that recommends a particular security in an impersonalized
fashion still qualifies for the bona fide publisher
exclusion. While a different outcome might be warranted if Lowe was recommending stocks he personally owned, the Court noted that the SEC presented
no evidence on this point. The Court also rejected
the SEC's argument that Lowe could not be "bona

fide" due to his previous run in with the SEC, as the Court noted that the term "bona fide" modifies the term "publication" and not the term "publisher." Finally, because the Court held that Lowe's publications clearly fell within the bona fide publisher exclusion, it found it unnecessary to reach the First Amendment issue.

A more modern case involving the bona fide publisher exclusion is *SEC v. Gun Soo Oh Park*, 99 F. Supp. 2d 889 (N.D. Ill. 2000). During the dot.com boom of the late 1990s, Mr. Park ran a website, part of which was fee based, named "Tokyojoe.com." The site was designed to promote Park's personal stock picking prowess. All in all, he collected over $1.1 million in fees.

The SEC alleged that Park was engaged in "scalping" and "touting." "Scalping" consists of pumping up stock prices while selling shares at the same time. "Touting," in this context, consists of promoting a given company's stock in exchange for free stock or other compensation from that company.

The SEC also alleged that Park was operating as an illegal investment adviser under the Advisers Act. However, pointing to *Lowe v. SEC*, 472 U.S. 181 (1985), Park insisted he was a bona fide publisher deserving of the bona fide publisher exclusion. Specifically, he claimed that he did not provide personalized investment advice, and thus what the SEC was really trying to do was regulate his First Amendment rights.

Unfortunately for Park, an alleged publisher must satisfy all three requirements set forth in *Lowe* before the bona fide publisher exclusion is available. In denying Park's motion to dismiss, the District Court found that the first requirement was not met because Park's website publication was not "bona fide." Indeed, it was littered with promotional material, effusive testimonials, misleading performance information and other "touts."

With respect to the second requirement, the Court found that Park's website may not have constituted a "general and regular" publication. According to the Court, to satisfy this requirement the publication cannot be timed to "specific market activity, or to events affecting or having the ability to affect the securities industry." According to the SEC, Park had been sporadically posting stock picks and sending out e-mails so as to take advantage of certain prices and inflate them or to sell or purchase his own shares of a particular stock profitably. If the SEC's allegations proved to be true, the Court stated that there would not be anything "general or regular" about Park's publications.

In terms of the third requirement, the Court was not entirely convinced that Park did not tell subscribers on an individualized basis to buy, sell or hold securities. Indeed, the Court seems to indicate that part of what Park was doing could be viewed as "personalized." He had sent e-mails containing stock picks directly to individual e-mail accounts. He had also personally answered individual questions posited by subscribers in his chat room.

Through his activities, some of his stock picks became stock picks of some of his individual subscribers as well. When Park thereafter talked about those stocks, he was talking about stocks that some of his subscribers actually did own.

(5) Government Securities Advisers

Under Advisers Act Section 202(a)(11)(E), a person who provides advice *solely* with respect to U.S. government securities is excluded from the definition of "investment adviser." Thus, a broker-dealer providing advice solely with respect to these securities would not be subject to the Advisers Act. However, that broker-dealer would remain subject to the requirements of the Exchange Act, as the Exchange Act does not exempt persons dealing exclusively in U.S. government securities from the definition of "broker" or "dealer."

(6) Nationally Recognized Statistical Rating Organizations

Under Advisers Act Section 202(a)(11)(F), a nationally recognized statistical rating organization ("NRSRO"), as defined in Exchange Act Section 3(a)(62), is excluded from the definition of "investment adviser." However, a NRSRO will not be excluded if it issues recommendations with respect to purchasing, selling or holding securities or manages assets, consisting in whole or in part of securities, on behalf of others. The NRSRO exclusion was recently added as part of the Credit Rating Agency Reform Act of 2006, an Act designed to improve competition in the ratings industry while reducing abusive practices and conflicts of interest. As a practical matter, each of the three major NRSROs (Moody's Investors Service Inc., Standard & Poor's Corp. and Fitch Ratings) is a registered investment adviser.

(7) Other Persons Excluded by the SEC Pursuant to Statutory Authority

Under Advisers Act Section 202(a)(11)(G) (formerly subparagraph (F)), the SEC may exclude any other person from the definition of investment adviser by rule, regulation or order if that person does not fall within the Congressional intent of Section 202(a)(11). Because subparagraph (G) requires the filing of a formal application with the SEC, the staff of the SEC cannot provide relief to parties requesting it in the form of a no-action letter.

The SEC has used its power under subparagraph (G) to exclude court-appointed trustees, receivers and guardians from the definition of investment adviser under the theory that court supervision of those individuals is a sufficient substitute to regulation under the Advisers Act. The SEC has also excluded persons who provide investment advisory services on a very narrow basis. For example, the SEC deemed a corporation that solely advised an affiliated company as falling outside the Congressional intent of Section 202(a)(11).

As mentioned earlier, the SEC also pointed to subparagraph (G) and Advisers Act Section 211(a) for the authority to adopt Advisers Act Rule 202(a)(11)–1, the former Broker–Dealer Safe Harbor. In an attempt to protect its turf, the Financial

Planning Association sued the SEC challenging its authority to adopt that Safe Harbor under subparagraph (G) of Advisers Act Section 202(a)(11). The U.S. District Court for the District of Columbia sided with the Financial Planning Association and vacated Advisers Act Rule 202(a)(11)–1. See *Financial Planning Assoc. v. SEC*, 482 F.3d 481 (D.C. Cir. 2007) and Nutshell Section 3B(3)d.

C. Governmental Entities

Governmental entities are completely carved out from regulation under the Advisers Act. Advisers Act Section 202(b) provides that the Act shall not apply to the United States, a state, or any political subdivision of a state, or any agency, authority, corporation or instrumentality of the U.S. or the states.

§ 4. EXEMPTION FROM REGISTRATION

Those falling within the definition of "investment adviser" and not excluded under Section 202(a)(11) may still be *exempt from registration* under the Advisers Act. Exempt advisers are not required to register with the SEC and are not subject to most provisions of the Act. This includes the Act's record-keeping requirements and performance fee restrictions. Notably, exempt advisers are still subject to the antifraud provisions of Advisers Act Section 206, as well as the antifraud provisions of the other Federal securities laws.

There are six categories of persons exempt from registration under Advisers Act Section 203(b):

· Intrastate advisers;

· Advisers to insurance companies only;

· Private investment advisers;

· Charitable organizations;

· Church plans; and

· Commodity trading advisers.

Each of these categories is considered below.

A. Intrastate Advisers

The Advisers Act is designed to regulate only those advisers engaged in interstate commerce. See Advisers Act Section 201. Accordingly, Advisers Act Section 203(b)(1) exempts from registration:

Any investment adviser all of whose clients are residents of the state within which such investment adviser maintains his or its principal office and place of business, and who does not furnish advice or issue analyses or reports with respect to securities listed or admitted to unlisted trading privileges on any national securities exchange[.]

Based on the foregoing, an adviser must satisfy two conditions in order to rely on the "intrastate adviser" registration exemption. First, an adviser is limited to serving clients who are residents of the state in which the adviser maintains his or its principal office and place of business. Second, an adviser must not furnish advice or issue analyses or reports with respect to securities listed, or securities admitted to unlisted trading privileges, on any national securities exchange. Because most investment advisers provide advice relating to exchange-traded securities, and thus do not satisfy the second condition, the intrastate adviser exemption has very limited utility.

B. Advisers to Insurance Companies Only

Consistent with the general Federal policy of permitting states to regulate insurance companies, Advisers Act Section 203(b)(2) exempts from registration any investment adviser whose only clients are insurance companies. Insurance companies themselves, by contrast, are neither excluded from the definition of "investment adviser" under Section 202(a)(11) nor exempt from registration. Thus, those falling within the definition of "investment adviser" based on their activities must register under the Advisers Act unless another exemption is available.

C. Private Investment Advisers

Relied on heavily by those advising *hedge funds*, *private equity funds* and *collateral debt obligation (CDO) funds*, Advisers Act Section 203(b)(3) (the "Private Adviser Registration Exemption") exempts from registration any investment adviser which:

(i) Has *fewer than 15 clients* during the course of the preceding 12 months;

(ii) Does not hold itself out generally to the public as an investment adviser; and

(iii) Does not act as an investment adviser to either a registered investment company or a business development company.

Each of these three conditions is discussed below.

(1) "Fewer than 15 Clients"

With respect to the first condition to the Private Adviser Registration Exemption, Advisers Act Rule 203(b)(3)–1 provides a nonexclusive safe harbor for determining who is a "client" of an investment adviser. Once determinations in this regard are made, it is possible to calculate the number of clients an investment adviser has. Subparagraph (a) of the Rule provides two general rules on counting clients, while subparagraph (b) provides several special rules.

Before discussing these rules, it is worth double underscoring that Advisers Act Section 208(d) makes it unlawful for any person *indirectly*, or through or by any other person, to do any act or thing which would be unlawful for such person to do directly under either the Advisers Act or the Advisers Act Rules. See Nutshell Section 57. Those considering playing "fast and loose" with the rules on counting clients should be mindful of Section 208(d).

a.   *General Rules on Counting Clients*

The first general rule on counting clients is found in subparagraph (a)(1) of Advisers Act Rule 203(b)(3)–1. It allows an adviser to count as a "single" client the following persons:

(i) a natural person and his minor children;

(ii) any relative, spouse, or relative of the spouse of that natural person who shares that person's principal residence; and

(iii) any accounts or trusts whose only primary beneficiaries are the individuals specified in clauses (i) and (ii) above.

The second general rule on counting clients is found in subparagraph (a)(2) of Advisers Act Rule 203(b)(3)–1. It allows an adviser to count as a "single" client any corporation, general or limited partnership, limited liability company (LLC) or business trust if one condition is met: the adviser must provide the legal organization with investment advice based on the *organization's objectives* rather than the individual investment objectives of the organization's owners. In other words, there is generally no need to "look through" an entity and count its individual investors as clients of the adviser when determining whether the adviser has "fewer than 15 clients." See Advisers Act Rule 203(b)(3)–1(a)(2)(i). In addition, two or more entities that meet the condition described above may be counted as a single "client" if those entities have identical owners. See Advisers Act Rule 203(b)(3)–1(a)(2)(ii).

Of course, the anti-"look through" language found in subparagraph (a)(2)(i) had allowed most hedge fund advisers to avoid registration with the SEC, unless the hedge fund adviser advised more than 14 hedge funds and other separately managed accounts. Effective February 2006, new Advisers

Act Rule 203(b)(3)–2 changed the way advisers were required to count clients. Under that Rule, an adviser to a so-called "private fund" had to "look though" the fund and count each shareholder, limited partner, member, and beneficial owner of that fund as a separate client of the adviser when determining whether the first condition to the Private Adviser Registration Exemption had been met. A "private fund" was essentially defined as a hedge fund under revised Advisers Act Rule 203(b)(3)–1(d) which permitted hedge fund investors to redeem any portion of their investment in the fund within two years from the purchase date of the investment.

Only four months after Rule 203(b)(3)–2 became effective, the U.S. Court of Appeals for the District of Columbia determined that the SEC did not have the authority to promulgate the Rule. See *Goldstein v. SEC*, 451 F.3d 873 (D.C. Cir. 2006). Calling the Rule "arbitrary," the Court vacated it and sent it back to the SEC for reconsideration. Thus, hedge fund advisers are once again entitled to count an entity as a "single" client so long as the provisions of subparagraph (a)(2)(i) of Rule 203(b)(3)–1 are met. See Nutshell Section 9E(1) for a full discussion of the *Goldstein* decision and its implications.

b. *Special Rules on Counting Clients*

Subparagraph (b) of Rule 203(b)(3)–1 contains several additional special rules for determining who is a client of an adviser. Subparagraph (b)(1) provides that an adviser must count as a separate client the owner of a legal organization if that owner receives investment advice separately and apart from the organization. Subparagraph (b)(2) qualifies subparagraph (b)(1) by not requiring advisers to count as a separate client an owner of a legal organization solely because that owner receives periodic reports from the adviser or is solicited by the adviser on behalf of the legal organization.

Subparagraph (b)(3) provides that a limited partnership or limited liability company is a client of any general partner, managing member or other person acting as an investment adviser to the partnership or limited liability company. Subparagraph (b)(4) provides that an adviser does not have to count as a client any person to whom the adviser provides investment advice without compensation, which, of course, is consistent with the definition of "investment adviser" found in Advisers Act Section 202(a)(11). Subparagraph (b)(5) applies to offshore advisers, *i.e.,* those advisers whose principal office and place of business are located outside the U.S. Under that subparagraph, offshore advisers do not have to count as clients persons who are not residents of the U.S.

(2) "Holding Itself Out" Generally to the Public

The second condition to the Private Adviser Registration Exemption is that the person in question must not hold himself or itself out generally to the public as an investment adviser. "Holding oneself out" as an adviser is an advertising/publicity-oriented notion. Thus, business cards, business stationery, a business listing in a telephone or building directory, a business website, and/or advertisements that indicate a person is an investment adviser or is seeking clients to advise satisfies this condition. Even encouraging existing clients to refer other potential clients ("word-of-mouth" advertising) is enough. The SEC has also indicated that seeking out a specific class of prospective clients, such as utility company pension plans, as opposed to the public at large *does not* change the analysis.

However, a person is not deemed to be holding himself or itself out generally to the public as an investment adviser, within the meaning of Advisers Act Section 203(b)(3), solely because that person participates in a non-public offering of interests in a limited partnership under the Securities Act. See Advisers Act Rule 203(b)(3)–1(c). Thus, a hedge fund adviser would not be deemed to be "holding itself out to the public" as an investment adviser solely because it participates in a private offering of the hedge fund's securities under the Securities Act.

(3) Registered Investment Companies and Business Development Companies

The third and final condition to the Private Adviser Registration Exemption is that the person in question must not act as an investment adviser to either an investment company registered as such under the Company Act or a business development company. The term "business development company," which is defined in Advisers Act Section

202(a)(22), is designed to cover venture capital funds. Indeed, in the Small Business Investment Incentive Act of 1980, Congress generally modeled the definition of business development company on the capital formation activities of venture capital funds. A business development company is like an investment company in that it is operated for the purpose of making investments in securities. However, unlike an investment company, it often purchases large equity stakes in the issuers of those securities and makes significant managerial assistance available to those issuers.

D. Charitable Organizations

Advisers Act Section 203(b)(4) exempts from registration any investment adviser that is a "charitable organization" as defined in Company Act Section 3(c)(10)(D). This exemption arose when the Advisers Act, as well as several other Federal securities laws, were amended as a result of the enactment of the Philanthropy Protection Act of 1995. The purpose of the Philanthropy Protection Act was to facilitate contributions to charitable organizations.

Importantly, Advisers Act Section 203(b)(4) also exempts any trustee, director, officer, employee or volunteer of a charitable organization if two conditions are met. First, the person must be acting within the scope of his employment or duties with the organization. Second, the person's advice, analyses or reports must only be provided to the charitable organization itself and certain charitable funds that are excluded from the definition of "investment company" under Company Act Section 3(c)(10)(D).

E. Church Plans

Advisers Act Section 203(b)(5) exempts three types of investment advisers from registration under the Advisers Act. First, it exempts any "church plan" as defined in Section 414(e) of the IRC. Second, it exempts any person or entity eligible to establish and maintain such a plan under the IRC. Lastly, it exempts any trustee, director, officer or employee of or volunteer for any such plan, so long as that person, acting in such capacity, provides investment advice exclusively to, or with respect to, any church plan that is excluded from the definition of "investment company" under Company Act Section 3(c)(14).

F. Commodity Trading Advisers

Advisers Act Section 203(b)(6) exempts from registration under the Advisers Act any investment adviser that is registered with the Commodity Futures Trading Commission as a "commodity trading adviser" if two conditions are met. First, the adviser's business cannot primarily consist of acting as an investment adviser. Second, the adviser must not act as an investment adviser to either an investment company registered under the Company Act or a business development company.

Advisers Act Section 203(b)(6) was added as part of the enactment of the Commodity Futures Modernization Act of 2000 (the "CFMA"). The CFMA reflected in large part Congress' attempt to settle the turf war between the SEC and the CFTC over which regulatory agency would regulate derivative instruments.

A SEC-registered investment adviser, by contrast, may have to register as a commodity trading adviser with the CFTC depending on its activities. See Nutshell Section 8.

III. FEDERAL AND STATE AUTHORITY OVER INVESTMENT ADVISERS

§ 5. REGULATORY SCHEME

A. Dual Regulatory Scheme (Pre–1997)

Until 1997, investment advisers typically fell under a dual regulatory scheme. This scheme subjected them to registration, fees, inspection and substantive regulation at both the Federal and state levels. In 1997, Congress implemented a bifurcated regulatory system upon passage of the Investment Advisers Supervision Coordination Act, which formed a part of the National Securities Markets Improvement Act of 1996 ("NSMIA"). This bifurcation resulted in a more efficient investment adviser regulatory scheme and largely relieved the SEC from its obligation to police investment advisers with small dollar amounts of assets under management.

B. Bifurcated Regulatory Scheme (1997 to Present)

As described below, each investment adviser is now generally subject to registration and regulation *primarily* at either the Federal or state level, but not both. The nature of an adviser's business and the dollar amount of its "assets under management" determine where it must register and by whom it is primarily regulated.

(1) Federal Registration and Regulation

a. *Mandatory Federal Registration*

Advisers Act Section 203A (aptly entitled "State and Federal Responsibilities") and Advisers Act Rules 203A–1 and 203A–2 control whether a given investment adviser must register with the SEC rather than with one or more of the states. Although certain language in that Section and those Rules appears to give an investment adviser leeway as to whether to register with the SEC or the states, it is generally interpreted much more narrowly in favor of SEC registration.

Synthesizing Section 203A with Rules 203A–1 and 203A–2 yields the following conclusion. Unless excepted from the definition of "investment adviser" or a registration exemption is available to it, an investment adviser *must register* with the SEC if it:

(i) has one or more investment company clients registered under the Company Act (see Section 203A(a)(1)(B));

(ii) has at least $30 million or more in "assets under management" (see Rule 203A–1(a)(1)(i));

(iii) maintains its principal office and place of business in a state that does not require registration of investment advisers (currently, only Wyoming does not) (see Section 203A(a)(1));

(iv) maintains its principal place of business outside the U.S., but has U.S. clients;

(v) is a nationally recognized statistical rating organization ("NRSRO") (*e.g.,* Moody's Investors Service Inc. and Standard & Poor's Corp.) that issues recommendations with respect to purchasing, selling or holding securities or manages assets, consisting in whole or in part of securities, on behalf of others (see Section 202(a)(11)(F), Rule 203A–2(a) and Nutshell Section 3B(6));

(vi) is a "pension consultant" (as defined in Rule 203A–2(b)(2)) with respect to assets of certain pension plans described in ERISA having an aggregate value of at least $50 million (see Rule 203A–2(b)); or

(vii) is affiliated with (*i.e.,* controls, is controlled by, or is under common control with) an SEC-registered investment adviser and shares the same principal office and place of business with that adviser (see Rule 203A–2(c)).

For purposes of category (vii) above, "control" means the power to direct or cause the direction of the management or policies of an investment adviser, whether through ownership of securities, by contract or otherwise. Any person that directly or indirectly has the right to vote 25% or more of the voting securities, or is entitled to 25% or more of the profits, of an investment adviser is presumed to control that investment adviser. See Rule 203A–2(c). "Principal office and place of business" means the executive office of the investment adviser from which the officers, partners or managers of that adviser direct, control and coordinate the activities of the adviser. See Rule 203A–3(c).

b. Optional Federal Registration

As described below, four types of investment adviser, pursuant to SEC rules, *have the option* to register at either the Federal or state level. Whether a particular adviser would choose to exercise its option to register with the SEC depends on whether it views the Federal regulatory regime as more or less burdensome than the state(s) regulatory regime(s) in question. Often, an adviser will register at the state level in order to avoid SEC inspections and regulations. In other instances, an adviser may seek the regulatory predictability of SEC registration over the unpredictability and potentially more burdensome state regulatory regime. For example, some states require investment advisers to maintain a minimum amount of net capital and, if the advisers have custody of clients' assets or discretionary authority over clients' accounts, to maintain a surety bond.

The first type consists of investment advisers that have "assets under management" of at least $25 million but less than $30 million and are not otherwise required to register with the SEC. See Advisers Act Rule 203A–1(a)(2).

The second type consists of newly-formed investment advisers that have a reasonable expectation of SEC registration eligibility within 120 days after registration. See Advisers Act Rule 203A–2(d). However, an investment adviser who avails itself of this option must withdraw its SEC registration if it ultimately fails to meet SEC registration eligibility within this time frame.

The third type consists of investment advisers whose "assets under management" are, at the time of its initial application to the SEC, less than $25 million but whose multi-state activities would require them to register as investment advisers in 30 or more states. Thereafter, at the time it files its annual updating amendment to its Form ADV with the SEC, an adviser must be required to register, under the laws of the various states, with at least 25 states if the adviser wants to continue being SEC-registered. Apparently, having to register with up to 24 states is not considered overly burdensome by the SEC, as an adviser who avails itself of this option must withdraw its SEC registration if it subsequently is required by the laws of fewer than 25 states to register at the state level. See Advisers Act Rule 203A–2(e).

The final type consists of so-called "internet investment advisers." To qualify as such, an adviser must provide investment advice to all its clients exclusively through an interactive website, although it may provide advice to fewer than 15 clients through *other means* during the preceding 12 months. An "interactive website" is defined as a website in which computer software-based models or applications provide investment advice to clients based on personal information each client supplies through the website. See Advisers Act Rule 203A–2(f).

c.   *"Assets Under Management"*

Because the dollar amount of most advisers' "assets under management" will determine whether they must register with the SEC or the states, understanding what constitutes "assets under management" and how they are calculated is imperative. Advisers Act Section 203A(a)(2) defines "assets under management" as "the securities portfolios with respect to which an investment adviser provides continuous and regular supervisory or management services." However, the Advisers Act itself provides no other real guidance on this issue. Instead, one must look to the instructions to Form ADV for further clarification.

General Instruction 5b to Form ADV describes a "securities portfolio" as an account or accounts of which securities represent at least 50% of the total value, with cash and cash equivalents being treated as securities for this purpose. Commodities, collectibles and real estate, however, are not treated as securities. If securities represent 50% or more of the total value of a given account, then the entire value of the account is used to determine the amount of the adviser's assets under management, rather than just the value of the portion consisting of securities. No deduction is made for securities purchased on margin. Accounts of clients that do not pay fees to the investment adviser are included in the calculation, as these accounts often reflect capital provided by the investment adviser itself, its affiliates, family members and, in the case of hedge funds, certain investors for whom fees are waived.

If an investment adviser has discretionary authority over a given account and provides it with ongoing supervisory or management services, that account is, of course, included in the "assets under management" calculation. General Instruction 5b(3)(b) to Form ADV also indicates that, under certain limited circumstances, nondiscretionary advisory arrangements may also count in that calculation.

d. State Authority Over SEC–Registered Investment Advisers

Advisers Act Section 203A(b)(1)(A) prohibits the various states from applying their laws requiring the registration, license or qualification of an investment adviser to a SEC-registered investment adviser. Nevertheless, a state may still require a SEC-registered adviser to file with it any documents filed with the SEC solely for notice purposes. See Nutshell Section 16. Moreover, a state may continue to register, license and qualify certain of a SEC-registered adviser's "supervised persons" (as defined in Advisers Act Section 202(a)(25)) if they also qualify as "investment adviser representatives" and have a place of business in that state. See Nutshell Section 5B(2)a.

In addition, all investment advisers remain subject to state general antifraud authority. Indeed, Advisers Act Section 203A(b)(2) explicitly provides state securities commissions (or equivalent entities) with the authority to investigate and bring enforcement actions with respect to fraud or deceit against an investment adviser or any person associated with an investment adviser. Associated persons include partners, officers and directors of an investment adviser, as well as any person directly or indirectly controlling or controlled by an investment adviser. See Advisers Act Section 202(a)(17).

(2) State Registration and Regulation

a. *Registration*

Generally, an investment adviser must register at the state level if it (i) is not required to register with the SEC, (ii) chooses not to register with the SEC when it has the option to do so, (iii) is not excepted from the "investment adviser" definition in Advisers Act Section 202(a)(11), and (iv) cannot avail itself of a registration exemption.

The SEC is prohibited from asserting a violation of Advisers Act Section 203 (or any provision of the Act to which an adviser becomes subject upon registration under Section 203) against any state-registered adviser which reasonably believed it had assets under management of less than $30 million and therefore was not required to register with the SEC. However, an adviser must be registered in the state in which it has its principal office and place of business. See Advisers Act Rule 203A–4.

Assuming state registration is required or permitted, in which state(s) must an investment adviser register? In general, whenever a person meets the statutory definition of "investment ad-

viser" of a given state and transacts business in
that state, he or it must register with that state.
Fortunately, most (but not all) states' investment
adviser statutes and regulations have been drafted
to closely reflect provisions of the Advisers Act,
including the definition of "investment adviser"
set forth in Advisers Act Section 202(a)(11). Moreover, under Advisers Act Section 222(d) (the "National De Minimus Standard"), a state may not
require an investment adviser to register with it
unless the adviser has a place of business located
within that state and, during the preceding 12–
month period, has had at least six clients who are
residents of that state.

Importantly, a state may also license, register or
otherwise qualify any *"investment adviser representative"* ("IAR") who has a place of business in that
state. See Advisers Act Section 203A(b)(1)(A). Under Advisers Act Rule 203A–3(a)(1), two requirements must be met before a person is considered an
IAR. First, the person in question must qualify as a
"supervised person" of the investment adviser. A
"supervised person" means any partner, officer,
director (or other person occupying a similar status
or performing similar functions) or employee of an
investment adviser, or other person who provides
investment advice on behalf of that adviser and is
subject to the supervision and control of that adviser. See Advisers Act Section 202(a)(25). However,
any "supervised person" who does not solicit, meet
with or otherwise communicate with clients of the
investment adviser on a regular basis, or who pro-

vides only advice that does not purport to meet the objectives or needs of specific individuals or accounts ("impersonal investment advice"), is not considered an IAR. See Advisers Act Rule 203A–3(a)(2).

Second, the person in question must have (i) more than five clients who are natural persons and (ii) an overall clientele more than 10% of which consists of natural persons. Thus, the focus primarily is on retail investors, as the term "natural persons," according to the SEC, covers all retail investors. Excluded, however, are businesses, charitable or educational institutions, investment companies, other institutional investors and, if they enter into performance fee contracts under Advisers Act Rule 205–3, high net worth individuals (referred to as "qualified clients" in this context).

State securities commissions (or equivalent entities) also have the explicit authority to investigate and bring enforcement actions with respect to fraud or deceit against an investment adviser or any person associated with an investment adviser. See Advisers Act Section 203A(b)(2). Associated persons include partners, officers and directors of an investment adviser, as well as any person directly or indirectly controlling or controlled by an investment adviser. See Advisers Act Section 202(a)(17).

> *b. SEC Authority Over State–Registered Investment Advisers*

The SEC retains authority over a state-registered investment adviser in four primary areas. First, the

SEC shares with the states the ability to investigate and bring enforcement actions with respect to fraud or deceit against an investment adviser or any of its associated persons. See Advisers Act Sections 203A(b)(2) and 206. Interestingly, however, *certain antifraud rules* under the Advisers Act do not apply to state-registered advisers. Indeed, Advisers Act Rules 206(4)–1 (advertising), 206(4)–2 (custody of clients' assets), 206(4)–3 (cash fee solicitations) and 206(4)–4 (financial and disciplinary information disclosure) only apply to advisers who either are, or are required to be, registered with the SEC.

Second, Advisers Act Section 205's prohibition against performance fees applies equally to state-registered advisers as well as to SEC-registered advisers. However, state-registered advisers, like their SEC-registered counterparts, may avail themselves of the exception relating to high net worth individuals (referred to as "qualified clients" in this context). See Advisers Act Rule 205–3.

Third, Advisers Act Section 206(3)'s prohibitions against principal and agency cross transactions apply to state-registered advisers. However, state-registered advisers, like their SEC-registered counterparts, may engage in agency cross transactions under certain conditions pursuant to Advisers Act Rule 206(3)–2. For a general discussion of principal and agency cross transactions, see Nutshell Section 31.

Finally, state-registered investment advisers, like their SEC-registered counterparts, must establish, maintain and enforce written procedures reasonably designed to prevent the misuse of material, non-public information. See Advisers Act Section 204A and Nutshell Sections 43 and 44.

(3) Transitioning From State Registration to SEC Registration

Form ADV requires an investment adviser to specify the amount of assets it has under management. A state-registered investment adviser must apply for registration with the SEC within 90 days of the date on which it files its annual updating amendment to its Form ADV with the state(s) reporting that its assets under management have increased to at least $30 million. See Advisers Act Rule 203A–1(b)(1). An adviser whose assets under management have increased to $25 million or more but not $30 million may, but is not required to, register with the SEC (assuming the adviser is not otherwise required to register with the SEC). Once registered with the SEC, the adviser will be subject to SEC regulations regardless of whether it also remains registered with one or more states. See General Instruction 11 to Form ADV and Nutshell Section 5B(1)b.

(4) Transitioning From SEC Registration to State Registration

Any SEC-registered adviser who files an annual updating amendment to its Form ADV with the SEC reporting that it no longer has $25 million of assets under management (or is not otherwise eligible for SEC registration) must file Form ADV–W withdrawing its SEC registration within 180 days of its fiscal year end. It must, of course, register as an investment adviser with the applicable state(s) during this time if it plans on continuing to operate as an investment adviser.

Until its Form ADV–W is filed, the investment adviser is considered registered with both the SEC and one or more states and, thus, is subject to both the Advisers Act and applicable state law. If, prior to filing its Form ADV–W with the SEC during the 180–day window, the investment adviser once again attains at least $25 million of assets under management (or otherwise becomes eligible for SEC registration), it need not file a Form ADV–W and may remain registered with the SEC. See Advisers Act Rule 203A–1(b)(2) and General Instruction 12 to Form ADV.

§ 6. REGISTRATION OF HEDGE FUND AND COLLATERALIZED DEBT OBLIGATION (CDO) ADVISERS

See Nutshell Sections 9 and 10 for a discussion of this topic.

§ 7. ERISA CONSIDERATIONS

A. Generally

Pension plans have become the single biggest contributor to the enormous growth of the investment management business which now stands at several trillion dollars. Because pension plan assets are the main driver of this growth, it is not surprising that in addition to voluminous SEC regulations, investment advisers find themselves subject to some Employee Retirement Income Security Act of 1974 ("ERISA") and U.S. Department of Labor ("DOL") regulations from time to time.

Investment advisers that manage pension assets may be inspected by the staff of the DOL, which administers and enforces ERISA. These inspections are much less frequent than SEC inspections because the DOL inspection staff is much smaller than the SEC inspection staff.

B. Registration and Qualification

Section 403 of ERISA requires any person who is the "investment manager" of any employee benefit plan to be a registered investment adviser (unless the adviser is a bank or insurance company). Prohibited Transaction Class Exemption 84–14 may also require an adviser to qualify as a "qualified professional asset manager" or QPAM in order to manage pension plan assets. A QPAM is:

> an independent fiduciary that is registered as an investment adviser and has more than $85 million in assets under its management and control, and either (A) shareholders' or partners' equity in excess of $1 million, or (B) payment of all of its liabilities, including any liabilities that may arise by reason of a breach or violation of a duty described in sections 404 and 406 of ERISA is unconditionally guaranteed by: (i) a person with a relationship to such

investment adviser if the investment adviser and such affiliate have shareholders' or partners' equity, in the aggregate, in excess of $1 million, or (ii) a bank, a savings and loan association, or an insurance company, or (iii) a registered broker-dealer that has a net worth in excess of $1 million.

A QPAM is permitted to engage in a wide variety of transactions with the affiliates described in ERISA Section 406(a)(1)(A) through (D).

C. Bonding

Section 412 of ERISA requires investment advisers to obtain a fiduciary bond to protect retirement plans from losses resulting from fraud and dishonesty by the adviser if the adviser "handles" or otherwise has investment discretion over retirement plan assets. The DOL defines "handling" broadly to include whenever an adviser exercises physical contact or control over the plan assets and has the power to transfer or negotiate the value of the assets. See 29 C.F.R. § 2580.412–6.

Most investment advisers, whether registered or unregistered, manage retirement assets and, therefore, are required by ERISA Section 412 to obtain a bond. The amount of the bond must be not less than 10% of the plan assets handled, subject to a $1,000 minimum and $500,000 maximum. Given the size of advisers' assets under management and the size of many frauds these days, these limits are low. In addition, the bond may not have any deductible and each retirement plan must be named as an insured party under the bond.

The ERISA bonding requirement does not apply to advisers that have capital and surplus of at least $1 million, are authorized to exercise trust powers or conduct insurance business, and are supervised by a Federal or state authority. Because most investment advisers are thinly capitalized, and many do not exercise trust powers or sell insurance, most advisers obtain ERISA bonds. The ERISA bonding requirement is in addition to the fidelity bonding requirement for investment companies imposed by Company Act Section 17(g) and Company Act Rule 17g–1.

D.   Other Potentially Applicable ERISA/DOL Regulations

ERISA regulations that also may apply to advisers include: ERISA Technical Bulletin 86–1 (May 22, 1986) concerning soft dollars; DOL Bulletin 94–2 (July 29, 1994) concerning proxy voting; DOL/Treasury Statement on Pension Investments (Jan. 31, 1989); Prohibited Transaction Class Exemption 77–4 (March 31, 1977) concerning affiliated mutual funds; and Prohibited Transaction Class Exemption 86–128 (Nov. 5, 1986) concerning using affiliated broker-dealers.

§ 8. CFTC CONSIDERATIONS

A. Generally

Many investment advisers use futures and commodity options to leverage their securities investments, hedge currencies and, generally, to enhance the yield of their portfolios. These investment advisers may have to register with the Commodity Futures Trading Commission ("CFTC") as a commodity trading adviser unless they can avail themselves of a statutory or regulatory exemption. The CFTC regulates commodities, including futures contracts, options on futures and other exchange-traded commodity instruments.

Section 1a(6) of the Commodity Exchange Act ("CEA") defines "commodity trading adviser" to be any person who, for compensation or profit (1) engages in the business of advising others about trading in futures contracts, commodity options or certain leverage transactions, or (2) as part of a regular business, issues or promulgates analyses or reports concerning these activities.

B. Exemption From Registering as a Commodity Trading Adviser

Similar to the Advisers Act, the CEA and related rules exempt the following persons from commodity trading adviser registration when their rendering of commodity trading advisory services is solely incidental to the conduct of their business: banks, trust companies, reporters, news publishers, lawyers, accountants, teachers, floor brokers, futures commission merchants and insurance companies. The CFTC has issued guidance in CFTC Interpretive Letter No. 94–29, 1994 WL 283961 (Mar. 15, 1994) concerning what constitutes "solely incidental," which is a facts and circumstances analysis.

Like the Advisers Act, CEA Section 4m provides that the CFTC registration requirements do not apply to any commodity trading adviser who, during the last twelve months, has not rendered commodity trading advice to more than fifteen persons and who does not hold itself out generally to the public as a commodity trading adviser. See Advisers Act Section 203(b)(3) (which allows fourteen (as opposed to fifteen) clients in a year) and Nutshell Section 4C(1). CFTC Rule 4.14(a)(10) sets forth an approach to determining who a person is for purposes of counting the fifteen maximum persons that is substantially similar to the approach taken by the SEC in Advisers Act Rule 203(b)(3)–1. See Nutshell Section 4C(1)a & b. Funds generally count as one person and are not "looked through" when counting the investors in each fund.

Importantly, CEA Section 4m(3) exempts from registration as a commodity trading adviser any SEC-registered investment adviser whose business does not consist primarily of acting as a commodity trading adviser. See CFTC Rule 4.14(a)(8).

SEC-registered investment advisers that engage in foreign currency futures transactions and transactions with options that are listed on commodities markets are not required to register with the CFTC as a commodity trading adviser, provided the investment adviser does not hold itself out to the public as a commodity trading adviser and all of its futures trading advice is directed solely to pools described in CFTC Rules 4.5, 4.13(a)(3) or 14.13(a)(4), or offshore pools in which all of the investors are non-U.S. persons. However, the investment adviser must file a notice with the National Futures Association stating that the adviser is relying on the CFTC Rule 4.14(a)(8) exemption for investment advisers.

C.   Exemption From Registering as a Commodity Pool Operator (CPO)

The CEA defines a commodity pool operator ("CPO") as any person who solicits or receives funds from participants for a commodity pool. The CFTC broadly defines commodity pool to be any privately offered collective investment fund that trades any amount of futures. CFTC Rule 4.13(a)(3) provides an exemption from registration for CPOs of commodity pools that are offered to: (1) accredited investors (as defined in Securities Act Rule 501(a)); (2) a trust that was formed by an accredited investor for the benefit of a family member; (3) a knowledgeable employee as defined in Company Act Rule 3c–5(a)(4); or (4) a qualified eligible person as defined under CFTC Rule 4.7(a)(2)(viii)(A), which includes, among other parties, certain CPO agents and affiliates.

CFTC Rule 4.13(a)(3) sets forth limits on the maximum amount of futures trading that is permitted in a commodity pool: (1) initial margin and premiums for futures cannot exceed five percent of the pool's liquidation value, after taking into account unrealized profits and unrealized losses on open positions (but excluding the in-the-money amount of purchased options); or (2) the aggregate net notional value of the pool's futures does not exceed 100% of the pool's liquidation value, after taking into account unrealized profits and unrealized losses on open positions.

Another exemption set forth in CFTC Rule 4.13(a)(4) exempts from registration CPOs of pools in which all natural persons are qualified eligible persons, and each non-natural person is either a qualified eligible person or an accredited investor.

These two exemptions under Rules 4.13(a)(3) and (a)(4) require a notice to be filed with the National Futures Association that the CPO is relying on the applicable exemption.

IV. HEDGE FUND AND COLLATERALIZED DEBT OBLIGATION (CDO) ADVISERS

§ 9. CURRENT REGISTRATION ENVIRONMENT

A. Overview

Traditionally, most hedge funds and their investment advisers have been able to avoid SEC registration by taking advantage of registration exemptions within both the Company Act and the Advisers Act. Those hedge fund advisers that avoid Advisers Act registration under Advisers Act Section 203(b) are not subject to that Act's recordkeeping and disclosure requirements. Furthermore, the SEC is without authority to conduct examinations of them. However, unregistered advisers are subject to the antifraud provisions of the Advisers Act, as well as the antifraud provisions of the other Federal securities laws.

Over the past two decades the SEC, lawmakers and others have become concerned over the substantial impact that hedge funds have had on both the national securities market and the national economy. This impact stemmed from the tremendous growth in the number of hedge funds and the assets invested in them, as well as the significant increase in their market activity, trading volume and use of debt financing (*i.e.,* leverage). The SEC in particular was concerned that it lacked the vital information necessary to develop regulatory policies with respect to hedge funds as those funds became more important financial market participants.

Due to its concerns, in 2002 the SEC requested that its staff conduct a study on hedge funds. In September 2003 the staff produced a study entitled the "Implications of the Growth of Hedge Funds." This study, in turn, provided the catalyst for the development and subsequent implementation of Advisers Act Rule 203(b)(3)–2 and certain related rule amendments (the "Hedge Fund Registration Provisions"). These Provisions, which are discussed below in depth, had the effect of requiring most hedge fund advisers to register with the SEC under the Advisers Act as of February 2006. They also subjected them to the recordkeeping and disclosure requirements of the Advisers Act, as well as SEC inspection.

The Hedge Fund Registration Provisions greatly impacted the hedge fund industry. Indeed, at the end of March 2006, 24% of the 10,000 investment advisers registered with the SEC were hedge fund advisers. Of the 2,400 registered hedge fund advisers, 46% had registered *after* the adoption of the new Provisions.

However, in June 2006, just four months after the Hedge Fund Registration Provisions went into effect, the U.S. Court of Appeals for the District of

Columbia, in a unanimous decision, vacated them. As discussed below in Nutshell Section 9E, the Court deemed the provisions "arbitrary" and labeled the SEC's justifications for promulgating them "unreasonable." See *Goldstein v. SEC*, 451 F.3d 873 (D.C. Cir. 2006).

Because the former Hedge Fund Registration Provisions provide tremendous insight into the way in which the SEC views hedge funds and their advisers, we provide full coverage of them below even though they are no longer effective.

B. Exemptions and Exclusions for Hedge Funds and Their Advisers

(1) What Is a Hedge Fund?

A hedge fund is essentially a "private" mutual fund. Like a mutual fund, it raises the capital necessary to purchase its own portfolio of securities and other assets by selling its own equity securities (typically limited partnership interests or LLC membership interests) to investors. Also like a mutual fund, a hedge fund typically pays its adviser an annual management fee based on a percentage of the fund's assets under management.

However, unlike a mutual fund, a hedge fund does not register its securities offering under the Securities Act nor does it register itself as an investment company under the Company Act. Rather, it takes advantage of registration exemptions available under both Acts and sells interests in its fund through private placements. Also unlike most mutual funds, hedge funds typically pay fund advisers a percentage of the funds' capital gains and appreciation in addition to an annual management fee, commonly called "carried interest." Hedge funds typically limit redemptions by investors to a specified percentage of their investments each quarter, as opposed to mutual funds that are required to satisfy redemptions daily. Finally, with respect to performance results, hedge funds seek to provide their investors with a positive absolute return rather than merely out perform a set benchmark, such as the S & P 500 stock index.

(2) Registration Exemptions Under the Company Act

There are two exclusions from the definition of "investment company" which allow hedge funds to avoid registration under the Company Act: Sections 3(c)(1) and 3(c)(7). Each is described below.

a. *Section 3(c)(1) Fund*

Section 3(c)(1) of the Company Act excludes from the definition of "investment company" any issuer of securities (a "Section 3(c)(1) fund") which satisfies two requirements. First, its outstanding securities must be beneficially owned by *100 or fewer investors*. Second, it must not make or propose to make a public offering of its securities under the Securities Act.

With respect to the first requirement, a corporate investor in a given Section 3(c)(1) fund is generally counted as a single investor. However, if the following two conditions are met the fund must "look through" the corporate investor and count each of the corporate investor's beneficial owners towards the 100 investor limitation. The first condition is that the corporate investor must either be a registered investment company or a company which is itself relying on registration exemptions found in Company Act Sections 3(c)(1) or 3(c)(7). The second condition is that the corporate investor must beneficially own 10% or more of the outstanding voting shares of the Section 3(c)(1) fund. See Company Act Section 3(c)(1)(A) and Company Act Rule 3c–1.

With respect to the second requirement, a Section 3(c)(1) fund is precluded from engaging in general solicitation and advertising and must have a demonstrable pre-existing relationship with its investors. To avoid registering its offering under the Securities Act, a Section 3(c)(1) fund will rely on Securities Act Section 4(2), the "private placement" exemption from Securities Act registration, and Securities Act Rule 506 of Regulation D, the safe harbor rule that the SEC promulgated under Section 4(2). Under Rule 506, an issuer is limited to selling its shares solely to investors meeting the definition of "accredited investor" found in Securities Act Rule 501(a) and up to 35 others (referred to as "purchasers") who do not meet that definition. For a natural person to qualify as an "accredited investor" under Securities Act Rule 501(a), she must either have (1) a net worth exceeding $1 million (*including* her principal residence), either alone or together with her spouse, or (2) an individual income in excess of $200,000 in each of the two most recent years, or joint income with her spouse in excess of $300,000 during that time, and a reasonable expectation of reaching the same income level in the current year. See Securities Act Rule 501(a)(5) & (6).

Importantly, a hedge fund cannot avail itself of any of the other Regulation D exemptive rules (*i.e.*, Rules 504 and 505) or Regulation A, because those rules and that regulation are based on Securities Act Section 3(b), the "small issue" exemption of the Securities Act, rather than Section 4(2). The SEC has deemed offerings conducted under those rules and that regulation "public" rather than "private," even though, in the case of Rule 505, general solicitation and advertising are prohibited. See Securities Act Rule 502(c).

b.   *Section 3(c)(7) Fund*

Section 3(c)(7) of the Company Act excludes from the definition of "investment company" any fund (a "Section 3(c)(7) fund") which satisfies two requirements. First, its outstanding securities must be owned *exclusively* by persons who, at the time of the acquisition of such securities, are *"qualified purchasers."* Second, it must not make or propose to make a public offering of its securities under the Securities Act.

With respect to the first requirement, the minimum qualifications of a "qualified purchaser" under the Company Act are significantly higher than those necessary to qualify as an "accredited investor" under the Securities Act. Under Company Act Section 2(a)(51), a "qualified purchaser" must have

$5 million or more in investments (*excluding* a principal residence) if a natural person; and $25 million or more in investments, if a corporation that invests on a discretionary basis. By contrast, for a natural person to qualify as an "accredited investor" under Securities Act Rule 501(a), she must either have (1) a net worth exceeding $1 million (*including* her principal residence), either alone or together with her spouse, or (2) an individual income in excess of $200,000 in each of the two most recent years, or joint income with her spouse in excess of $300,000 during that time, and a reasonable expectation of reaching the same income level in the current year. See Securities Act Rule 501(a)(5) & (6).

Unlike a Section 3(c)(1) fund, a Section 3(c)(7) fund seemingly can have an unlimited number of "qualified purchasers." However, two limits do exist. First, a 3(c)(7) fund runs the risk of becoming a "back door" reporting company under the Exchange Act if it has too many investors. In this regard, a fund must be careful not to reach the 500 investor mark, because at that point it will become a reporting company under the Exchange Act if it also has $10 million in assets under management. See Exchange Act Section 12(g) and Exchange Act Rule 12g–1. Second, as the number of investors in a given Section 3(c)(7) fund grows, the likelihood that the fund has engaged in general solicitation also increases.

With respect to the second requirement, a Section 3(c)(7) fund must neither make nor propose to make a public offering of its securities under the Securities Act. The discussion and analysis of this requirement is substantially similar to that involving a Section 3(c)(1) fund. See Nutshell Section 9B(2)a.

Most hedge funds and private equity funds rely on Section 3(c)(7) to exempt them from registration under the Company Act. However, it is not unusual for their advisers to form parallel funds relying on the Section 3(c)(1) exemption in order for employees and friends and family—most of whom do not meet the "qualified purchaser" standard—to participate.

(3) Registration Exemption Under the Advisers Act

Hedge fund investment advisers traditionally rely on the Private Adviser Registration Exemption of the Advisers Act to avoid registration with the SEC and the states. Advisers Act Section 203(b)(3) exempts an investment adviser from Advisers Act registration provided that the adviser (a) has fewer than fifteen clients during the preceding twelve-month period, (b) does not hold itself out generally to the public as an investment adviser, and (c) is not an adviser to any investment company registered under the Company Act. See Nutshell Section 4C.

Prior to 2006, there was generally no need to "look through" an entity advisee and count its individual investors when determining whether the adviser had "fewer than 15 clients." However, under Advisers Act Rule 203(b)(3)–1(a)(2)(i), the adviser must provide the entity with investment advice based on the *entity's objectives* rather than the individual investment objectives of its owners. Thus, by directly advising legal organizations rather than individual investors, investment advisers could indirectly advise hundreds of individual investors without having to register with the SEC.

Effective February 2006, the SEC's Hedge Fund Registration Provisions, which contained a "look through" provision, forced most hedge fund advisers to register under the Advisers Act. The U.S. Court of Appeals for the District of Columbia, however, vacated the Provisions in June 2006. See *Goldstein v. SEC*, 451 F.3d 873 (D.C. Cir. 2006). Currently, therefore, there is no "look through" provision impacting on the determination of the number of an adviser's clients other than Advisers Act Rule 203(b)(3)–1(a)(2)(i), which continues in full force and effect.

Because the former Hedge Fund Registration Provisions provide tremendous insight into the way in which the SEC views hedge funds and their advisers, we provide full coverage of them below even though they are *no longer effective*.

C. Conditions That Led to the Implementation of the Former Hedge Fund Registration Provisions

The SEC believed that Congress did not intend the Private Adviser Registration Exemption to ex-

empt advisers to wealthy and sophisticated clients
from Advisers Act registration. Instead, the SEC
believed that Congress intended to create a limited
exemption for advisers whose activities were not
national in scope and instead consisted of providing
advice to a small number of investors primarily
consisting of close friends and family members.
Unlike the Securities Act which provides an offering
exemption for transactions involving investors who
have sufficient knowledge and experience to fend
for themselves (*i.e.*, Securities Act Section 4(2)), the
Advisers Act is intended to protect all types of
investors who have entrusted their assets to a professional investment adviser.

In the early 2000s, the SEC began to believe its
current regulatory program was inadequate with
respect to hedge funds and that it could not effectively deter or detect fraud by unregistered investment advisers. The SEC's perceived inadequacy was
based on its inability to obtain information on unregistered advisers, which, in turn, stemmed from
its lack of authority to examine records or compel
information disclosure. Furthermore, the SEC was
concerned about the amount of useful information
investors were receiving about hedge funds and
their advisers, potential conflicts of interest between hedge funds and their advisers, and the manner in which hedge fund advisers valued fund assets.

For these reasons, the SEC adopted the Hedge
Fund Registration Provisions. As discussed in more
detail below, these Provisions included new Advis-

ers Act Rule 203(b)(3)–2, which contained a "look through" provision for use in counting "clients" in the context of certain "private funds" (thus rendering the "single client" provision of Advisers Act Rule 203(b)(3)–1(a)(2)(i) unavailable to advisers of these private funds). They also amended Advisers Act Rule 203(b)(3)–1 by adding a definition of a "private fund" in subparagraph (d) of that Rule. Until the U.S. Court of Appeals for the District of Columbia handed down *Goldstein v. SEC*, 451 F.3d 873 (D.C. Cir. 2006), the "look through" element of the Hedge Fund Registration Provisions had the intended effect of requiring most hedge fund advisers to register with the SEC, as the Private Adviser Registration Exemption of Section 203(b)(3) was no longer available to them.

D. The *Former* Hedge Fund Registration Provisions

(1) The Starting Point: Definition of a "Private Fund"

The SEC's former Hedge Fund Registration Provisions were specifically targeted to those advisers whose activities involved so-called "private funds." Before a fund was labeled a "private fund," it had to satisfy three conditions. First, the fund had to be excluded from the definition of "investment company" under either Company Act Section 3(c)(1) or 3(c)(7). Second, the fund must have provided its equity owners with the opportunity to redeem any portion of their ownership interest within two years of the purchase of such interest. Lastly, the fund must have been marketed based on the skills, ability and expertise of its investment adviser.

The second condition—the two-year redemption provision—had been added to ensure that long term investment vehicles, such as private equity funds and venture capital funds, did not inadvertently fall into the definition of a "private fund." Indeed, the SEC believed that a two-year redemption period was sufficient to capture most hedge funds in the definition of a "private fund."

The unintended effect of the two-year redemption provision was that some new hedge fund advisers, and many existing ones, drafted fund governance provisions (or altered existing ones) in order to deny new investors the ability to redeem their interests before two years. By requiring new investors to sign two-year lock up agreements, advisers were again able to avoid registering under the Advisers Act.

(2) Counting "Clients" Under the Former Hedge Fund Registration Provisions

Former Advisers Act Rule 203(b)(3)–2 required an adviser to "look through" any "private fund" and count each owner of that fund, such as its shareholders, limited partners, members or beneficiaries, as a separate client of that adviser. If the total number of owners exceeded fourteen, then the adviser could not avail itself of the Private Adviser Registration Exemption of Advisers Act Section 203(b)(3). Unless another registration exemption was available, the adviser had to register with the SEC, assuming the threshold requirements for SEC registration were met. See Nutshell Section 5B(1)a & b for a discussion of those requirements.

The former Rule allowed an adviser holding an ownership stake in its own fund (which is typical) to exclude itself as a client, regardless of the form of ownership stake it held. Furthermore, certain knowledgeable advisory personnel were excluded from the count because they were considered "qualified clients" under current Advisers Act Rule 205–3(d)(1)(iii).

If the investors in a "private fund" included a registered investment company, then the investment adviser to that fund had to count the owners of that investment company for purposes of the Private Adviser Registration Exemption. This rule applied whether or not the registered investment company's ownership stake in the "private fund" was direct or indirect. However, when counting the owners of the investment company, the general provisions of current Advisers Act Rule 203(b)(3)–1(a)(1), which give guidance with respect to when certain persons count as a "single" client, continued to apply.

The SEC stated that former Rule 203(b)(3)–2 also applied to hedge fund advisers whose investors included a "fund of funds" that was itself a "private fund." The adviser was required to look through the "top tier" private fund and count that fund's investors as clients to determine whether the Private Adviser Registration Exemption was available.

Finally, the SEC had rejected the possibility of exempting offshore fund advisers who were subject to the regulations of a foreign jurisdiction. Thus, under former Rule 203(b)(3)–2, offshore advisers were required to count each investor that was a U.S. resident as a client, but not investors who were not U.S. residents. As a result, any offshore adviser who advised more than fourteen clients who were residents of the U.S. had to register with the SEC. If an investor was a non-U.S. resident at the time of his investment and subsequently became a resident of the U.S., an offshore fund did not have to count him towards the fourteen U.S. resident investor limitation.

With the demise of the Hedge Fund Registration Provisions, prior SEC staff guidance and letters addressing offshore advisers continue to apply. Thus, the substantive provisions of the Advisers Act generally do not apply to offshore advisers with respect to such advisers' dealings with offshore funds and offshore clients. Any offshore adviser registered with the SEC under the Advisers Act must continue to comply with the Act and the rules promulgated thereunder with respect to any U.S. clients and prospective U.S. clients it may have. See Subcommittee on Private Investment Entities of the Amer. Bar Assoc., SEC No–Action Letter, 2005 WL 3334980 (avail. Dec. 8, 2005).

(3) Amendments to Advisers Act Rule 205–3

Current Advisers Act Rule 205–3(a) permits registered advisers to charge a performance fee to "qualified clients" only. "Qualified clients" are generally either natural persons or companies each of whom (1) has at least $750,000 under management with the investment adviser or (2) has a net worth of more than $1.5 million at the time of the investment. See Advisers Act Rule 205–3(d)(1).

Unregistered advisers, of course, are not subject to the performance fee prohibition in Advisers Act Section 205(a)(1). By requiring advisers to register under the former Hedge Fund Registration Provisions and, as a result, be subject to Rule 205–3, the SEC hoped to limit retail investor access to hedge funds (the concept of "retailization"). Indeed, each investor who would be charged a performance fee would have to have satisfied the "qualified client" requirements, thus preventing retail investors with modest net worths from investing in the first place.

E. The Demise of the Former Hedge Fund Registration Provisions

(1) *Goldstein v. SEC*

In June 2006, just four months after the Hedge Fund Registration Provisions went into effect, the U.S. Court of Appeals for the District of Columbia, in a unanimous decision, vacated them. The Court deemed the Provisions "arbitrary" and labeled the SEC's justifications for promulgating them "unreasonable." See *Goldstein v. SEC*, 451 F.3d 873 (D.C. Cir. 2006).

The Provisions had been challenged by Phillip Goldstein, an investment advisory firm that co-

owns Kimball & Winthrop and Opportunity Partners L.P. The thrust of the challenge involved former Advisers Act Rule 203(b)(3)–2's equation of the
term "client" with the term "investor." In promulgating the former Rule, the SEC concluded that
since the term "client" is not defined in the Advisers Act, the statute was ambiguous as to the method of counting clients. Therefore, the SEC enacted
the former Rule to clarify that "investors" in a
fund, and not just the fund itself, would be considered "clients" when determining how many clients
an adviser has for purposes of the Private Adviser
Registration Exemption. The SEC argued that such
an interpretation was reasonable, especially against
the background of hedge funds becoming increasingly important to the national markets.

The Court, however, disagreed with the SEC over
the proper interpretation of the term "client." The
Court stated that just because a term is susceptible
to several meanings does not authorize an agency to
choose any plausible meaning. The "words of a
statute should be read in context," and read consistently with the overall statutory scheme.

The Court's main concern was that if former Rule
203(b)(3)–2 were allowed to equate an "investor"
with a "client," a hedge fund adviser would, in
effect, owe a fiduciary duty to both the entity and
the entity's individual investors. Such a rule would
create conflicts of interests for advisers and force
them to be "servants of two masters." Moreover,
the Court pointed out that the SEC's position would
result in the term "client" having two different

meanings within the Advisers Act itself. Investors in hedge funds would count as "clients" for purposes of determining whether the Private Adviser Registration Exemption were available, but would not count as "clients" as to the fiduciary obligations that advisers owe under Advisers Act Section 206. The Court criticized the SEC for being unable to explain why this should be the case.

The SEC also defended former Rule 203(b)(3)–2 by arguing that the organizational form of most hedge funds is merely a "legal artifice" used by advisers to escape registration by having less than fifteen "clients." The Court conceded this point. However, it responded by noting that in this area of the law, form matters and it dictates to whom a fiduciary duty is owed.

Ultimately, the Court stated that the SEC had not adequately explained how the relationship between investors in hedge funds and advisers had changed so as to justify treating those investors as "clients." In effect, former Rule 203(b)(3)–2 allowed funds with less than one hundred clients to escape Company Act registration via Company Act Section 3(c)(1), but required the registration of advisers to funds with more than fourteen clients under the Advisers Act.

Using a harsh tone to vacate the Rule, the Court stated that "the [SEC's] interpretation [fell] outside the bounds of reasonableness." As a result, the SEC had exceeded its authority. Indeed, the Court found that the SEC's "interpretation of the word 'client'

[came] very close to violating the plain language of the statute." By refusing to allow the SEC to manipulate the meaning of a single term used in the Advisers Act, the Court precluded the SEC from creating a "hook" on which to hang more comprehensive regulation of hedge funds.

(2) Where Do We Go From Here?

The SEC ultimately chose not to appeal the *Goldstein* decision and decided instead to pursue a separate rulemaking agenda. In this regard, the SEC first proposed and later adopted a new antifraud rule based on Advisers Act Section 206(4). In addition, the SEC has proposed redefining the term "accredited investor" in an attempt to limit the ability of retail investors to invest in hedge funds.

a.   *Advisers Act Rule 206(4)–8*

In December 2006 the SEC proposed new Advisers Act Rule 206(4)–8, later adopting it as proposed with an effective date of September 10, 2007. Under the Rule, it is a fraudulent, deceptive or manipulative act, practice or course of business within the meaning of Advisers Act Section 206(4) for an investment adviser to a "pooled investment vehicle" to:

- · make any untrue statement of a material fact or omit to state a material fact necessary to make the statements made, in light of the circumstances under which they were made, not misleading, to any investor or prospective investor in a pooled investment vehicle; or

·   otherwise engage in any act, practice, or course
    of business that is fraudulent, deceptive, or ma-
    nipulative with respect to any investor or pro-
    spective investor in a pooled investment vehicle.

See Advisers Act Rule 206(4)–8(a)(1) & (2). The
SEC will consider a fact to be material for purposes
of the Rule if there is a substantial likelihood that a
reasonable investor in making an investment decision would consider it as having significantly altered the total mix of information available. See,
e.g., *Basic Inc. v. Levinson*, 485 U.S. 224 (1988);
TSC Indus. v. Northway, Inc., 426 U.S. 438 (1976).

The Rule applies to all investment advisers so
long as they advise a pooled investment vehicle. A
"pooled investment vehicle" is defined to include
any investment company and any company that
would be an investment company but for the exclusions in Company Act Sections 3(c)(1) and (7). See
Advisers Act Rule 206(4)–8(b). Thus, the Rule only
applies to pooled investment vehicles that are either
registered in the U.S. as investment companies or
are excluded from registration in reliance on Company Act Section 3(c)(1) or (7). Importantly, the
Rule does not apply to prospective investors in a
pooled investment vehicle until the pool is either
registered with the SEC or has accepted an investment by a U.S. person (as defined in Regulation S
under the Securities Act) in reliance on either Company Act Section 3(c)(1) or (7). Advisers to private
equity funds, hedge funds, venture capital funds,
distressed funds, funds of funds, CDOs and regis-

tered investment companies are all subject to the Rule.

The Rule's prohibitions apply to advisers to pooled investment vehicles regardless of whether the vehicle is offering, selling or redeeming securities, or whether the investment adviser is merely communicating with current or prospective investors. Because Rule 206(4)–8 lacks a "scienter" or knowledge requirement, it imposes a low negligence threshold for liability on a pooled investment vehicle's adviser, while also covering conduct that is recklessly or deliberately deceptive. However, the Rule provides neither a pooled investment vehicle nor its investors with a private right of action against the vehicle's adviser. Instead, the SEC will enforce the Rule by bringing civil and administrative enforcement actions against investment advisers that violate the Rule.

The Rule does not delineate any per se frauds, thus making each claim of investment adviser fraud under the Rule a case-by-case factual inquiry. The staff of the SEC intentionally did not include specific examples of fraudulent activity within the Rule itself in an effort to deny would-be fraudsters a roadmap for circumventing the Rule. In the Rule's proposing release, however, the SEC indicated that fraudulent activity would include "false or misleading statements made, for example, to existing investors in account statements as well as to prospective investors in private placement memoranda, offering circulars, or responses to 'requests for proposals.' " Prohibition of Fraud by Advisers to Certain Pooled

Investment Vehicles; Accredited Investors in Certain Private Investment Vehicles, Advisers Act Rel. No. 2576, 2006 WL 3814994 (Dec. 27, 2006) ("Release No. 2576").

b. *Proposed Securities Act Rule 509*

The SEC also has proposed a new Rule 509 to Regulation D under the Securities Act designed to limit the "retailization" of hedge funds and other private investment vehicles. See Release No. 2576. The proposed Rule would only apply to offerings by "private investment vehicles," defined to cover investment funds, excluding venture capital funds, that would be "investment companies" under the Company Act but for the exclusion contained in Company Act Section 3(c)(1) (so-called "3(c)(1) Funds"). "Venture capital fund" would have the same meaning as "business development company" in Advisers Act Section 202(a)(22).

Under the proposed Rule, a natural person would have to qualify as an "accredited natural person" before he could participate in an offering by a private investment vehicle. To do so, he would have to satisfy a *two-step test*. First, he would have to meet the definition of an "accredited investor" in Securities Act Rule 501(a)(5) or (6). See Nutshell Section 9B(2)a. Second, he would have to have $2.5 million or more in "investments" (adjusted for inflation every five years) at the time of his investment in the vehicle. Note that investment funds relying on the exclusion provided by Company Act Section 3(c)(7) (so-called "3(c)(7) Funds") are excluded from the definition of "private investment vehicle" because they are already subject to a similar two-step test (offers and sales must be made to "qualified purchasers" (as defined in Company Act Section 2(a)(51)(A)) who are also accredited investors under Securities Act Rule 501(a)).

The definition of "investments" would be similar to that contained in Company Act Section 2a51–1. Investments of a natural person acting on his own behalf (and not jointly with a spouse) would only include 50% of (a) any of his investments held jointly with his spouse and (b) any investments in which he shares a community property or similar ownership interest with his spouse. When spouses make a joint investment, however, the full amount of their investments (whether made jointly or separately) would be included for purposes of determining whether each spouse is an accredited natural person. Importantly, investments would not include real estate that is used by a natural person or certain family members for personal purposes or as a place of business, or in connection with a trade or business.

Proposed Rule 509 limits the "retailization" of hedge funds from a statistical perspective. By increasing the requirements that must be met to qualify as an "accredited natural person," the SEC has estimated that the number of qualifying households would be reduced from the current level of around 8.5% to only 1.29% (an 88% reduction). In this regard, the SEC is leaning heavily on the assumption that the value of a natural person's aggregate investments is an appropriate proxy for financial sophistication.

As mentioned earlier (see Nutshell Section 9B(2)b), most hedge funds and private equity funds rely on Company Act Section 3(c)(7) to exempt them from registration under the Company Act. However, it is not unusual for their advisers to form parallel funds relying on the Section 3(c)(1) exemption in order for employees and friends and family—most of whom do not meet the "qualified purchaser" standard of Section 3(c)(7)—to participate. Thus, it is this group that will most likely feel the pinch of the proposed Rule if and when it is adopted.

Not surprisingly, investors not qualifying as "accredited natural persons" under the proposed Rule, particularly those who do currently qualify as "accredited investors" under Securities Act Rule 501(a), have reacted negatively to the proposed Rule and are putting up a fierce fight. This is particularly true in that the proposed Rule would not grandfather current accredited investors who would not meet the new accredited natural person standard so that they could make future investments in private investment pools, even those in which they currently are invested. In one instance of potential "blinking" by the SEC, the SEC has sought comment in a subsequent release on whether the definition of "accredited natural person" should include an income standard of $400,000 ($600,000 together with one's spouse) as an alternative to the $2.5 million investments standard. See Revisions of Limited Offering Exemptions in Regulation D, Securities Act Rel. No. 8828, 2007 WL 2239110 (Aug. 3, 2007).

c.　Other Initiatives

The Federal government as well as several states have considered regulating hedge funds. Congress has considered new legislation which would have the effect of regulating hedge fund advisers along the lines of the former Hedge Fund Registration Provisions. In terms of the states, Connecticut, which is considered to be the state with the second or third largest concentration of hedge funds (with New York being the first), has taken the lead. It formed a Hedge Fund Unit within its Department of Banking in early 2006. The seven-person Unit encompasses a broad set of market participants in addition to hedge funds. While its primary focus is on manipulative conduct, it does not conduct examinations per se.

As hedge fund regulation is a moving target, readers are strongly advised to check current rules and regulations.

(3) Withdrawing Registration

Hedge fund advisers who registered with the SEC pursuant to the former Hedge Fund Registration Provisions were entitled to deregister following the *Goldstein* decision. So long as an adviser meets the requirements of the Private Adviser Registration Exemption in Advisers Act Section 203(b)(3), it is free to do so. To deregister with the SEC, a registered investment adviser must file Form ADV–W with the SEC. Form ADV–W is filed electronically through the Investment Adviser Registration Depository ("IARD"). See Advisers Act Rule 203–2 and Nutshell Section 15C. Perhaps surprisingly, the SEC has indicated that, although many hedge fund advisers did withdraw registration after the *Goldstein* decision, a significant number voluntarily maintained their registration. Consequently, the net registration loss since the decision has not been as significant as had been anticipated.

Deregistration for many hedge fund advisers was problematic because they held themselves out generally to the public as investment advisers and/or the number of their clients grew larger than 14 during the time they were registered. In other words, they took actions that disqualified them from using the Private Adviser Registration Exemption.

Nevertheless, the SEC indicated that these advisers could still take advantage of the Private Adviser Registration Exemption if, by the time they withdrew their SEC registration, they ceased holding themselves out as investment advisers and had reduced the number of their clients to 14 or fewer. However, the SEC required these advisers to withdraw their registration by no later than February 1, 2007. For the first 12 months following these advisers' withdrawal, the SEC allowed them, for the purposes of assessing their eligibility under the Private Adviser Registration Exemption, to determine the number of clients they had by reference to a period of time beginning on the date of their withdrawal even though that period may have been less than 12 months.

Advisers who registered due to the former Hedge Fund Registration Provisions who decided to remain registered with the SEC were entitled to take advantage of certain benefits extended to them by the vacated Provisions. Specifically, these advisers are permitted to:

· Present their past performance information for periods prior to the effectiveness date of the Provisions (February 10, 2005), even if they do not otherwise have all of the supporting records otherwise required by Advisers Act Rule 204–2(a)(16). Each such adviser must continue to preserve any of its books and records that relate to its performance for periods prior to February 10, 2005;

· Continue charging a performance fee to investors and other advisory clients who were their investors or clients prior to February 10, 2005, regardless of whether those investors or clients meet the definition of a "qualified client," as such term is defined in Advisers Act Rule 205–3(c); and

· Deliver audited financial statements of a fund of funds, meeting certain requirements, to investors within 180 days of the fund's fiscal year, rather than within 120 days (as required for other types of hedge funds).

§ 10.   APPLICABILITY OF ADVISERS ACT TO UNREGISTERED HEDGE FUND AND CDO ADVISERS

A.   Registration Exemption

As discussed in Nutshell Section 9B(3), investment advisers to hedge funds typically take advantage of the Private Adviser Registration Exemption of Advisers Act Section 203(b)(3) by having less than 15 advisory clients; therefore, they do not register with the SEC. Each adviser considers its fund (whether it takes the legal form of a limited partnership, limited liability company or business trust) to be its "client" rather than the individual investors in the fund. This position was embraced by the U.S. Court of Appeals for the District of Columbia in *Goldstein v. SEC*, 451 F.3d 873 (D.C. Cir. 2006), when it vacated the Hedge Fund Registration Provisions. In reaching its decision, the Court stated that hedge fund advisers are "concerned with the fund's performance, not with each investor's financial condition."

Collateralized debt obligations (CDOs) are a relatively new innovation in the structured finance market that allow investors to invest in a diversified portfolio of bonds and equities with different risk profiles. CDO advisers (often called collateral managers) actively manage and trade their CDO portfolios. CDOs typically have different classes of investors based upon the seniority of the bonds and equity holders.

Like hedge fund advisers, collateral managers generally take the position that each CDO counts as one "client" for purposes of counting the 14 permissible clients under the Private Adviser Registration Exemption. To date, neither the SEC nor the courts has commented on this position. However, the Court in *Goldstein* suggested that the SEC may be justified in treating different classes of investors in a fund as clients, stating "[i]f there are certain characteristics present in some investor-adviser relationships that mark a 'client' relationship, then the [SEC] should have identified those characteristics and tailored [the Hedge Fund Registration Provisions] accordingly." If the SEC were to pursue the Court's suggestion that different classes of investors in a CDO could be counted as clients, collateral managers would be required to advise significantly fewer funds. For instance, if a given CDO had four classes of debt and one class of equity, that fund would count as five clients instead of one client; thus, the collateral manager would be permitted to advise only one more similarly structured fund comprised of five classes, instead of 13 additional funds. It is your co-authors' view that the SEC would have to adopt a rule that applies the *Goldstein* Court's dicta before that dicta should be considered the law.

B. Antifraud Provisions

Most importantly, both hedge fund advisers and collateral managers (whether they are required to be registered with the SEC or not) are subject to the antifraud provisions of Section 206 of the Advisers Act. In July 2007, the SEC Enforcement Division established a special hedge fund antifraud working group to investigate and sanction hedge fund advisers that engage in insider trading.

C. Principal Transactions

Collateral managers actively manage their CDOs. From time to time a given collateral manager's trading may result in a principal transaction that requires client consent. Because it is unclear who the CDO "client" is and there are no applicable SEC rules, industry practice varies concerning how client consent should be obtained for purposes of Advisers Act Section 206(3). Some collateral managers obtain consent from a CDO's board of directors. That board is typically comprised of representatives from a Cayman Islands administrator who presumably know nothing about the details of the principal transaction. Other collateral managers obtain consent from representatives of the debt investors in the CDO. Still others obtain consent from a representative committee established at the time the CDO is formed for the specific purpose of reviewing the fairness of each principal and agency cross transaction. Finally, some collateral managers do not obtain client consent for each principal transaction and instead rely on a general blanket consent provision included in the charter documents of the CDO at the time of its formation. Your co-authors believe that obtaining client consent from representatives of debt investors or from a representative committee are the preferred practices. For more on principal and agency cross transactions, see Nutshell Sections 31B(1) & (2).

V. REGISTRATION AND FORM ADV

§ 11. GENERALLY

Unless exempt from registration under Advisers Act Section 203(b), an investment adviser must register as such with either the SEC or one or more state securities regulators. See Nutshell Section 5B. Regardless of whether registration is required at either the Federal or state level, an adviser must do so on Form ADV, the "Uniform Application for Investment Adviser Registration," which the SEC and the North American Securities Administrators Association jointly developed. In addition, existing SEC-registered advisers and those registering with the SEC for the first time also use Form ADV to make required *notice filings* with state securities regulators. See Nutshell Section 16.

Form ADV is broken down into two parts. Part 1 provides regulators with technical and background information about an adviser. Part II describes the services of an adviser and the scope of its activities. An adviser may also use Part II as a disclosure document for current and prospective clients. Such use satisfies Advisers Act Rule 204–3(a)'s requirement that an adviser furnish each existing and prospective advisory client with a written disclosure statement. See Nutshell Section 23B. Of course, advisers use Form ADV as a shield against liability for fraud, as they would any disclosure-oriented document.

The information that an adviser sets forth in its Form ADV must be both truthful and complete. Under Advisers Act Section 207, it is unlawful for an adviser to intentionally make any untrue statement of a material fact in any "registration application or report" filed with the SEC. Also pursuant to that Section, it is unlawful for an adviser to intentionally omit to state any material fact which is required to be stated in any such application or report.

The SEC's approval or denial of an applicant's Form ADV, as well as the suspension of an existing adviser's registration, is discussed in Nutshell Section 15.

§ 12. FORM ADV

Form ADV consists of two parts: Part 1 and Part II. Part 1 is itself divided into two parts: Part 1A and 1B. Each of these is considered below.

A. Part 1A of Form ADV

All advisers registering with either the SEC or any of the state securities regulators must complete Part 1A. Through a series of questions, Part 1A elicits information about the adviser, its business practices, the persons who own and control the adviser, and the persons who provide investment advice on the adviser's behalf.

Part 1A is broken down into the following 12 Items:

Item 1, identifying information—requires information about the identity of the adviser, where the adviser is doing business, and where a regulator can contact the adviser.

Item 2, SEC registration—requires information necessary to determine whether the adviser is eligible to register with the SEC.

Item 3, form of organization—requires information concerning the form of entity the adviser has chosen (*e.g.*, corporation, partnership, sole proprietorship, etc.), the state or country in which the adviser is organized, and the adviser's fiscal year end.

Item 4, successions—requires information concerning succession if the adviser is succeeding to the business of an existing registered investment adviser.

Item 5, information about advisory business—requires information about the adviser's employees, clients, compensation arrangements, assets under management, and advisory activities. Item 5 information helps the SEC understand the adviser's business, prepare for on-site examinations and formulate regulatory policy.

Item 6, other business activities—requires information about the adviser's non-advisory business activities. The adviser is required to indicate whether it is also, among other things, a broker-dealer, a registered representative of a broker-dealer, a futures commission merchant, a commodity trading adviser, a real estate broker, an insurance broker or a bank.

Item 7, financial industry affiliations—requires information about the adviser's financial industry affiliations and activities. Item 7 information helps identify areas in which conflicts of interest may occur between the adviser and its clients. In particular, the adviser must indicate the nature of an adviser's "related persons" (*e.g.*, a broker-dealer, an investment company, a bank) and, in certain cases, the identity of such persons. A "related person" is defined to include (1) all of the adviser's officers, partners or directors (or any person performing similar functions), (2) all persons directly or indirectly controlling, controlled by, or under common control with the adviser, and (3) all of the adviser's employees (other than those performing only clerical, administrative, support or similar functions).

Item 8, participation/interest in client transactions—requires information about the adviser's participation and interest in its clients' transactions. This would include the adviser buying securities from or selling securities to any client as a principal, effecting securities transactions as a broker for any client for compensation, and buying and selling securities for itself that it also recommends to clients. Like Item 7 information,

Item 8 information helps identify areas in which conflicts of interest may occur between the adviser and its clients. Also like Item 7, Item 8 requires information about the adviser's "related persons."

Item 9, custody of client assets—requires information about whether the adviser or its related persons have custody of any client assets.

Item 10, control persons—requires information about the identity of every person that controls the adviser, either directly or indirectly.

Item 11, disciplinary history—requires information about the adviser's disciplinary history and the disciplinary history of the adviser's advisory affiliates. The SEC uses this information to determine whether to grant or deny an adviser's application for registration, revoke an adviser's registration or place limitations on an adviser's activities as an investment adviser. It also uses the information to identify potential problem areas to focus on during on-site examinations.

Item 12, small business—requires information from advisers meeting the definition of "small business" or "small organization" under Advisers Act Rule 0–7. The SEC uses this information to determine the effect of its regulations on small entities. Only advisers registered or registering with the SEC which have assets under management of less than $25 million need respond to Item 12.

Part 1A also requires advisers to complete the following disclosure schedules:

Schedule A asks for information about the adviser's direct owners and executive officers.

Schedule B asks for information about the adviser's indirect owners.

Schedule C is used to update the information required by Schedules A and B.

Schedule D is used to provide additional information required by certain items in Part 1A.

Disclosure Reporting Pages ("DRPs"), which are also considered schedules, ask for details about disciplinary events involving the adviser or persons affiliated with the adviser.

B. Part 1B of Form ADV

Part 1B of Form ADV requires an adviser to answer additional questions required by state securities authorities. *Accordingly, an adviser which is either registered or registering with the SEC need not complete Part 1B.*

As seen below, Part 1B consists of two items, the second of which is comprised of multiple subitems:

Item 1, state(s) in which adviser is registering—requires the adviser to indicate in which state(s) it is registering by checking the box next to the appropriate state abbreviation(s).

Item 2A, person responsible for supervision/compliance—requires identifying information about the person responsible for the adviser's supervision and compliance.

Item 2B, bond/capital information—requires information about the adviser's bond and/or capital if its home state requires such information.

Item 2C, denial, revocation or payout on bond—requires information about whether a bonding company has ever denied, paid out on, or revoked a bond for the adviser. If so, the adviser must complete a Bond DRP.

Item 2D, unsatisfied judgments or liens—requires information about whether the adviser has any unsatisfied judgments or liens against it. If so, it must complete a Judgment/Lien DRP.

Item 2E, arbitration claims—requires information about whether the adviser, any advisory affiliate or any management person either has been or currently is the subject of an arbitration claim (a) alleging damages in excess of $2500 and (b) involving an investment or investment-related business, embezzlement, bribery, forgery, counterfeiting, extortion, or, broadly, dishonest, unfair or unethical practices. If so, the adviser must complete an Arbitration DRP.

Item 2F, civil, administrative or SRO proceedings—requires information about whether the adviser, any advisory affiliate or any management person either has been or currently is the subject of a civil, administrative, or self-regulatory organization ("SRO") proceeding involving an investment or investment-related business, embezzlement, bribery, forgery, counterfeiting, extortion, or, broadly, dishonest, unfair or unethical practices. If so, the adviser must complete a Civil Judicial Action DRP.

Item 2G, other business activities—requires information about any other business activities in which the adviser is engaged.

Item 2H, financial planning services—requires information about the dollar amount of investments made based on any financial planning services provided by the adviser during its last fiscal year.

Item 2I, custody of client assets—requires information and details concerning whether the adviser withdraws advisory fees directly from clients' accounts or requires a client to prepay more than $500 in advisory fees six or more months in advance.

Item 2J, sole proprietorship—requires the adviser to state if it is a sole proprietor and, if so, to state if it has passed certain licensing exams (*e.g.,* the Series 65 examination). It also asks the adviser whether it has any investment advisory professional designations (*e.g.,* Certified Financial Planner).

C. Part II of Form ADV

Part II of Form ADV focuses on the services and business practices of the adviser. Most advisers use Part II in order to comply with the Brochure Rule (*i.e.,* Advisers Act Rule 204–3). Under this Rule, an investment adviser that is registered or required to be registered under Advisers Act Section 203 generally must furnish each advisory client and prospective advisory client with a written disclosure statement (*i.e.*, a "brochure") within a specified time frame. A brochure must consist of Part II of an adviser's Form ADV or contain at least the information required by Part II of that Form. See Nutshell Section 23B. Advisers who provide a written disclosure statement other than Part II need not follow the same format as Part II so long as the statement contains at least the information required by Part II. See Nathan and Lewis Securities, SEC No–Action Letter, 1990 WL 286885 (avail. July 19, 1990).

In April 2000, the SEC proposed amending Part II of Form ADV. See Advisers Act Rel. No. 1862 (Apr. 5, 2000). The amendments (which, among other things, would rename Part II as "Part 2") have not been adopted at this time. Therefore, advisers must continue to use Part II, as it currently exists. As seen below, Part II requires an adviser to complete 14 items covering a wide variety of information:

Item 1, services and fees—requires information about the advisory services the adviser offers and the fees that the adviser charges. A description of the offered services and the adviser's basic fee schedule, among other information, must be set forth on Schedule F to Form ADV.

Item 2, types of clients—requires information about the types of clients (*e.g.*, individuals, investment companies, trusts, etc.) to which the adviser generally provides investment advice.

Item 3, types of investments—requires information about the types of investments (*e.g.*, equity securities, corporate debt securities, investment company securities, etc.) about which the adviser offers investment advice.

Item 4, security analysis methods/investment strategies—requires information about the adviser's security analysis methods, such as charting, fundamental or technical analysis. The adviser also must disclose the investment strategies it uses to implement any investment advice given to clients. These strategies may include, among others, long-term purchases of securities (securities held at least one year), short-term purchases of securities (securities sold within one year), trading (securities sold within 30 days), short sales, option writing and margin transactions. Finally, the adviser must provide the main sources of information (*e.g.*, financial newspapers, public company annual reports and other SEC filings, company press releases, etc.) that it uses in formulating its advice.

Item 5, educational and business experience—requires information about any general standards of education or business experience that the adviser requires of those involved in determining or giving investment advice to clients. Any such standards must be described on Schedule F to Form ADV.

Item 6, background information—requires the name, year of birth, formal post-high school education and preceding five year business background of the adviser's principal executive officer and each individual who determines general investment advice given to clients. Disclosure is made on Schedule F to Form ADV.

Item 7, other business activities—requires information about business activities other than the provision of investment advice in which the adviser engages. Disclosure must also be made with respect to any products or services other than investment advice that the adviser sells to clients.

Item 8, financial industry affiliations—requires information about the adviser's other financial industry activities or affiliations, such as being a registered broker-dealer, a registered commodity trading adviser or a real estate broker.

Item 9, participation/interest in client transactions—requires information about whether the adviser or its related persons participate or have other interests in client transactions. This would include an adviser buying securities from or selling securities to any client as a principal, effecting securities transactions as a broker for any client for compensation, and buying and selling securities for itself that it also recommends to clients.

Item 10, minimum account requirements—requires the adviser to disclose whether it provides investment supervisory services, manages investment advisory accounts or holds itself out as providing financial planning or some similarly termed services *and* imposes a minimum dollar value of assets or other conditions for starting or maintaining an account. "Investment supervisory services" means the giving of continuous advice as to the investment of funds on the basis of the individual needs of each client. See Advisers Act Section 202(a)(13).

Item 11, client account reviews—if the adviser provides investment supervisory services, manages investment advisory accounts or holds itself out as providing financial planning or some similarly termed services, it must describe who reviews client accounts and how the reviews are conducted. With respect to reviewers, the adviser must provide the number of reviewers, their titles and functions, the instructions they received from the adviser on performing reviews, and the number of accounts assigned to each reviewer. With respect to the actual reviews themselves, the adviser must disclose their frequency, the factors that trigger them, and the different levels of review conducted. In addition, the adviser must describe the nature and frequency of regular client account reports provided to clients.

Item 12, discretion over accounts—requires the adviser to disclose whether it or any related person has the authority to determine, without obtaining specific client consent, the securities to be bought or sold, the amount of the securities to be bought or sold, the broker or dealer to be used, and the commission rates to be paid. If the adviser or a related person suggests brokers to clients, the adviser must describe the factors considered in selecting brokers in determining the reasonableness of their commissions. If the value of products, research and services given to the adviser or a related person is a factor, additional disclosure is required.

Item 13, additional compensation—requires information about any additional compensation received by the adviser. Specifically, the adviser has to disclose any arrangements, whether oral or in writing, whereby the adviser or a related person is paid cash by, or receives some economic benefit from, a non-client in connection with giving advice to clients. The adviser must also disclose whether it or a related person directly or indirectly compensates any person for client referrals.

Item 14, balance sheet—requires the adviser to provide a balance sheet for its most recent fiscal year if it either (a) has custody of client funds or securities (unless the adviser is registered or registering with the SEC) or (b) requires a client (or provides a client with the option) to prepay more than $500 in advisory fees six or more months in advance. Disclosure is made on Schedule G to Form ADV. Item 14 disclosure is designed to assist clients in evaluating the financial ability of the adviser to fulfill its client obligations.

To the extent an adviser is using Part II of Form ADV to satisfy the Brochure Rule, it must disclose any other information to its clients or prospective clients, even if not specifically required by the Bro-

chure Rule, if disclosure is required by any other
provision of the Advisers Act, the rules thereunder,
or any other Federal or state law. See Advisers Act
Rule 204–3(e). This would certainly include disclosure about certain material financial and disciplinary information as mandated by Advisers Act Rule
206(4)–4. See Nutshell Section 23C.

In the event that an adviser renders substantially
different types of advisory services to different advisory clients, it may be entitled to omit certain
information from the brochure it delivers to a particular client or prospective client. Specifically, an
adviser may omit any information required by Part
II of Form ADV from the brochure furnished to a
client or prospective client if that information is
applicable only to a type of investment advisory
service or fee which is not rendered or charged, or
proposed to be rendered or charged, to that client or
prospective client. See Advisers Act Rule 204–3(d).

§ 13. FILING FORM ADV

An adviser must complete Form ADV electronically using the Investment Adviser Registration Depository ("IARD") if it is either (a) filing with the
SEC (and submitting notice filings to any of the
state securities authorities) or (b) filing with a state
securities authority that requires advisers to submit
Form ADV through the IARD. The IARD website
(*www.iard.com*) contains detailed instructions that
an adviser can follow when filing through the IARD.
In order to get started, an adviser must complete an

IARD Entitlement Package and submit it to the NASD, which currently operates the IARD but will likely be replaced by FINRA in the future. With respect to SEC registration, a Form ADV is considered "filed" with the SEC upon its acceptance by the IARD (assuming the appropriate filing fee has been paid), thus subjecting the adviser to potential liability under Advisers Act Section 207. That Section prohibits material misstatements or omissions in SEC filings. See Advisers Act Rule 203–1(c) & (d).

An adviser may submit a paper version of Form ADV rather than an electronic version if it is either (1) filing with the SEC or a state securities authority that requires electronic filing and the adviser has been granted a continuing hardship exemption (as discussed below) or (2) filing with a state securities authority that permits (but does not require) electronic filing and the adviser chooses not to file electronically.

Advisers Act Rule 203–3 provides two "hardship exemptions" from the electronic filing requirement. The SEC may grant an adviser a "temporary hardship" exemption from a required electronic filing if the adviser experiences unanticipated technical difficulties that prevent it from submitting that filing to the IARD system. However, that filing must be filed electronically with the IARD no later than seven business days after the filing was due. By contrast, the SEC may grant an adviser a "continuing hardship" exemption if the adviser qualifies as a "small business." To qualify as a "small business," an adviser must be required to answer Item 12 of Part 1A of Form ADV and must answer "no" to each applicable question in that Item. An adviser seeking either a temporary or continuing hardship exemption must file for the exemption (obviously in paper format) on Form ADV–H. See Advisers Act Rule 203–3(a)(2)(i) & (b)(2).

An adviser is not required to file a copy of Part II of its Form ADV with the SEC, so long as the adviser maintains a copy of its Part II (and any brochure it delivers to clients) in its files. The copy of Part II maintained in the adviser's files is considered "filed" with the SEC, thus subjecting the adviser to potential liability under Advisers Act Section 207. That Section prohibits material misstatements or omissions in SEC filings. See Advisers Act Rules 203–1(b)(2) & 204–1(c).

An adviser must pay the NASD an initial filing fee when it first electronically files Part 1A of Form ADV. Thereafter, the adviser must pay an annual filing fee each time it files its annual updating amendment. No portion of either fee is refundable, and a Form ADV will not be considered "filed" with the SEC until the adviser has paid the filing fee. See Advisers Act Rule 203–1(d).

§ 14. AMENDING FORM ADV

An adviser must amend its Form ADV *at least annually* within 90 days of the end of its fiscal year. See Advisers Act Rule 204–1(a)(1). According to General Instruction 4 to Form ADV, an adviser must update its responses to *all items* in its annual amendment.

An adviser must amend its Form ADV more frequently than annually (*i.e.*, it must file so-called "interim amendments") if the instructions to Form ADV so require. See Advisers Act Rule 204–1(a)(2). General Instruction 4 states that an adviser must amend its Form ADV "promptly" if information previously provided in (a) certain responses becomes *inaccurate in any way* and (b) certain other responses becomes *materially inaccurate*.

A summary of an adviser's duty to amend its Form ADV is set forth in Table 1:

TABLE 1

AMENDMENTS TO FORM ADV			
PART/ITEM	ANNUAL AMENDMENTS ONLY	INTERIM AMENDMENT FOR *ANY* CHANGE	INTERIM AMENDMENT FOR *MATERIAL* CHANGE
PART 1A			
Item 1, identifying information		X	
Item 2, SEC registration	X		
Item 3, form of organization		X	
Item 4, successions			X
Item 5, information about advisory business	X		
Item 6, other business activities	X		
Item 7, financial industry affiliations	X		
Item 8, participation/interest in client transactions			X
Item 9, custody of client assets		X	
Item 10, control persons			X

AMENDMENTS TO FORM ADV			
PART/ITEM	ANNUAL AMENDMENTS ONLY	INTERIM AMENDMENT FOR *ANY* CHANGE	INTERIM AMENDMENT FOR *MATERIAL* CHANGE
Item 11, disciplinary history		X	
Item 12, small business	X		
PART 1B			
Item 1, state(s) in which adviser is registering		X	
Item 2A, person responsible for supervision/compliance		X	
Item 2B, bond/capital information		X	
Item 2C, denial, revocation or payout on bond		X	
Item 2D, unsatisfied judgments or liens		X	
Item 2E, arbitration claims		X	
Item 2F, civil, administrative or SRO proceedings		X	
Item 2G, other business activities			X
Item 2H, financial planning services	X		
Item 2I, custody of client assets		X	
Item 2J, sole proprietorship	X		
PART II			
Non-material changes	X		
Material changes			X

Any amendment that an adviser files under Advisers Act Rule 204–1 is considered a "report" within the meaning of Advisers Act Sections 204 and 207. See Advisers Act Rule 204–1(e). Among other things, Advisers Act Section 207 makes it unlawful for any person to willfully make any untrue statement of a material fact in any report filed with the SEC under Section 204, or to willfully omit to state in any such report any material fact which is required to be stated therein.

Advisers file amendments with the IARD in a process similar to the filing of an original Form ADV. See Advisers Act Rule 204–1(b) & (d) and Nutshell Section 13.

§ 15. ADVISER QUALIFICATION, DISQUALIFICATION AND WITHDRAWAL

A. Qualification of Advisers

Surprisingly, if not shockingly, the Advisers Act imposes no capital, financial or educational requirements or examinations that must be satisfied before a person can register as an investment adviser with the SEC. As discussed below, however, the Advisers Act disqualifies certain persons from becoming investment advisers under the Act. In most cases, SEC registration occurs relatively quickly and inexpensively. This contrasts markedly with broker-dealers whose registration is expensive and who must meet specified testing requirements. Many states take an approach different from that of the SEC by requiring that individuals associated with a state-registered adviser pass certain examinations, such as the Series 65.

Unless an applicant consents to a longer period of time, the SEC has a statutorily-mandated 45 days from the date the applicant files its Form ADV to either grant its request for registration or institute proceedings to determine whether registration should be denied. The SEC will grant registration if it finds that the applicant qualifies to register with the SEC (as opposed to with one or more states) under Advisers Act Section 203A and the requirements of Advisers Act Section 203 are satisfied. See Advisers Act Section 203(c)(2). In practice, however, the SEC grants most registrations within 21 days of their filing date.

A SEC-approved applicant may not represent or imply in any manner whatsoever that it has been sponsored, recommended or approved, or that its abilities or qualifications have in any respect been passed upon, by the United States or any agency or officer thereof. However, an approved applicant may state that it is registered under the Advisers Act so long as the effect of such registration is not misrepresented. See Advisers Act Section 208(a) & (b). In this regard, the staff of the SEC does not prohibit use of the phrase "Registered Investment Adviser" on an adviser's stationery, business cards or other marketing materials; however, aggressive promotion based on SEC registration is frowned upon. Compare Mandell Fin. Group, SEC No–Action Letter, 1997 WL 274828 (avail. May 21, 1997), with In the Matter of FinArc, LLC, Advisers Act Rel. No. 1763, 1998 WL 667628 (Sept. 29, 1998).

In a similar vein, an adviser must use care in representing itself as an "investment counsel" or using the name "investment counsel" as descriptive of its business. Indeed, it is unlawful for an adviser to do so unless (1) its principal business consists of acting as an investment adviser and (2) a substantial part of its business consists of rendering investment supervisory services. See Advisers Act Section 208(c).

If the SEC decides to institute proceedings to determine whether a given applicant's registration should be denied, it must provide the applicant with the grounds for denial under consideration and an opportunity for a hearing. While the SEC must normally conclude its proceedings within 120 days of the date on which the applicant filed its Form ADV, the SEC may unilaterally extend them for up to 90 days if it finds good cause for such an extension and publishes its reasons for doing so. An applicant must consent to any extension beyond 90 days. See Advisers Act Section 203(c)(2).

The SEC may deny registration if the applicant does not qualify to register with the SEC in the first place, if the applicant fails to comply with the requirements of the registration process, or if the SEC determines that the applicant's registration would be subject to revocation or suspension under Advisers Act Section 203(e), which is discussed in the subsection below.

B. Disqualification of Advisers

Advisers Act Section 203(e) provides the SEC with the authority to deny, suspend (for a period not exceeding 12 months) or revoke an adviser's registration or to impose sanctions or limitations on its activities due to specified disqualifying events on the part of the adviser or its associated persons. Disqualifying events include, among others, the filing of a materially false or misleading application for registration, a conviction within the preceding 10 years of any felony, an SEC bar or suspension from being associated with an investment adviser, or the violation of any provision of the Federal securities laws. See generally Section 203(e)(1)-(9).

Advisers Act Section 203(f) gives the SEC similar authority over any person associated with or seeking to become associated with an investment adviser who is or has engaged in similar disqualifying events. For these purposes, the definition of "person associated with an investment adviser" covers all controlled persons and employees, including clerical and ministerial persons. It is unlawful for a disqualified person to associate with an adviser and for an adviser to allow such disqualified person to associate with it. For purposes of Section 203(f), it is irrelevant whether the adviser affirmatively allows a disqualified person to associate with it or stands by passively while it happens. See *SEC v. Washington Investment Network*, 475 F.3d 392 (D.C. Cir. 2007).

C. Adviser Withdrawal

A SEC-registered adviser may voluntarily withdraw its registration in one of two ways. First, a registered adviser may assign its registration to another firm that succeeds to its business as an investment adviser. See Advisers Act Section 203(g). The successor adviser will become registered with the SEC if, within 30 days from its succession, it files an application for registration with the SEC that the SEC does not deny.

Second, a registered adviser may withdraw from registration by filing a Form ADV–W with the SEC. See Advisers Act Section 203(h). Form ADV–W is considered a "report" within the meaning of Advisers Act Sections 204 and 207; therefore, it must be completed fully, accurately and truthfully. The Form itself requires an adviser to provide specific information about its efforts to wind up its advisory business, especially as it relates to custody of client assets, the assignment of advisory contracts and the future storage of books and records. Form ADV–W becomes effective 60 days after acceptance by the IARD, thus providing the SEC with a window of opportunity to impose conditions upon an adviser's withdrawal or, in more extreme instances, to suspend or revoke the adviser's registration. See Advisers Act Rule 203–2. Registered advisers who deregister must maintain certain required books and records for five years and notify the SEC of their location under Advisers Act Rule 204–2(e).

§ 16. STATE NOTICE FILINGS

Advisers Act Section 203A(b)(1)(A) prohibits the states from requiring the registration, licensing or qualification of SEC-registered advisers. Nonetheless, that Section allows state securities authorities to require advisers applying for registration with the SEC or amending their existing SEC registration to provide them with copies of their SEC filings. These filings are referred to as "notice filings." Notice filings are generally required in any state in which an adviser has six or more clients or a place of business. The typical notice filing consists of Part 1A of Form ADV, a consent to service of process and the payment of a filing fee. An adviser can usually submit the filing electronically through the IARD. The SEC will automatically send notice filings to state securities authorities if the adviser so requests on Part 1A of its Form ADV.

While a state is prohibited from requiring the registration, licensing or qualification of a SEC-registered adviser, it may continue to license, register or otherwise qualify any *"investment adviser representative"* ("IAR") who has a place of business in that state. See Advisers Act Section 203A(b)(1)(A) and Nutshell Section 5B(2)a.

VI. ADVERTISING BY INVESTMENT ADVISERS

§ 17. INTRODUCTION

If nothing else, the investment advisory industry is, indeed, a competitive one. While the desire of a given adviser to differentiate itself from others plays out in a myriad of ways, perhaps none is more ripe for abuse than adviser advertising. Acknowledging this, the SEC pays particular attention to adviser advertisements during its periodic inspections. False or misleading statements in advertisements—especially those regarding performance results—are among the most common subjects of SEC deficiency letters and enforcement actions.

In this regard, the SEC broadly relies on the general antifraud prohibitions contained in Advisers Act Section 206(4). That Section makes it unlawful for any adviser "[t]o engage in any act, practice, or course of business which is fraudulent, deceptive, or manipulative." Section 206(4) directs the SEC to establish rules and regulations that define, and prescribe means reasonably designed to prevent, "such acts, practices, and courses of business as are fraudulent, deceptive, or manipulative." The SEC has done so by promulgating Advisers Act Rule

206(4)–1 (the "Advertising Rule"), a rule which either restricts or prohibits outright four specific categories and one general category of adviser advertising. It has also provided substantial guidance in this area through a multitude of no-action letters.

§ 18. WHAT IS AN "ADVERTISEMENT"?

The term "advertisement" is defined in subsection (b) of the Advertising Rule. The term is broadly defined as any notice, circular, letter or other written communication addressed to *more than one person*, or any notice or other announcement in any publication or by radio or television, that offers an investment adviser's advisory services, including any communications intended to induce existing clients to continue or renew advisory services. Communications distributed electronically are considered advertisements and are subject to the same restrictions as communications on paper or by radio or television. Accordingly, an adviser should be aware that information posted on its website, as well as an e-mail sent to more than one person, may constitute an "advertisement" under the Advertising Rule.

Importantly, *oral* person-to-person communications do not fall within the definition of "advertisement," and thus are not subject to the prohibitions contained in the Advertising Rule. Nevertheless, they are still subject to the general antifraud provisions of Advisers Act Section 206. *Written* person-to-person communications, by contrast, may fall within the definition of "advertisement." Indeed, because the written materials used to pitch one prospective client generally do not vary in any substantive way from those used to pitch others, those materials may be considered to be publicly disseminated. See Investment Company Institute, SEC No–Action Letter, 1998 WL 235022 (avail. Sept. 23, 1988).

Advisers are generally required to maintain copies of their advertisements pursuant to Advisers Act Rule 204–2(a)(11). See Nutshell Section 46D.

§ 19. PROHIBITIONS AND RESTRICTIONS UNDER THE ADVERTISING RULE

The Advertising Rule (*i.e.,* Advisers Act Rule 206(4)–1) either restricts or prohibits outright four specific categories and one general category of adviser advertising. Each of these categories is discussed below. These prohibitions only apply to investment advisers who are registered or required to be registered as investment advisers under Advisers Act Section 203. See Advisers Act Rule 206(4)–1(a). Those not required to be registered would, of course, remain subject to the general antifraud provisions of Advisers Act Section 206.

A. Specific Prohibitions and Restrictions

(1) Testimonials

Under the Advertising Rule, an adviser may not, directly or indirectly, publish, circulate or distribute any advertisement "[w]hich refers, directly or indirectly, to any *testimonial* of any kind concerning the investment adviser or concerning any advice, analysis, report or other service rendered by such investment adviser." Advisers Act Rule 206(4)–1(a)(1). A "testimonial" includes any statement of an advisory customer's experience regarding the adviser's advisory services or a customer's endorsement of those services. Of course, the quintessential testimonial is a letter to the adviser from a "satisfied" customer. See Richard Silverman, SEC No–Action Letter, 1985 WL 54061 (avail. Mar. 27, 1985).

The testimonial prohibition reflects the concern that statements of a particular advisory customer's experience or endorsement are likely to give rise to a fraudulent or deceptive implication or mistaken inference that the experience of that customer is typical of the experience of all the adviser's clients. See Gallagher and Assoc., Ltd., SEC No–Action Letter, 1995 WL 447626 (avail. July 10, 1995). In situations where this concern does not exist, the SEC staff has granted no-action relief. Thus, advertisements including an unbiased third party's opinion of an adviser's performance, rather than the opinion of an actual advisory customer, are permissible. See New York Investors Group, Inc., SEC No–Action Letter, 1982 WL 29455 (avail. Sept. 7, 1982).

So too are advertisements that include unbiased third-party ratings of an adviser's performance, even if those ratings are based on survey findings of the adviser's actual customers, so long as the ratings do not emphasize favorable client responses or ignore unfavorable responses. See DALBAR, Inc., SEC No–Action Letter, 1998 WL 136415 (avail. Mar. 24, 1998).

The mere mention of specific client names in an adviser's advertisement raises concerns under the Advertising Rule, because the names used could help influence the decision of a potential customer. While the staff of the SEC does not consider advertisements that include client lists to be "testimonials," it does believe those ads remain subject to Advisers Act Section 206(4), as well as subsection (a)(5) of the Advertising Rule. Thus, an adviser must use "objective criteria" (*e.g.,* account size, geographic location), rather than "performance-based criteria," when selecting clients for inclusion in a client list. See, e.g., In the Matter of Reservoir Capital Mgt., Inc., Advisers Act Rel. No. 1717, 1998 WL 193159 (Apr. 24, 1998); Cambiar Investors, Inc., SEC No–Action Letter, 1997 WL 528245 (avail. Aug. 28, 1997); Denver Investment Advisors, Inc., SEC No–Action Letter, 1993 WL 313090 (avail. July 30, 1993).

(2) Past Specific Recommendations

Under the Advertising Rule, an adviser may not, directly or indirectly, publish, circulate or distribute any advertisement "[w]hich refers, directly or indirectly, to *specific recommendations* of such investment adviser which were or would have been profitable to any person[,]'' except in certain limited situations. Advisers Act Rule 206(4)–1(a)(2). The SEC's obvious concern in this regard is that an adviser will only advertise its profitable recommendations in an effort to garner new customers and keep existing ones, thereby giving the false impression that the adviser's acumen is better than it actually is.

Subparagraph (a)(2) of the Advertising Rule, however, does allow an advertisement to contain *all* the recommendations made by the adviser within the immediately preceding period of not less than one year, or offer to provide a list (free of charge) of all such recommendations. Such an advertisement or list, as the case may be, must contain the following additional disclosures:

(i) the name of each security recommended;

(ii) the date and nature (whether to buy, sell or hold) of each recommendation;

(iii) the market price of each security at the time when it was recommended;

(iv) the price at which each recommendation was to be acted upon;

(v) the market price of each such security as of the most recent practicable date; and

(vi) the following cautionary legend set forth on the first page and in print or type as large as the largest print or type used in the body or text:

"It should not be assumed that recommendations made in the future will be profitable or will equal the performance of the securities in this list."

Importantly, subparagraph (a)(2)'s restrictions cover both traditional advertisements as well as creative attempts at advertising. For example, the SEC staff has stated that an adviser may violate these restrictions by providing prospective clients with selected past copies of an adviser's newsletter, under the theory that the adviser would send only those copies containing the most profitable recommendations. See Starr and Kuehl, Inc., SEC No–Action Letter, 1976 WL 9116 (avail. Apr. 17, 1976).

In situations where the concerns about past specific recommendations do not exist, the SEC staff has granted no-action relief. Thus, an adviser's communication to its existing clients that contains past specific recommendations generally is not viewed as an advertisement so long as the securities mentioned are, or recently were, held by each of those clients and the context of the communication does not suggest that its purpose is to promote the adviser's advisory services. See Investment Counsel Assoc. of Amer., Inc., SEC No–Action Letter, 2004 WL 892243 (avail. Mar. 1, 2004). Similarly, an adviser is entitled to respond to an unsolicited request by a client, prospective client or consultant for specific information about the adviser's past specific recommendations, as such response is not technically an "advertisement."

The SEC has also indicated that certain related materials not subject to subparagraph (a)(2) of the Advertising Rule may, nevertheless, run afoul of subparagraph (a)(5)'s prohibition on advertisements containing "any untrue statement of a material fact, or which is otherwise false or misleading." These include an advertisement containing selected past specific recommendations accompanied by an offer to furnish the remainder in a separate list; and an advertisement containing selected past specific recommendations without indicating whether those recommendations were or would have been profitable, unless the adviser selected the specific securities using an objective, non-performance-based criteria. See Franklin Mgt., Inc., SEC No–Action Letter, 1998 WL 853257 (avail. Dec. 10, 1998).

(3) Charts, Graphs and Formulae

Under the Advertising Rule, an adviser is prohibited from advertising that any chart, graph, formula or other device can, by itself, guide an investor as to what securities should be bought or sold or when to buy or sell them. Similarly, an advertisement may not suggest that such tools will assist an investor in determining what securities should be bought or sold or when to buy or sell them, unless the advertisement prominently discloses the limitations and difficulties of their use. See Advisers Act Rule 206(4)–1(a)(3). This restriction embodies an implicit value judgment by the SEC that no device can successfully make investment decisions without the aid of some human judgment.

For example, in Investor Intelligence (John Anthony), SEC No–Action Letter, 1975 WL 8971 (avail. Nov. 30, 1975), an individual who described himself as "a self acclaimed [psychic] medium dealing in [f]inancial matters only" sought the SEC's permission to advertise his unique skills. In declining to grant such permission, the SEC noted that the "predictive value of extrasensory perception or similar claimed capabilities has not been scientifically established." It added that the individual's "claim that [he had] special mental capabilities which enable [him] to make predictions relating to securities values would constitute, in [the SEC's] view, a representation that [he was] offering a device which can be used in the selection of securities" in violation of subparagraph (a)(3) of the Advertising Rule.

(4) Free Services

Under the Advertising Rule, an advertisement may not contain any statement that any report, analysis or other service will be provided free of charge unless such report, analysis or other service actually is or will be furnished entirely free without any direct or indirect condition or obligation. See Advisers Act Rule 206(4)–1(a)(4).

B. General Prohibition

As mentioned previously, the Advertising Rule contains a general prohibition on false or misleading advertising. Specifically, an adviser is prohibited from, directly or indirectly, publishing, circulating or distributing any advertisement "[w]hich contains any untrue statement of a material fact, or which is otherwise false or misleading." Advisers Act Rule 206(4)–1(a)(5). In an attempt to provide advisers guidance as to what type of advertisements could run afoul of this general prohibition, the SEC staff has suggested that advisers consider each prospective advertisement in light of the following three factors: (1) the advertisement's form and content; (2) any implications or inferences arising out of the advertisement when viewed in its total context; and (3) the sophistication of the client or prospective clients at whom the advertisement is targeted. See, e.g., Bypass Wall Street, Inc., SEC No–Action Letter, 1992 WL 19987 (avail. Jan. 7, 1992).

Utilizing subparagraph (a)(5) of the Advertising Rule, the SEC has brought enforcement actions against an adviser who had, for example: (1) exaggerated the amount of assets under management, the number of its employees and the length of its operations (see In the Matter of Boston Investment Counsel, Inc. and Robert E. Campanella, Advisers Act Rel. No. 1801, 1999 WL 373782 (June 10, 1999)); (2) overstated its investment performance (see In re Reservoir Capital Mgt., Inc., Advisers Act Rel. No. 1717, 1998 WL 193159 (Apr. 24, 1998)); (3) disclosed gross performance figures while burying net-of-fee performance figures on an unnumbered page in the back of its brochure (see In the Matter of Bell Capital Mgt., Inc., Advisers Act Rel. No.

1813, 1999 WL 641795 (Aug. 6, 1999)); and (4) developed a mutual fund timing and selection strategy, advertised that strategy's performance based on its retroactive application, and failed to disclose with sufficient prominence or detail that the advertised performance did not represent the results of actual trading using client assets (see In the Matter of LBS Capital Mgt., Inc., Advisers Act Rel. No. 1644, 1997 WL 401055 (July 18, 1997)).

§ 20. ADVERTISING PERFORMANCE INFORMATION

A. Generally

Advisers are well aware that one of the best ways to attract new clients is to advertise performance information that reveals a stellar track record. While the advertising of mutual fund performance is heavily regulated by the Securities Act, the Company Act and by the rules of the NASD (soon to be replaced by those of FINRA), this is not the case with respect to investment adviser performance. Indeed, the Advisers Act does not specifically address the issue of performance advertising. Nevertheless, performance advertising is subject to the general prohibition regarding false or misleading advertisements contained in the Advertising Rule. See Advisers Act Rule 206(4)–1(a)(5).

Historically, the SEC took the position that it was inherently misleading to include performance information in an adviser's advertisement, because such an advertisement implies that past performance can be repeated. See, e.g., A.R. Schmeidler & Co., SEC No–Action Letter, 1976 WL 12236 (avail. June 1, 1976). Today, the SEC accepts the fact that advisers can use performance information in their advertising without necessarily being misleading so long as certain guidelines are followed and disclosures made. Through a series of no-action letters, the staff of the SEC has provided significant guidance on the issue of performance advertising. Of particular importance in this regard is Clover Capital Mgt. Inc., SEC No–Action Letter, 1986 WL 67379 (avail. Oct. 28, 1986), which is discussed below, and its progeny.

An adviser must maintain all accounts, books, internal working papers and any other records or documents "that are necessary to form the basis for or demonstrate the calculation of the performance or rate of return of any or all managed accounts" in, among other things, any advertisement. See Advisers Act Rule 204–2(a)(16) and Nutshell Sections 20 & 46D.

B. Actual or Model Performance Information

An adviser generally advertises one of two types of performance information. First, it may advertise the performance of some or all of the *actual* client portfolios it has under management. Second, it may advertise the performance of a *fictional* account (a "model portfolio") established as of a certain date which it manages just like its actual client portfolios. An adviser may prefer to advertise the performance of a model portfolio, rather than an actual client portfolio, because it can demonstrate its competence and investment style without violating client confidentiality and misrepresenting its performance to the public. Indeed, depending on the adviser, the performance of a model portfolio may provide an excellent proxy for the adviser's investment approach and track record.

An adviser's dissemination of its performance information, in turn, generally takes place in one of two ways. First, an adviser may publicly disseminate that information through widely distributed advertisements. Second, an adviser may present performance information in connection with one-on-one sales pitches made to prospective institutional clients and wealthy individuals.

The permutations created when combining the two types of performance information with the two manners of dissemination are explored below.

(1) Advertising Actual Performance Information to the Public

When an adviser advertises its "actual" performance information to the public, that information may be based either on a "composite" or on select accounts, so long as the exclusion of certain accounts does not cause the presentation to be misleading. See Nicholas-Applegate Mutual Funds, SEC No–Action Letter, 1996 WL 450350 (avail. Aug. 6, 1996). A "composite" is the aggregation of portfolios or asset classes, which are managed with a similar strategy or investment objective, into a single performance presentation. Composites ensure that all accounts sharing a particular investment style, strategy and objective are included in performance presentations, thus providing a more complete record than the use of a "representative account" or partial composite that leaves out accounts that have terminated. See Assoc. for Investment Mgt. & Research, SEC No–Action Letter, 1996 WL 729385 (avail. Dec. 18, 1996).

As discussed below, when providing actual performance information, an adviser must provide prospective clients with (i) performance information *generally* on a "net-of-fee" basis and (ii) certain mandatory narrative disclosures.

a. Net of Fees

In Clover Capital Mgt. Inc., SEC No–Action Letter, 1986 WL 67379 (avail. Oct. 28, 1986), the SEC staff stated that actual performance information must be presented on a "net-of-fee" basis instead of a gross basis. Thus, subject to one exception described in the following paragraph, actual performance information must be presented *after* the deduction of advisory fees, brokerage or other commissions, and any other applicable charges. While initially the SEC staff also required the deduction of custodial fees, it subsequently reversed its position under the theory that most clients select custodians and pay custodial fees directly. See Investment Company Institute, SEC No–Action Letter, 1987 WL 108068 (avail. Aug. 24, 1987).

In Assoc. for Investment Mgt. & Research, SEC No–Action Letter, 1996 WL 729385 (avail. Dec. 18, 1996), the SEC staff allowed an adviser to distribute an advertisement that presented both gross and net-of-fee performance information, at least with respect to composite performance. However, the staff required that gross and net performance information be presented with "equal prominence." In addition, it required the information to be presented in a manner that would allow a prospective client to easily compare the two.

When an adviser is advertising composite performance, the SEC staff allows the deduction of either actual fees or a "model fee." An adviser may prefer to deduct a "model fee" because it simplifies the calculation of composite performance. However, the model fee an adviser chooses must represent the highest fee charged to any account included in the composite during the performance period. In addition, the advertisement must disclose that performance information reflects a deduction of the highest fee charged. See J.P. Morgan Investment Mgt., Inc., SEC No–Action Letter, 1996 WL 282573 (avail. May 7, 1996).

b.   *Mandatory Disclosure*

The SEC staff in *Clover* required advertisements containing actual performance information to set forth the following six disclosure items:

(i) The effect of material market or economic conditions on the actual results portrayed;

(ii) Whether and to what extent the actual results portrayed reflect the reinvestment of dividends or other earnings;

(iii) The possibility of loss if the advertisement also suggests or makes claims about potential profits;

(iv) All material facts relevant to the comparison of the adviser's actual results to those of an index if the advertisement compares the adviser's actual results to those of an index;

(v) Any material conditions, objectives or strategies used to obtain the actual results portrayed (*e.g.,* that managed accounts contained equity stocks managed with a view towards capital appreciation); and

(vi) If applicable, that the actual results portrayed relate only to a select group of the adviser's clients, the basis on which the selection was made, and the effect of this practice on the actual results portrayed, if material. (Note: this disclosure must be made "prominently.")

(2) Advertising Model Performance Information to the Public

As mentioned earlier, an adviser may advertise the performance of a *fictional* account (a "model portfolio") established as of a certain date which it manages just like its actual client portfolios. When doing so, however, an adviser must provide prospective clients with (i) model performance information on a "net-of-fee" basis and (ii) certain mandatory narrative disclosures noted below.

a. Net of Fees

In Clover Capital Mgt., Inc. SEC No–Action Letter, 1986 WL 67379 (avail. Oct. 28, 1986), the SEC staff stated that model performance information must be presented on a "net-of-fee" basis instead of a gross basis. Thus, model performance information must be presented *after* the deduction of advisory fees, brokerage or other commissions, and any other applicable charges. While initially the SEC staff also required the deduction of custodial fees, it subsequently reversed its position under the theory that most clients select custodians and pay custodial fees directly. See Investment Company Institute, SEC No–Action Letter, 1987 WL 108068 (avail. Aug. 24, 1987). Note that the gross-of-fee presentation exception available to advertisements containing actual performance information is not available in the context of model performance information.

b. Mandatory Disclosure

The SEC staff in *Clover* required advertisements containing model performance information to set forth the following nine disclosure items:

(i) The effect of material market or economic conditions on the model results portrayed;

(ii) Whether and to what extent the model results portrayed reflect the reinvestment of dividends or other earnings;

(iii) The possibility of loss if the advertisement also suggests or makes claims about potential profits;

(iv) All material facts relevant to the comparison of the adviser's model results to those of an index if the advertisement compares the adviser's model results to those of an index;

(v) Any material conditions, objectives or strategies used to obtain the model results portrayed (*e.g.*, that the model portfolio contained equity stocks managed with a view towards capital appreciation);

(vi) The limitations inherent in model results, particularly the fact that such results do not represent actual trading and that they may not reflect the impact that material economic and market factors might have had on the adviser's decision-making if the adviser were actually managing clients' money;

(vii) Any material changes in the conditions, objectives or investment strategies of the model portfolio occurring during the time period portrayed in the advertisement and the effect of any such change on the model results portrayed;

(viii) Whether any of the securities contained in, or the investment strategies followed with respect to, the model portfolio no longer relate, or only partially relate, to the type of advisory services currently offered by the adviser (*e.g.*, the model includes some types of securities that the adviser no longer recommends for its clients); and

(ix) Whether the adviser's clients had investment results materially different from the results portrayed in the model.

(3) "One–On–One" Presentations

An adviser may make one-on-one presentations to prospective clients that contain either actual or model performance information. While an adviser generally must exclude "gross-of-fee" performance information from advertisements directed to the general public, the adviser may include it when making "one-on-one" presentations. See Investment Company Institute, SEC No–Action Letter, 1988 WL 235405 (avail. Sept. 23, 1988). This reflects the SEC's belief that only wealthy individuals and institutional investors receive one-on-one pitches in the first place, and that they are generally in a position to bargain with the adviser about fees.

As a condition to an adviser providing "gross-of-fee" performance information during one-on-one presentations, however, the staff of the SEC requires the adviser to disclose the following information to prospective clients in writing:

(i) That performance figures do not reflect a deduction of investment advisory fees;

(ii) That the client's return will be reduced by the advisory fees and any other expenses the adviser may incur in the management of the client's investment advisory account;

(iii) That the investment advisory fees are described in Part II of the adviser's Form ADV; and

(iv) A representative example (*e.g.,* a table, chart, graph, or narrative) that shows the effect an investment advisory fee, compounded over a period of years, could have on the total value of the client's portfolio.

See Investment Company Institute, SEC No–Action Letter, 1988 WL 235405 (avail. Sept. 23, 1988).

C. AIMR Performance Presentation Standards

In order to assist prospective clients in comparing investment manager performance and to promote consistency in the calculation of such performance, the Association for Investment Management and Research ("AIMR"), a trade association for investment advisers, developed standards for the calculation and presentation of performance information. Among other things, the standards take a restrictive view towards the elimination of accounts when calculating performance information. Although not endorsed by the SEC, the AIMR standards are well-known and accepted. Adherence to them is, in fact, demanded by many clients, particularly institutions. Accordingly, many advisers advertise that they are "AIMR compliant." Those who do so knowing that this is not in fact true could be held liable for making false and misleading statements. See, e.g., In the Matter of Schield Mgt. Co., Advisers Act Rel. No. 1872, 2000 WL 694288 (May 31, 2000).

§ 21. PORTABILITY OF PERFORMANCE INFORMATION

It is relatively common for a successful portfolio manager who works for an investment adviser to leave to start his own advisory business or to join another existing adviser who offers him a better compensation package. In this regard, the question arises as to whether that manager should be able to advertise or otherwise publicize his performance track record from his previous place of employment in order to attract clients to his new endeavor or employer.

The SEC is concerned that advertisements containing previous track records could be misleading under Advisers Act Rule 206(4)–1(a)(5). For example, it would be misleading for a person who advertises the performance results of accounts managed at his prior place of employment when he had been only one of several persons responsible for selecting securities for those accounts. Indeed, he would be giving the false impression that he, alone, was responsible for the performance results. It would be similarly misleading if that person had been the only one responsible for selecting the securities in his prior place of employment when he now is one of several persons responsible for managing accounts at his new place of employment. See, e.g., Great Lake Advisors, Inc., SEC No–Action Letter, 1992 WL 105179 (avail. Apr. 3, 1992). The SEC, however, did permit for the first time a mutual fund portfolio manager to use her prior investment performance record at a new advisory firm for a new mutual fund in 1996. See Bramwell Growth Fund, SEC No–Action Letter, 1996 WL 450346 (avail. Aug. 7, 1996).

As detailed in Horizon Asset Mgt., LLC, SEC No–Action Letter, 1996 WL 554956 (avail. Sept. 13, 1996), the SEC staff takes the position that advertisements that include prior performance results of accounts managed by a predecessor entity would not, in and of itself, be misleading under subparagraph (a)(5) of the Advertising Rule if the following six conditions are satisfied:

(i) the person or persons who manage accounts at the new adviser were also those *primarily responsible* for achieving the prior performance results at the former adviser;

(ii) the accounts managed at the former adviser are so similar to the accounts currently under management at the new adviser that the performance results would provide relevant information to prospective clients;

(iii) all accounts that were managed in a substantially similar manner at the former adviser are advertised unless the exclusion of any such account would not result in materially higher performance being advertised;

(iv) the advertisement is consistent with SEC staff interpretations (*i.e., Clover* and its progeny) with respect to the advertisement of performance results;

(v) the advertisement includes all relevant disclosures, including that the performance results were from accounts managed at another entity; and

(vi) as required by Advisers Act Rule 204–2(a)(16), the new adviser retains the records necessary to demonstrate the calculation of the performance or rate of return that is included in the advertisements.

Horizon itself involved a no-action request from a new adviser whose investment advisory committee would consist of three persons. One of those persons—the controlling manager—would be responsible for all investment decisions of the committee. Although other committee members could provide advice, the controlling manager would have final decision-making authority and the ability to manage investment portfolios notwithstanding that advice. The controlling manager previously owned and operated an investment adviser unaffiliated with the new adviser. Although he was an employee of the predecessor adviser, the controlling manager was substantially responsible for all investment decisions made by that firm. Subject to the new adviser satisfying the six conditions listed above, the staff of the SEC noted that it would not be misleading for the new adviser to advertise the performance record of the predecessor adviser if the controlling manager was the person actually responsible for making the investment decisions at the predecessor firm, and that those decisions going forward at the new adviser need not be made with the consensus of the other members of the committee.

One problematic area in this regard is the adviser's ability to comply with the sixth condition noted above, which incorporates Advisers Act Rule

204–2(a)(16). That Rule generally requires an investment adviser to keep all documents that are necessary to form the basis for or demonstrate the calculation of the performance or rate of return of managed accounts that is included in advertisements. This requirement also applies to the use by an investment adviser of a *predecessor's* performance data. See Great Lake Advisors, Inc., SEC No–Action Letter, 1992 WL 105179 (avail. Apr. 3, 1992).

Understandably, many predecessors are either reluctant or unwilling to provide another adviser with the documents necessary to make this showing. However, where the predecessor publicly publishes net asset values contemporaneously with the management of the prior account in question (including a mutual fund), a new adviser could satisfy Advisers Act Rule 204–2(a)(16) by calculating performance based on that public information and by retaining the worksheets that support those calculations. Such calculations, however, may be problematic if the amounts and payment dates of any dividend payments or distributions made by the account in question are not known. See Salomon Brothers Asset Mgt. Inc. and Salomon Brothers Asset Mgt. Asia Pacific Ltd., SEC No–Action Letter, 1999 WL 528854 (avail. July 23, 1999).

VII. THE ADVISORY RELATIONSHIP

§ 22. SOLICITATION AND REFERRAL ARRANGEMENTS

A. "Solicitors" Generally

Investment advisers often rely on affiliated persons and/or third parties (*e.g.,* brokers, insurance agents, financial planners, accountants or lawyers) to introduce prospective clients to them. The person making the referral is called a "solicitor." When a referral arrangement truly does not involve the adviser compensating the solicitor, no conflicts of interest arise and the arrangement is not suspect. However, when a solicitor is compensated, whether with a cash payment or otherwise, the conflicts that arise are a cause for concern.

The SEC has long believed that the payment of referral fees by investment advisers raises serious problems under the antifraud provisions of Advisers Act Section 206. In the SEC's view, these arrangements pose an inherent conflict of interest because the solicitor is financially motivated to refer a prospective client to an adviser who will pay a referral fee. However, that adviser may be different from the adviser best suited to that client's needs. At a minimum, Section 206 requires that this conflict be disclosed to the prospective client.

B.   Cash Compensation

(1) Background of the Cash Solicitation Rule

The SEC considered two alternative methods by which to address the inherent conflicts of interest and biases that exist when a solicitor is compensated for referring clients to a particular investment adviser. The SEC initially considered imposing an outright ban on such referral compensation. However, the SEC had second thoughts, apparently persuaded by commentators' views that client referral expenditures were a necessary and acceptable form of advertising within the investment advisory industry.

The SEC instead embraced the second alternative of allowing referrals while regulating certain aspects of them. Thus, the SEC adopted Advisers Act Rule 206(4)–3 (the "Cash Solicitation Rule") under the authority provided to it by Advisers Act Section 206(4). The Cash Solicitation Rule allows a solicitor to receive cash compensation for his referrals, so long as certain requirements are met. By definition, non-cash solicitation arrangements are not covered by the Cash Solicitation Rule, but are still subject to the antifraud provisions of Advisers Act Section 206.

(2) Requirements of the Cash Solicitation Rule

Before an investment adviser that is registered or required to be registered under Advisers Act Section 203 may pay a *cash fee*, either directly or indirectly, to a solicitor with respect to solicitation activities, the investment adviser must satisfy the provisions of the Cash Solicitation Rule. Attempts to disguise cash referral fees as "fees for services rendered," "consulting fees" or "brokerage commissions" have been met with disdain by the SEC. For purposes of the Rule, "solicitor" is defined to include any person who, directly or indirectly, solicits any client for, or refers any client to, an investment adviser. "Client," in turn, includes both existing clients and prospective clients. See Advisers Act Rule 206(4)–3(d)(1) & (2).

Generally speaking, "solicitation activities" include any activities designed to steer a prospective client to a particular investment adviser. While normally it is a solicitor that steers a prospective client towards an investment adviser, "solicitation activities" is defined broadly enough to include the opposite as well. That is, the solicitor can provide the name of the prospective client to the investment adviser so that the adviser can contact that client.

Activities designed to help a prospective client select an investment adviser in a generic sense are generally not considered "solicitation activities." For example, a person who compiles a list of prospective advisers for a prospective client to consider, and, importantly, does not have any real financial interest in promoting one adviser over another, is generally not engaged in "solicitation activities." See Nat'l Football League Players Assoc., SEC No–Action Letter, 2002 WL 100675 (avail. Jan. 25, 2002). Indeed, activities should not constitute "solicitation activities" if they do not give rise to the inherent conflict of interest involved when a solicitor is financially motivated to refer a prospective client to an adviser who will pay a referral fee.

The Cash Solicitation Rule sets forth the following five types of requirements which, if applicable under the circumstances, must be satisfied: (i) those relating to the investment adviser; (ii) those relating to the solicitor; (iii) those relating to the need for a written solicitation agreement; (iv) those relating to disclosure; and (v) those relating to the supervision of solicitors. While each type is discussed below, it is important to remember that compliance with the Cash Solicitation Rule does not relieve any person of any fiduciary or other obligation to which such person may be subject under the law. See Advisers Act Rule 206(4)–3(c).

Table 2 below summarizes the requirements of the Cash Solicitation Rule and sets forth the corresponding sections of the Nutshell which discuss those requirements.

TABLE 2

Cash Solicitation Rule Requirements
(Advisers Act Rule 206(4)–3)

		TYPE OF SOLICITOR	
REQUIREMENT	AFFILIATED SOLICITOR	UNAFFILIATED SOLICITOR PROMOTING *IMPERSONAL* ADVISORY SER-VICES	UNAFFILIATED SOLICITOR PROMOTING *PERSONALIZED* ADVISORY SER-VICES
Registration of investment adviser seeking solicitation services	Always 22B(2)a*	Always 22B(2)a*	Always 22B(2)a*
Prohibition on engagement of *disqualified* solicitor	Always 22B(2)b*	Always 22B(2)b*	Always 22B(2)b*
Written solicitation agreement between adviser and solicitor	Always 22B(2)c*	Always 22B(2)c*	Always 22B(2)c*
Specific provisions required in written solicitation agreement	No 22B(2)c1*	No 22B(2)c2(a)*	Yes 22B(2)c2(b)*
Disclosure of solicitor's affiliation/position to prospective clients	Yes 22B(2)d1*	Not applicable 22B(2)d2(a)*	Not applicable 22B(2)d2(b)*
Disclosure of terms of solicitation agreement	No 22B(2)d1*	No 22B(2)d2(a)*	Yes 22B(2)d2(b)*
Supervision of solicitor by adviser	No 22B(2)e*	No 22B(2)e*	Yes 22B(2)e*

* Refers to section of the Nutshell which discusses the requirement.

a. *Investment Adviser Requirements*

In order to rely on the Cash Solicitation Rule, an adviser must be registered as such under Advisers Act Section 203. See Advisers Act Rule 206(4)–3(a)(1)(i). An adviser that is required to be registered but has failed to do so is prohibited from paying a cash referral fee to a solicitor. Advisers that are excluded from the definition of "investment adviser" under Section 202(a)(11) or are exempt from registration under Section 203(b) need not comply with the Cash Solicitation Rule.

b. Solicitor Requirements

An investment adviser may not engage as a solicitor any person who has been disqualified under any of the disqualification provisions set forth below. All and all, those provisions essentially lead to the following conclusion: an adviser cannot utilize the services of a solicitor if, under the Advisers Act, the adviser could not hire that person directly as an employee of the adviser. Specifically, under Advisers Act Rule 206(4)–3(a)(1)(ii), an adviser cannot make a cash payment to any solicitor who:

(i) is subject to an SEC order issued under Advisers Act Section 203(f);

(ii) has been convicted within the previous ten years of any felony or misdemeanor involving conduct described in Advisers Act Section 203(e)(2)(A)-(D);

(iii) has been found by the SEC to have engaged, or has been convicted of engaging, in any of the conduct specified in paragraph (1), (5) or (6) of Advisers Act Section 203(e); or

(iv) is subject to an order, judgment or decree described in Advisers Act Section 203(e)(3).

Advisers Act Section 203, which is referred to in all four of the disqualification provisions set forth above, authorizes the SEC to bar a person from associating with an investment adviser under certain conditions. However, it does not require the

SEC to do so. Accordingly, when the Cash Solicitation Rule was adopted, the SEC expressed its willingness, under the appropriate circumstances, to allow a person who is subject to a SEC order under Advisers Act Sections 203(e) or (f) to nevertheless be engaged as a solicitor subject to appropriate disclosure of the statutory disqualification to prospective clients. See, e.g., Dougherty & Co. LLC, SEC No–Action Letter, 2003 WL 22204509 (avail. July 3, 2003).

c.   *Requirement of a Written Solicitation Agreement*

An investment adviser may only pay a cash fee to a solicitor pursuant to a written solicitation agreement to which the adviser is a party. See Advisers Act Rule 206(4)–3(a)(1)(iii). An adviser must keep a copy of the agreement as part of the records required to be kept under Advisers Act Rule 204–2(a)(10). See Nutshell Section 46E. As discussed below, whether *additional requirements* apply to the written solicitation agreement depends on the identity of the solicitor and the type of advisory services the adviser is planning on providing to a prospective client.

1.   Affiliated Solicitors

No additional requirements apply to the written solicitation agreement when the solicitor in question is a partner, officer, director or employee of either the investment adviser or an affiliate of that adviser. For these purposes, ''affiliate'' means a person which controls, is controlled by, or is under common control with the investment adviser. However, the status of the solicitor with the adviser or affiliate, as the case may be, and any affiliation between the adviser and the affiliate must be disclosed to the client at the time of the solicitation or referral. See Advisers Act Rule 206(4)–3(a)(2)(ii).

2. Unaffiliated Solicitors

(a) Promotion of Impersonal *Advisory Services*

Additional requirements also do not apply to the written solicitation agreement when the solicitor in question is soliciting prospective clients with respect to an adviser who will provide "impersonal advisory services" only. See Advisers Act Rule 206(4)–3(a)(2)(i). While this applies whether the solicitor is affiliated or unaffiliated with the adviser in question, affiliated solicitors are already separately carved out due to their investment adviser affiliation as discussed in the preceding subsection.

An adviser provides "impersonal advisory services" when he provides investment advisory services solely by means of (i) written materials or oral statements which do not purport to meet the objectives or needs of the specific client, (ii) statistical information containing no expressions of opinion as to the investment merits of particular securities, or (3) any combination of the foregoing services. See Advisers Act Rule 206(4)–3(d)(3).

(b) Promotion of Personalized *Advisory Services*

Additional requirements, however, do apply to the written solicitation agreement in all other cases, *i.e.,* when the solicitor is an *unaffiliated third party* soliciting prospective clients with respect to an adviser who will provide *personalized* advisory services. In this situation, the written agreement must satisfy the following three conditions:

(i) It must describe the solicitation activities to be engaged in by the solicitor on behalf of the investment adviser and the compensation to be received in exchange;

(ii) It must contain an undertaking by the solicitor to perform his duties in a manner consistent with the adviser's instructions and with the provisions of the Advisers Act and the rules thereunder; and

(iii) It must require the solicitor, at the time of any solicitation activities for which compensation will be paid, to provide each client with a current copy of the investment adviser's written disclosure statement (*i.e.,* "brochure") required by Advisers Act Rule 204–3, as well as a separate written disclosure document (the "solicitor's disclosure document") which essentially provides identification information about the solicitor and adviser and describes the arrangement (especially the financial one) between the two (see Advisers Act Rule 206(4)–3(a)(2)(iii)(A)).

d.   *Disclosure Requirements*

The degree of disclosure the solicitor must make to a prospective client depends on the identity of the solicitor and the type of advisory services the adviser is planning on providing to that client.

1.   Affiliated Solicitors

Advisers Act Rule 206(4)–3(a)(2)(ii) governs disclosure by a solicitor who is a partner, officer, director or employee of either the investment adviser or an affiliate of the adviser. For these purposes, "affiliate" means a person which controls, is controlled by, or is under common control with the investment adviser. Such a solicitor must disclose to clients at the time of the solicitation or referral his status with the investment adviser or affiliate, as the case may be, and any affiliation between the adviser and the affiliate. Affiliation need not be disclosed in a separate disclosure document but instead could be inferred from objective circumstances. For example, a solicitor could present his business card which also carries the adviser's name or identifying logo on it. The SEC does not require any additional disclosure based on its assumption that clients are often aware that an affiliated person's recommendations are biased. Because affiliation is disclosed, the SEC does not mandate disclosure of the terms of the solicitation agreement as potential clients generally understand that the solicitor is being paid.

2.   Unaffiliated Solicitors

(a) Promotion of Impersonal *Advisory Services*

When an unaffiliated solicitor's activities are limited to promoting an adviser's "impersonal advisory services," a solicitor is not required to disclose the terms of the solicitation agreement to a prospective client. See Advisers Act Rule 206(4)–3(a)(2)(i). An adviser provides "impersonal advisory services" when he provides investment advisory services solely by means of (i) written materials or oral statements which do not purport to meet the objectives or needs of the specific client, (ii) statistical information containing no expressions of opinion as to the investment merits of particular securities, or (iii) any combination of the foregoing services. See Advisers Act Rule 206(4)–3(d)(3).

Because the SEC believes that potential clients generally understand that those soliciting with respect to the provision of an adviser's impersonal advisory services are doing so as paid salespersons, the SEC does not mandate disclosure of the terms of the solicitation agreement. However, the solicitor's activities must exclusively relate to the adviser's impersonal advisory business. An adviser will lose the protection of this provision if solicitation is made as to any other types of advisory services offered by the adviser, even if the client ultimately chooses to purchase only the impersonal services.

  (b) Promotion of Personalized *Advisory Services*

The most stringent disclosure requirements are imposed when the solicitor is an *unaffiliated third party* soliciting prospective clients with respect to the provision of *personalized* advisory services. This should come as no surprise, as this scenario gives rise to the conflict of interest about which the SEC is most concerned. See Nutshell Section 22A. Under Advisers Act Rule 206(4)–3(a)(2)(iii)(A), such a solicitor is required to provide each client with a current copy of the investment adviser's written disclosure statement (*i.e.*, "brochure") required by Advisers Act Rule 204–3, as well as a separate written disclosure document (the "solicitor's disclosure document") satisfying the delivery requirements of subparagraph (b) of Rule 204–3. See Nutshell Section 23B(2).

The solicitor's disclosure document must contain the following:

· The names of the solicitor and the adviser;

· The nature of the relationship between the solicitor and the adviser;

· A statement that the solicitor will be compensated for his solicitation services by the adviser;

· The terms of the compensation arrangement between the solicitor and the adviser, including a description of the compensation that the adviser has paid or will pay to the solicitor; and

· Disclosure of any additional charges that will be incurred by the client as a result of the cash solicitation agreement, such as a separate advisory fee or a higher advisory fee.

See Advisers Act Rule 206(4)–3(b).

Importantly, subparagraph (a)(2)(iii)(B) of Advisers Act Rule 206(4)–3 requires an adviser to obtain from a client, either prior to or at the time the advisory contract is entered into, a signed and dated acknowledgment of receipt of both the adviser's brochure and the solicitor's disclosure document. An adviser must keep a copy of the acknowledgment as part of the records required to be kept under Advisers Act Rule 204–2(a)(15). See Nutshell Section 46E.

e. Supervisory Requirements

The SEC imposes a supervisory requirement on an adviser when the solicitor in question is an *unaffiliated third party* soliciting prospective clients with respect to the provision of *personalized* advisory services. Under Advisers Act Rule 206(4)–3(a)(2)(iii)(C), an adviser must make a bona fide effort to ascertain whether the solicitor has complied with the terms of the solicitation agreement and must have a reasonable basis for believing that the solicitor has, in fact, complied. This supervisory requirement surely underscores the SEC's concern about cash compensation flowing to unaffiliated third party solicitors.

C. Non–Cash Compensation

The Cash Solicitation Rule does not cover non-cash solicitation arrangements. Because non-cash compensation also presents conflicts of interest, it is generally subject to the antifraud provisions of Advisers Act Section 206. At a minimum, this means that an adviser must fully disclose non-cash compensation arrangements with solicitors in its Form ADV.

One form of non-cash compensation arises when an adviser directs brokerage transactions to a broker in exchange for client referrals. Once again, the referred clients may not have been referred to an adviser best suited for their needs, but rather simply to one who compensated a broker through directed brokerage. Moreover, existing clients may not be aware of the extra expenses that may be incurred as a result of the adviser directing transactions to a preferred broker, as opposed to a broker who is able to offer the most competitive commission rates. Any such arrangement must be disclosed pursuant to the provisions of Advisers Act Section 206. For more on adviser directed brokerage, see Nutshell Section 36.

D. Registration Status of Solicitors

(1) Solicitor for an SEC–Registered Investment Adviser

a. *Registration Under the Advisers Act*

Whether a given solicitor must register as an investment adviser under the Advisers Act solely because of his solicitation activities on behalf of a SEC-registered investment adviser depends on the identity of the solicitor and the type of advisory services the adviser is planning on providing to solicited clients.

An *affiliated* solicitor normally may avoid separately registering under the Advisers Act due to his affiliation with an investment adviser who is so registered. Indeed, an affiliated solicitor normally qualifies as a "person associated with an investment adviser" under Advisers Act Section 202(a)(17). Thus, like other employees of an adviser, he need not register separately as an investment adviser under the Advisers Act.

The registration requirements relating to an *unaffiliated* third party solicitor whose activities are limited to promoting an adviser's *impersonal* advisory services are not clear cut. In fact, the SEC has stated that such a solicitor may have to register depending on the particular facts and circumstances applicable to that solicitor and his activities. See Advisers Act Rel. No. 688, 1979 WL 174269 (July 12, 1979) ("Release 688").

An *unaffiliated* third party solicitor who solicits prospective clients with respect to the provision of *personalized* advisory services need not register under the Advisers Act so long as he complies with the Cash Solicitation Rule. See Release 688 and Nutshell Section 22B. According to the SEC, the reason for this is twofold. First, such a solicitor is substantially similar to an employee of the adviser due to the solicitor's need to comply with the Cash Solicitation Rule's requirements. Second, under that Rule the adviser has an obligation to supervise the solicitor's activities.

Finally, the registration status of solicitors who receive non-cash compensation or who otherwise operate outside of the purview of the Cash Solicitation Rule is less clear. If the solicitor is deemed to be "engaged in the business" of advising, then he would be required to register as an investment adviser. One slightly convoluted way to reach this conclusion is to view the solicitor as indirectly giving investment advice about securities due to the fact that he is giving advice about the expertise of investment advisers. And, of course, he is being compensated (albeit not in cash) for that advice.

b.   *Registration Under State Law*

NSMIA preempted a great deal of state regulation of investment advisers registered under Advisers Act Section 203(b) and their advisory personnel. Specifically, a state may not license or register any person who qualifies as a "supervised person" of a SEC-registered investment adviser, *unless* that person also qualifies as an "investment adviser representative" ("IAR") of a SEC-registered adviser. See Advisers Act Section 203A(b)(1). However, if a solicitor has a place of business in a given state and also qualifies as an IAR, that state may subject him to its licensing, registration and qualification requirements. See Advisers Act Section 203A(b)(1)(A) and Nutshell Section 5B(2)a.

Under Advisers Act Rule 203A–3(a)(1), two requirements must be met before a person is considered an IAR. First, the person must qualify as a "supervised person" of the investment adviser subject to one exception discussed below. A "supervised person" means any partner, officer, director (or other person occupying a similar status or performing similar functions) or employee of an investment adviser, or other person who provides investment advice on behalf of that adviser and is subject to the supervision and control of that adviser. See Advisers Act Section 202(a)(25).

Second, the "supervised person" must have (i) more than five clients who are natural persons and (ii) an overall clientele more than 10% of which consists of natural persons. Excluded from the universe of "natural persons" are businesses, charitable or educational institutions, investment companies, other institutional investors and, if they enter into performance fee contracts under Advisers Act Rule 205–3, high net worth individuals (referred to as "qualified clients" in this context).

Importantly, an exception is made with respect to any "supervised person" who does not solicit, meet with or otherwise communicate with clients of an investment adviser on a regular basis, or who provides only advice that does not purport to meet the objectives or needs of specific individuals or accounts ("impersonal investment advice"). Such a person is not considered an IAR. See Advisers Act Rule 203A–3(a)(2).

Because only an *affiliated* solicitor can, by definition, qualify as a "supervised person," an *unaffiliated* solicitor will always be subject to any applicable state licensing and registration requirements.

(2) Solicitor for a State–Registered Investment Adviser

A solicitor for a state-registered investment adviser must comply with any applicable state licensing and registration requirements. These vary from state to state, but can include qualification and examination requirements as well as registration requirements.

§ 23. DISCLOSURE REQUIREMENTS RELATING TO CLIENTS AND PROSPECTIVE CLIENTS

A. Introduction

To help the public make informed decisions regarding the selection and retention of investment advisers, the SEC has adopted several disclosure rules. The two most important are Advisers Act Rules 204–3 (commonly referred to as the "Brochure Rule") and 206(4)–4. The Brochure Rule requires registered investment advisers to deliver or offer to deliver to clients and prospective clients a written disclosure statement (*i.e.,* a brochure). Advisers Act Rule 206(4)–4, which was promulgated by the SEC pursuant to its authority under the anti-fraud provisions of Advisers Act Section 206, requires registered investment advisers to promptly disclose to clients certain material financial and disciplinary events.

Importantly, Advisers Act Rules 204–3 and 206(4)–4 establish *minimum* disclosure requirements. Compliance with them does not relieve an investment adviser of any obligation under Federal or state law to disclose any other information to clients or prospective clients. See Advisers Act Rule 204–3(e). As a general matter, an investment adviser, as a fiduciary, has a duty to disclose to clients all material facts about the advisory relationship. This duty is enforceable under Advisers Act Section 206. See Nutshell Section 28C(1).

B. The "Brochure Rule"

(1) General Provision

Under Advisers Act Rule 204–3(a), an investment adviser that is registered or required to be registered under Advisers Act Section 203 generally must furnish each advisory client and prospective advisory client with a written disclosure statement. This disclosure statement (hereinafter referred to as a "brochure") may be either a copy of Part II of the adviser's Form ADV or a written document containing at least the information required by Part II of that Form. Advisers who provide a written disclosure statement other than Part II need not follow the same format as Part II so long as the statement contains at least the information required by Part II. See Nathan and Lewis Securities, Inc., SEC No–Action Letter, 1990 WL 286885 (avail. July 19, 1990).

To demonstrate compliance with the Rule, an adviser typically has a client expressly acknowledge receipt of a brochure in the written advisory contract between the adviser and the client. An adviser must keep a copy of each brochure and any amendment or revision thereto given, or offered to be given, to any client or prospective client who subsequently becomes a client as part of the records required to be kept under Advisers Act Rule 204–2(a)(14). See Nutshell Section 46C.

(2) Timing of Delivery

The timing of a brochure's delivery is very important. Generally, an adviser must deliver a brochure not less than 48 hours *prior* to "entering into" any written or oral investment advisory contract with a client or prospective client. If, however, the client has the right to terminate the advisory contract without penalty within five business days after entering into it, the adviser has until the time the contract is entered into to deliver the brochure. See Advisers Act Rule 204–3(b)(1). "Entering into" an advisory contract does not include an extension or renewal of an existing contract unless there has been a material change to it. See Advisers Act Rule 204–3(g)(2).

Moreover, an adviser must, on an annual basis and without charge, deliver or offer in writing to deliver upon a client's written request a brochure to each of its advisory clients. See Advisers Act Rule 204–3(c)(1). If a client makes such a written request, the adviser must deliver the brochure within seven days of receipt of that request. To demonstrate at least partial compliance with the Rule, an adviser typically includes language on each client's fourth quarter account statement informing the client of his or her right to make a written request for a brochure.

Under subparagraphs (b)(2) and (c)(2) of Advisers Act Rule 204–3, two exceptions to the delivery requirement exist. First, a brochure need not be delivered when an adviser enters into an advisory contract with a registered investment company, so long as that contract meets the requirements of Company Act Section 15(c). Second, delivery need not be made in connection with a contract for impersonal advisory services; however, with respect to any client paying $200 or more for those services, an adviser must make to that client a written offer to deliver a brochure. See Advisers Act Rule 204–3(c)(3). A contract for "impersonal advisory services" essentially is one that provides investment advisory services which do not purport to meet the objectives or needs of specific individuals or accounts. See Advisers Act Rule 204–3(g)(1).

(3) Contents of Brochure

A brochure must consist of Part II of an adviser's Form ADV or contain at least the information required by Part II of that Form. As described in greater detail in Nutshell Section 12C, Part II requires a wide variety of information. This includes information about an adviser's background and business practices, the types of business services it provides, fees it charges, how it analyzes securities, any conflicts of interest affecting it, and its role in the client's securities transactions. Importantly, an adviser must disclose any other information to its clients or prospective clients, even if not specifically required by the Brochure Rule, if disclosure is required by any other provision of the Advisers Act, the rules thereunder, or any other Federal or state law. See Advisers Act Rule 204–3(e). This would certainly include disclosure about certain material financial and disciplinary information as mandated by Advisers Act Rule 206(4)–4. See Nutshell Section 23C.

In the event an adviser renders substantially different types of advisory services to different advisory clients, it may be entitled to omit certain information from the brochure it delivers to a particular client or prospective client. Specifically, an adviser may omit any information required by Part II of Form ADV from the brochure furnished to a client or prospective client if that information is applicable only to a type of investment advisory service or fee which is not rendered or charged, or proposed to be rendered or charged, to that client or prospective client. See Advisers Act Rule 204–3(d).

(4) Wrap Fee Program Disclosure

For a discussion of a wrap fee brochure, its contents and its delivery requirements, see Nutshell Section 42.

(5) Hedge Fund Advisers

Investment advisers to hedge funds typically take advantage of the Private Adviser Registration Exemption of the Advisers Act and, therefore, do not register with the SEC. Each adviser considers its fund (whether it legally takes the form of a limited partnership, limited liability company or business trust) to be its "client" rather than the individual investors in the fund. This position, of course, was embraced by the U.S. Court of Appeals for the District of Columbia in *Goldstein v. SEC*, 451 F.3d

873 (D.C. Cir. 2006). See Nutshell Section 9E. Accordingly, an unregistered hedge fund adviser typically does not deliver a brochure to each investor in its fund. Rather, it will distribute a private placement memorandum or offering circular to prospective fund investors. It will distribute this disclosure document, which, among other things, will provide details about the fund and the adviser, in order to satisfy disclosure obligations under the Securities Act.

(6) Solicitors

For a discussion of the disclosure requirements applicable to solicitors, see Nutshell Section 22B(2)d.

C. Adverse Financial Conditions and Certain Disciplinary Events

(1) Generally

Advisers Act Section 206(4) makes it unlawful for any investment adviser to use any means of interstate commerce to engage in any act, practice or course of business which is fraudulent, deceptive or manipulative. The SEC, under the authority granted to it by Section 206(4), promulgated Advisers Act Rule 206(4)–4 to clarify financial and disciplinary information that advisers must disclose to their clients and prospective clients.

Specifically, an adviser must disclose two types of information under Rule 206(4)–4 to any client or prospective client. First, an adviser must disclose all material facts relating to any financial condition that is reasonably likely to impair its ability to meet contractual commitments to clients. However, disclosure need only be given to each client or prospective client if the adviser (i) has discretionary authority, either express or implied, over the client's account, (ii) has custody over the client's funds or securities, or (iii) requires the client to prepay more than $500 in advisory fees six or more months in advance. See Advisers Act Rule 206(4)–4(a)(1). Disclosure under any of these circumstances makes perfect sense given that a client of a financially troubled adviser could wind up losing his prepaid fees, incurring costs associated with locating another adviser or, in the worst-case scenario, having the capital hungry adviser purloin his assets.

Importantly, the SEC has not provided any guidance in the Rule as to what specific adverse financial conditions would require disclosure to clients or prospective clients. It is safe to assume that conditions such as bankruptcy and insolvency, which would clearly have a material adverse effect on an adviser's ability to operate, would qualify. However, other lesser events, such as the appointment of a receiver, would also potentially qualify.

Second, an adviser must disclose all material facts relating to any legal or disciplinary event that is material to the evaluation of the adviser's integrity or ability to meet contractual commitments to clients. See Advisers Act Rule 206(4)–4(a)(2). This disclosure is in addition to the disciplinary matters that an adviser must routinely disclose on Part 1A (Item 11) of its Form ADV. See Nutshell Section 12A. Events relating to a "management person" of the adviser also must be disclosed. See Advisers Act Rule 206(4)–4(b). A "management person" is a person with the power to exercise, directly or indirectly, a controlling influence over the management or policies of a corporate adviser or to determine the general investment advice given to clients. See Advisers Act Rule 206(4)–4(d)(1).

Legal or disciplinary events occurring within the previous 10 years are covered by Rule 206(4)–4, although those that were resolved in the adviser's or management person's favor or subsequently reversed, suspended or vacated are excluded. Moreover, as explained in Nutshell Section 23C(2) below, the SEC has created a rebuttable presumption, under subparagraph (b) of the Rule, that disclosure of certain specified legal or disciplinary events is required.

Whether or not a given legal or disciplinary event is "material" to an evaluation of the adviser's integrity or ability to meet contractual commitments to clients depends on many factors. According to the staff of the SEC, one must look at "the distance of the entity or individual involved in the disciplinary event from the advisory function; the nature of the infraction that led to the disciplinary event; the severity of the disciplinary sanction and the time elapsed since the date of the disciplinary event." Douglas Capital Mgt., Inc., SEC No–Action Letter, 1988 WL 233565 (avail. Jan. 11, 1988).

The SEC has made it clear that an adviser's compliance with Rule 206(4)–4 will not relieve that adviser from any other disclosure requirement under the Advisers Act, the rules or regulations thereunder, or any other Federal or state law. See Advisers Act Rule 206(4)–4(f).

(2) Legal or Disciplinary Events Presumptively Subject to Disclosure

Pursuant to Advisers Act Rule 206(4)–4(b), the SEC has created a rebuttable presumption that disclosure of the following legal or disciplinary events is required:

- A criminal or civil action in which the person was (i) convicted or pleaded guilty or no contest to a felony or misdemeanor, or is a named subject of a pending criminal proceeding, so long as the action involved an "investment-related" (see discussion below) business or various specified acts, such as fraud or bribery, (ii) found to have been "involved" (see discussion below) in a violation of an investment-related statute or regulation or (iii) the subject of any order, judgment or decree permanently or temporarily enjoining the person from, or otherwise limiting the person from, engaging in any investment-related activity;

- An administrative proceeding before the SEC, any other Federal regulatory agency or any state agency in which the person (i) was found to have caused an investment-related business to lose its authorization to do business or (ii) was (a) found to have been involved in a violation of an investment-related statute or regulation and (b) the subject of an order by the agency denying, suspending or revoking the authorization of the person to act in, or barring or suspending the person's association with, an investment-related business, or otherwise significantly limiting the person's investment-related activities.

· A self–regulatory organization ("SRO") proceeding in which the person (i) was found to have caused an investment-related business to lose its authorization to do business or (ii) was (a) found to have been involved in a violation of the SRO's rules and (b) the subject of an order by the SRO barring or suspending the person from membership or from association with other members, or expelling the person from membership, fining the member more than $2,500, or otherwise significantly limiting the person's investment-related activities.

For purposes of the events listed above, the term "investment-related" is broadly defined to include activities pertaining to securities, commodities, banking, insurance or real estate. Additionally, the term "involved" means acting or abetting, causing, counseling, commanding, inducing, conspiring with or failing reasonably to supervise another in doing a specified act. See Advisers Act Rule 206(4)–4(d)(3) & (4).

(3) Timing and Delivery of Disclosure

With respect to *current* clients, an adviser must disclose information "promptly" under Advisers Act

Rule 206(4)–4. Unfortunately, the SEC has not provided guidance as to what "promptly" means in this context. With respect to *prospective* clients, an adviser must disclose that information no less than 48 hours prior to entering into any written or oral investment advisory contract. If, however, the prospective client has the right to terminate the advisory contract without penalty within five business days after entering into it, the adviser has until the time the contract is entered into to deliver the information. See Advisers Act Rule 206(4)–4(c).

Registered investment advisers are entitled to disclose Rule 206(4)–4 information to clients and prospective clients in their brochures. However, the delivery of the brochure must satisfy the timing requirements described in the preceding paragraph. See note following Advisers Act Rule 206(4)–4. If an adviser is unable to satisfy those timing requirements with its brochure, then it must furnish existing clients and prospective clients with a separate disclosure statement, such as a letter, that complies with both the disclosure and timing requirements of Rule 206(4)–4.

With respect to the disclosure of SEC enforcement actions, the SEC has on occasion required an adviser to send an actual copy of the SEC's opinion or order to the adviser's existing and prospective clients, despite the fact that Rule 206(4)–4 does not mandate this form of disclosure. See, e.g., In the Matter of Boston Investment Counsel, Inc. and Robert E. Campanella, Advisers Act Rel. No. 1801, 1999

WL 373782 (June 10, 1999); In the Matter of Valicenti Advisory Services, Inc. and Vincent R. Valicenti, Advisers Act Rel. No. 1774, 1998 WL 798699 (Nov. 18, 1998). The Second Circuit Court of Appeals has affirmed the SEC's power in this regard. See *Valicenti Advisory Services, Inc. v. SEC*, 198 F.3d 62 (2d Cir. 1999).

§ 24. ADVISORY AGREEMENTS

A. Necessity of a Writing?

The Advisers Act does not explicitly require contracts between investment advisers and their clients to be in writing. While Advisers Act Section 205(a) implies that this should be the case, the SEC has indicated the opposite in its rulemaking. See, e.g., Advisers Act Rules 204–3 & 206(4)–4.

Obviously, having a written advisory contract with each client makes both business and common sense. A written advisory contract may provide an investment adviser with significant legal protection. By detailing the exact responsibilities of the adviser and the client in a written contract, misunderstandings down the road can be avoided. Additionally, a written contract can evidence the adviser's disclosure and/or the client's acknowledgment of certain legally disclosable information. See Nutshell Sections 23B & C.

Despite the Advisers Act's lack of explicitness on the necessity of having a written contract, other laws dictate that advisory contracts be in writing in certain situations. For example, Company Act Section 15(a) requires written advisory contracts between advisers and their registered investment company clients. Advisory contracts with pension plan clients are also typically in writing given ERISA's requirement that the investment adviser acknowledge in writing that it is a fiduciary with respect to a pension plan client. See ERISA Section 3(38). Finally, investment advisers registered at the state level may need to have written advisory contracts based on state law rather than the Advisers Act.

B. General Contractual Provisions

Subject to three explicit prohibitions discussed in Nutshell Section 24C, a given investment adviser and its clients have, as a general matter, a great deal of flexibility with respect to the terms contained in their advisory contracts. In fact, it is not unusual for an investment adviser to have several custom-tailored contractual templates for different types of clients (*e.g.*, institutional versus retail). Having said that, advisers should ensure that any written advisory contract is consistent with the adviser's Form ADV and other regulatory filings.

Most written advisory contracts contain provisions covering most if not all of the following topics:

- · Advisory fees payable by the client, including the amount, timing and manner of payment;
- · Scope of services to be provided by the adviser to the client;
- · Scope and frequency of investment reports to be provided by the adviser to the client;

- Identity of the custodian of the assets in the client's account;
- Scope of the adviser's liability to the client for negligence, misfeasance or bad faith;
- Dispute resolution mechanism;
- Each party's ability to terminate, assign and/or amend the agreement;
- Client's acknowledgment of receipt of certain mandatory disclosures from the adviser;
- Indemnification; and
- Choice of law

C. Contract Prohibitions

Subject to a number of exceptions, Advisers Act Section 205(a) prohibits an investment adviser, unless exempt from registration pursuant to Advisers Act Section 203(b), from entering into, extending, renewing or performing any investment advisory contract that:

(i) compensates the adviser by allowing it to share in the capital gains upon or capital appreciation of any of the client's funds (the "Performance Fee Prohibition");

(ii) allows the adviser to assign the contract without the consent of the client (the "Assignment Prohibition"); or

(iii) does not require the adviser, if a partnership, to notify the client of any change in the membership of the partnership within a reasonable time after the change.

The importance of complying with Section 205(a) is made crystal clear in Advisers Act Section 215(b). That section provides that any advisory contract made in violation of any provision of the Advisers Act shall be *void* with respect to the violating party.

Note that Section 205(a)'s prohibitions do not apply to any adviser exempt from registration under the Advisers Act. See Nutshell Section 4. Thus, for example, they would not apply to any hedge fund adviser qualifying as a "private investment adviser" under Section 203(b)(3). Moreover, Section 205(a)'s Performance Fee Prohibition has a great many exceptions listed in Section 205(b), while Section 205(e) gives the SEC the authority to carve out other persons it determines do not need the protections of that Prohibition. These exceptions, as well as other matters pertinent to an advisory contract, are discussed in the remainder of this subsection.

(1) Performance Fees

Advisers Act Section 205(a)(1) sets forth the Performance Fee Prohibition. Before discussing that Prohibition, a general understanding of the ways in which clients typically compensate their investment advisers is needed.

a. *Fee Arrangements Generally*

As a general matter, the type and amount of fee that a given investment adviser charges is constrained only by market forces. Thus, it is between the adviser and the client to determine the appropriate fee that the client must pay. The typical fee is a percentage of assets under management (*i.e.*, an "asset-based fee") charged on a periodic basis such as monthly or quarterly. That percentage sometimes drops as assets under management grow and hit certain predetermined levels (*a.k.a.* "break points"), reflecting the achievement of "economies of scale" by the adviser.

b. Regulation of Potentially Abusive Fee Arrangements

Congress saw fit to regulate potentially abusive fee arrangements in two respects. The first relates to a so-called "performance fee" or "carried interest." A performance fee arrangement essentially allows the adviser to receive a share of profits generated in a client's account. However, a performance fee typically would not be owed until after the account has achieved a certain level of investment performance or a specified percentage increase. Thus, the better a client's account performs, the more money the adviser could potentially receive.

While most performance fees relate to increased performance, they can also be tied to the prevention or limitation of a decrease in account value. For example, a performance fee could be contingent upon a given client's account either not decreasing in value at all or avoiding a specified amount of capital depreciation agreed to in advance by the investment adviser and the client. See generally Contingent Advisory Compensation Arrangements,

Advisers Act Rel. No. 721, 1980 WL 19231 (May 16, 1980).

Congress' concern over performance fees was related to the perverse incentives those fees may create. Indeed, an investment adviser which is to receive a share of a client's profits may decide to "swing for the bleachers" (*i.e.,* invest the client's money in more risky investments) in order to hit a grand slam in which it would participate financially. If, instead, the adviser strikes out, it will not be significantly penalized for its poor performance. Of course, it is easier to take greater risks when you are gambling with someone else's money or, to quote Congress, engaging in a strategy of "heads I win and tails you lose." Accordingly, significant limitations exist on an investment adviser's ability to charge a performance fee as detailed in the next subsection.

Congress was also concerned about abusive fee arrangements between investment advisers and registered investment companies (*i.e.,* mutual funds). To prevent abuse in this context, Company Act Section 36(b) imposes a fiduciary duty on advisers of mutual funds with respect to the compensation they receive from those funds and their shareholders. Both the SEC and fund shareholders are entitled to bring suit against a fund adviser who has breached its fiduciary duty. "To be guilty of a violation of § 36(b), . . . the adviser-manager must charge a fee [to the mutual fund] that is so disproportionately large that it bears no reasonable relationship to the services rendered and could not have been the product of arm's-length bargaining." *Gar-*

tenberg v. Merrill Lynch Asset Mgt., Inc., 694 F.2d 923 (2d Cir. 1982).

In this regard, the *Gartenberg* Court took note of Congress' mandate that it "look at all the facts in connection with the determination and receipt of such compensation, including all services rendered to the fund or its shareholders and all compensation and payments received." The Court thus espoused the following factors—some substantive and others procedural in nature—that have proved to be of enduring significance in subsequent litigation under Company Act Section 36(b):

· The adviser's cost in providing the service to the fund;

· The nature and quality of the service;

· The extent to which the adviser realizes economies of scale as the fund grows larger;

· Rates charged by other advisers to similar funds;

· The expertise of the fund's independent directors;

· Whether the independent directors are fully informed about all the facts bearing on the adviser's service and fee; and

· The extent of care and conscientiousness with which the independent directors perform their duties with respect to the adviser's fee.

The above-cited factors take into account all the circumstances that bear on an adviser's compensation. Thus, the integrity of the process by which the fund's directors review and approve an advisory contract is covered. Process, however, is not dispositive in this regard. Indeed, the Court cautioned that even if the fund's directors "endeavored to act in a responsible fashion," the adviser's fees still could be so "disproportionately large as to amount to a breach of fiduciary duty [by those directors]."

c.   *Performance Fee Prohibition*

1.   General Restriction

Under Advisers Act Section 205(a)(1), an investment adviser that is not exempt from registration under Advisers Act Section 203(b) is prohibited from entering into an advisory contract that provides for compensation to the adviser on the basis of a share of capital gains upon or capital appreciation of the funds or any portion of the funds of a client. Importantly, the Prohibition does not apply to fees based on other measures of performance, such as interest or dividends. See James R. Waters, SEC No–Action Letter, 1995 WL 498690 (June 1, 1995). Moreover, the Prohibition is subject to a number of important exceptions as described in the following subsection.

2.   Exceptions to the Performance Fee Prohibition

Under Advisers Act Section 205(b)(1), the Performance Fee Prohibition does not apply in the context of, or with respect to: (a) asset-based fees; (b) fulcrum fees; (c) business development companies; (d) Section 3(c)(7) funds; (e) non-U.S. resident clients; and (f) so-called "qualified clients." Each exception is discussed below.

(a) Asset–Based Fees

The Performance Fee Prohibition does not apply to an advisory contract which provides for compensation based upon the total value of a fund averaged over a definite period or as of a definite date or dates. See Advisers Act Section 205(b)(1). This type of compensation is the traditional asset-based fee. Pursuant to it, the adviser receives a fee based on a percentage of the client's assets under management, either averaged over a definite period of time or measured on a specific date or dates.

Capital gains and capital appreciation, of course, increase a client's assets under management and thus are naturally subjected to an asset-based fee. Therefore, it is necessary to exclude the traditional asset-based fee from the Performance Fee Prohibition. Moreover, the policy considerations behind the Performance Fee Prohibition do not exist in the asset-based fee context. Indeed, the adviser is penalized for any poor performance because any loss, depreciation or other reduction in the client's account reduces the adviser's fee as measured in gross dollars.

(b) Fulcrum Fees

(I) Generally

The Performance Fee Prohibition also does not apply to an advisory contract with a registered investment company or any other person with investment assets in excess of $1 million so long as one condition is met. That condition is that the performance fee must qualify as a so-called *"fulcrum fee."* See Advisers Act Section 205(b)(2). Simply put, the adviser's base fee in a fulcrum fee arrangement will be increased or decreased proportionately depending on whether the adviser's performance compares favorably or unfavorably to the investment record of an index of securities prices (*e.g.,* S & P 500, Russell 2000, Dow Jones Industrial Average) or such other measure of investment performance as the SEC may embrace through a rule, regulation or order. Thus, the policy considerations behind the Performance Fee Prohibition do not exist in a fulcrum fee context as the adviser is now speculating with both the client's money as well as its own. Indeed, the adviser is penalized for any poor performance relative to the market index by having to return a portion of its base fee.

In the context of a fulcrum fee, over performance may occur in both rising and falling markets. For example, if the S & P 500 increases by 5% in a given year, but a client's account with a fulcrum fee in place increases by 6%, then the adviser will receive its performance fee. If, however, the S & P 500 decreases by 10% in a given year, but a client's account only falls by 8%, then the adviser will also receive its performance fee even though the client's account fell in value during that year.

Under performance likewise may occur in both rising and falling markets. For example, if the S & P 500 increases by 5% in a given year, but a client's account with a fulcrum fee in place increases by only 4%, then the adviser will have to return a part of its base fee. If, however, the S & P 500 decreases by 10% in a given year, but a client's account falls by 12%, then the adviser will have to return a part of its base fee even though the S & P 500 also lost value during that year.

(II) Choosing an Appropriate Index

An adviser has flexibility in selecting an index of security prices for use in a fulcrum fee arrangement. Advisers Act Section 205(c) states that an index of securities prices "shall be deemed appropriate unless the [SEC] by order shall determine otherwise." When choosing an index, an adviser must look closely at the investment objectives, diversification of holdings, volatility of investments and types of securities owned by the investment company or other "in excess of $1 million" clients and compare them with the attributes of the index under consideration. See Company Act Rel. No. 7113, 1972 WL 121274 (Apr. 18, 1972).

The staff of the SEC has shot down a number of proposed indices when it believed they were inappropriate in light of the investment company or client accounts in question. For example, an investment adviser sought approval to use inflation (as measured by the Consumer Price Index (CPI)) as the index against which to measure performance of his performance-based investment management service. He argued that his clients were primarily seeking to meet long-term financial goals such as college education for children and retirement. Because his clients were most interested in making their investments grow faster than the goods and services for which the proceeds from the investments were earmarked, he naturally believed the most suitable measure of whether his clients were achieving this goal was how their investment performance compared to inflation (as measured by the CPI). The staff of the SEC, however, disagreed. It pointed out that the adviser's proposal ran contrary to Advisers Act Section 205(b)(2), because the CPI was not an "index of security prices" and the SEC had not deemed the CPI to be a measure of investment performance. See James R. Waters, SEC No–Action Letter, 1995 WL 498690 (June 1, 1995).

(III) Making the Comparison

With respect to investment company clients with fulcrum fee arrangements, the SEC has provided guidance in the form of two rules to aid advisers in determining whether they have earned performance fees. Advisers Act Rule 205–1 delineates how to calculate "investment performance" of an investment company and the "investment record" of an appropriate index of securities prices for any period of time. Because it is crucial to use consistent time periods when measuring performance in the context of a fulcrum fee arrangement, Advisers Act Rule 205–2 defines the "specified period" over which performance is measured.

The SEC requires advisers to use a sufficiently long period of time to provide a reasonable basis for determining the adviser's performance. In the SEC's view, this appears to be intervals of at least one year so as to minimize the possibility that performance payments will be based upon random or short-term fluctuations. Interim performance fee payments to advisers are likewise prohibited, although the SEC does allow the "specified period" to be computed on a rolling basis. See Company Act Rel. No. 7113, 1972 WL 121274 (Apr. 18, 1972).

(c) Business Development Companies

Advisers Act Section 205(b)(3) relates to business development companies. The term "business development company," which is defined in Advisers Act Section 202(a)(22), is designed to cover venture capital funds. Indeed, in the Small Business Investment Incentive Act of 1980, Congress generally modeled the definition of business development company on the capital formation activities of venture capital funds. A business development company is like an investment company in that it is operated for the purpose of making investments in securities. However, unlike an investment company, it often purchases large equity stakes in the issuers of those securities and makes significant managerial assistance available to those issuers.

Under Advisers Act Section 205(b)(3), the Performance Fee Prohibition does not apply to an advisory contract with a business development company so long as several conditions are met that are designed to reign in the adviser's total compensation. First, the compensation provided to the adviser must not exceed 20% of the realized capital gains upon the funds of the business development company over a specified period or as of definite dates, computed net of all realized capital losses and unrealized capital depreciation. Second, any performance fee received by the adviser must be a fulcrum fee satisfying the provisions of Advisers Act Section 205(b)(2). See Nutshell Section 24C(1)c2(b). Finally, the business development company can neither have (i) outstanding options, warrants or rights to purchase voting securities of the company in the hands of its directors, officers, employees or general partners nor (ii) a profit-sharing plan for its directors, officers, employees or general partners.

(d) Section 3(c)(7) Funds

Under Advisers Act Section 205(b)(4), the Performance Fee Prohibition does not apply to an advisory contract with a company (a "Section 3(c)(7) fund") excepted from Company Act registration pursuant to Section 3(c)(7) of the Company Act. Securities of a Section 3(c)(7) fund are sold through private placements targeted only to "qualified purchasers." See Nutshell Section 9B(2)b. It is presumed that a Section 3(c)(7) fund's investors are sophisticated to the point where the protections of the Performance Fee Prohibition are unnecessary.

(e) Non–U.S. Resident Clients

Under Advisers Act Section 205(b)(5), the Performance Fee Prohibition does not apply to an advisory contract between an adviser and a person who is not a resident of the U.S.

(f) *"Qualified Clients"*

Under Advisers Act Section 205(e), the SEC, by rule or regulation, has the authority to exempt any other person from the Performance Fee Prohibition if it determines that he does not need the protections of the Prohibition based on such factors as his financial sophistication, net worth, knowledge of and experience in financial matters, amount of assets under management and relationship with a registered investment adviser. Pursuant to its authority, the SEC has excluded advisory contracts between investment advisers and so-called "qualified clients" from the Prohibition. See Advisers Act Rule 205–3(a).

The term "qualified client" is defined in Advisers Act Rule 205–3(d)(1). Included within the definition are, among others:

· Any natural person or "company" (see discussion below) with at least $750,000 under management with the investment adviser immediately after entering into the advisory contract;

· Any natural person or company who the adviser reasonably believes has a net worth (either alone or together with a spouse in the case of a natural person) of more than $1.5 million at the time the advisory contract is entered into;

· Any natural person or company who the adviser reasonably believes is a "qualified purchaser" under Company Act Section 2(a)(51)(A) (and therefore could also invest in a Section 3(c)(7) fund) at the time the advisory contract is entered into; and

· Any natural person who, immediately prior to entering into the contract, is an executive officer, director, trustee, general partner or person serving in a similar capacity of the investment adviser, or is an employee of the investment adviser who has participated in the investment activities of such adviser for at least the last 12 months.

The term "company" as used above is defined in Advisers Act Rule 205–3(d)(2). The definition requires an adviser to "look through" certain entities to determine whether each equity owner of those entities meets the definition of a "qualified client." Specifically, an adviser must look through a registered investment company, a Section 3(c)(1) fund or a business development company.

d. Hedge Fund Advisers

The Performance Fee Prohibition does not apply to advisers that are exempt from Advisers Act registration under Advisers Act Section 203(b). Because many hedge fund advisers are exempt under the Private Adviser Registration Exemption of Section 203(b)(3), they are not restricted from charging a performance fee. Nor are they restricted in the type of performance fee they charge. Thus, an exempt hedge fund adviser could (and generally does) charge a performance fee that is not a fulcrum fee.

The performance fee typically is 20% of the profits generated during each measurement period. However, because investors in a given hedge fund may invest at different times, each investor typically pays a performance fee only on profits beyond her contribution (known as her "high-water mark").

e.   *NASD Conduct Rule 2330(f)*

Persons who are dually registered as both an investment adviser under the Advisers Act and a broker-dealer under the Exchange Act must be cognizant of NASD Conduct Rule 2330(f). This Rule generally prohibits a broker-dealer (or its associated persons) from sharing directly or indirectly in the profits or losses of a client's account. However, that prohibition does not apply to performance fee arrangements of Dual Registrants if certain conditions are met. Those conditions essentially mirror those in Advisers Act Rule 205–3 dealing with "qualified clients." See Nutshell Section 24C(1)c2(f).

On July 30, 2007, a new self-regulatory organization, the Financial Industry Regulatory Authority ("FINRA"), was created through the consolidation of the NASD and the member regulation, enforcement and arbitration operations of the NYSE. Accordingly, readers should be aware that a FINRA analog to NASD Conduct Rule 2330(f) will likely replace that NASD rule in the near future.

(2) Assignment of Advisory Contracts

Under Advisers Act Section 205(a)(2), an investment adviser that is not exempt from registration under Advisers Act Section 203(b) generally may not enter into, extend, renew or perform any investment advisory contract unless the contract prohibits assignment by the adviser without the client's consent. Thus, this requirement applies to both SEC- and state-registered advisers. Assignments of advisory contracts with registered investment companies are subject to more stringent regulation under the Company Act. Specifically, Company Act Section 15(a)(4) requires the automatic termination of such contracts in the event of their assignment.

One of the more difficult issues arising in the context of an assignment of an advisory contract is whether the sale or transfer of an ownership interest in, or a merger, consolidation or reorganization of, an adviser constitutes an "assignment" for purposes of Advisers Act Section 205(a)(2). The term "assignment" itself is broadly defined in Advisers Act Section 202(a)(1). The term includes the direct or indirect transfer of (a) an investment advisory contract by an adviser or (b) a controlling block of the adviser's outstanding voting securities by a security holder of the adviser. However, Advisers Act Rule 202(a)(1)–1 makes it clear that a transaction that does not result in a change of actual control or management of an investment adviser is not an assignment for purposes of Section 205(a)(2).

Assuming that an adviser seeks to assign an advisory contract, may that adviser employ a "negative consent" procedure to obtain the necessary client consent? A negative consent procedure is one in which the adviser notifies its client in advance about an upcoming assignment. That notification will state that, if the adviser does not hear an affirmative objection from the client within a prescribed period of time, then the client will be deemed to have given his consent. The use of negative consents has become a standard industry practice. See Templeton Inv. Counsel Ltd., SEC No–Action Letter, 1986 WL 67662 (avail. Jan. 2, 1986); Jennison Associates Capital Corp., SEC No–Action Letter, 1985 WL 55687 (avail. Dec. 2, 1985); Scudder, Stevens & Clark, SEC No-Action Letter, 1985 WL 54004 (avail. Mar. 18, 1985).

(3) Notification of Change in Partnership

Advisers Act Section 205(a)(3) imposes an additional requirement on an advisory contract between a client and an investment adviser that is organized as a partnership and is not exempt from registration under Advisers Act Section 203(b). That contract must provide that the investment adviser will notify its client of any change in the membership of the partnership within a reasonable period of time after such change.

D. Other Notable Provisions in Advisory Contracts

(1) Disclaimer of Liability/Indemnification Provisions

Almost every investment advisory contract has a disclaimer of liability/indemnification provision similar to the following which seeks to protect the adviser and its officers and directors:

> Except as otherwise may be provided under provisions of applicable state law or Federal securities law which cannot be waived or modified hereby, the Adviser shall not be liable for any error of judgment or mistake of law or for any loss arising out of any investment or for any act or omission in carrying out its duties hereunder, provided that it acted in good faith and in a manner it reasonably believed to be in, or not opposed to, the best interests of the Client and provided that the omission, act or conduct that was the basis for such loss was not the result of fraud, gross negligence (as defined under [Delaware] law) or willful misconduct. (As used in this paragraph, the term "Adviser" shall include agents, consultants, officers, directors, partners, shareholders and employees of the Adviser as well as the [limited liability] company itself). The Client will indemnify and hold the Adviser harmless from and against any and all claims, liabilities, losses, damages, costs and expenses, including legal fees and expenses, arising out of or in connection with any action taken or omitted by the Adviser, unless such action or omission is finally adjudicated to have resulted from the Adviser's fraud, gross negligence or willful misconduct.

Investment advisers should not enter into investment advisory contracts that do not contain this protective provision.

The first sentence of the provision quoted above (beginning "Except as otherwise may be provided ...") ensures that the provision complies with Advisers Act Section 215(a). That Section voids any condition, stipulation or provision binding any person to waive compliance with any provisions of the Advisers Act or with any rule, regulation or order thereunder. Thus, any advisory contract that purports to allow an adviser to operate liability free under a standard of care lower than that required by the Advisers Act itself is invalid.

Despite the last clause of the first sentence of the provision quoted above (beginning "provided that the omission, act or conduct ..."), the SEC has historically taken the position that an investment adviser may not limit its liability to "gross negligence" or "willful misconduct" in an advisory contract. Because applicable law may require a greater degree of care by a fiduciary, any advisory contract using those adjectives may mislead clients into believing that they have waived a right of action based on the adviser's ordinary negligence or misconduct. See, e.g., Auchincloss & Lawrence Inc., SEC No–Action Letter, 1974 WL 10979 (avail. Feb. 8, 1974). Nevertheless, it is standard industry practice to attempt to limit an adviser's liability in this way. Moreover, Company Act Section 17(h) takes a similar position as it prohibits any organizational instrument (*e.g.,* articles of association or by-laws) of a registered investment company "to protect any director or officer of such company against any liability to the company or to its security holders to which he would otherwise be subject by reason of willful misfeasance, bad faith, gross negligence or reckless disregard of the duties involved in the conduct of his office."

(2) Arbitration Provisions

An investment advisory contract typically includes a provision requiring the client and the adviser to settle any dispute arising out of the contract by arbitration rather than adjudication. The SEC has taken the position that arbitration provisions may mislead clients into believing that they cannot exercise their rights of action under the Federal securities laws. Accordingly, the SEC has viewed these provisions as violative of the antifraud provisions of Advisers Act Section 206. See, e.g., McEldowney Fin. Services, SEC No–Action Letter, 1986 WL 67330 (avail. Oct. 17, 1986).

Two Supreme Court decisions, however, throw into substantial doubt the correctness of the SEC's position on arbitration provisions. In *Shearson/American Express, Inc. v. McMahon*, 483 U.S. 1056 (1987), the Supreme Court held that arbitration agreements between brokerage firms and their customers are enforceable with respect to claims brought under the Exchange Act. Similarly, in *Rodriguez de Quijas v. Shearson/American Express, Inc.*, 490 U.S. 477 (1989), the Supreme Court upheld arbitration agreements with respect to claims brought under the Securities Act.

It is worth noting that the Supreme Court underscored in both of the aforementioned opinions that

a self-regulatory organization subject to SEC oversight would conduct the arbitrations. Because investment advisers who are not Dual Registrants are
not members of any self-regulatory organization,
arbitrations involving those advisers would not be
subject to SEC oversight. Whether this is a mean-
ingful distinction to the Supreme Court has yet to
be decided.

(3) Termination Provisions

Pointing to an adviser's fiduciary duties under
Advisers Act Section 206, the staff of the SEC has
indicated that a client has the right to terminate
any advisory relationship without penalty. Therefore, an adviser cannot impose a termination fee on
the client, except to the extent that fee directly
relates to services previously provided by the adviser to the client. Consistent with that, an adviser
generally must refund the portion of any prepaid
advisory fees attributable to time periods after the
termination of the contract.

The advisory contract typically spells out whether
the client must provide the adviser with any advanced written notice prior to terminating the contract. When the client is a registered investment
company, however, Company Act Section 15(a)(3)
allows either the board of directors or the holders of
the majority of the outstanding voting securities of
such company to cancel an advisory contract at any
time without penalty upon 60 days written notice to
the adviser.

§ 25. REPORTS PROVIDED
TO CLIENTS

The Advisers Act does not expressly require investment advisers to provide clients with periodic statements regarding the activity in their accounts. The SEC, however, has implied that it expects investment advisers offering discretionary asset management services to send (or designate another person to send) periodic statements to clients. Traditionally, most advisers provide their clients with quarterly account statements. They generally include in the fourth quarter account statement their annual offer to deliver their brochure in accordance with Advisers Act Rule 204–3(c). See Nutshell Section 23B(2).

Investment advisers that have custody of client assets also must comply with the requirements of Advisers Act Rule 206(4)–2. This Rule requires either an adviser or a qualified custodian to send to each client, at least quarterly, an itemized statement showing the assets held in custody at the end of the period and setting forth all transactions in the client's account during the period. For more on the custody of clients' funds or securities, see Nutshell Section 28D.

§ 26. PRIVACY OF CONSUMER
FINANCIAL INFORMATION

A. Generally

The Gramm–Leach–Bliley Financial Modernization Act of 1999 ("GLBA") established the first

Federal privacy mandate for all financial institutions, including investment advisers registered with the SEC, brokers, dealers and investment companies. The SEC adopted Regulation S–P to implement the requirements of Title V of the GLBA. Regulation S–P imposes notice requirements and restrictions on an investment adviser's ability to disclose nonpublic personal information about consumers. This is important because investment advisers generally gather detailed client financial information as part of the account opening process.

An investment adviser must provide an initial and annual notice to its natural person clients about its privacy policies and practices. See Rules 4 & 5 of Reg. S–P. These notices must describe the conditions under which the adviser may disclose nonpublic personal information about clients to nonaffiliated third parties. They must also provide a method for clients to prevent the investment adviser from disclosing that information to certain nonaffiliated third parties by "opting out" of that disclosure, subject to various exceptions as stated in the Regulation.

Regulation S–P also requires investment advisers registered with the SEC to adopt policies and procedures that safeguard customer information and records. See Rule 30(a) of Reg. S–P. Additionally, investment advisers have a duty to take reasonable measures to protect discarded client information and records from unauthorized access or use. See Rule 30(b)(2)(ii) of Reg. S–P.

B. Information Covered by Regulation S–P

Regulation S–P protects only "nonpublic personal information." Rule 3(t)(1) of Regulation S–P defines such information as "personally identifiable financial information" and "any list, description or other grouping of consumers (and publicly available information pertaining to them) that is derived using any personally identifiable financial information that is not publicly available information." Rule 3(u)(1) of Regulation S–P defines "personally identifiable financial information" as any information:

· a consumer provides to an investment adviser to obtain a financial product or service from that adviser;

· about a consumer resulting from any transaction involving a financial product or service between an investment adviser and that consumer; or

· an investment adviser obtains about a consumer in connection with providing a financial product or service to that consumer.

Publicly available information about a consumer is not covered by Regulation S–P, and an investment adviser can disclose information it reasonably believes is publicly available without complying with any of the provisions of the Regulation. Publicly available information is information that is lawfully available to the public from one of three sources: (1) Federal, state or local government records (*e.g.*, real estate records or security interest filings); (2) widely-distributed media (*e.g.*, a telephone book, television or radio program, or newspaper); and (3) disclosures to the general public that are required to be made by Federal, state or local law. See Rule 3(v)(1) of Reg. S–P. An investment adviser will be deemed to have a "reasonable belief" that information is publicly available if it has confirmed, or the consumer has represented to it, that the information is publicly available from one of the three sources described above.

C. Clients Covered by Regulation S–P

Regulation S–P protects nonpublic personal financial information that was obtained from an individual in connection with financial products and services primarily for personal, family or household purposes. The provision does not cover information about companies or about individuals who obtain financial products or services primarily for business, commercial or agricultural purposes. See Rule 1(b) of Reg. S–P.

Regulation S–P also makes a distinction between "consumers" and "customers" of an investment adviser. A "consumer" is a person who obtains or has obtained a financial product or service from the adviser that is to be used primarily for personal, family or household purposes, or by that person's legal representative. See Rule 3(g)(1) of Reg. S–P. A "customer," by contrast, is a consumer that has a *continuing relationship* with the adviser. See Rules 3(j) & (k)(1) of Reg. S–P. Thus, "customer" is a subset of "consumer."

The major implication of the consumer/customer distinction is for purposes of the Regulation's notice requirements. An adviser generally must provide a *customer* with notice no later than the time the customer enters into an advisory contract (whether in writing or orally) with the adviser. See Rules 4(a)(1) & (c)(3)(iii) of Reg. S–P. An adviser is required to give a *consumer* notice of its privacy policies and practices only if the adviser intends to disclose nonpublic personal information to nonaffiliated third parties, subject to certain exceptions discussed in Nutshell Section 26G. See Rule 4(a)(2) of Reg. S–P and Nutshell Sections 26E & G.

D. Investment Advisers Covered by Regulation S–P

Regulation S–P covers only investment advisers registered with the SEC, including foreign advisers that are registered with the SEC. Thus, the provisions of Regulation S–P do not apply to advisers that are not required to register with the SEC. This would include hedge fund and private equity fund advisers relying on the Private Adviser Registration Exemption found in Advisers Act Section 203(b)(3). Hedge funds and private equity funds themselves are not subject to Regulation S–P because they are excluded from investment company registration pursuant to Company Act Section 3(c)(1) or 3(c)(7).

E. Notice Requirements

An adviser is required to provide a *customer* with an initial notice no later than the time the customer enters into an advisory contract (whether in writing or orally) with the adviser. See Rules 4(1)(2) & (c)(3)(iii) of Reg. S–P. Thereafter, an adviser is required to provide a customer with an annual notice that accurately reflects its privacy policies and practices. "Annually" means at least once in any period of 12 consecutive months during which a relationship between the adviser and customer exists. See Rule 5(a)(1) of Reg. S–P.

By contrast, an adviser is required to give a *consumer* notice of its privacy policies and practices only if the adviser intends to disclose nonpublic personal information to nonaffiliated third parties, subject to certain exceptions discussed in Nutshell Section 26G. Moreover, an adviser is required to provide a consumer with a clear and conspicuous revised notice that describes any amended privacy policies and practices with a reasonable opportunity to opt out prior to disclosing any nonpublic personal information about the consumer to a nonaffiliated third party. See Rule 8(a) of Reg. S–P.

Pursuant to Rule 6(a) of Regulation S–P, an adviser is required to include in its initial notice (Rule 4), annual notice (Rule 5) and any revised notice (Rule 8) the following information:

(1) The categories of nonpublic personal information the adviser collects;

(2) The categories of nonpublic personal information the adviser may disclose;

(3) The categories of affiliates and nonaffiliated third parties to which the adviser discloses non-

public personal information, subject to certain exceptions;

(4) The categories of nonpublic personal information about former customers that the adviser discloses and the categories of affiliates and non-affiliated third parties to which the adviser discloses this information;

(5) The categories of nonpublic personal information that the adviser may disclose under agreements with third party service providers and joint marketers and the categories of third parties providing the services;

(6) An explanation of the consumer's right to opt out of the disclosure of nonpublic personal information to nonaffiliated third parties, and the methods by which a consumer may opt out;

(7) Any disclosures that the adviser made under the Fair Credit Reporting Act regarding the ability of the consumer to opt out of disclosures of information among affiliates;

(8) A description of the adviser's policies and practices for protecting the confidentiality and security of nonpublic personal information; and

(9) A statement, if applicable, that the adviser makes disclosures to other nonaffiliated third parties as permitted by law.

The required privacy notice must be "clear and conspicuous" and must accurately reflect the investment adviser's privacy policies and practices. "Clear and conspicuous" means phrases that are designed to call attention to the nature and significance of the information contained in the notice. See Rule 3(c)(1) of Reg. S–P. An adviser may combine its privacy notice with other required disclosures in a single document, such as the adviser's brochure, so long as the privacy notice is clear and conspicuous. See Investment Company Institute, SEC No–Action Letter, 2001 WL 345815 (avail. Apr. 10, 2001).

F. Opt Out Options

Under Rule 10(a)(1) of Regulation S–P, and subject to certain exceptions contained in Rules 13 through 15, an investment adviser can disclose nonpublic personal information about a consumer to a nonaffiliated third party only if the following conditions are met:

(i) The adviser has provided the consumer with an initial notice of the adviser's privacy policies and practices pursuant to Rule 4;

(ii) The adviser has provided the consumer with an *opt out notice* pursuant to Rule 7;

(iii) The adviser has given the consumer a reasonable opportunity, before disclosing the information to the nonaffiliated third party, to opt out of the disclosure; and

(iv) The consumer does not opt out.

Rule 7 of Regulation S–P governs the form of the opt out notice advisers must provide to consumers.

An opt out notice is subject to the "clear and conspicuous requirements" of Rule 3(c)(1). The notice must (i) state that the adviser will disclose or reserves the right to disclose nonpublic personal information about the consumer to a nonaffiliated third party, (ii) state that the consumer has the right to opt out of that disclosure and (iii) set forth reasonable means by which the consumer may exercise the opt out right. See Rule 7(a)(1) of Reg. S–P.

Reasonable means of opting out include: (i) designating a check-off box in a prominent position on the relevant form with the opt out notice; (ii) including a reply form together with the opt out notice; (iii) providing an electronic means to opt out, such as a form that can be sent via electronic mail or a process at the adviser's website, if the consumer agrees to the electronic delivery of information; or (iv) providing a toll-free telephone number that consumers may call to opt out. See Rule 7(a)(2)(ii) of Reg. S–P. Regulation S–P also provides examples of *unreasonable* opt out means, including an adviser requiring the consumer to write his own opt out letter. See Rule 7(a)(2)(iii) of Reg. S–P. A consumer who does not exercise the right to opt out does not lose that right and may exercise the right at any time. See Rule 7(f) of Reg. S–P.

An adviser must comply with a consumer's opt out direction as soon as reasonably practical after the adviser receives it. See Rule 7(e) of Reg. S–P. A *consumer's* decision to opt out will remain in effect until revoked by the consumer in writing or, if the consumer agrees, electronically. See Rule 7(g) of Reg. S–P.

A *customer's* opt out direction continues to apply to the nonpublic personal information that an adviser collected during or related to the customer relationship even after that relationship terminates. If the former customer subsequently establishes a new customer relationship with the adviser, the opt out direction that applied to the former relationship does not apply to the new relationship. See Rule 7(g) of Reg. S–P.

G. Exceptions

(1) Generally

Rules 13 through 15 of Regulation S–P set forth three exceptions to the disclosure notice and opt out requirements. Pursuant to these exceptions, which are discussed in detail in the following subsections, advisers can share nonpublic personal information with certain nonaffiliated third parties without providing consumers with an initial notice and/or the right to opt out.

Nonaffiliated third parties that receive nonpublic financial information from advisers pursuant to Rules 13 through 15 of Regulation S–P are prohibited from disclosing that information either directly or through an affiliate to any person not affiliated with the adviser unless the disclosure would be lawful if made directly by the adviser. See Rule 11 of Reg. S–P. The Regulation does not make advisers responsible for monitoring the regulatory compliance of third parties with whom information is shared. However, the SEC may take enforcement action against third parties that use the information in a way not authorized by the Regulation.

(2) Service Providers and Joint Marketing

Under Rule 13(a)(1) of Regulation S–P, the opt out requirements (Rules 7 and 10) do not apply when an adviser provides nonpublic personal information about a consumer to a nonaffiliated third party to enable that third party to perform services for the adviser or functions on behalf of the adviser. However, two conditions must be met. First, the adviser must provide an initial notice to the consumer in accordance with Rule 4. Second, the adviser must enter into a contractual agreement with the third party that prohibits the third party from disclosing or using the information other than to carry out the purposes for which the adviser disclosed the information. This would include ordinary course of business use permitted pursuant to an exception in Rule 14 or 15.

The exception under Rule 13(a)(1) is most often utilized when a nonaffiliated third party markets an adviser's products or services pursuant to joint agreements between the adviser and one or more financial institutions. A "joint agreement" means a written contract pursuant to which an adviser and one or more financial institutions jointly offer, endorse or sponsor a financial product or service. See Rules 13(b) & (c) of Reg. S–P.

(3) Processing and Servicing Transactions

The initial notice requirements (set forth in Rule 4 and also incorporated into Rule 13) and opt out requirements (Rules 7 and 10) do not apply if an adviser discloses nonpersonal public information about a consumer in connection with the following: (1) effecting, administering or enforcing a transaction that a consumer requests or authorizes; (2) processing or servicing a financial product or service that a consumer requests or authorizes; or (3) maintaining or servicing the consumer's account with the adviser. See Rule 14(a) of Reg. S–P. There is no contract requirement in connection with this exception.

(4) Other Exceptions to Notice and Opt Out Requirements

The initial notice requirements (set forth in Rule 4 and also incorporated into Rule 13) and opt out requirements (Rules 7 and 10) also do not apply if an adviser discloses nonpersonal public information about a consumer in certain other situations, including the following:

(1) With the consent or at the direction of the consumer;

(2) To protect the confidentiality or security of the adviser's records pertaining to the consumer, service, product or transaction;

(3) To prevent fraud or unauthorized transactions;

(4) To persons acting in a fiduciary or representative capacity on behalf of the consumer;

(5) To comply with Federal, state, or local laws, rules or other applicable legal requirements;

(6) To comply with the properly authorized civil, criminal or regulatory investigation, or subpoena or summons by Federal, state or local authorities; or

(7) To respond to judicial process or government regulatory authorities.

See Rule 15(a) of Reg. S–P.

H. Establishing Procedural Safeguards

Rule 30(a) of Regulation S–P requires an adviser to adopt written policies and procedures that address administrative, technical and physical safeguards for the protection of customer records and information. These policies and procedures must be reasonably designed to:

(1) Ensure the security and confidentiality of customer records and information;

(2) Protect against any anticipated threats or hazards to the security or integrity of customer records and information; and

(3) Protect against unauthorized access to or use of customer records or information that could result in substantial harm or inconvenience to any customer.

Rule 30(b) of Regulation S–P requires an adviser that maintains or otherwise possesses consumer report information for business purposes to properly dispose of the information by taking reasonable measures to protect against unauthorized access to or use of the information in connection with its disposal. Reasonable measures include burning, pulverizing or shredding of paper records; destruction or erasure of electronic records so that information cannot be read or reconstructed; and, after conducting due diligence on a third party, contracting with that third party to destroy records in a manner consistent with the Rule.

I. Relationship to State Laws

Regulation S–P preempts any state law to the extent that law is inconsistent with the provisions of the Regulation, but only to the extent of the inconsistency. See Rule 17(a) of Reg. S–P. However, Regulation S–P does not preempt any state law that is not inconsistent with the provisions of the Regulation if the protection such law affords any consumer is greater than the protection provided by the Regulation. See Rule 17(b) of Reg. S–P.

VIII. PERFORMANCE OF DUTIES

§ 27. INTRODUCTION

The core of an investment adviser's business–how it provides advice and manages accounts—is subject only to a few specific mandates and prohibitions:

(i) Advisers Act Section 206(3) imposes specific requirements for principal transactions and agency cross transactions for client accounts;

(ii) Advisers Act Rule 206(4)–2 sets forth requirements for advisers that have custody or possession of client securities or funds;

(iii) Exchange Act Section 28(e) sets the standard for use of soft dollar products and services; and

(iv) Management of retirement plans and account assets are subject to the requirements of ERISA and/or the IRC.

The Advisers Act's mandates and prohibitions are less extensive than those that apply to broker-dealers or registered investment companies. Instead, most of what investment advisers do falls under the general antifraud prohibitions found in Advisers Act Sections 206(1) and (2) and the general fiduciary duties that are implicitly enforced through those prohibitions.

§ 28. GENERAL FIDUCIARY OBLIGATIONS OF INVESTMENT ADVISERS

A. Concept of Fiduciary Duty

"Fiduciary duty" is the general principle that defines an investment adviser's duties in managing client accounts or otherwise providing investment advice. This principle grows out of the common law of agency and the law of trusts which typically impose special duties upon those who occupy a relationship of trust and confidence with their clients. Moreover, although not expressly set forth in the Advisers Act, the U.S. Supreme Court in *SEC v. Capital Gains Research Bureau, Inc.*, 375 U.S. 180 (1963) held that Advisers Act Section 206 imposes fiduciary duties on investment advisers by operation of law.

In *Capital Gains*, the SEC sought an injunction forcing a registered investment adviser, who published the "Capital Gains Report," to disclose to his clients his "scalping" activities. "Scalping" (also referred to as "front running") is the practice of buying particular securities *before* recommending them to your clients. When the clients buy those securities, the prices of those securities generally rise. The investment adviser then sells his holdings at a nice little profit.

The SEC argued that Section 206 of the Advisers Act mandated disclosure of "scalping." Neither the

District Court nor the Second Circuit agreed, as they both believed that Section 206 was

designed to prevent fraud "in the technical sense," *i.e.*, an investment adviser had to have an "intent to deceive" that led to "actual client damages." Of particular importance to the courts was the lack of proof that the investment advice contained in the "Capital Gains Reports" was unsound or was based on bribes paid to tout stocks.

The U.S. Supreme Court disagreed with the lower courts, holding instead that Congress did intend Section 206 to cover "nondisclosure of material facts" as well as "technical fraud" in order to effectuate the Advisers Act's remedial purposes. According to the Court, whenever an investment adviser might personally benefit from investment advice, a conflict of interest is created. In order for a client or potential client to protect himself in this situation, he must be able to evaluate whether the investment adviser is serving "two masters" or only one, "especially if one of the masters happens to be [personal] economic interest."

It is important to note that *Capital Gains* does not hold that Section 206 prohibits the existence of the conflict. Rather, it only requires that a conflict of interest be properly disclosed to the adviser's client or potential client.

Turning back to the Advisers Act, Section 206(1) prohibits classic fraud, *i.e.,* intentionally fraudulent and deceptive practices. Section 206(2) prohibits a much broader range of conduct that "operates as a fraud or deceit" upon an existing client or prospective client. According to the *Capital Gains* decision, deliberate dishonesty or intent to commit "fraud" in the traditional sense or intent to injure clients is not required to show a violation of Section 206(2). Rather, an adviser may violate Section 206(2) if it fails to act with "the utmost good faith" with respect to its clients and/or fails to satisfy its affirmative duty to disclose all material facts and conflicts of interest to them.

B.   General Application

Fiduciary duties apply to all advisers, whether registered with the SEC or not, as Advisers Act Section 206 applies irrespective of registration. Thus, they apply to hedge fund and private equity advisers relying on the Private Adviser Registration Exemption under Advisers Act Section 203(b)(3). Moreover, they apply to advisers that provide individualized discretionary management services as well as to those that merely provide impersonal investment advice through publications or otherwise.

C.   Specific Fiduciary Responsibilities

Fiduciary duties of an adviser which are generally enforceable under Advisers Act Section 206 include those discussed below.

(1) Disclosure

An investment adviser has a duty to disclose all material facts relating to the offer of its services to a prospective client as well as conflicts of interest. Two particular areas of concern in this context are investment adviser advertising and the use of solicitors to refer clients to advisers. Advisers Act Rule 206(4)–1 addresses investment adviser advertising (see Nutshell Chapter VI), while Rule 206(4)–3 addresses cash payments for client solicitations (see Nutshell Section 22B).

An investment adviser has an obligation to existing clients to disclose all material facts about the advisory relationship as well as conflicts of interest. This is an affirmative duty to disclose rather than simply a duty to respond to a client's request for information. Of course, when an adviser does respond to a client's request for information, any evasiveness on the part of the adviser may constitute a violation of Section 206. See *SEC v. Washington Investment Network*, 475 F.3d 392 (D.C. Cir. 2007). Information is "material" if there is a substantial likelihood that a reasonable client would attach importance to it.

(2) Loyalty and Fairness

An investment adviser has a duty to act only in the best interests of its clients and to treat its clients fairly. Among other things, this means that an adviser must place the interests of its clients above its own interests when a conflict may be present. The investment adviser must disclose the existence of any conflict and obtain the client's consent to the relevant arrangement. Disclosure is needed to ensure the client makes an informed decision. Additionally, an adviser must treat each client fairly, and any preferential practices must be adequately disclosed to its clients in its Form ADV or otherwise. See Nutshell Section 33.

(3) Care

a. *Implied Duty*

The SEC has taken the position that an implied duty of care exists under Advisers Act Section 206 whenever an adviser recommends securities to a customer. Before the *Capital Gains* decision, this implied duty was grounded in the shingle theory whereby an adviser, by hanging up a "shingle" to conduct business, impliedly represented that it would use due care in providing investment advice and otherwise conduct its business in an equitable and professional manner.

b. *Informed Basis*

Advisers are expected to familiarize themselves with the facts on which they base their recommendations, although the extent of their fiduciary duty to investigate the securities they recommend is not clear. Nevertheless, advisers have been held liable for failing to disclose they were relying on someone else's analysis, especially when the accuracy of the information was in question.

(4) D & O/E & O Insurance

In addition to having an ERISA bond (see Nutshell Section 7C), many investment advisers voluntarily obtain directors' and officers' errors and omissions insurance policies (D & O/E & O), which is not required by the Advisers Act or Company Act.

Registered and unregistered advisers typically obtain D & O/E & O insurance to induce highly qualified individuals to serve as the adviser's officers and directors.

The amounts of coverage principally depend upon the amount of assets under management and the risk profile of the adviser. These policies generally have deductibles and may be joint policies with the adviser's funds, subject to certain requirements if the funds are registered investment companies. See Company Act Rule 17d–1.

Unlike an ERISA bond which covers theft and losses resulting from dishonesty, D & O/E & O policies insure against losses resulting from officers' and directors' negligence.

D. Custody and Possession

(1) The Custody Rule

The SEC promulgated Advisers Act Rule 206(4)–2 (the "Custody Rule") to insulate a client's assets from unlawful activities by an adviser that has "custody" of that client's securities or funds. These unlawful activities would typically arise when the adviser faces severe financial difficulties, including insolvency. For purposes of the Rule, "custody" means holding, directly or indirectly, client funds or securities, or having any authority to obtain possession of them. See Advisers Act Rule 206(4)–2(c)(1). Examples of "custody" provided by the SEC in subsection (c)(1) of the Custody Rule include:

- Possession of client funds or securities, excluding (a) those the adviser received inadvertently so long as the adviser sends them back to the sender promptly but in any case within three business days of receiving them and (b) checks drawn by clients and made payable to third parties;

- Any arrangement, including a general power of attorney, under which the adviser is authorized or permitted to withdraw client funds or securities maintained with a custodian upon the adviser's instruction to the custodian; and

- Any capacity that gives the adviser or the adviser's supervised person legal ownership of or access to client funds or securities, including being a trustee of a trust or a general partner of a limited partnership, a managing member of a limited liability company or holding a comparable position for another type of pooled investment vehicle.

Under the Custody Rule, it is considered a fraudulent, deceptive or manipulative act, practice or course of business within the meaning of Advisers Act Section 206(4) for an adviser to have custody of client funds or securities unless three conditions are met. First, a "qualified custodian" must maintain the client's funds and securities either in (1) a separate account for each client under that client's name or (2) accounts that contain only the adviser's clients' funds and securities, under the adviser's name as agent or trustee for the clients. See Advisers Act Rule 206(4)–2(a)(1). Generally speaking, a "qualified custodian" includes certain banks, registered broker-dealers, registered futures commission merchants and foreign financial institutions (so long as they customarily hold financial assets for their customers and segregate customer assets from their own proprietary assets). See Advisers Act Rule 206(4)–2(c)(3).

Second, an adviser must provide notice to its clients concerning the custodial arrangement. This means that an adviser must notify each client in writing of the qualified custodian's name, address and the manner in which the client's funds or securities are maintained. An adviser must send this notice promptly when a client opens her account and following any changes to this information. See Advisers Act Rule 206(4)–2(a)(2). A client may designate an independent representative to receive, on her behalf, the custodial arrangement notice, so long as the independent representative is not materially connected with the adviser. See Advisers Act Rules 206(4)–2(a)(4) & (c)(2). Additionally, an adviser must continue to disclose on its Form ADV that it has custody of client funds or securities.

Third, either the adviser or the qualified custodian must, at least quarterly, send each client an account statement identifying the amount of funds and of each security in the client's account at the end of the period and setting forth all transactions in the account during that period. See Advisers Act Rule 206(4)–2(a)(3). A client may designate an independent representative to receive, on her behalf, account statements, so long as the independent representative is not materially connected with the adviser. See Advisers Act Rules 206(4)–2(a)(4) & (c)(2).

If the qualified custodian is sending the account statements, the adviser must have a reasonable basis for believing that the qualified custodian has met its obligations in this regard. See Advisers Act Rule 206(4)–2(a)(3)(i). If the adviser is sending out the statements, however, an independent public accountant must verify all of the securities and funds through an actual examination at least once during each calendar year (and irregular from year to year) at a time chosen by the accountant without prior notice or announcement to the adviser (*a.k.a.* a "surprise" audit). Within 30 days after the accountant completes its examination, it must file a certificate on Form ADV–E with the SEC. If the accountant finds any material discrepancies during the course of its examination, it must notify the SEC within one business day of its finding. See Advisers Act Rule 206(4)–2(a)(3)(ii)(A)-(C).

Although not listed as a condition to an adviser having custody of a client's funds or securities, it is worth noting that an adviser having such custody must maintain certain additional records under Advisers Act Rule 204–2(b). These include a journal or other record showing all purchases, sales, receipts and deliveries of securities (including certificate numbers) for that client's account and all other debits and credits to that account. See Nutshell Section 46H.

(2) Exceptions to the Custody Rule

The Custody Rule (or certain aspects of it) is subject to four notable exceptions. First, an adviser is entitled to have shares of an open-end mutual fund it holds for clients held by the mutual fund's transfer agent in lieu of a qualified custodian. See Advisers Act Rule 206(4)–2(b)(1).

Second, an adviser need not comply with any aspects of the Custody Rule with respect to certain "privately offered securities." "Privately offered securities" means securities that are (1) acquired from the issuer in a transaction or chain of transactions not involving any public offering, (2) in uncertificated form (*i.e.*, that ownership is recorded only on the books of the issuer or its transfer agent) and (3) transferable only with the prior consent of the issuer or holders of the outstanding securities of the issuer. However, with respect to privately offered securities held for the account of a private fund (*e.g.*, a hedge fund), this exception is only available if the fund itself is audited, and the audited financial statements are distributed, in the manner described in the following paragraph. See Advisers Act Rule 206(4)–2(b)(2).

Third, an adviser is not required to comply with the account statement delivery requirement with respect to the account of any private fund that is subject to audit at least annually and distributes its audited financial statements prepared in accordance with GAAP to all beneficial owners within 120 days of the end of its fiscal year, or in the case of a "fund of funds" within 180 days of the end of its fiscal year. See Advisers Act Rule 206(4)–2(b)(3). This exception is referred to as the "annual audit exception." For purposes of this exception, "fund of funds" means a private fund that invests 10% or more of its total assets in other pooled investment vehicles that are not, and are not advised by, a related person of that private fund. See Advisers Act Rule 206(4)–2(c)(4). Advisers to "funds of funds" receive 180 days rather than only 120 days because they cannot complete their final fund audits prior to the completion of the audits for the underlying funds in which they invest. See Subcommittee on Private Investment Entities of the Amer. Bar Assoc., SEC No–Action Letter, 2005 WL 3334980 (avail. Dec. 8, 2005).

Finally, an adviser need not comply with the Custody Rule with respect to the account of a registered investment company. Instead, a registered investment company and the adviser must comply with the custody provisions of Company Act Section 17(f) and the seven custody rules promulgated thereunder. See Advisers Act Rule 206(4)–2(b)(4), Company Act Section 17(f) & Company Act Rules 17f–1 through –7.

E. Proxies

The Advisers Act does not require advisers to vote proxies for their clients. Nor does it impose standards on how advisers who choose to vote proxies should do so. Similarly, the Company Act does not address the exercise of voting rights by investment advisers to registered investment companies. Nonetheless, an adviser's fiduciary duty attaches to proxy voting and other ownership attributes of client securities, and advisers therefore who choose to vote proxies must do so in the best interests of their clients. Moreover, the SEC has promulgated rules under both the Advisers Act and the Company Act that address proxy voting procedures, disclosure and recordkeeping.

It is also worth noting that NASD Conduct Rule 2260 ("Forwarding of Proxy and Other Materials") permits a beneficial owner of stock held of record by an NASD member to designate a registered investment adviser to receive and vote proxies and receive related materials. However, the investment adviser must have investment discretion over the account pursuant to the advisory contract and the beneficial owner must designate in a writing that the investment adviser is to vote proxies and receive other shareholder materials.

On July 30, 2007, FINRA was created through the consolidation of the NASD and the member regulation, enforcement and arbitration operations of the NYSE. Accordingly, readers should be aware that a FINRA analog to NASD Conduct Rule 2260 will likely replace that NASD rule in the near future.

(1) Proxy Voting Under the Advisers Act

Investment advisers who exercise voting authority with respect to client securities must adhere to

Advisers Act Rule 206(4)–6 (the "Proxy Voting Rule"). It does not matter whether a given client granted explicit (through, for example, the advisory contract) or implicit (through, for example, an over-all grant of discretionary authority) proxy voting authority to the adviser. Moreover, advisers who exercise voting authority are required to keep addi-tional detailed books and records relating to their proxy voting activities in accordance with Advisers Act Rule 204–2(c)(2). See Nutshell Section 46I.

Under the Proxy Voting Rule, it is considered a fraudulent, deceptive or manipulative act, practice or course of business within the meaning of Advis-ers Act Section 206(4) for an adviser to exercise voting authority with respect to client securities unless three conditions are met. First, the adviser must adopt and implement written policies and procedures that are reasonably designed to ensure that the adviser votes client securities in the best interests of clients. These procedures must include how the adviser addresses material conflicts that may arise between the adviser's interests and those of the adviser's clients. See Advisers Act Rule 206(4)–6(a).

Second, the adviser must disclose to clients how they may obtain information from the adviser about how the adviser voted their securities. See Advisers Act Rule 206(4)–6(b). However, a given client is only entitled to learn how his adviser voted *his* securities, as opposed to the securities of all the adviser's clients. Moreover, except for advisers to registered management investment companies, advisers are not required to make public their proxy voting record.

Third, the adviser must describe to its clients the adviser's proxy voting policies and procedures and, upon request, furnish a copy of the policies and procedures to the requesting client. See Advisers Act Rule 206(4)–6(c). The logical place for this description is in the adviser's brochure.

(2) Proxy Voting Under the Company Act

Company Act Rule 30b1–4, which applies to registered management investment companies (*i.e.*, the vast majority of mutual funds), requires each fund to file an annual report on Form N–PX not later than August 31 of each year that contains that fund's proxy voting record for the most recent 12–month period ended June 30. In addition, these funds must disclose the policies and procedures they use with respect to proxy voting in their Statements of Additional Information, which are filed with the SEC and available to fund shareholders upon request. In cases where a fund's board delegates proxy voting to the fund's adviser (which is typically the case), the fund is required to disclose the adviser's proxy policies and procedures. Of course, such delegation must be subject to the board's continuing oversight.

F. Pursuing Claims Against Third Parties

Client claims against issuers of securities or third parties for misstatements or other actionable events under the securities laws may arise from time to time. The Advisers Act does not impose any express duty on investment advisers to pursue these claims on behalf of clients or to provide specific support to clients who choose to do so. The SEC has not taken a contrary position. However, the terms of an advisory agreement may, of course, impose general responsibilities on an adviser in this regard.

§ 29. SUITABILITY

A. Generally

As fiduciaries, advisers have an implicit duty under Advisers Act Section 206 to provide, among other things, only suitable investment advice to clients. This duty has been articulated primarily in SEC enforcement actions. In order to satisfy this duty, an adviser must make a reasonable inquiry into the financial situation and condition, investment experience, risk tolerance and general investment objectives of each client. Once the adviser has obtained that information, it must provide the client with suitable investment advice based upon that information.

B. Proposed Advisers Act Suitability Rule Abandoned

In 1994, the SEC proposed a suitability rule under the Advisers Act. See Advisers Act Rel. No. 1406, 1994 WL 84902 (Mar. 16, 1994). The SEC's proposal would have required advisers to maintain records of a client's financial situation, investment experience and investment objectives. The SEC withdrew its proposal from its regulatory agenda in 1996, and informally stated that it would not give further consideration to the proposal. Nevertheless, the proposed suitability rule provides significant insight into the SEC's thinking on the issue of suitability under the Advisers Act.

The proposed suitability rule would have required an investment adviser to satisfy a duty of inquiry. Thus, prior to making any investment recommendations, an adviser would have had to inquire into each client's financial situation, investment experience and investment objectives. An adviser would have been required to update the appropriate information obtained from each client "periodically so that the adviser [could] adjust its advice to reflect changed circumstances." According to the SEC, the required scope of a suitability inquiry would vary depending on what was "reasonable under the circumstances." Thereafter, an investment adviser could not give investment advice to the client unless the adviser reasonably determined that the advice was suitable for that client based on that client's information.

C. Dual Registrants

In addition to their suitability obligations under the Advisers Act, investment advisers that are also registered broker-dealers (*i.e.*, "Dual Registrants") are subject to other suitability obligations. The most important suitability rule for these purposes is NASD Conduct Rule 2310 ("Recommendations to Customers (Suitability)"). Other suitability obligations are imposed under the Exchange Act (see Exchange Act Rule 15g–9), the various securities exchanges and state law.

On July 30, 2007, FINRA was created through the consolidation of the NASD and the member regulation, enforcement and arbitration operations of the NYSE. Accordingly, readers should be aware that a FINRA analog to NASD Conduct Rule 2310 will likely replace that NASD rule in the near future.

§ 30. BEST EXECUTION

A. Generally

Investment advisers have a duty to seek the most favorable terms reasonably available under the circumstances when executing clients' securities transactions through brokers. This duty is referred to as the duty of "best execution." While not expressly imposed by the Advisers Act, this duty derives from an adviser's general fiduciary obligations to its clients.

The duty of best execution only applies when the investment adviser, rather than the client herself, is responsible for choosing among different brokers to execute the client's securities transactions. Some clients, particularly large institutional investors, specifically instruct their advisers to use a specific broker to effect securities transactions for them (a process referred to as "directed brokerage"). For more on client directed brokerage, see Nutshell Section 35.

B. What Constitutes Best Execution?

Put bluntly, "best execution" does not mean that an adviser must place trades through brokers charging the lowest possible commissions. Indeed, the SEC has underscored that best execution is not determined by the "lowest possible commission cost" but rather by the best "qualitative execution." See Exchange Act Rel. No. 23170, 1986 WL 630442 (Apr. 23, 1986) ("Release No. 23170"). According to Release No. 23170, to achieve best execution an adviser must "execute securities transactions for clients in such a manner that the client's total costs or proceeds in each transaction is most favorable under the circumstances."

An adviser must consider the full range and quality of a broker's services when determining whether "best execution" has been achieved. In addition to commission rates, these include execution capability, financial responsibility and responsiveness to the adviser. While not binding on the SEC, the Investment Company Institute has also counseled advisers to consider a broker's "trading expertise, reputation and integrity, facilities, financial services offered, willingness and ability to commit capital, access to underwritten offerings and secondary markets, reliability both in executing trades and keeping records, fairness in resolving disputes, and with respect to any particular trade, the timing and size of the order, available liquidity and current market conditions." Report by the Investment Company Institute on Brokerage Allocation Practices (Mar. 1998). An adviser is required to disclose the factors it considers when determining best execution in Part II of its Form ADV. See Nutshell Section 12C.

C. Conflicts of Interest

Two notable conflicts of interest arise in the context of "best execution." First, a conflict arises when an investment adviser seeks to have an affiliated broker execute client trades. Indeed, there is a financial incentive for the adviser to send trade orders to its affiliated broker regardless of whether that broker offers an adviser's clients best execution.

Second, some brokerage arrangements (referred to as "soft dollar arrangements") call for a broker to provide the adviser with products or services (other than securities execution) in return for directing client securities transactions to that broker. Most soft dollar arrangements involve brokers providing securities research reports to investment advisers, thus theoretically and indirectly benefitting the clients of those advisers. Because of the inherent conflicts of interest involved in soft dollar arrangements, the SEC has scrutinized them very closely. These arrangements and the SEC's regulation of them are discussed in detail in Nutshell Section 34.

D. Continuing Duties

An adviser has an ongoing duty of best execution. The SEC requires advisers to "periodically and systematically evaluate the execution performance of broker-dealers executing their transactions" in order to ensure continuing compliance with their duty of best execution. See Release No. 23170. Accordingly, an adviser should strongly consider establishing a trading oversight committee to measure the costs and quality of trades. Additionally, an adviser should maintain records evidencing the process used for broker selection and monitoring, the controls designed to prevent conflicts of interest and the materials prepared for the consideration of the trading oversight committee.

§ 31. PRINCIPAL AND CROSS TRANSACTIONS

A. Generally

Two types of transactions—the principal transaction and the agency cross transaction—create conflicts of interest that could allow an investment adviser to put its own interests ahead of those of its client (in the case of a principal transaction) or the interests of one client over those of another client (in the case of an agency cross transaction). Therefore, Advisers Act Section 206(3) prohibits these types of transactions unless the adviser discloses to the client the capacity in which it is acting and obtains that client's consent prior to their execution. While Section 206(3) on its face only applies to advisers, the staff of the SEC has taken the position that it also applies to principal and agency cross transactions effected by affiliates of advisers (*i.e.*, those who control, are controlled by, or are under common control with, an adviser). See Advisers Act Release No. 1732, 1998 WL 400409 (July 17, 1998).

B. Types of Transactions and Their Regulation

Advisers Act Section 206(3) covers the purchase and sale of securities in connection with principal transactions and agency cross transactions. For purposes of Section 206(3), the staff of the SEC interprets "purchase and sale" in accordance with its plain meaning. Accordingly, a purchase and sale of securities is not implicated when a client grants a security interest in securities to a Dual Registrant when establishing a margin account; nor is one involved if the client's securities are liquidated in order to meet a margin call. Furthermore, a purchase and sale of securities does not occur when securities are transferred or loaned on behalf of a client to facilitate a short sale. See Goldman, Sachs & Co., SEC No–Action Letter, 1999 WL 123998 (avail. Feb. 22, 1999).

(1) Principal Transactions

Advisers Act Section 206(3) covers "principal transactions." A principal transaction involves an investment adviser, acting as *principal for its own account* or the proprietary account of an affiliate, knowingly buying securities from, or selling them to, a client's account. This gives rise to a conflict of interest, as the adviser is acting both as an adviser to the client and as a private investor. In the worst-case scenario, an adviser could unload undesirable securities that it personally owns onto its advisory client.

The SEC also includes "riskless principal transactions" within the universe of "principal transactions" subject to Advisers Act Section 206(3). See In the Matter of ABN AMRO–NSM Int'l Funds Mgt., B.V., Advisers Act Rel. No. 1767, 1998 WL 668122 (Sept. 30, 1998). A "riskless principal transaction" occurs when a Dual Registrant purchases or sells a security that trades on a principal basis for an advisory client, and thus includes most over-the-counter (OTC) securities and debt securities. The adviser, on behalf of the client, will locate a buyer or seller for a particular security and then simultaneously sell or buy that security for the client through an offsetting transaction in the adviser's own account (hence the "riskless" aspect of the transaction to the adviser). The adviser normally charges the client a mark-up or mark-down rather than a commission. Because the security passes through the adviser's account on the way to or from the client's account, the SEC lumps riskless principal transactions together with ordinary principal transactions. It is also worth noting that fees paid for a riskless principal transaction in which both legs of the transaction are executed at the same price and are reported under the NASD's trade reporting rules are considered "commissions" for purposes of the "soft dollar" safe harbor found in Exchange Act Section 28(e). See Nutshell Section 34B.

Advisers Act Section 206(3) prohibits an investment adviser that is "acting as an investment adviser" from engaging in any principal transaction *unless* the adviser, before the completion of *each* transaction, (a) makes written disclosure to the client of the capacity in which it is acting and (b) obtains the client's consent to that transaction. A client's prospectively provided blanket consent to principal transactions is *insufficient* to satisfy the trade-by-trade disclosure and consent requirements. Moreover, any adviser engaging in principal transactions must satisfy its fiduciary duties to its clients. This means, among other things, that the adviser must determine that a given principal transaction is in the best interests of the client involved in that transaction.

(2) Agency Cross Transactions

Advisers Act Section 206(3) also covers "agency cross transactions." An agency cross transaction is only relevant when an investment adviser is a Dual Registrant or affiliated with a broker-dealer. An agency cross transaction is a trade between an adviser's advisory client, on the one hand, and one of that adviser's brokerage clients, on the other hand. The adviser or its broker-dealer affiliate acts as broker for its advisory client and for the party on the other side of the transaction. See Advisers Act Rule 206(3)–2(b). As a result of the trade, the adviser (if it is a Dual Registrant) or its broker-dealer affiliate receives a commission. An agency cross transaction gives rise to a conflict of interest as an adviser could favor its advisory client over its brokerage client, or vice versa.

Advisers Act Section 206(3)'s trade-by-trade disclosure and consent requirements apply to agency cross transactions; however, Advisers Act Rule 206(3)–2 provides substantial relief from those requirements. This Rule relaxes Section 206(3)'s prior disclosure and consent requirements for agency cross transactions (but *not* principal transactions) if the adviser provides certain mandatory disclosures to the client and the client *prospectively* authorizes agency cross transactions in writing. Specifically, pursuant to subsection (a) of Rule 206(3)–2, the following five requirements must be met:

(1) The advisory client must execute a written consent prospectively authorizing the investment adviser to effect agency cross transactions on her behalf after the adviser makes full written disclosure to the client that the adviser will act as broker for, receive commissions from, and have a potential conflicting division of loyalties and responsibilities regarding, both parties to the transactions;

(2) The investment adviser must send a written confirmation to each client at or before the completion of each transaction that describes the terms of the transaction and the total compensation received by the adviser or any affiliated broker-dealer;

(3) The investment adviser must send to each client, at least annually, a written disclosure statement identifying the total number of agency cross transactions that occurred during the period since the date of the last such statement and the total amount of all commissions or other remu-

neration received or to be received by the investment adviser in connection with the transactions
during that period;

(4) Each written disclosure statement and confirmation must include a conspicuous statement
that the written consent previously provided by
the client may be revoked at any time through a
written notice to the adviser; and

(5) No agency cross transaction may be effected
in which the same investment adviser recommended the transaction to both seller and purchaser.

Notwithstanding the safe harbor it provides, Advisers Act Rule 206(3)–2 does not relieve an investment adviser of any of its fiduciary duties, including
the duty of best execution. Thus, an adviser must
continue to act in the best interests of its advisory
clients when effecting agency cross transactions.
Nor does the Rule relieve an adviser from any
disclosure obligation which may be imposed under
subparagraphs (1) or (2) of Advisers Act Section 206
or by other applicable provisions of the Federal
securities laws. See Advisers Act Rule 206(3)–2(c).

(3) Internal Cross Transactions

Although not covered by Advisers Act Section
206(3), it is helpful to understand another type of
cross transaction referred to as an "internal cross
transaction." An internal cross transaction is a
trade between two advisory client accounts of the
same investment adviser over which the investment

adviser has discretionary authority. No broker is used to effect the trade, and thus no commission is paid (other than the customary advisory fee). If this were not the case, the adviser could be deemed to be acting as a broker and the transaction, therefore, would constitute an agency cross transaction subject to Section 206(3).

While internal cross transactions do not have to satisfy the trade-by-trade disclosure and consent requirements of Advisers Act Section 206(3), an adviser still must make full disclosure concerning internal cross trading on its Form ADV. Moreover, the adviser should ensure that internal cross trades are fair to, and in the best interests of, both clients.

An adviser can assure fairness by adopting pricing procedures analogous to those set forth in Company Act Rule 17a–7. That Rule is an exemptive rule that permits affiliated investment companies to engage in a purchase and sale transaction of securities so long as:

(i) The transaction is consistent with the investment policy of each of the participating investment companies;

(ii) The transaction complies with the pricing procedures specified in the Rule;

(iii) No brokerage fee or other remuneration, other than a customary transfer fee, is paid in connection with the transaction; and

(iv) The board of directors of each investment company, including a majority of the directors who are not "interested persons" as defined in Company Act Section 2(a)(19), approves certain actions specified in the Rule.

§ 32. INVESTMENTS IN INVESTMENT COMPANIES

If an investment adviser invests client assets in an investment company (*i.e.*, a mutual fund) or other pooled investment vehicle, the client may in effect be paying two layers of advisory fees: (a) one fee at the account level payable to the client's adviser; and (b) another fee at the mutual fund or pooled investment vehicle level payable to the adviser of that fund or vehicle. "Pyramiding" of fees, however, could potentially work to the disadvantage of the client.

The client's adviser has a fiduciary duty under Advisers Act Section 206 to disclose to prospective clients that, in addition to the fee paid to the adviser directly by a client, each fund or other vehicle in which the client's assets may be invested also imposes its own advisory fees and other expenses. This duty applies whether or not the adviser also manages the underlying fund or vehicle.

Problems also arise when one investment company invests in another investment company. In addition to the problem of fee and expense "pyramiding" discussed above, the exercise of control of an investment company by a fund holding company, or a group of related fund holding companies, could be disadvantageous to the other investors in the controlled company. For example, a fund holding company could unduly influence prudent management of the controlled investment company by threatening to redeem its large stake in that investment company. While outright ownership of the securities of one investment company by another investment company is not prohibited, significant limitations exist. See Company Act Section 12(d)(1).

§ 33. ALLOCATION AND AGGREGATION ISSUES

A. Allocation of Securities Among Clients

(1) Generally

In most instances, investment opportunities are limited. Thus, when an adviser seeks to purchase or sell a particular security on behalf of more than one client account, the adviser will often need to allocate the purchase and sale opportunity among those accounts. An adviser has a fiduciary duty to allocate investment opportunities fairly among its eligible accounts and may not favor one account at the expense of another. The staff of the SEC has indicated that an adviser allocating trading opportunities on a pro rata basis generally would satisfy the adviser's duty to make fair allocations, although other methods could also satisfy this duty. See Pretzel & Stouffer, SEC No–Action Letter, 1995 WL 737153 (avail. Dec. 1, 1995); SMC Capital, Inc., SEC No–Action Letter, 1995 WL 529274 (avail. Sept. 5, 1995).

Allocation conflicts were particularly prevalent during the 1990s as some advisers decided to allocate securities among client accounts in a way that favored certain clients over other clients. In one case, an adviser that managed two mutual funds, on the one hand, and part of the assets of an employee profit-sharing plan affiliated with the adviser, on the other hand, would place orders for the purchase of securities without designating which client was to be the owner of the securities. Once it was clear that a given trade would be profitable, the securities relating to it would be allocated disproportionately towards the affiliated employee profit-sharing plan. Among other things, the SEC charged the portfolio manager engaged in these activities with violating Advisers Act Section 206(2). That Section makes it unlawful for an adviser to engage in any transaction, practice or course of business which operates as a fraud or deceit upon any client or prospective client. See In the Matter of Kemper Financial Services, Inc., Advisers Act Rel. No. 1387, 1993 WL 431535 (Oct. 20, 1993).

The SEC has also brought enforcement actions against advisers who inappropriately allocated shares in "hot IPOs." In one instance, the adviser allocated the shares to a limited group of favored clients but failed to adequately disclose the practice to all its clients. See In the Matter of Account Mgt. Corp., Advisers Act Rel. No. 1529, 1995 WL 579449 (Sept. 29, 1995). Similarly, another adviser allocated such shares disproportionately towards performance-based fee accounts and away from asset-based fee accounts. Since hot IPO shares tend to "pop" up in value, the adviser reaped greater rewards by pursuing an allocation strategy that steered the shares into the performance-based accounts. Not surprisingly, the adviser's allocation practices were not adequately disclosed to all the adviser's clients. See In the Matter of McKenzie Walker Investment Mgt., Inc., Advisers Act Rel. No. 1571, 1996 WL 396091 (July 16, 1996).

(2) "Hot IPOs" and NASD Conduct Rule 2790

On the topic of "hot IPOs," it is worth noting that the NASD limits the ability of Dual Registrants and their personnel to participate in any new issuances of equity securities. NASD Conduct Rule 2790 ("Restrictions on the Purchase and Sale of IPOs of Equity Securities") generally prohibits a NASD member from selling any "new issue" (and not just "hot issues" as was the case with prior NASD Conduct Rule 2110) to any account in which a "restricted person" has a beneficial interest.

The term "restricted person" includes most associated persons of a NASD member, most owners and affiliates of a broker-dealer, and certain other classes of persons. The Rule requires a member, before selling shares of a new issue to any account, to meet certain "preconditions for sale." These generally require the member to obtain a representation from the beneficial owner of the account that the account is eligible to purchase new issues in accordance with the Rule. The Rule also contains a series of general exemptions.

NASD Conduct Rule 2790 is designed to protect the integrity of the public offering process, thereby maintaining investor confidence. It does so by ensuring that:

(i) NASD members, when acting as underwriters, make bona fide public offerings of securities at the offering price;

(ii) Members do not withhold securities in a public offering for their own benefit or use such securities to reward persons who are in a position to direct future business to members; and

(iii) Industry insiders, including NASD members and their associated persons, do not take advantage of their "insider" position to purchase "new issues" for their own benefit at the expense of public customers.

On July 30, 2007, FINRA was created through the consolidation of the NASD and the member regulation, enforcement and arbitration operations of the NYSE. Accordingly, readers should be aware that a FINRA analog to NASD Conduct Rule 2790 will likely replace that NASD rule in the near future.

B. Aggregation of Client Orders

"Aggregating trades" (also known as "bunching trades") occurs when an adviser places a single, large trade order (an "aggregated order") for a particular security on behalf of multiple client accounts. While the adviser could place a single, small trade order for that security on behalf of each and every client account, doing so would be highly inefficient. Indeed, trade aggregation may provide the adviser with the leverage necessary to obtain more favorable execution and lower brokerage commissions.

Trade aggregation, however, gives rise to a conflict of interest. Through it, an adviser has the ability to favor one client over another. This stems from the adviser's ability to select the accounts that will participate in the trade and the quantity in which they will participate. An adviser, however, must satisfy its fiduciary duty of acting in the best interests of its clients by determining, in advance of placing any aggregated order, how it will treat each participating client fairly through that order. Moreover, the adviser must continue to seek best execution for the aggregated order and disclose its aggregation policy to its clients. If an aggregated order is filled through multiple transactions occurring over the course of a single trading day, an adviser must ensure that each participating client receives the average share price for those multiple transactions.

Additional guidance on trade aggregation exists with respect to advisers who aggregate trades on behalf of investment company clients. In order to avoid violating Company Act Section 17(d) and Company Act Rule 17d–1, an adviser who aggregates trades involving investment company clients must disclose its practice and engage in it for the exclusive purpose of achieving lower brokerage commissions. See Owen T. Wilkinson & Assoc., Inc., SEC No–Action Letter, 1987 WL 108842 (avail. Dec. 30, 1987). Moreover, when an adviser seeks to aggregate orders on behalf of investment company clients as well as the adviser's own proprietary accounts (such as another pooled investment vehicle in which the adviser and its personnel may have invested), the staff of the SEC requires the adviser to satisfy a number of stringent conditions, including the following:

(i) The adviser must prepare a written statement (referred to as an "allocation statement") listing each participating client account and specifying how the aggregated order will be allocated among those accounts. An allocation statement must be prepared *before* the adviser places an aggregated order;

(ii) The aggregated order must be allocated on a pro rata basis if the order is only partially filled; and

(iii) If the actual allocation that the adviser makes deviates from that contained in the allocation statement, the adviser must ensure that the deviation is fair and equitable to all participating client accounts. Moreover, the adviser must explain the deviation and the reasons behind it in writing to its compliance officer no later than one hour after the markets open on the next trading day. The compliance officer must approve the deviation.

See Pretzel & Stouffer, SEC No–Action Letter, 1995 WL 737153 (avail. Dec. 1, 1995); SMC Capital, Inc., SEC No–Action Letter, 1995 WL 529274 (avail. Sept. 5, 1995).

§ 34. SOFT DOLLARS

A. Historical Background

Prior to the mid–1970s, commission rates on national exchanges had been fixed by custom and regulation since the founding of the New York Stock Exchange nearly 200 years earlier. During this time of fixed rates, broker-dealers could not compete against one another on the basis of the commissions they charged for executing orders. Therefore, they found other ways to stand out in the crowd. For example, they often attracted order execution business from institutional money managers by offering them brokerage functions and research reports. These ancillary services essentially amounted to non-cash "rebates" payable to the customers placing trades with a particular broker-dealer. In the world of mutual funds and investment advisers, these non-cash "rebates" are referred to as "*soft dollars*."

In June 1975, Congress passed legislation deregulating commission rates as part of the Securities Acts Amendments of 1975. Among other things, those Amendments added Exchange Act Section 6(e)(1). That Section prohibits national securities exchanges from imposing any schedule, or fixing rates, of commissions, allowances, discounts, or other fees charged by its members.

In light of Exchange Act Section 6(e)(1), the question arose as to how a competitive environment of commission rates would impact on the brokerage practice of providing research and other services (*i.e.*, soft dollars) to brokerage customers, including investment advisers. In particular, investment advisers were concerned that they would have to allocate brokerage solely on the basis of the lowest execution costs. If that were the case, they would not be able to take into consideration the value of soft dollar benefits received from broker-dealers when determining whether they satisfied their fiduciary duty of best execution. Moreover, many advisers were concerned that useful research would become more difficult to obtain. Indeed, advisers believed that many broker-dealers which produced proprietary "Street" research might reduce or even eliminate their research departments if they thought they could no longer be compensated through commissions for their work product. In order to allay industry concerns in this regard, Congress included a safe harbor in the Securities Acts Amendments of 1975—namely, Exchange Act Section 28(e).

B. Exchange Act Section 28(e) Safe Harbor

Although this discussion of Exchange Act Section 28(e) is focused on investment advisers, that Section actually applies to a broad category of persons known as "money managers." The term "money managers" includes all persons who exercise investment discretion with respect to a client account. These include investment advisers, mutual fund portfolio managers, fiduciaries of bank trust funds and money managers of pension plans and hedge funds. See Exchange Act Rel. No. 54165, 2005 WL 4843294 (July 18, 2006) ("Release No. 54165").

Investment advisers, as fiduciaries, are obligated to act in the best interests of their clients. They cannot use client assets, including client commissions, to benefit themselves, absent client consent. Investment advisers who obtain brokerage and research services with client commissions do not have to purchase those services with their own money, thus creating an obvious conflict of interest for them. For purposes of Section 28(e), the term "commissions" includes not only normal brokerage commissions but also fees paid for a riskless principal transaction in which both legs of the transaction are executed at the same price and are reported under the NASD's trade reporting rules. For more on riskless principal transactions, see Nutshell Section 31B(1).

Exchange Act Section 28(e) is designed to address the conflict of interest arising when an investment adviser receives soft dollar benefits in exchange for paying brokerage commissions that are higher than the lowest commission available at that time. Pursuant to Section 28(e)(1), so long as one condition is met, an investment adviser will not be deemed to have acted unlawfully or to have breached a fiduciary duty under state or Federal law by paying commissions on behalf of a client that are higher than otherwise available to obtain brokerage and research services (*i.e.*, soft dollars). That one condition is as follows:

> An adviser must determine in good faith that the commission paid was reasonable in relation to the value of the brokerage and research services provided by the broker, viewed in terms of either that particular transaction or the adviser's overall responsibilities with respect to the accounts as to which it exercises investment discretion.

Conduct not protected by Section 28(e) may constitute a breach of fiduciary duty (*e.g.*, failure to seek best execution) as well as a violation of the Federal securities laws, particularly the Advisers Act and the Company Act, as well as ERISA. In addition, an adviser's compliance with the Section 28(e) safe harbor does not immunize it from the antifraud provisions of the Federal securities laws.

C. Complying With Exchange Act Section 28(e)

Determining whether a particular product or service falls within the safe harbor of Exchange Act Section 28(e) is a three step process:

· *First*, an adviser must determine whether the product or service is *eligible* "research" under Section 28(e)(3)(A) or (B) or *eligible* "brokerage" under Section 28(e)(3)(C).

· *Second*, the adviser must determine whether the eligible product or service actually provides *lawful and appropriate assistance* in the performance of its investment decision-making responsibilities (thus benefitting clients). If a given product or service serves both an investment decision-making function and functions not related to that process (a so-called "*mixed-use*" product or service), an adviser must make a reasonable allocation of the costs of the product or service between itself and its clients.

· *Third*, the adviser must make a good faith determination that the amount of client commissions paid is reasonable in light of the value of the eligible products or services provided by the broker-dealer.

The three-step process set forth above gives rise to a number of important issues. In Release No. 54165, the SEC provided interpretive guidance on a number of these issues, including the following:

· What constitutes eligible "research" services?

· How should third-party research be treated under Section 28(e)?

· What constitutes eligible "brokerage" services?

· How should "mixed-use" products or services be treated under Section 28(e)?

· How does an adviser make a "good faith determination" that the commissions paid are reasonable in relation to the value of the eligible brokerage and research services received?

· What is the importance of, and the connection between, the terms "provided by" and "effecting" in the context of Section 28(e)?

Each of these issues is discussed below.

(1) "Research Services" Under Section 28(e)

A broker provides "research services" under Exchange Act Section 28(e)(3)(A) or (B) insofar as he:

(A) furnishes *advice*, either directly or through publications or writings, as to the value of securities, the advisability of investing in, purchasing, or selling securities, and the availability of securities for purchasers or sellers of securities; or

(B) furnishes *analyses* and *reports* concerning issuers, industries, securities, economic factors and trends, portfolio strategy, and the performance of client accounts.

The eligibility of a particular research service under the Section 28(e) safe harbor depends on its subject matter and whether it constitutes advice, analysis or a report. The form the research takes (*e.g.*, electronic, paper or oral discussions) is irrelevant to the eligibility analysis under the safe harbor.

As seen in subsections (A) and (B) of Section 28(e)(3), the subject matter of the advice, analyses and reports constituting "research" is generally securities, issuers, industries and the financial markets. However, as also seen above, it is not necessarily limited to those topics. Indeed, a report concerning political factors that are interrelated with economic factors could potentially fall within the scope of the Section 28(e) safe harbor.

According to the SEC, an important common element among the advice, analyses and reports potentially eligible as "research" is that all contain substantive content, *i.e.*, the expression of reasoning or knowledge. Thus, in determining whether a product or service is eligible as "research" under Section 28(e), the adviser must conclude that it reflects the expression of reasoning or knowledge and relates to the subject matter identified in Section 28(e)(3)(A) or (B). Products or services that the SEC has indicated *are eligible* as "research" under Section 28(e) include the following:

- · Traditional research reports analyzing the performance of a particular company or stock;

- · Discussions with research analysts relating to the advisability of investing in securities;

- · Meetings with corporate executives to obtain oral reports on the performance of a company;

- · Seminars or conferences if they provide substantive content relating to issuers, industries, securities and other eligible subject matters;

- · Software that provides analyses of securities portfolios; and

- · Corporate governance research (including corporate governance analytics) and corporate governance rating services if they reflect the expression of reasoning or knowledge relating to issuers or other eligible subject matters.

a. Guidance on Specific Products and Services

1. Mass–Marketed Publications

In Release No. 54165, the SEC stated its belief that Section 28(e) *should not* protect an adviser's purchase of publications that are mass-marketed. Instead, mass-marketed publications are more properly considered as overhead expenses of an adviser. Mass-marketed publications are those publications that are intended for and marketed to a broad, public audience, rather than the specialized interests of a small readership. Subscriptions for mass-marketed publications are typically inexpensive.

By contrast, publications that are not mass-marketed are eligible for the safe harbor of Section 28(e) if they qualify as "research" under that Section. Publications that are not mass-marketed, and thus could be eligible research under the safe harbor, are typically marketed to a narrow audience, directed to readers with specialized interests in particular industries, products or issuers, and expensive in terms of subscription cost. Examples would include financial newsletters and other financial and economic publications that are not targeted to a wide, public audience. Trade magazines and technical journals concerning specific industries or product lines may also be eligible as research if they are marketed to, and intended to serve the interests of, a narrow audience, rather than the general public.

The SEC has indicated that the method of distribution of the publication does not determine whether it is mass-marketed. Rather, the publication's marketing rather that its availability is an important criterion for determining the applicability of the safe harbor. If the publication is marketed to a narrow audience, such as investment professionals, and designed to serve the specialized interests of that audience, it still may be eligible as research under Section 28(e) even if it can be accessed over the Internet by the general population.

   2.   Inherently Tangible Products and Services

Products or services that do not reflect the expression of reasoning or knowledge are not eligible as research under the safe harbor. Because products and services with inherently tangible or physical attributes lack these, they are *not* eligible as research under Section 28(e). According to the SEC, examples of these *ineligible* products and services include:

- · Office equipment and office furniture;
- · Computer hardware, including computer terminals;
- · Computer accessories;
- · Telephone lines, transatlantic cables and computer cables (although the products or services delivered over them may be eligible);
- · Business supplies;
- · Salaries (including research staff);
- · Office rent;
- · Accounting fees and software;

· Website design;

· Software for operating systems, administrative functions and e-mail;

· Internet service;

· Legal expenses;

· Personnel management;

· Marketing;

· Utilities;

· Membership dues (including initial and maintenance fees paid on behalf of the adviser or any of its employees to any organization, representative, lobbying group or firm);

· Professional licensing fees;

· Word processing; and

· Equipment maintenance and repair services.

In addition, expenses for travel, entertainment and meals associated with attending seminars, and travel and related expenses associated with arranging trips to meet corporate executives, analysts or other individuals, are not eligible under the safe harbor. This is true even though those seminars, corporate executives, analysts or other individuals may themselves provide eligible research under the safe harbor.

3.   Market Research

Although eligible research typically relates to issuers, securities and industries, it may also include "market research." Market research consists of advice, analyses and reports regarding the market for securities, and includes advice on market color and execution strategies. According to the SEC, market research that may be eligible as "research" under Section 28(e) includes:

· Pre-trade and post-trade analytics, software and other products that depend on market information to generate market research, including research on optimal execution venues and trading strategies; and

· Advice from broker-dealers on order execution, including advice on execution strategies, market color and the availability of buyers and sellers, as well as software that provides these types of market research.

Some of these products and services may contain functionality that is not eligible research or brokerage under the safe harbor. In addition, other products or services that are eligible research or brokerage may sometimes be used by an adviser in a way that does not provide lawful and appropriate assistance in investment decision-making. Accordingly, care should be taken when evaluating these products and services, as they could constitute mixed-use items. For more on mixed-use items, see Nutshell Section 34C(3).

4. Third–Party Research

The SEC has stated that independent research products developed by third parties should be accorded equal treatment with proprietary research products developed by broker-dealers that execute trades. In this regard, the SEC believes that third-party research arrangements can benefit advised accounts by providing greater breadth and depth of research. In particular, an adviser may utilize third-party arrangements to obtain specialized research that is particularly beneficial to its advised accounts. For a discussion of third-party research in the context of Section 28(e)'s requirement that research be "provided by" an executing broker-dealer, see Nutshell Section 34C(5)b.

5. Data

According to the SEC, data services, including those that provide market data or economic data, could constitute eligible "reports" under the safe harbor if they satisfy the subject matter criteria and provide lawful and appropriate assistance in the investment decision-making process. For example, because market data (*e.g.*, stock quotes, last sale prices and trading volumes) contain aggregations of information on a current basis related to the subject matter identified in Section 28(e), they contain substantive content and thus constitute "reports concerning ... securities" within the meaning of Section 28(e)(3)(B). Other data are eligible under the safe harbor if they reflect substantive content, *i.e.*, the expression of reasoning or knowledge, related to the subject matter identified in Section 28(e). In this regard, the SEC believes that company financial data and economic data (such as unemployment and inflation rates or gross domestic product fig-

ures) may be eligible as research under Section
28(e).

6. Proxy Services

Proxy service providers offer a range of services
to investment advisers. Some of the services may
satisfy the standards for eligible "research" under
the safe harbor while others may not. Proxy services, therefore, generally must be treated as mixed-
use items. See Nutshell Section 34C(3). For example, on the one hand, reports and analyses on issuers, securities and the advisability of investing in
securities that are transmitted through a proxy
service may fall within the Section 28(e) safe harbor. On the other hand, other services such as the
handling of the mechanical aspects of voting, including casting, counting, recording and reporting
votes, would not be eligible. These ineligible services constitute administrative overhead expenses of
the adviser and thus are not eligible under Section
28(e).

b. *"Lawful and Appropriate Assistance"*

It is not enough for products or services to be
eligible as "research" under Section 28(e)(3)(A) or
(B). In addition, those products or services must
provide the adviser with "lawful and appropriate
assistance" in making investment decisions. The
focus, therefore, is on *how* the adviser uses the
eligible research. If the adviser uses it to help
perform the adviser's investment decision-making
responsibilities, the "lawful and appropriate assis-

tance" requirement is satisfied. If, however, the adviser uses it for another purpose, such as to help it market its own services, that requirement would not be satisfied and, as a result, the eligible research would not fall within the safe harbor.

(2) Eligibility Criteria for "Brokerage" Under Section 28(e)

A broker provides "brokerage services" under Exchange Act Section 28(e)(3)(C) insofar as he:

> effects securities transactions and performs functions incidental thereto (such as clearance, settlement and custody) or required in connection therewith by rules of the SEC or a self-regulatory organization of which he is a member or in which he is a participant.

Thus, Section 28(e)(3)(C) not only describes the brokerage products and services that are eligible under the safe harbor, but it also provides that functions "incidental thereto" are also eligible. Additionally, functions that are required by SEC or SRO rules are eligible. For example, in certain circumstances, the use of electronic confirmation and affirmation of institutional trades is required in connection with settlement processing. See, e.g., NASD Rule 11860(a)(5) and NYSE Rule 387(a)(5) (or their forthcoming FINRA analogs).

Clearance, settlement and custody services in connection with trades effected by the broker are explicitly identified as eligible incidental brokerage services. According to the SEC, the following post-trade services relate to functions incidental to executing a transaction and thus are eligible under the safe harbor as "brokerage services":

- Post-trade matching of trade information;
- Other exchanges of messages among broker-dealers, custodians and institutions related to the trade;
- Electronic communication of allocation instructions between institutions and broker-dealers;
- Routing settlement instructions to custodian banks and broker-dealers' clearing agents;
- Short-term custody related to effecting particular transactions in relation to clearance and settlement of the trade; and
- Comparison services required by SEC or SRO rules.

a. *Temporal Standard*

According to the SEC, "brokerage" services under the safe harbor must relate to the execution of securities transactions. The SEC views the execution of transactions as a process. Services related to the execution of securities transactions begin when an adviser communicates with a broker-dealer for the purpose of transmitting an order for execution. They end when funds or securities are delivered or credited to the advised account or the account holder's agent. Accordingly, the SEC employs a *temporal standard* in order to distinguish between "brokerage services" that are eligible under Section 28(e) and those products and services, such as overhead, that are not eligible.

Under the SEC's temporal standard, communications services related to the execution, clearing and settlement of securities transactions and other functions incidental to effect securities transactions (*e.g.*, connectivity service between the adviser and the broker-dealer and other relevant parties such as custodians) are eligible under Section 28(e)(3)(C). Moreover, trading software used to route orders to market centers, software that provides algorithmic trading strategies, and software used to transmit orders to direct market access ("DMA") systems are within the temporal standard and thus are eligible "brokerage" under the safe harbor.

It is important to note that, unlike research services (see Nutshell Section 34C(1)b), brokerage services *can include* connectivity services and trading software when they are used to transmit orders to a broker. This is because the transmission of orders has traditionally been considered a core part of the brokerage service. The SEC believes that mechanisms to deliver research, by contrast, are separable from the research and investment decision-making process, and thus cannot be considered "research" for purposes of Section 28(e).

Connectivity services eligible for "brokerage" under the safe harbor include:

· Dedicated lines between a broker-dealer and the adviser's order management system ("OMS");

- Lines between a broker-dealer and an OMS operated by a third-party vendor;

- Dedicated lines providing direct dial service between the adviser and the trading desk at a broker-dealer; and

- Message services used to transmit orders to broker-dealers for execution.

b. *Ineligible Overhead*

The SEC has indicated that a number of products and services are not "brokerage" under the safe harbor. This is because they are not sufficiently related to order execution and fall outside the temporal standard for "brokerage" under the safe harbor. Accordingly, they are properly characterized as overhead, *i.e.*, part of the adviser's cost of doing business. These include:

- Hardware, such as telephones or computer terminals;

- Software functionality used for recordkeeping or administrative purposes (such as managing portfolios); and

- Quantitative analytical software used to test "what if" scenarios relating to adjusting portfolios, asset allocation or portfolio modeling (whether or not provided through OMS).

Furthermore, the SEC has stated that an adviser cannot use client commissions under the safe harbor to meet its compliance responsibilities. These responsibilities include:

· Performing compliance tests to analyze information over time in order to identify unusual patterns, including, for example, an analysis of the quality of brokerage executions for the purpose of evaluating the adviser's fulfillment of its duty of best execution;

· Creating trade parameters for compliance with regulatory requirements, prospectus disclosure or investment objectives; and

· Stress-testing a portfolio under a variety of market conditions or to monitor style drift.

Finally, trades to correct adviser errors and related services in connection with errors are not eligible under the safe harbor. Indeed, errors are not related to the initial trade for a client within the meaning of Section 28(e)(3)(C); rather, they are separate transactions to correct the adviser's error and do not benefit the advised accounts. For more on trading errors, see Nutshell Section 38.

c. *Custody*

While Section 28(e)(3)(C) explicitly includes "custody" within the scope of the safe harbor, the SEC believes that only *short-term* custody, and not *long-term* custody, is covered. According to the SEC, short-term custody related to effecting a particular transaction, as well as the clearance and settlement of that transaction, falls within the safe harbor because it is tied to processing the trade between the time the order is placed and settlement of the trade (*i.e.*, it falls within the temporal standard). By contrast, long-term custody would not fall within the safe harbor because it is provided post-settlement (*i.e.*, it falls outside the temporal standard) and relates to long-term maintenance of securities positions. Moreover, many advisory clients pay for their own long-term custody through contractual arrangements made directly with custodians.

(3) "Mixed–Use" Items

Certain products or services obtained with client commissions have a mixed use, *i.e.*, they benefit both the advisory client and the adviser. Mixed-use products may include trade analytical software (which may sometimes be put to administrative use), proxy voting services and OMS. Advisers face a conflict of interest in obtaining mixed-use products or services with client commissions. In this regard, advisers may be tempted to use client commissions to pay for all of the product or service rather than only for the portion that actually benefits clients.

When a product or service has a mixed use, an adviser must in good faith make a reasonable allocation of the cost of the product or service according to its use. Client commissions may only be used to fund the portion of the mixed-use product's cost that the adviser has reasonably allocated to the client. The adviser must use its own funds to pay the remaining portion (*i.e.*, the amount allocated to the adviser). Because the allocation determination itself poses a conflict of interest for the adviser, that conflict must be disclosed to the client. Moreover, the adviser must keep adequate books and records concerning allocations so as to be able to make the required good faith showing.

In deciding how to allocate costs for a particular mixed-use product or service, an adviser should make a good faith, fact-based analysis of how it and its employees use the product or service. Relevant factors to consider would include, among others, the amount of time the product or service is used for eligible purposes versus ineligible purposes, the relative utility (measured by objective metrics) to the adviser of the eligible versus ineligible uses, and the extent to which the product is redundant with other products employed by the adviser for the same purpose. See Release No. 54165 and Exchange Act Rel. No. 23170, 1986 WL 630442 (Apr. 23, 1986).

(4) An Adviser's Good Faith Determination as to Reasonableness Under Section 28(e)

In order to avail itself of the safe harbor under Section 28(e), an adviser must make a good faith determination that the commissions paid are reasonable in relation to the value of the eligible research and brokerage services received. The adviser has the burden of proof in this regard. In the context of research, if a broker-dealer also offers its research for an unbundled price, that price should inform the adviser as to the research's market value and help the adviser make its good faith determination.

An adviser may not obtain eligible products and services in order to camouflage the payment of higher commissions to broker-dealers for ineligible services, such as shelf space or client referrals. In this situation, the adviser could not make the determination, in good faith, that the commission rate was reasonable in relation to the value of the Section 28(e) eligible products, because the commission incorporates a payment to the broker-dealer for non-Section 28(e) services. In this regard, an adviser to a registered investment company should take note of Company Act Rule 12b–1(h) which prohibits a fund from using brokerage commissions to pay for distribution of the fund's shares.

(5) Linkage Between "Provided by" and "Effecting" Under Section 28(e)

Section 28(e) requires that the broker-dealer "providing" eligible research to an adviser also be involved in "effecting" the trade on behalf of that adviser. The statutory linkage between the party providing the research and the one effecting the trade was principally intended to preclude the practice of paying "give-ups."

The quintessential "give-up" occurred when a mutual fund (or its adviser or underwriter) directed an executing broker-dealer to pay a portion of the commission payment to another broker-dealer that was a member of the same exchange as the executing broker-dealer. The give-up often was payment for other services (that may have been unrelated to the trade) provided to the fund (or its adviser or underwriter) by the give-up recipient. This created a conflict of interest between the interest of fund shareholders in paying lower commission charges and the interest of the adviser and underwriter in stimulating the sale of additional fund shares by paying split commissions. The sale of additional fund shares generated additional fees for the adviser but did not necessarily benefit existing fund shareholders.

a. Separation of Execution and Research

Since the mid–1970s, specialization and innovation in the financial industry have resulted in the functional separation of order execution and research. Efficient execution venues provide good, low-cost execution while research providers offer valuable research ideas that can benefit managed accounts. In light of this, some advisers have entered into arrangements (so-called "Section 28(e) arrangements") to execute trades through one broker-dealer and to obtain research and other services from a different broker-dealer. The SEC has indicated its belief that the separation between execution and research is beneficial to advisory clients and that Section 28(e) arrangements that promote the functional allocation of these services are not the same as "give-ups." See Release No. 54165.

Nevertheless, the SEC believes that the statutory term "effecting" requires that, in order for an adviser to use the safe harbor, a broker-dealer that is "effecting" the trade must (a) perform at least one of four minimum functions and (b) take steps to see that the other functions have been reasonably allocated to the other broker-dealers involved in the arrangement in a manner that is fully consistent with their obligations under SRO and SEC rules. The four functions are:

(i) Taking financial responsibility for all customer trades until the clearing broker-dealer has received payment (or securities). This means that one of the broker-dealers in any arrangement must be at risk for the customer's failure to pay;

(ii) Making and/or maintaining records relating to customer trades required by SEC and SRO rules, including blotters and memoranda of orders;

(iii) Monitoring and responding to customer comments concerning the trading process; and

(iv) Generally monitoring trades and settlements.

   b. "Provided by" in the Context of Third–Party Research Arrangements

Section 28(e) requires a broker-dealer receiving commissions for "effecting" transactions to "provide" the brokerage or research services to an adviser. The SEC has interpreted this to allow advisers to use client commissions to pay for research produced by someone other than the executing broker-dealer (so-called "third-party research") in certain circumstances. Third-party research arrangements are not rendered ineligible if the adviser participates in selecting the research services or products that the broker-dealer will provide. In addition, the third-party may send the research directly to the adviser. See Release No. 54165 and

Goldman, Sachs & Co., SEC No–Action Letter, 2007 WL 516135 (avail. Jan. 17, 2007).

According to the SEC, the following attributes help determine whether the broker-dealer effecting transactions for the advised accounts has satisfied the "provided by" element, thus making the Section 28(e) safe harbor available to an adviser:

(i) The broker-dealer pays the research preparer directly;

(ii) The broker-dealer reviews the description of the services to be paid for with client commissions under the safe harbor looking for red flags that indicate the services are not within Section 28(e) and agrees with the adviser to use client commissions only to pay for those items that reasonably fall within the safe harbor; and

(iii) The broker-dealer develops and maintains procedures so that research payments are documented and paid for promptly. Prompt payment is relevant because it ensures that the research and the payment are linked, thereby preserving the statutory language requiring that the broker-dealer that "effects" the transactions for the advised accounts "provides" the research.

§ 35. CLIENT DIRECTED BROKERAGE

Some clients, particularly large institutional investors or qualified plan sponsors acting on behalf of plans, explicitly instruct their investment advisers to use a specific broker to effect securities transactions for them (a process referred to as "directed brokerage"). Directed brokerage arrangements typically involve the use of the client's commission dollars to obtain services that directly and exclusively benefit that client alone. For example, a client may recapture a portion of its commissions in the form of a rebate or use that portion for client-related expenses such as sub-transfer agent fees, consultants' fees or administrative service fees.

In a directed brokerage arrangement, an adviser no longer has a duty of best execution, as the client has directed the adviser to place the client's trades through one or more specified brokers. However, the adviser does have a duty of disclosure. Specifically, an adviser is required to disclose to the client any potentially adverse consequences that may arise due to a directed brokerage arrangement. These consequences may include the impairment of the adviser's ability to obtain best execution for the client and the client's failure to benefit from any volume commission discounts on aggregated orders that the adviser places. See In the Matter of Mark Bailey & Co., Advisers Act Rel. No. 1105, 1988 WL 901756 (Feb. 24, 1988). Additionally, if an adviser has a policy of effecting non-directed trades prior to placing directed trades, the adviser needs to disclose this policy as well.

Directed brokerage arrangements, however, do not implicate the soft dollar safe harbor provided by Exchange Act Section 28(e). This is because those arrangements do not involve the exercise of discretion by the adviser in the selection of the broker. Nor do they result in the provision of any products or services to the adviser. For more on the soft dollar safe harbor, see Nutshell Section 34.

§ 36. ADVISER BENEFITTING FROM BROKERAGE

A. Generally

A conflict of interest arises when an adviser (rather than a client) directs brokerage to a particular broker-dealer to compensate that broker-dealer for referring clients to the adviser. Indeed, the referred clients may not have been referred to an adviser best suited for their needs, but rather simply to one who compensated a broker through adviser directed brokerage. Moreover, existing clients of that adviser may not be aware of the extra expenses that may be incurred as a result of that adviser directing transactions to a preferred broker, as opposed to a broker who is able to offer the most competitive commission rates.

The Cash Solicitation Rule (Advisers Act Rule 206(4)–3) by its own terms only authorizes cash referral fees to brokers and other "solicitors" if specified conditions are met. See Nutshell Section 22B. Because the SEC may question the propriety of non-cash compensation under Advisers Act Section 206, an adviser must fully disclose in its Form ADV any arrangements by which it directly or indirectly compensates any person for client referrals. See Form ADV, Part 1A, Item 8.F.

B.   Investment Company Clients

(1) Adviser Liability

During the late 1990s and early 2000s, certain advisers to registered investment companies entered into "preferred shelf space" arrangements with broker-dealers. Pursuant to these arrangements, an adviser would compensate a broker-dealer for increasing the visibility of the adviser's advised funds within the broker-dealer's distribution system. This compensation often took the form of adviser directed brokerage in violation of Company Act Rule 12b–1(h). An adviser would benefit by the sale of additional shares of its advised funds, as its management fee was based on a percentage of each fund's assets under management. Typically, the adviser would not disclose the arrangement with the shareholders of its advised funds, nor would the broker-dealer make disclosure to its customers.

For example, the SEC alleged that Putnam Investment Management, LLC ("Putnam") entered into preferred marketing arrangements with over 80 broker-dealers whereby the broker-dealers provided services designed to promote the sale of the mutual funds advised by Putnam. More than 60 broker-dealers received directed brokerage commissions from the funds' portfolio transactions. All these arrangements were based primarily upon negotiated formulae relating to gross or net fund sales and/or the retention of fund assets.

The SEC's order found that Putnam willfully violated Advisers Act Section 206(2), because Putnam, as a fiduciary, had a duty to disclose to the board of directors of the Putnam funds any potential conflict of interest created by the use of fund brokerage commissions to satisfy the preferred marketing arrangements with the broker-dealers. In addition, the SEC found that Putnam violated Company Act Section 34(b) which prohibits any person from making materially misleading statements or omissions in an investment company registration statement. In this regard, neither the Putnam funds' prospectuses nor Statements of Additional Information adequately disclosed that Putnam directed fund brokerage commissions to satisfy the negotiated preferred marketing arrangements. Without admitting or denying the findings in the SEC's order, Putnam agreed to pay $40 million in civil penalties to settle the charges. See In the Matter of Putnam Investment Mgt., LLC, Advisers Act Rel. No. 2370, 2005 WL 673295 (Mar. 23, 2005).

(2) Broker–Dealer Liability

With respect to an adviser's investment company clients, NASD rules do allow a fund or its adviser, in allocating brokerage, *to consider* the activities of a broker-dealer in selling shares of the fund. NASD Conduct Rule 2830(k), also known as the Anti–Reciprocal Rule, permits NASD members to execute portfolio transactions for investment companies that follow a policy of considering prior fund sales as a factor when selecting broker-dealers, but prohibits NASD members from conditioning their sale of fund shares on the receipt of fund brokerage.

Under the terms of the Rule, this recognition of fund sales still must be consistent with the adviser's duty to seek best execution for fund portfolio transactions.

Many broker-dealers were targeted for their activities in connection with preferred shelf space arrangements involving adviser directed brokerage. For example, in 2004 the SEC alleged that Edward D. Jones & Co., L.P. ("Edward Jones"), a registered broker-dealer under the Exchange Act, entered into revenue-sharing arrangements with seven mutual fund families, which Edward Jones designated as "Preferred Mutual Fund Families." According to the SEC order, Edward Jones told the public and its clients that it was promoting the sale of the Preferred Families' mutual funds because of the funds' long-term investment objectives and performance. At the same time, Edward Jones failed to disclose that it received tens of millions of dollars from the Preferred Families each year, on top of commissions and other fees, for selling their mutual funds. Edward Jones also failed to disclose that such payments were a material factor in becoming and remaining an Edward Jones Preferred Family member.

The SEC stated that, when customers purchase mutual funds, they must be told about the full nature and extent of any conflict of interest that may affect the transaction. Edward Jones failed to inform investors that it was being paid undisclosed compensation by the fund families whose shares they were pushing. Without admitting or denying the findings in the SEC's order, Edward Jones agreed to pay $75 million in civil penalties to settle the charges. See In the Matter of Edward D. Jones & Co., L.P., Exchange Act Rel. No. 50910, 2004 WL 3177119 (Dec. 22, 2004).

Both the NASD and the NYSE made additional allegations that went beyond those of the SEC in the Edward Jones matter. The NASD found that Edward Jones gave preferential treatment to the funds of three of the Preferred Mutual Fund Families in exchange for millions of dollars in adviser directed brokerage from those Families. The NASD alleged that this violated its "Anti–Reciprocal Rule" which prohibits regulated firms from favoring the distribution of shares of particular mutual funds on the basis of brokerage commissions to be paid by the fund companies. The NYSE found that Edward Jones' conduct was inconsistent with just and equitable principles of trade and failed to adhere to good business practices in violation of NYSE Rules 476 and 401.

On July 30, 2007, FINRA was created through the consolidation of the NASD and the member regulation, enforcement and arbitration operations of the NYSE. Accordingly, readers should be aware that FINRA analogs will likely replace the NASD rule and NYSE rules discussed in this subsection.

§ 37. AFFILIATED BROKERAGE

A conflict of interest arises when an adviser itself executes client transactions (as a Dual Registrant) or through an affiliated broker-dealer. Because the adviser keeps the commission revenue generated through this so-called *"affiliated brokerage,"* it has a strong monetary incentive to engage in it. In addition, the adviser, like any broker-dealer, has a financial incentive to engage in excessive trading on behalf of client accounts (and activity referred to as *"churning"*) to generate additional commission revenue.

An adviser in this situation remains subject to its fiduciary duty under Advisers Act Section 206, including its duty to obtain best execution for any transaction that it or its affiliate executes. It also must disclose to its clients that it or its affiliate will receive commissions for effecting client trades in Part II of its Form ADV. Moreover, if a given affiliated brokerage transaction also constitutes a principal transaction (including a riskless principal transaction), and thus the adviser or its affiliate has a proprietary interest in the transaction itself, the adviser must comply with Advisers Act Section 206(3). See Nutshell Section 31B(1). Similarly, if a given affiliated brokerage transaction also constitutes an agency cross transaction, the adviser must comply with Advisers Act Rule 206(3)–2. See Nutshell Section 31B(2).

Affiliated brokerage transactions that an adviser or its affiliate effects on behalf of registered investment company clients are governed by Company Act Section 17(e)(2). This Section restricts the commission on any such affiliated brokerage transaction to "the usual and customary broker's commission" if the sale is effected on a securities exchange. Company Act Rule 17e–1 establishes guidelines with respect to what is "usual and customary" brokerage commissions. Among other things, that Rule requires a commission to be "reasonable and fair" compared to the commission received by other brokers in connection with comparable transactions involving similar securities being purchased or sold on a securities exchange during a comparable period of time. A mutual fund's board of directors, including a majority of directors who are not "interested persons" (as defined in Company Act Section 2(a)(19)), must adopt procedures reasonably designed to ensure that affiliated brokerage transaction commissions satisfy the "reasonable and fair" standard.

§ 38. TRADING ERRORS

The term "trading error" is used broadly to refer to a variety of errors that can occur in the execution of trades for client accounts. Examples include purchases instead of sales, trades for the wrong accounts, and trades that are executed on terms other than what the adviser intended. The greater the number of clients an adviser has, and the greater the number of transactions the adviser effects on behalf of its clients, the more inevitable trading errors become.

The Advisers Act does not use the terms "error" or "trading error" and does not contain any specific provisions addressing an adviser's responsibility for trading errors. However, the staff of the SEC has stated that an adviser, as a fiduciary, must effect client trades correctly (something also required by an adviser's common law duty of care). The staff also requires an adviser itself to shoulder the cost of correcting trading errors. The adviser should not attempt to correct errors by selling securities to, or purchasing securities from, other client accounts. See In the Matter of M & I Investment Mgt. Corp., Advisers Act Rel. No. 1318, 1992 WL 160038 (June 30, 1992). As discussed in Nutshell Section 34C(2)b, an adviser may not correct trading errors through the use of soft dollars.

§ 39. KEY MAN LIFE INSURANCE

With respect to investment performance, many investment advisers are entirely dependent on several key portfolio managers. As a result of the importance of these key personnel, advisers often obtain key man life insurance on the lives of the key personnel for the benefit of the adviser. This is a standard industry practice for both registered and unregistered advisers. Large investors in private equity and hedge funds often insist that advisers obtain key man insurance as a precondition to their investment.

IX. WRAP FEE PROGRAMS

§ 40. GENERALLY

A wrap fee program is named as such because the services of discretionary portfolio management, trade execution, asset allocation and administrative services are "wrapped" together and provided to the client for a single fee. That fee is based on the amount of assets in the client's wrap fee account. The SEC has defined a wrap fee program slightly more elaborately as an "advising program under which a specified fee or fees not based directly upon transactions in a client's account is charged for investment advisory services (which may include portfolio management or advice concerning the selection of other investment advisers) and the execution of client transactions." See Advisers Act Rule 204–3(g)(4) & Form ADV: Glossary of Terms, definition 35.

Wrap fee programs were first introduced in the early 1990's and have become increasingly popular since then. They have gained in popularity because, similar to mutual funds, wrap fee programs pool the assets of multiple clients. Each of these clients typically is investing an amount of money less than the minimum investment required for an individually managed account but significantly more than the minimum account size of most mutual fund accounts. Through pooling, these clients gain access to the more successful investment advisers who usually cater only to investors with high account minimums. However, unlike mutual funds, wrap fee programs provide individual investment advice directly from the adviser to the client, rather than indirectly through a fund entity.

Wrap fee "sponsors" are subject to the Advisers Act and do not fall within the broker-dealer exclusion. Because wrap fee programs have become increasingly popular in the investment community, the SEC has determined that extra disclosure about them is needed. In addition to preparing and filing Form ADV, wrap fee program sponsors must disclose additional information under Schedule H of that Form. See Advisers Act Rule 204–3(f)(1). "Sponsors," in this regard, are defined to include those who sponsor, organize or administer the program or select, or provide advice to clients regarding the selection of, other investment advisers in the program. See Form ADV: Glossary of Terms, definition 33.

A. Wrap Fees Are Negotiable

Wrap fees are generally based on a percentage of the client's assets under management. This is different from the usual relationship between an investor and a broker where fees are charged based on how often an investor trades. The investor will usually be able to negotiate the percentage charged by the adviser if the investor is willing to invest enough assets. The wrap fee is a novel way of dealing with the inherent conflict of interest that exists in the broker-investor relationship that rewards the broker for buying and selling securities, regardless of the result, rather than for performance. This incentive to produce as many trades as possible from each investor per year is referred to as "churning."

The wrap fee, however, has given rise to another incentive that works against the investor's interests. Instead of having the incentive to churn, advisers have the incentive to execute as few trades as possible in order to do the least amount of work for the set fee which will be earned regardless of how many trades are executed. This process is called "reverse churning."

B. Wrap Fee Program Structures

Wrap fee programs are usually "sponsored" by large brokerage firms. Sponsors are typically responsible for marketing the program to the public and administering the program with respect to those who invest their money in wrap fee accounts.

When the brokerage firm sponsors a wrap fee program, a representative of the brokerage firm will conduct the initial interview with the client and maintain the relationship. The initial interview consists of determining the client's investment objectives and risk tolerance, as well as the selection of a portfolio manager. Because a firm may have thousands of clients, cost-effective management may be difficult. Therefore, the firm will typically pool clients together who have similar investment objectives. The firm will then form a model portfolio for each individual client in the group, entering into new trades for individual clients on a discretionary basis from time to time. These new trades may be executed without the prior permission of the client, as wrap fee accounts are discretionary in nature.

§ 41.   REGISTRATION REQUIREMENTS

A.   Generally

The SEC and most states classify those who advise others on the selection of an investment adviser or receive compensation for referring clients to investment advisers as investment advisers themselves. Therefore, a brokerage firm which acts as a sponsor for a wrap fee program must register as an investment adviser under the Advisers Act.

B.   Broker–Dealer Exclusion Not Available

In a wrap fee program, a brokerage firm usually will receive a fee for services rendered as the sponsor of the program. This will disqualify the brokerage firm from availing itself of the broker-dealer exclusion to the definition of investment adviser found in Advisers Act Section 202(a)(11)(C). See Nutshell Section 3B(3). The exclusion is also unavailable because the very nature of a wrap fee program is the providing of advice which is included in the set wrap fee.

C. Company Act and Securities Act Concerns

Given that a wrap fee program will group similar client accounts together, provide those accounts with the same investment management advice and place the same securities in those accounts, wrap fee programs generally give rise to concerns under both the Company Act and the Securities Act. Indeed, does the operation of a given wrap fee program create an investment company that must be registered under the Company Act? Does the program give rise to a new security that must be registered under the Securities Act before it may be offered to the public?

To address both concerns, the SEC adopted Company Act Rule 3a–4. This rule provides a nonexclusive safe harbor from the definition of "investment company" for certain investment advisory programs, including wrap fee programs. Moreover, its preliminary note states that "[t]here is no registration requirement under Section 5 of the Securities Act of 1933 with respect to programs that are organized and operated in the manner described in Rule 3a–4." Thus, compliance with the Rule eliminates both concerns mentioned above.

The key to Rule 3a–4 compliance is to ensure that each wrap fee client receives *individualized treatment*, including the opportunity to place investment restrictions on the management of his account and the right to receive disclosure documents in connection with securities held in his account. Specifically, the Rule provides for:

· *Individualized management*—each client's account must be managed on the basis of the client's financial situation and investment objectives, and in accordance with any reasonable restrictions imposed by the client on the management of the account;

· *Collection of client information*—the sponsor of the program must obtain sufficient information from each client to be able to provide individualized investment advice to the client;

· *Sponsor and portfolio manager availability*—the sponsor and portfolio manager must be reasonably available to consult with each client;

· *Annual client contact*—the sponsor must at least annually contact each client to determine whether any changes have occurred with respect to the client's financial situation or investment objectives, and whether the client wants to change or impose new investment restrictions on the management of the accounts;

· *Imposition of investment restrictions*—each client must have the ability to impose reasonable restrictions on the management of the client's account;

· *Quarterly notices*—the sponsor must at least quarterly send to each client a written notice instructing the client to contact the sponsor if there have been any changes to the client's financial situation or investment objectives, or if the client wants to change or impose new investment restrictions on the management of the account, and provide a means for contacting the sponsor;

· *Quarterly account statements*—each client must be provided with a quarterly account statement containing a description of all activity in the client's account; and

· *Indicia of securities ownership*—each client must retain certain indicia of ownership of all securities and funds in the account.

While the Rule does not include provisions requiring the adoption of written compliance policies and procedures, the SEC has indicated that sponsors must monitor and demonstrate compliance with the Rule. Accordingly, the SEC has strongly encouraged sponsors to adopt such written policies and procedures. See Status of Investment Advisory Programs under the Investment Company Act of 1940, Advisers Act Rel. No. 1623, 1997 WL 134316 (Mar. 24, 1997).

§ 42. DISCLOSURE REQUIREMENTS

A. Wrap Fee Brochure

Once wrap fee programs became prominent in the industry, the SEC amended Form ADV and Advisers Act Rule 204–3 to require sponsors to provide a separate wrap fee brochure to each client and prospective client of a wrap fee program. A wrap fee brochure must contain at least the information required by Schedule H of Form ADV. An adviser must deliver the wrap fee brochure in lieu of the disclosure brochure (typically Part II of Form ADV) mandated by Advisers Act Rule 204–3(a). See Advisers Act Rule 204–3(f)(1). While an adviser can insert additional information into its wrap fee brochure that goes beyond the information required by Schedule H, that additional information must solely relate to the wrap fee programs that the adviser sponsors. While a wrap fee sponsor need not deliver its standard disclosure brochure, the portfolio manager who actually manages a client's assets must deliver its standard disclosure brochure to the client.

Sponsors of mutual fund asset allocation programs are not required to deliver a wrap fee brochure. Instead, they must deliver their standard disclosure brochure (typically Part II of Form ADV). Additionally, each client will receive the prospectus for each mutual fund into which his assets are placed.

If an investment adviser offers more than one wrap fee program, it may omit from the wrap fee brochure it furnishes to clients and prospective clients of a particular wrap fee program any information required by Schedule H that is not applicable to those clients or prospective clients. See Advisers Act Rule 204–3(f)(2). In addition, an adviser need not furnish a wrap fee brochure to clients and prospective clients of a given wrap fee program if another investment adviser is required to furnish and does furnish a wrap fee brochure to all clients and prospective clients of that program. See Advisers Act Rule 204–3(f)(3).

B. Contents

Unlike certain other parts of Form ADV, which are in the "check-the-box" format, advisers must complete Schedule H in a narrative form. The following is a list of the information that an adviser must include in Schedule H and thus must also include in its wrap fee brochure:

(1) *Fees*—The amount of the wrap fee charged for each program along with a table setting forth the fee schedule.

(2) *Additional charges*—Any fees that the client may pay in addition to the wrap fee and the circumstances under which these fees may be paid.

(3) *Comparability*—The cost of the services if they were provided separately and the factors that bear upon the relative cost of the program (*e.g.,* the amount of trading activity conducted in an account).

(4) *Compensation for recommendation*—If applicable, a statement disclosing that the person recommending the program to the client receives compensation as a result of the client participating in the program.

(5) *Portfolio manager selection/review*—The method for selecting portfolio managers, including the basis for which portfolio managers are recommended or chosen for particular clients, and the circumstances under which the sponsor will replace a portfolio manager.

(6) *Performance data for portfolio manager*—The name of the person who reviews the manager's performance to determine accuracy and the industry standards under which performance may be calculated.

(7) *Client information*—A description of the information about the client that the sponsor relays to the portfolio manager.

(8) *Conflicts of interest*—If any relationship presents a conflict between the interests of the sponsor and those of the client, the sponsor must explain the nature of that conflict.

C. Delivery of the Brochure

The SEC allows advisers to deliver electronic versions of their wrap fee brochures to clients and potential clients so long as the SEC's guidelines for delivery of disclosure documents through electronic media are satisfied. Nevertheless, many advisers still deliver paper copies, despite the added expense, because many of their customers feel more comfortable with a concrete document in their hands, rather than reading the document from a computer screen.

D. Updating

Once any information in a wrap fee brochure becomes materially inaccurate, the sponsor must file an amendment to the brochure as quickly as possible. Many sponsors satisfy this requirement by simply "stickering" their existing wrap fee brochure. A sticker is a supplement attached to the existing wrap fee brochure indicating what information is being added or what existing information is being amended. When the wrap fee brochure is ultimately revised, information contained in the sticker should be incorporated into the brochure itself.

X. PROPRIETARY AND INSIDER TRADING

§ 43. GENERALLY

The U.S. Supreme Court in *SEC v. Capital Gains Research Bureau, Inc.*, 375 U.S. 180 (1963), held that Advisers Act Section 206 imposes fiduciary duties on investment advisers by operation of law. Given their position within the financial services industry, many advisers and their personnel are in a position to exploit their informational advantage to the benefit of themselves and to the detriment of their clients. Such acts of exploitation could constitute a breach of their fiduciary duties and potentially violate Federal insider trading prohibitions (most notably Exchange Act Section 10(b) and Exchange Act Rule 10b–5). In fact, the conflict addressed by the Supreme Court in *Capital Gains* was the potential ability of an adviser and its personnel to engage in "scalping" or "front running," *i.e.*, exploiting their knowledge of impending client recommendations to their own benefit and thus to the detriment of their clients. See Nutshell Section 28A.

Advisers Act Section 204A specifically addresses the prevention of insider trading by advisers who are subject to the recordkeeping requirements of the Advisers Act (*i.e.*, Advisers Act Section 204 and the rules promulgated thereunder). It imposes on each such adviser an affirmative obligation to adopt written policies and procedures reasonably designed, taking into consideration the nature of the adviser's business, to prevent the misuse of material, nonpublic information by the adviser or "any person associated with such investment adviser." The term "person associated with an investment adviser" means any partner, officer or director of such adviser (or any person performing similar functions), or any person directly or indirectly controlling or controlled by such adviser, including any employee of such adviser. See Advisers Act Section 202(a)(17). Section 204A also authorizes the SEC to promulgate rules and regulations to require specific policies or procedures reasonably designed to prevent insider trading. In this regard, the SEC has promulgated Advisers Act Rule 204A–1, which, among other things, requires an investment adviser to adopt a code of ethics.

§ 44.   CODE OF ETHICS

A.   Generally

Advisers and their employees are dissuaded from breaching their fiduciary duties through personal trading activities or from engaging in insider trading by Advisers Act Rule 204A–1 (the "Ethics Code Rule"). The Ethics Code Rule requires an investment adviser which is registered or required to be registered under Advisers Act Section 203 to establish, maintain and enforce a written code of ethics. According to subparagraph (a) of the Ethics Code Rule, an adviser's written code of ethics must include, at a minimum, the following five things:

(1) *Standards of business conduct*—A standard (or standards) of business conduct that the adviser requires of its "supervised persons," which standard must reflect the adviser's fiduciary obligations and those of the adviser's supervised persons;

(2) *Compliance with applicable Federal securities laws*—Provisions requiring supervised persons to comply with all applicable Federal securities laws, including the Exchange Act, SOX, the Company Act, the Advisers Act, Title V of the GLBA, the Bank Secrecy Act (as it applies to investment companies and investment advisers), and any rules adopted thereunder by the SEC or the Department of the Treasury;

(3) *Securities transactions reports*—Provisions that require all the adviser's "access persons" to report, and for the adviser to review, their personal securities transactions and holdings periodically;

(4) *Self-reporting of violations*—Provisions requiring supervised persons to report any violations of the adviser's code of ethics promptly to the adviser's chief compliance officer or, provided the adviser's chief compliance officer also receives reports of all violations, to other persons the adviser designates in its code of ethics. An adviser must keep a record of any violation of its code of

ethics and any action taken as a result of the violation. See Advisers Act Rule 204–2(a)(12)(i) & (ii) and Nutshell Section 46F; and

(5) *Provision of code and receipt acknowledgment*—Provisions requiring the adviser to provide each of its supervised persons with a copy of its code of ethics and any amendments thereto, and requiring each supervised person to provide the adviser with a written acknowledgment of her receipt of the code and any amendments.

The distinction between an adviser's "supervised persons" and its "access persons" is discussed below in Nutshell Section 44B. Personal security transactions reporting is discussed in Nutshell Section 44C.

A sample adviser's code of ethics may be found at *www.nyls.edu/jhaas*.

B. Distinction Between a "Supervised Person" and an "Access Person"

The Ethics Code Rule imposes minimum requirements on an adviser's code of ethics. These requirements mostly apply to an adviser's "supervised persons," while on one occasion they apply to an adviser's "access persons." Accordingly, it is important to understand the distinction between the two terms.

Advisers Act Rule 204A–1(a)(1), (2), (4) and (5) require an adviser's code of ethics to contain standards or provisions applicable to an adviser's "supervised persons." The term "supervised person" means any partner, officer, director (or other person occupying a similar status or performing similar functions), or employee of an investment adviser, or other person who provides investment advice on behalf of the investment adviser and is subject to the supervision and control of the investment adviser. See Advisers Act Section 202(a)(25).

By contrast, only Advisers Act Rule 204A–1(a)(3) relating to personal securities transactions and holdings applies to "access persons." "Access persons" is a *subset* of "supervised persons," with "access" essentially referring to access to nonpublic information about client trading activities or client recommendations. Specifically, Advisers Act Rule 204A–1(e)(1) defines an "access person" as any *supervised person* of an investment adviser who either:

(A) Has access to nonpublic information regarding any clients' "purchase or sale of securities," or nonpublic information regarding the portfolio holdings of any "reportable fund"; or

(B) Is involved in making securities recommendations to clients, or who has access to such recommendations that are nonpublic.

If the primary business of an investment adviser is providing investment advice, all of that adviser's directors, officers and partners are presumed to be access persons. See Advisers Act Rule 204A–1(e)(1)(ii). An adviser must keep a record of the names of persons who are currently, or were within the past five years, access persons of the adviser.

See Advisers Act Rule 204–2(a)(13)(ii) and Nutshell Section 46F.

For purposes of the definition of "access person," the term "reportable fund" means any registered investment company for which an adviser serves as an "investment adviser" (as defined in Company Act Section 2(a)(20)). The term also includes any registered investment company whose investment adviser or principal underwriter is an affiliate of the adviser in question (*i.e.*, controls, is controlled by, or is under common control with that adviser). See Advisers Act Rule 204A–1(e)(5) & (9). The phrase "purchase or sale of a security" not only includes the purchase or sale of a particular security in the traditional sense, but it also includes the writing of an option to purchase or sell that security. See Advisers Act Rule 204A–1(e)(8).

C. Reporting Requirements Under the Ethics Code Rule

One way access persons are dissuaded from breaching their fiduciary duties through personal trading activities or from engaging in insider trading is by virtue of the extensive recordkeeping requirements imposed upon them. Specifically, the Ethics Code Rule requires access persons to submit two types of reports to the adviser's chief compliance officer or other persons designated in the adviser's code of ethics: holdings reports and transaction reports. Each type of report is discussed below.

(1) Holdings Reports

An adviser's code of ethics must require each access person to submit to the adviser's chief compliance officer or other persons designated in the adviser's code a report of that access person's current securities holdings. See Advisers Act Rule 204A–1(b)(1). The contents of each holdings report must contain, at a minimum, three pieces of vital information as specified in Advisers Act Rule 204A–1(b)(1)(i)(A)-(C).

First, a holdings report must set forth the following (to the extent applicable) for each "reportable security" in which an access person has any direct or indirect "beneficial ownership": the title and type of security; exchange ticker symbol or CUSIP number for the security; number of shares; and principal amount. The term "reportable security" has the same meaning as the term "security" as such is defined in Advisers Act 202(a)(18), except it excludes certain non-manipulable securities including direct U.S. government obligations, commercial paper and shares of money market funds. See Advisers Act Rule 204A–1(e)(10). The term "beneficial ownership" has the same meaning as the same defined term has in Exchange Act Rule 16a–1(2)(a). An access person may state in her holdings report that the report should not be construed as an admission that she has any direct or indirect beneficial ownership in one or more of the securities included in that report. See Advisers Act Rule 204A–1(e)(3).

Second, a holdings report must include the name of any broker, dealer or bank with which the access person maintained an account in which any securities are held for her direct or indirect benefit.

Lastly, a holdings report must include the date the access person submits the report.

An access person must submit both initial and annual holdings reports, subject to two exceptions described below. An access person must submit her initial holdings report no later than 10 days after she becomes an access person, and the information must be current as of a date no more than 45 days prior to the date she becomes an access person. Thereafter, she must submit an annual report at least once each 12–month period on a date she selects, and the information must be current as of a date no more than 45 days prior to the date the report is submitted. See Advisers Act Rule 204A–1(b)(1)(ii). An adviser must keep a record of each holdings report that an access person submits. See Advisers Act Rule 204–2(a)(13)(i) and Nutshell Section 46F.

Importantly, a holdings report need not be filed in two specified instances. First, a holdings report need not be filed with respect to securities held in accounts over which the access person had no direct or indirect influence or control. Second, a holdings report need not be filed by an adviser with only one access person (*i.e.*, the adviser herself), so long as the adviser maintains records of all of her holdings that the Ethics Code Rule would otherwise require her to report. See Advisers Act Rule 204A–1(b)(3)(i) & (d).

(2) **Transaction Reports**

An adviser's code of ethics must require each access person to submit to the adviser's chief compliance officer or other persons designated in the adviser's code a quarterly securities transaction report. See Advisers Act Rule 204A–1(b)(2). The contents of each transaction report must contain, at a minimum, the following five pieces of information specified in Advisers Act Rule 204A–1(b)(2)(i)(A)-(E):

(A) To the extent applicable for each "reportable security" involved, the date of the transaction, title, exchange ticker symbol or CUSIP number, interest rate and maturity date, number of shares and principal amount;

(B) The nature of the transaction (*i.e.*, purchase, sale or any other type of acquisition or disposition);

(C) The price of the security at which the transaction was effected;

(D) The name of the broker, dealer or bank with or through which the transaction was effected; and

(E) The date the access person submits the report.

An adviser must keep a record of each transaction report that an access person submits. See Advisers Act Rule 204–2(a)(13)(i) and Nutshell Section 46F.

Each access person must submit a transaction report no later than 30 days after the end of each calendar quarter. Each report must cover, at a minimum, all transactions occurring during the quarter. See Advisers Act Rule 204A–1(b)(2)(ii).

Importantly, a transaction report need not be filed in four specified instances. First, a transaction report need not be filed with respect to securities held in accounts over which the access person has no direct or indirect influence or control. Second, a transaction report need not be filed with respect to transactions effected pursuant to an automatic investment plan. Third, a transaction report need not be filed if it would duplicate information contained in broker trade confirmations or account statements that the adviser holds in its records, so long as the adviser receives the confirmations or statements no later than 30 days after the end of the applicable calendar quarter. Lastly, a transaction report need not be filed by an adviser with only one access person (*i.e.*, the adviser herself), so long as the adviser maintains records of all of her transactions that the Ethics Code Rule would otherwise require her to report. See Advisers Act Rule 204A–1(b)(3) & (d).

D.   Pre–Approval of Certain Investments

Another way access persons are dissuaded from breaching their fiduciary duties through personal trading activities or from engaging in insider trading is by requiring advisers to pre-approve certain investments made by them. Specifically, an adviser's code of ethics must require each access person to obtain the adviser's approval before he directly or indirectly acquires beneficial ownership in any security in an "initial public offering" or a "limited offering." See Advisers Act Rule 204A–1(c). An "initial public offering" or "IPO" is an offering of securities registered under the Securities Act, the issuer of which, immediately before the registration, was not subject to the reporting requirements of the Exchange Act. A "limited offering" means an offering of securities that is exempt from registration under the Securities Act by virtue of Securities Act Sections 4(2) (the "private placement" transactional exemption) or 4(6) or pursuant to Rule 504, 505 or 506 of Securities Act Regulation D. See Advisers Act Rule 204A–1(e)(6) & (7).

This pre-approval requirement allows an adviser the opportunity to evaluate potential conflicts of interest between an access person and the adviser's clients. For example, in the context of an IPO, an adviser can evaluate whether an access person is seizing an investment opportunity that should be presented first to an eligible client. The access person also may have received the investment opportunity as a *quid pro quo* for directing brokerage to a particular broker-dealer. In any event, an adviser must keep a record of any decision, and the reasons supporting the decision, to approve an access person's acquisition of securities issued in an IPO or limited offering for at least five years after the end of the fiscal year in which the approval is granted.

See Advisers Act Rule 204–2(a)(13)(iii) and Nutshell Section 46F.

E.   Analogous Rules for Advisers With Mutual Fund Clients

Investment advisers to registered investment companies (*e.g.,* mutual funds) must adhere to Company Act Section 17(j) and Rule 17j–1 promulgated thereunder. Section 17(j) makes it unlawful for an investment adviser and other enumerated persons to "engage in any act, practice, or course of business in connection with the purchase or sale, directly or indirectly, by such person of any security held or to be acquired" by a registered investment company advisee in contravention of SEC rules and regulations. The SEC promulgated Company Act Rule 17j–1 to flesh out this restriction.

Rule 17j–1 makes it illegal for a mutual fund's investment adviser and most of the adviser's personnel to defraud the fund in any way through the purchase or sale, directly or indirectly, by the adviser or such personnel of any security which, within the most recent 15 days, is or has been held by the fund or is being or has been considered by the fund or the adviser for purchase by the fund. See Company Act Rule 17j–1(b). In addition, every fund must adopt a code of ethics containing provisions reasonably necessary to prevent such fraudulent activity, and each access person of a fund must submit initial and annual securities holdings reports and quarterly securities transaction reports. See Company Act Rule 17j–1(c)-(f). The requirements relating to a fund's code of ethics, as well as those relating to the reporting requirements of access persons, are substantially similar to those relating to an adviser and its access persons discussed previously in this Nutshell Section 44.

XI. RECORDKEEPING REQUIREMENTS

§ 45. ADVISERS ACT SECTION 204

Advisers Act Section 204 provides the primary basis for the recordkeeping obligations of advisers. It requires advisers to make and maintain for prescribed periods all records that the SEC may require by rule as necessary or appropriate in the public interest or for the protection of investors. It also grants the SEC the authority to examine the records maintained by advisers on a reasonable periodic or special basis.

Pursuant to the authority granted to it, the SEC has promulgated Advisers Act Rule 204–2 (the "Recordkeeping Rule"). This Rule sets forth the books and records that an investment adviser must maintain. It also serves as the primary basis for the SEC's inspection program. Other securities and non-securities laws and regulations may also require advisers to keep other books and records beyond those specified in the Recordkeeping Rule.

§ 46. REQUIRED BOOKS AND RECORDS

The Recordkeeping Rule lists all the books and records which an adviser that is registered or re-

quired to be registered under Advisers Act Section
203 must keep. These books and records can be
broken down into the following nine categories:

(A) Adviser formation, governance and ownership
documents;

(B) Accounting and related records;

(C) Client relationship records;

(D) Marketing and performance information;

(E) Solicitor records (if applicable);

(F) Code of ethics and personal and proprietary
trading information;

(G) Portfolio management and trading records;

(H) Custody records (if applicable); and

(I) Proxy related records (if applicable).

Each of these categories is discussed in the subsections below.

According to the Recordkeeping Rule, an adviser
must arrange and index the records in a way that
permits the easy location, access and retrieval of
any particular record. An adviser also must separately store, for the time period required for preservation of the original record as specified in the
Recordkeeping Rule, a duplicate copy of the record
on any medium allowed under the Rule. Finally, an
adviser must promptly provide any of the following
that the SEC (through its examiners or other representatives) may request:

(i) A legible, true and complete copy of any record in the medium and format in which it is stored;

(ii) An eligible, true and complete printout of the record; and

(iii) Means to access, view and print the record.

See Advisers Act Rule 204–2(g)(2)(ii)(A)-(C).

A. Adviser Formation, Governance and Ownership Documents

An investment adviser must retain its formation, governance and ownership documents. Each such record must be maintained in the principal office of the investment adviser and preserved until at least three years after termination of the adviser's business. These documents include, depending on the type of entity involved:

- Partnership articles and any amendments thereto;
- Certificate or articles of incorporation or corporate charter and any amendments thereto;
- Minute books or other records documenting governance actions; and
- Stock certificate books of, or similar evidences of ownership in, the investment adviser and, if applicable, any predecessor.

See Advisers Act Rule 204–2(e)(2).

B. Accounting and Related Records

An investment adviser must retain its accounting and related records. Each such record must be maintained for at least five years from the end of the fiscal year during which the last entry was made on such record. Accounting and related records must be maintained in an appropriate office of the adviser during the first two years and in an easily accessible place thereafter. See Advisers Act Rule 204–2(e)(1). These records include:

· All journals, including cash receipts and disbursements records, and any other records of original entry forming the basis of entries in any ledger;

· All general and auxiliary ledgers (or other comparable records) reflecting asset, liability, reserves, capital, income and expense accounts;

· All check books, bank statements, canceled checks and cash reconciliations of the adviser;

· All bills or statements (or copies thereof), paid or unpaid, relating to the business of the adviser; and

· All trial balances, financial statements and internal audit working papers relating to the business of the adviser.

See Advisers Act Rule 204–2(a)(1), (2) & (4)-(6).

C. Client Relationship Records

An investment adviser must maintain virtually all communications between the adviser and its clients. A record of each communication must be maintained for at least five years from the end of the fiscal year during which the communication occurred or, in the case of a written agreement, five years after its termination. Each record must be maintained in an appropriate office of the adviser during the first two years and in an easily accessible place thereafter. See Advisers Act Rule 204–2(e)(1). These records include:

- · All written advisory contracts (or copies thereof) entered into by the adviser with any clients or otherwise relating to the business of the adviser. Thus, not only would client contracts be covered, but so too would employment agreements, lease agreements and agreements with service providers;

- · A list or other record of all accounts in which the adviser is vested with any discretionary power with respect to the funds, securities or transactions of any client;

- · All powers of attorney and other evidences of the granting of any discretionary authority by any client to the adviser, or copies thereof;

- · Originals of all written communications received and copies of all written communications sent by the adviser relating to:

  (i) any recommendation made or proposed to be made and any advice given or proposed to be given;

  (ii) any receipt, disbursement or delivery of funds or securities; or

  (iii) the placing or execution of any order to purchase or sell any security.

Excluded from the foregoing are:

(a) any unsolicited market letters and other similar communications of general public distribution not prepared by or for the adviser; and

(b) a record of the names and addresses of the persons to whom any notice, circular or other advertisement offering any report, analysis, publication or other investment advisory service, so long as the communication was sent to more than 10 persons (except that if the communication was distributed to persons named in any list, the adviser must retain a copy of the communication and a memorandum describing the list and its source).

· Copies of Part II of the adviser's Form ADV, or any brochure prepared in lieu thereof (*e.g.,* a wrap fee brochure), and any amendment or revision thereto, given or sent to any client or prospective client in accordance with the provisions of Advisers Act Rule 204–3, and the record of the dates that each such written statement, and each such amendment or revision thereof, was given, or offered to be given, to any client or prospective client who subsequently becomes a client.

See Advisers Act Rule 204–2(a)(7)-(10) & (14).

D. Marketing and Performance Information

An investment adviser must retain its marketing, performance information and related records. Rec-

ords relating to marketing materials and performance information used in marketing materials must
be maintained for at least five years from the end of
the fiscal year during which the marketing materials were last used. Each record must be maintained
in an appropriate office of the adviser during the
first two years and in an easily accessible place
thereafter. See Advisers Act Rule 204–2(e)(3)(i).
These records include:

· A copy of each notice, circular, advertisement,
  newspaper article, investment letter, bulletin or
  other communication the adviser circulates or
  distributes, directly or indirectly, to 10 or more
  persons (other than persons connected with the
  adviser);

· A memorandum of the adviser indicating the
  reasons for any recommendation to purchase or
  sell a specific security contained in any communication mentioned in the proceeding bullet
  point if such communication itself does not state
  the reasons for the recommendation;

· If the adviser includes performance information
  in any communication mentioned in the first
  bullet point, all accounts, books, internal working papers and any other records or documents
  that are necessary to form the basis for or
  demonstrate the calculation of the performance
  or rate of return of any or all managed accounts
  or securities recommendations. With respect to
  managed accounts, the retention of all account
  statements, if they reflect all debits, credits and

other transactions in a client's account for the period of the statement, and all worksheets necessary to demonstrate the calculation of the performance or rate of return of those accounts, is sufficient.

See Advisers Act Rule 204–2(a)(11) & (16).

E. Solicitor Records

Although an adviser may use solicitors to solicit prospective clients, it must follow Advisers Act Rule 206(4)–3 if it makes cash payments to solicitors. See Nutshell Section 22B. Records relating to any cash solicitation arrangement must be maintained for at least five years after the client relationship relating to that arrangement terminates. Each record must be maintained in an appropriate office of the adviser during the first two years and in an easily accessible place thereafter. See Advisers Act Rule 204–2(e)(1). These records include:

· A copy of each written solicitation agreement with the solicitor;

· A copy of any written disclosure document, if any, used by a solicitor pursuant to Advisers Act Rule 206(4)–3; and

· All written acknowledgments of receipt obtained from clients with respect to their receipt of the adviser's brochure as required by Advisers Act Rule 204–3 and, if applicable, the solicitor's written disclosure document as required by Advisers Act Rule 206(4)–3.

See Advisers Act Rules 204–2(a)(10) & (15) and 206(4)–3(a)(1) (note thereto).

F. Code of Ethics and Personal and Proprietary Trading Information

Investment advisers and their employees are dissuaded from breaching their fiduciary duties through personal trading activities and from violating the Federal securities laws by engaging in insider trading by virtue of Advisers Act Rule 204A–1 (the "Ethics Code Rule"). The Ethics Code Rule requires advisers that are registered or required to be registered under Advisers Act Section 203 to establish, maintain and enforce a written code of ethics.

Code of ethics-related records that an adviser must maintain include the following:

· A copy of the adviser's code of ethics that is currently in effect and copies of any previous codes that were in effect within the past five years;

· A record of any violation of the adviser's code of ethics and of any action taken as a result of the violation, which record must be maintained at least five years following the date of the violation in an easily accessible place, the first two years in an appropriate office of the adviser;

· A record of all written acknowledgments of receipt of the adviser's code of ethics and any amendments thereto from each person who is currently, or within the past five years was, a "supervised person" of the investment adviser;

· A record of the holdings reports and transaction reports made by each "access person" of the adviser, including any information in lieu of such reports as allowed in the Ethics Code Rule, which record must be maintained at least five years following the date of the report in question in an easily accessible place, the first two years in an appropriate office of the adviser;

· A record of the names of persons who are currently, or within the past five years were, access persons of the adviser; and

· A record of any decision, and the reasons supporting the decision, by the adviser to approve the acquisition of securities in an initial public offering or limited offering by access persons as provided in the Ethics Code Rule for at least five years after the end of the fiscal year in which the approval was granted.

See Advisers Act Rules 204–2(a)(12) & (13) and (e)(1).

For a general discussion of the Ethics Code Rule, as well as the distinction between "supervised persons" and "access persons," see Nutshell Section 44.

G. Portfolio Management and Trading Records

An investment adviser must maintain a wide variety of records relating to its portfolio management and trading activity. These records must be maintained for at least five years from the end of the fiscal year during which the underlying transactions occurred. Each record must be maintained in an appropriate office of the adviser during the first two years and in an easily accessible place thereafter. See Advisers Act Rule 204–2(e)(1). These records include:

· A memorandum of each order given by the adviser for the purchase or sale of any security, of any instruction received by the adviser from the client concerning the purchase, sale, receipt or delivery of a particular security, and of any modification or cancellation of any such order or instruction. The required memoranda must:

(i) show the terms and conditions of the order, instruction, modification or cancellation;

(ii) identify the person connected with the adviser who recommended a transaction to the client and the person who placed the order;

(iii) show the account for which the order was entered, the date of entry, and the bank, broker or dealer by or through whom the transaction was executed where appropriate; and

(iv) include a designation, where appropriate, that the order was entered pursuant to the exercise of discretionary power;

· For each client who receives "investment super-visory or management service" (*i.e.*, an adviser's provision of continuous advice regarding the investment of funds based on the individual needs of each client (see Advisers Act Section 202(a)(13))):

 (i) a separate record showing the securities purchased and sold, and the date, amount and price of each such purchase and sale; and

 (ii) information from which the adviser can promptly furnish the name of each client who has a current position in a security, and the current amount or interest of such client;

· Research reports and other materials received from any source if used in the process of making recommendations (excluding unsolicited market letters and other similar communications of general public distribution not prepared by or for the adviser);

· Copies of all written agreements entered into concerning soft dollar arrangements (for more on these arrangements, see Nutshell Section 34); and

· An "allocation statement" for each aggregated order that the adviser places that specifies the client accounts participating in the order and indicating how the adviser intends to allocate securities among those clients. If the adviser deviates from that statement, it must provide a written statement explaining the deviation. For more on the aggregation of client orders, see Nutshell Section 33B.

See Advisers Act Rules 204–2(a)(3), (7) & (10) and (c)(1).

H. Custody Records

An investment adviser who has custody or possession of client funds or securities must maintain certain additional records. "Custody" means holding, directly or indirectly, client funds or securities, or having any authority to obtain custody of them. See Advisers Act Rule 206(4)–2(c)(1) and Nutshell Section 28D. Custody records must be maintained for at least five years from the end of the fiscal year during which the underlying transactions occurred. Each record must be maintained in an appropriate office of the adviser during the first two years and in an easily accessible place thereafter. See Advisers Act Rule 204–2(e)(1). These records include:

· A journal or other record showing all purchases, sales, receipts and deliveries of securities (including certificate numbers) for all custody accounts and all other debits and credits to such accounts;

· A separate ledger account for each custody client showing all purchases, sales, receipts and deliveries of securities, the date and price of each such purchase and sale, and all debits and credits;

· Copies of confirmations of all transactions effected by or for the account of any custody client; and

· A record for each security in which any custody client has a position, which record shall show the name of each such client having any interest in such security, the amount or interest of each such client, and the location of each such security.

See Advisers Act Rule 204–2(b)(1)-(4).

I. Proxy Related Records

An investment adviser who exercises voting authority with respect to client securities must maintain certain additional records with respect to those clients. Proxy voting generally is covered by Advisers Act Rule 206(4)–6 (the "Proxy Voting Rule"). See Nutshell Section 28E. Proxy related records must be maintained for at least five years from the end of the fiscal year during which the record was created. Each record must be maintained in an appropriate office of the adviser during the first two years and in an easily accessible place thereafter. See Advisers Act Rule 204–2(e)(1). These records include:

· Copies of all internal policies and procedures required by the Proxy Voting Rule;

· A copy of each proxy statement that the adviser receives regarding client securities. An adviser may rely on a third party or the SEC's EDGAR system to satisfy this requirement;

· A record of each vote cast by the adviser on behalf of a client. An adviser may rely on a third party to satisfy this requirement;

· A copy of any document created by the adviser that was material to making a decision on how to vote proxies on behalf of a client or that memorializes the basis for that decision; and

· A copy of each written client request for information on how the adviser voted proxies on behalf of a client, and a copy of any written response by the investment adviser to any client request (whether written or oral) for information on how the adviser voted proxies on behalf of the requesting client.

See Advisers Act Rule 204–2(c)(2)(i)-(v).

§ 47. MEANS OF STORAGE

The records that the Recordkeeping Rule requires investment advisers to maintain are voluminous. The SEC, however, allows these records to be maintained and preserved for the requisite time periods in paper format, micrographic media (including microfilm, microfiche or any similar medium) or electronic storage media. See Advisers Act Rule 204–2(g)(1).

If an investment adviser utilizes electronic storage media, it must establish and maintain a number of procedures. These include procedures to:

(i) maintain and preserve the records, so as to reasonably safeguard them from loss, alteration or destruction;

(ii) limit access to the records to properly authorized SEC personnel (including its examiners and other representatives); and

(iii) reasonably ensure that any reproduction of a non-electronic original record on electronic storage media is complete, true and legible when retrieved.

See Advisers Act Rule 204–2(g)(3).

§ 48. FOREIGN ADVISERS

Non-resident SEC-registered investment advisers are subject to the same recordkeeping requirements as domestic advisers. However, to satisfy their recordkeeping requirements, non-resident advisers have two options: (1) they may notify the SEC in writing of the location in the United States where a copy of the requisite books and records will be maintained; or (2) they may maintain the books and records wherever they choose, but they must agree to furnish the SEC at their expense with all required books and records that the SEC demands within 14 days of any demand. See Advisers Act Rule 204–2(j)(1) & (3).

Under Advisers Act Rule 0–2(b)(2), a "non-resident" adviser includes:

(i) An individual who resides in any place not subject to the jurisdiction of the U.S.;

(ii) A corporation that is incorporated in or that has its principal office and place of business in any place not subject to the jurisdiction of the U.S.; and

(iii) A partnership or other unincorporated organization or association that has its principal office and place of business in any place not subject to the jurisdiction of the U.S.

XII. CHIEF COMPLIANCE OFFICERS (CCOs) AND ISSUES RELATING TO THEM

§ 49. NECESSITY OF A CHIEF COMPLIANCE OFFICER

Advisers Act Rule 206(4)–7(c) requires an adviser who is registered or required to be registered under Advisers Act Section 203 to designate a chief compliance officer ("CCO") to administer its compliance policies and procedures. The Rule does not require an adviser to hire an additional employee to serve as CCO, as the prospect of this had been the source of complaint when the SEC was considering making a CCO mandatory. Instead, an adviser may simply give the title and responsibility to an existing employee who qualifies as a "supervised person" under Advisers Act Section 202(a)(25).

The SEC provides some resources to help CCOs perform their obligations more effectively. The SEC's CCOutreach program, sponsored jointly by the Office of Compliance Inspections and Examinations and the Division of Investment Management, is designed to enable the SEC and its staff to better communicate and coordinate with mutual fund and investment adviser CCOs. The program provides a forum to discuss compliance issues in a practical way, to share experiences, and to learn about effective compliance practices. The program features a number of elements, including regional seminars at various locations across the country and an annual national seminar in Washington, D.C.

In addition, the staff of the SEC publishes *ComplianceAlert*, an online newsletter. Designed to assist CCOs of SEC-registered investment advisers, investment companies, broker-dealers and transfer agents with their compliance functions, *ComplianceAlert* is only available on the SEC's website, *www.sec.gov*. It helps CCOs learn more about common deficiencies and weaknesses that SEC staff examiners have found during recent examinations of SEC-registered entities, thus enabling them to proactively fine tune their compliance programs.

§ 50. ROLE OF THE CHIEF COMPLIANCE OFFICER

According to the SEC, a CCO is responsible for administering an adviser's written policies and procedures designed to prevent violation, by the adviser and its "supervised persons," of the Advisers Act and the Advisers Act Rules. See Advisers Act Rule 206(4)-(7)(a) & (b). Needless to say, a CCO should be competent and knowledgeable regarding the Advisers Act and empowered with full responsibility and authority to develop and enforce appropriate policies and procedures for the firm.

A typical CCO will be responsible for ensuring that he or she (1) builds compliance consciousness into daily operations, (2) monitors the effectiveness of compliance activities and (3) communicates instances of non-compliance to appropriate administrators for corrective action. In addition, a CCO will usually be responsible for compiling quarterly compliance reports and performing departmental inspections. Thus, the compliance officer should have a position of sufficient seniority and authority within the organization to compel others to adhere to the compliance policies and procedures.

The SEC has noted that having the title of CCO does not, in and of itself, carry supervisory responsibilities. Thus, the SEC would not necessarily sanction a CCO for failure to supervise other investment advisory personnel. However, a CCO who does have supervisory responsibilities could be sanctioned, subject to the defense set forth in Advisers Act Section 203(e)(6). That Section provides that a person shall not be deemed to have failed to reasonably supervise another person if:

(i) the adviser had adopted procedures reasonably designed to prevent and detect violations of the Federal securities laws;

(ii) the adviser had a system in place for applying those procedures; and

(iii) the supervising person had reasonably discharged his supervisory responsibilities in accordance with those procedures and had no reason to believe the supervised person was not complying with those procedures.

A. On-going CCO Responsibilities

The on-going responsibilities of a CCO are numerous. The following is a discussion of the most significant of these.

Registration and disclosure—At the outset, the CCO should ensure that all registration requirements mandated by the SEC have been fulfilled. In addition, Advisers Act Rule 204–3 requires that Part II of an adviser's Form ADV, or a comparable brochure, be offered to prospective clients for advisory services, and to existing clients on an annual basis.

Best execution/Soft dollar relationships—The CCO should review the reports used to monitor the commissions paid and soft dollar credits generated. Specifically, soft dollar policies, decision-making controls, safe harbor compliance, and soft dollar invoices and contracts should be reviewed.

Client directed brokerage—When a client instructs the adviser to direct brokerage transactions to a particular broker-dealer, the CCO should ensure that the adviser retains written documentation of those instructions in the client's file. When a client seems to have chosen a less than reputable broker-dealer whose quality of services is suspect, the CCO should make sure that the adviser informs the client of the substandard quality and gives the client a more sound recommendation.

Proxy voting—The CCO should ensure that proxy voting policies are carried out in a satisfactory manner and without a conflict of interest. Proxy voting records should be easily obtainable by any client who wishes to know how the adviser voted proxies on her behalf.

Privacy—The adviser should have and the CCO should ensure that there are procedures in place that will secure the confidentiality of clients' non-public personal information. Procedures should also be in place to inform clients about the adviser's privacy policy and material changes to that policy.

Trading procedures—The CCO should ensure that fair allocation of trades among clients occurs by reviewing trade activities and trade tickets. Also, the CCO should ensure that no conflict of interest is present because, as a fiduciary, the adviser must place the client's interest ahead of its own.

Advisory/Solicitor agreements—The CCO should ensure that procedures exist for the maintenance and continuing review of the contracts governing all advisory accounts. Description of services to be performed under the contract, fees to be charged and conflict of interest disclosure are some specific areas of the advisory contract that should be reviewed on a periodic basis. The same type of procedures should be in place with respect to solicitor agreements.

Electronic communications—The CCO should ensure that employees are made aware of the adviser's written communication policies governing electronic communications such as e-mails or instant messaging, whether it be random sampling or document retention for a number of years.

Business recovery—The CCO should ensure that the adviser has policies and procedures in place to maintain compliance in the event of a disaster. Contact information for key personnel responsible for maintenance of the system should be readily accessible. There should also be a process for the backup of critical data and operations systems along with a list of where operations could be continued. The CCO should concern himself or herself with potential scenarios that the adviser may face and continuously update the recovery plan accordingly.

Complaints—Policies and procedures should be in place to accurately record and properly respond to customer complaints. In this regard, an adviser must keep written copies of the complaints on hand for easy access by regulators. In addition, the adviser should retain all internal discussions and communications about the substance of any complaint.

Code of ethics/Insider trading—The adviser should have policies and procedures in place to monitor and identify employee compliance with its code of ethics. The adviser should have strict procedures in place for review of personal trading practices to ensure propriety. This requires employees to make personal trading and holdings reports. Any sanctions or actions taken against an employee during the period should be properly documented.

Books and records—Under Advisers Act Rule 204–2, procedures must be in place for the preservation of a multitude of adviser records for a specified period of time, in a specified place and in a satisfactory manner. These records may be used by the SEC and other regulatory bodies in determining whether any compliance or other violation has occurred.

Regulatory examinations—After a regulatory examination, the adviser should discuss any pending regulatory responses with the CCO. Any future policies and procedures implemented in response to the regulatory examination should also be reviewed by the CCO.

Financial and business status—Any changes in the adviser's overall business condition, including financial stability and operational soundness, should be discussed with the CCO. This includes reviewing the adviser's financial statements on a periodic basis. Also, the CCO should be notified of any new or pending regulations that would have an impact on the adviser's business.

Valuation of securities—The CCO should ensure that procedures exist to fairly value clients' portfolio holdings. This is especially important when the adviser's management fee is based on the value of assets under management. There should be a process for a review of the valuations, because some securities, such as ones the trading in which has been halted or are otherwise thinly traded, are hard to value.

Monitoring of investment performance—Controls for the monitoring of account performance should exist. Comparisons should be made against benchmarks, indices or other established markets. A review structure should be in place for these comparisons.

Advertising—Procedures should exist for the monitoring of advertising material to ensure the accuracy of any claimed performance and that no fraudulent or misleading statements have been made. These procedures should include guidelines and training on satisfactory advertising material, the designation of persons to review all advertising material, and the retention of all advertising pieces approved for distribution.

New hire training and orientation—The adviser should have an orientation program in place to acclimate new employees to the adviser's culture of compliance. These orientation programs should concentrate on the code of ethics, client privacy, record-keeping requirements and emergency contact information.

B. CCO Responsibilities During On-site SEC Visit or Review of Procedures

The CCO of an adviser has several major responsibilities when an SEC on-site inspection has been scheduled. (See Nutshell Section 53 for a discussion of SEC inspections.) The CCO should communicate to the visiting inspection team the following aspects of the adviser's business:

(1) Initial Interview

(i) The adviser's expectations, objectives and goals should be communicated, such as:

    a. Current issues and regulatory developments

    b. Most recent SEC examination letter and response thereto

    c. Special areas of interest to review

(ii) The organization and culture of compliance should be reviewed, including:

    a. Management's view of compliance

    b. Supervisory structure

    c. Escalation or corporate "whistleblower" process in place

    d. Types of clients

    e. Compensation structure

    f. Trade allocation procedures

    g. List of affiliates and their businesses

    h. New employee orientation

    i. Ongoing training

    j. Privacy policy

    k. Risk identification and mitigation techniques

    l. Processes for testing and evaluating procedures

    m. Procedures for maintenance of books and records

    n. Review of advertising material

    o. Business recovery testing efforts

(2) Walk Through of Operations

(i) Understand and observe the adviser's trading operations, including:

    a. Extent of pre-trade and post-trade compliance

    b. Order handling process

    c. Process for selection of approved brokers

    d. Negotiation of commission rates

    e. Soft dollar and directed brokerage arrangements

    f. Monitoring of personal trading

    g. Allocation of IPOs and block trades to clients

    h. Asset segregation procedures

    i. Affiliated transactions

    j. Trading error procedures

    k. Controls ensuring completeness of trade communication

    l. End of day cash management strategies

    m. Maintenance of books and records

(ii) Portfolio management operations:

    a. Money market procedures (if applicable)

    b. Monitoring of performance against benchmarks

  c. Trade allocation and management of other accounts

  d. Controls ensuring completeness of trade communication

  e. Communication with trading floor

  f. Code of ethics reporting

  g. Extent of pre-trade and post-trade compliance monitoring

  h. Board reporting

  i. Review of fund shareholder reports (if applicable)

  j. Portfolio manager disclosure requirements

  k. End of day cash managements strategies

  l. Affiliated transactions

  m. Maintenance of books and records

(iii) CCO's process for testing and evaluating policies and procedures:

  a. Fulfillment of "action statements" from adviser policies

  b. Monitoring and assessment of risk

  c. Process for reviewing trade activities

  d. Management of assets in accordance with restrictions

  e. Monitoring of performance against benchmarks

  f. Review of advertising material

    g. Most recent SEC examination letter and response thereto

    h. Asset segregation procedures

    i. Exchange Act Form 13D, F and G reporting

(iv) Exit interview:

    a. Summary of findings and recommendations

    b. Establishment of communications channels

    c. Consensus of further reporting requirements

    d. Establish periodic meetings to review strategy and outlook

C. NASAA Best Practices

While the SEC is responsible for inspecting SEC-registered investment advisers, state securities examiners are responsible for inspecting state-registered investment advisers. In this regard, the North American Securities Administrators Association ("NASAA") has released a series of recommended best practices that investment advisers should consider in order to improve their compliance practices and procedures. Advisers—whether registered with one or more states or the SEC—should consider using this information to help strengthen their compliance programs and minimize the potential for regulatory violations.

The NASAA's best practices were developed in 2007 after a nationwide series of coordinated examinations of investment advisers by 43 state and provincial securities examiners revealed a significant number of problem areas. The greatest number of deficiencies that the examinations identified involved registration, unethical business practices, books and records, supervisory/compliance, and privacy. Specifically:

· *Registration issues*—these included inconsistencies between Parts 1 and II of Form ADV, the failure to amend Form ADV in a timely manner, and the failure to provide or offer to provide a disclosure brochure to clients annually.

· *Business practice deficiencies*—these included contract deficiencies, unsuitable recommendations, excessive fees, and misrepresenting qualifications, services, or fees.

· *Books and records issues*—these included the failure to maintain suitability data and financial records.

· *Supervisory/compliance deficiencies*—these included the failure to have any written supervisory/compliance procedures.

· *Privacy issues*—these included the failure to create a privacy policy and to provide privacy notices initially and annually.

Based on the results of the 2007 coordinated exams, the NASAA recommended the following 13 best practices as a guide to assist advisers in the development of compliance practices and procedures:

1. Review and revise your Form ADV and disclosure brochure annually to reflect current and accurate information.

2. Review and update all contracts.

3. Prepare and maintain all required records including financial records.

4. Prepare and maintain client profiles which show suitability information.

5. Prepare a written compliance and supervisory procedures manual relevant to the type of business you operate.

6. Prepare and distribute a privacy policy initially and annually.

7. Keep accurate financials statements.

8. Make timely filings in the jurisdiction in which you are registered.

9. Maintain an adequate surety bond, if required.

10. Calculate and document fees correctly in accordance with contracts and your Form ADV.

11. Review and revise all advertisements, including website and performance advertising, for accuracy.

12. Implement appropriate custody safeguards, if applicable.

13. Review solicitor agreements, disclosure and delivery procedures.

§ 51. COMPLIANCE MANUAL

An adviser uses a compliance manual to inform its employees of the policies and procedures used to minimize compliance lapses. If the adviser has many different departments, a compliance manual will typically be produced for each department. Each department-specific compliance manual will emphasize the procedures and issues that would most commonly be encountered within that department, so as to focus employees' attention on those areas.

The compliance manual will also call for periodic checks of the compliance policies and procedures that the adviser has in place. This practice gives the adviser an insight into what more can be done to strengthen its "culture of compliance" and thus, potentially, avoid serious sanctions by curing problems in advance.

A sample adviser compliance manual may be found at *www.nyls.edu/jhaas*.

XIII. COMPLIANCE, INSPECTION AND ENFORCEMENT UNDER THE ADVISERS ACT

§ 52. GENERALLY

During the early years of the Advisers Act, investment adviser compliance was not a major SEC priority. By the 1980s, adviser compliance had become a more significant focus of the SEC's inspection and enforcement programs, with the SEC bringing an increasing number of enforcement actions against investment advisers.

Concerns over the adequacy of the SEC's oversight resources led to amendments of the Advisers Act in 1997 as part of NSMIA. These amendments divided oversight of investment advisers between the SEC and the states. See Nutshell Section 5B. The effect of the 1997 amendments, in conjunction with budgetary and organizational changes, was to increase the attention the SEC paid to adviser compliance, inspections and enforcement.

SEC-registered advisers can expect routine, indepth inspections by SEC personnel to determine whether they are in compliance with the Advisers Act's provisions. A failure to comply can result in, depending on the severity of the infraction, mild sanctions to revocation of an adviser's registration.

Routine inspections, however, are not the only tool in the arsenal of the SEC. The SEC can conduct more intrusive investigations if it has a reasonable suspicion of Advisers Act violations.

In order to minimize actual or potential Advisers Act violations, an adviser must have extensive internal controls to monitor high-risk areas, as outlined by the SEC. Also, an adviser must maintain and be ready to produce documents that reflect the adviser's day-to-day business, such as individual securities transactions, as well as other documents and records that are mandatory under the Act. Occasionally, an adviser will suspect that it has committed a violation and launch its own internal investigation.

The SEC will allow an adviser to correct many violations on its own without imposing sanctions. If a violation is serious enough, however, such as any of the specific situations mentioned in Nutshell Section 55A, sanctions will almost certainly result. When a violation warrants sanctions, the determination of what those sanctions will be is ultimately left to the SEC's Division of Enforcement. In dispensing punishment, the SEC will look to see if any mitigating factors exist.

§ 53. SEC INSPECTIONS

The SEC's authority to conduct inspections of advisers is found in Advisers Act Section 204. That Section states that the SEC may conduct "periodic, special or other examinations at any time or from time to time." Inspections are carried out by the SEC's Office of Compliance Inspections and Examinations (the "OCIE"). There are three types of inspections that the SEC carries out: (1) routine; (2) cause; and (3) sweep. Each is discussed below.

A. Routine Inspections

Through routine inspections, the SEC determines whether an adviser has violated, is violating or likely will violate the Advisers Act if precautions are not taken. SEC personnel carry out routine inspections every two to four years, depending on the size of the adviser's firm and its risk profile. The larger the firm and the greater the risk to which the firm is exposed, the more likely the firm can expect a routine inspection every two years. For example, the 20 largest advisers, as determined by assets under management, are inspected every two years automatically. Conversely, a smaller, less risky firm will likely be on a four year examination cycle.

The SEC determines an adviser's risk profile by looking at quantitative factors provided in the adviser's Form ADV. However, it also takes into account the firm's "culture of compliance," which covers a number of qualitative factors.

Quantitative factors include:

- · Total assets under management

- · Number of clients

- · Custody of client assets

- Use of affiliated entities to conduct client transactions
- Types of fees charged
- Types of products offered (*e.g.*, wrap fee programs and hedge fund investments)

Qualitative factors include:

- *Strategic compliance vision*—Are the adviser's internal policies and procedures tailored to reduce the likelihood of a compliance lapse in the areas identified by the SEC as most likely to result in an enforcement action?

- *Risk identification*—Has the adviser conducted a thorough analysis of its business situation and addressed its specific challenges when trying to reduce risk of non-compliance?

- *Control points*—Does an adviser have automated internal controls to complement other levels of control in order to minimize risk of non-compliance?

- *Documentation*—Does an adviser document the specific compliance risks faced by each of its departments in order to see that each is aware of the major compliance challenges it faces and knows the proper protocol to reduce non-compliance? Also, does the adviser conduct annual reviews of each department to see which, if any, is most susceptible to non-compliance?

- *Accountable personnel*—Has the adviser appointed a specific person to be held accounta-

> ble to manage each control point and see that it is working properly?

The Director of the OCIE set forth these qualitative factors as well as the Office's approach to the timing of routine examinations in an April 23, 2003 speech. The speech can be viewed in its entirety at *www.sec.gov/news/speech/spch042303lar.htm*.

A sample SEC inspection document request letter may be found at *www.nyls.edu/jhaas*.

(1) Inspection Process

SEC personnel view a routine examination as a three-step process:

(i) *Preparation*—the OCIE staff prepares for the on-site inspection by familiarizing itself with the adviser's past compliance history and with its business practices by viewing the adviser's Form ADV. In addition, the staff may look through any complaints that clients may have filed against the adviser. Once the staff has completed this initial review, it will send the adviser a list of all the books and records the adviser should make available to the inspection team upon its arrival.

(ii) *On-site examination*—The OCIE staff will usually begin its on-site examination by speaking with senior management in charge of risk control, such as the chief compliance officer and other risk managers. These meetings provide the OCIE staff with a more in-depth understanding of the adviser's compliance system and how it interacts with the adviser's business. The staff will then test the internal controls in specific areas of the adviser's business that are violation-prone by reviewing the adviser's books and records as well as individual securities transactions involving the firm, its clients and its employees.

(iii) *Evaluation*—After the on-site examination, the OCIE staff will leave the adviser's premises and evaluate the information collected. After the analysis is completed, the staff will prepare a report of their findings and any recommendation for corrective action. The staff will then present the report to its SEC supervisors who will then determine the appropriate action to take.

In a May 2000 letter, the OCIE outlined the problem areas which it deemed to be most susceptible to non-compliance. It also indicated that these problem areas would receive extra attention during routine examinations. These areas include:

- Inadequate disclosure of material facts
- Unfair trade allocation practices
- Advertising violations
- Overstated performance claims
- Personal trading violations
- Advisory agreement problems
- Failure to maintain proper books and records
- Referral arrangement problems
- Brokerage duty violations
- Violations dealing with custody of client assets

· Failure to remedy instances of past non-compliance

· Inadequate internal controls and supervisory procedures

See OCIE Letter to Registered Investment Advisers, on Areas Reviewed and Violations Found During Inspections (May 1, 2000) (available at *www.sec.gov/ divisions/ocie/advltr.htm*).

(2) Examination Results

The OCIE staff informs the adviser of the results of its examination in one of three ways:

(i) *No findings letter*—When the OCIE staff finds no violations at the adviser, it will send a no findings letter. Such a letter is unlikely, as less than 15 percent of all inspections result in a finding of no violations.

(ii) *Deficiency letter*—When the OCIE staff concludes that the adviser has committed minor violations that are correctable or has internal control weaknesses, it will send a deficiency letter. In the letter, the staff will identify those weaknesses or violations and the adviser will have 30 days to respond with exactly what corrective action it intends to take to remedy the problems. This is by far the most common result of an inspection, accounting for nearly 80 percent of inspections on an average year.

(iii) *Enforcement referral*—When the OCIE staff finds extensive or significant violations, it will refer the case to the SEC's Division of Enforcement. This is a rare result, accounting for only five percent of inspections in an average year.

B. Cause Inspections

The SEC's Division of Enforcement carries out cause inspections. These inspections are triggered when the SEC has reason to believe a violation of the Advisers Act has occurred or is likely to occur. The procedure of this more thorough inspection is outlined in Nutshell Section 55.

C. Sweep Inspections

A sweep inspection is a focused inspection that concentrates on a particular group of advisers. These advisers typically deal in a specific area of business that the SEC deems to be at a heightened risk of non-compliance. Instead of a generalized focus, a sweep inspection will focus on that specific area and check for violations within that area exclusively.

§ 54. INSPECTION PHASES

When the OCIE staff notifies an adviser that an inspection is imminent, the adviser can take several steps to lessen the likelihood that the OCIE staff will find a violation and demand corrective action. Because an inspection is virtually guaranteed to occur every four years at the very least, an adviser may prepare for it even before notification. In fact, steps can be taken even during the inspection itself and after the inspection to minimize any finding of deficiency by the OCIE staff.

Throughout the inspection process, the adviser should treat the inspection seriously and not just as an unwelcome interruption. By assisting the inspection team and convincing it that the firm takes its internal controls and compliance requirements seriously, the adviser can facilitate the completion of the inspection as expeditiously as possible. If the adviser does not take an inspection seriously, or delays production of necessary materials that the OCIE staff requests, the inspection team may become suspicious and dig deeper, or suggest harsher measures when a violation is found in order to convince the adviser that compliance should be taken more seriously.

A. Pre–Inspection Phase

An adviser should take several steps before an inspection starts, including the following:

(i) *Prepare in advance*—The adviser's CCO should be responsible for managing the compliance workload. Each department should have its own written compliance manual addressing the challenges that it will likely face. The CCO should conduct annual assessments of compliance performance for each department so that violation-prone areas can be quickly improved without the threat of sanctions by the OCIE. In addition, the adviser should anticipate the books and records that the inspection team will likely review. The adviser should make these books and records easily accessible and identifiable for when an inspection occurs.

(ii) *Mock inspections*—The adviser's CCO may hire a third-party inspection firm to conduct a "mock inspection" of the adviser's compliance procedures, records and compliance manual. The results of the mock inspection can be assessed by the CCO and other senior management of the adviser in confidence by having the "mock investigation" firm contract directly with the adviser's outside counsel so as to establish attorney-client privilege.

(iii) *Educate employees*—An adviser should engender a "culture of compliance." To do so, it should educate its employees as to the purpose of the inspection team's visit, what the team will be looking for, and the employees' potential role in an upcoming inspection. Also, during the annual review process, the CCO should periodically review each employee's compliance record to ensure that he or she understands the compliance obligations borne by his or her position.

(iv) *Appoint a main contact person*—The adviser should appoint a main contact person for the inspection team in order to achieve a high level of coordination. Normally, the adviser's CCO will assume this role. Employees should keep conversations between themselves and the inspection team to a minimum whenever the main contact person is not present. The main contact person should handle the "walk through" of the adviser that the inspection team will likely request. Finally, the main contact person should track the documents that the inspection team has requested and keep a record of all employees the team has interviewed.

B. On–Site Inspection Phase

During the on-site inspection, an adviser should keep the following three tips in mind:

(i) *Treat the inspection team with respect*—The adviser should have a separate, quiet work-area available for the inspection team when it arrives. Either an office or conference room where the team will be able to conduct interviews and review documents without interruption is ideal. Disagreements between the adviser and the team over the legal requirements to produce certain documents should be handled respectfully and carefully. Indeed, the adviser should recognize that the inspection team is merely doing its job.

(ii) *Do not stall the inspection team*—The inspection team will include seasoned professionals who know when they are being stalled. Stalling raises the team's level of suspicion that a large violation may be found if a more in-depth investigation were to be conducted. When the team requests the production of certain documents, the adviser should see to it that those documents are given in the time frame suggested by the team. If delays are unavoidable, the adviser should immediately communicate the reason for the delay.

(iii) *Correct the problem*—During the on-site inspection, the OCIE staff may notify the adviser of certain areas of concern that have come to the inspection team's attention. These areas of concern should be addressed immediately. Decisive and immediate action shows the inspection team that the adviser takes its compliance responsibilities seriously. It also can serve as a mitigating factor and convince the staff to suggest less extreme action in the event an enforcement referral is an option. Even if an enforcement referral is ultimately given, the SEC's Division of Enforcement may take into account such remedial efforts in its determination of the proper sanctions.

C. Post–Inspection Phase

After the inspection is over, an adviser should keep the following in mind:

(i) *Arrange an exit interview*—An inspection team often will grant an exit interview to the adviser before leaving its premises. An exit interview allows the adviser to discover what a team has found and possibly give an explanation or point out a simple misunderstanding that led to the finding of a violation. Also, the exit interview may give the adviser advanced warning of what the likely result of the inspection will be, whether it is an enforcement referral or a deficiency letter with minor infractions.

(ii) *Confidentiality*—Confidential and proprietary information that an adviser provides to the SEC during inspections is accessible to the public, including the adviser's competitors, through a request under the Freedom of Information Act ("FOIA"). To prevent this result, an adviser may request confidential treatment from the SEC by promptly submitting a letter that identifies the information for which confidentiality is being sought. The adviser should follow this course when it has submitted material it deems confidential *during* an inspection. When the SEC requests that an adviser send documents to it *after* the inspection, the information for which confidentiality is being sought should be produced separately from other information for which confidentiality is *not* being sought. Also, such information must fall within designated categories in order to qualify for confidential treatment. For example, one category is commercial or financial information of the kind that is not customarily disclosed by the adviser to the public. Even if the SEC grants a request for confidentiality, a third-party may still obtain the documents under the FOIA if its reason is deemed substantial.

(iii) *Receipt of deficiency letter*—If the adviser receives a deficiency letter, it will have 30 days to address and resolve the deficiencies contained in the letter. Thus, upon receipt of a deficiency letter, immediate action should be taken. The adviser should then accurately describe all steps that are being taken to correct the problem in a letter addressed to the SEC staff. Indeed, the SEC will check to see if the problem has been resolved during its next inspection and that the actions that the adviser has claimed to have taken were actually taken.

§ 55. ENFORCEMENT

Pursuant to Advisers Act Section 209(b), the SEC may elect to use its investigative authority when it reasonably believes that a violation of the Adviser's Act is about to occur or has already occurred. Investigations are handled by the SEC's Division of Enforcement and are more serious than inspections. Because of this, the powers granted to an investigative team are broad. For example, investigative teams are allowed to subpoena witnesses and compel attendance. If the violation is serious enough, the Advisers Act provides for criminal prosecution of the culprits. Criminal prosecutions, which are a rare occurrence, are handled by the U.S. Attorney General, not the SEC.

A. Advisers Act Sections 203(e) and (f)

Advisers and their personnel, unlike broker-dealers, are not subject to the regulatory authority of a self-regulatory organization such as FINRA. Instead, only the SEC and, to a much more limited extent, state securities authorities, police advisers.

Section 203 of the Advisers Act gives the SEC the power to impose and enforce administrative sanctions. The SEC may impose sanctions if it finds that the adviser or a person associated with an adviser has:

(1) willfully made any false or misleading statements in an application for registration or a report required to be filed with the SEC;

(2) been convicted during the ten years prior to an application for registration of certain felonies or, more specifically, crimes involving dishonesty, as determined by the SEC;

(3) been convicted during the ten years prior to an application for registration of any crime not described in (2) above which is punishable by imprisonment of one or more years;

(4) been temporarily or permanently enjoined by a court from engaging in any activity within the broader financial services industry;

(5) willfully violated any provision of the Federal securities laws or comparable statutes;

(6) aided and abetted a violation by another person of the Federal securities laws or comparable statutes or, subject to certain exceptions, has failed to properly supervise a person who commits such a violation;

(7) been barred by the SEC from being associated with an investment adviser;

(8) been found by a foreign financial regulatory body to have engaged in conduct comparable to that outlined in (1)–(7) above; or

(9) committed a state securities law violation.

See Advisers Act Section 203(e)(1)-(9).

While Section 203(e) outlines the specific activities that can potentially result in sanctions, Section 203(f) specifically empowers the SEC to impose sanctions on any person associated, or seeking to become associated, with any adviser which itself is subject to sanctions under Section 203(e). These sanctions range from censure to revocation of the ability of the person in question to associate with an adviser for up to 12 months.

B. Failure to Supervise

Among other things, Advisers Act Section 203(e)(6) allows the SEC to impose sanctions on an adviser and its managers for a failure to properly supervise those under the adviser's supervision. For example, in In the Matter of Applied Financial Group, Inc. and Dennis Holcombe, Advisers Act Rel. No. 2436, 2005 WL 2413652 (Sept. 30, 2005), the SEC found that the adviser and the supervisor of the adviser's CCO had failed to properly supervise the CCO who had misappropriated approximately $5.4 million of the assets of four profit-sharing plans advised by the adviser. The SEC fined the adviser $50,000 and the supervisor $25,000. It also suspended the supervisor from acting in any supervisory capacity with any investment adviser for a period of 12 months.

Alleged subsection (6) violations are generally not black or white and thus must be determined on a case-by-case basis. Importantly, a failure to supervise allegation will fail against a given adviser or individual if two conditions are met. First, the adviser in question must have established procedures, and a system for applying those procedures, which would reasonably be expected to prevent and detect, insofar as practicable, any violation by a supervised person. Second, the adviser and its personnel must have reasonably discharged their duties and obligations incumbent upon them by reason of those procedures and system without reasonable cause to believe that those procedures and system were not being complied with. See Advisers Act Section 203(e)(6)(A) & (B).

C. Adviser "Cooperation"

An adviser, under certain circumstances, will find that "self-reporting" certain of its violations to the SEC is often a desirable route to take. Indeed, when determining the proper action to take in light of a violation, the SEC will consider and "credit" a firm for its level of cooperation on the matter. Such credit makes sense because when the adviser actively seeks out, self-reports and takes measures to rectify illegal conduct, the SEC saves significant resources by not having to take those steps itself.

There are four broad areas that the SEC takes into account when determining the level of credit to give to an adviser: self-policing; self-reporting; remediation; and cooperation with law enforcement. All are self-explanatory except perhaps for "remediation." Remediation refers to how well the adviser appropriately disciplines wrongdoers, improves internal controls to correct its shortcomings in light of a violation, and compensates those who have been adversely affected by the violation. The SEC, however, is not bound to consider an adviser's corrective measures when determining appropriate sanctions in light of a violation. The violation may be so egregious that no amount of corrective action and cooperation will prevent the SEC from handing down serious sanctions.

The SEC has outlined 13 specific areas into which it will look and the questions it will ask when determining whether an adviser is "credit worthy." These specific areas of inquiry were originally outlined by the SEC in an October 23, 2001 report pursuant to Exchange Act Section 21(a), and have since been applied to investment advisers. They are:

(1) What is the nature of the misconduct involved? Did it result from inadvertence, honest mistake, simple negligence, reckless or deliberate indifference to indicia of wrongful conduct, willful misconduct or unadorned venality? Were the adviser's auditors misled?

(2) How did the misconduct arise? Is it the result of pressure placed on employees to achieve specific results, or a tone of lawlessness set by those in control of the adviser? What compliance procedures were in place to prevent the misconduct now uncovered? Why did those procedures fail to stop or inhibit the wrongful conduct?

(3) Where in the adviser's organization did the misconduct occur? How high up in the chain of command was knowledge of, or participation in, the misconduct? Did senior personnel participate in, or turn a blind eye toward, obvious indicia of misconduct? How systemic was the behavior? Is it symptomatic of the way the entity does business, or was it isolated?

(4) How long did the misconduct last? Was it a one-quarter, or one-time, event, or did it last several years?

(5) How much harm has the misconduct inflicted upon investors and other constituencies?

(6) How was the misconduct detected and who uncovered it?

(7) How long after discovery of the misconduct did it take to implement an effective response?

(8) What steps did the adviser take upon learning of the misconduct? Did the firm immediately stop the misconduct? Are persons responsible for any misconduct still with the adviser? If so, are they still in the same positions? Did the adviser promptly, completely and effectively disclose the existence of the misconduct to the regulators? Did the adviser cooperate completely with appropriate regulatory and law enforcement bodies? Did the adviser identify what additional related misconduct is likely to have occurred? Did the adviser take steps to identify the extent of damage to investors and other constituencies? Did the adviser appropriately recompense those adversely affected by the conduct?

(9) What processes did the adviser follow to resolve many of these issues and ferret out necessary information?

(10) Did the adviser commit to learn the truth, fully and expeditiously? Did it do a thorough review of the nature, extent, origins and conse-

quences of the conduct and related behavior? Did management oversee the review? Did adviser employees or outside persons perform the review? If outside persons, had they done other work for the adviser? If the review was conducted by outside counsel, had management previously engaged such counsel? Were scope limitations placed on the review? If so, what were they?

(11) Did the adviser promptly make available to the SEC staff the results of its review and provide sufficient documentation reflecting its response to the situation? Did the adviser identify possible violative conduct and evidence with sufficient precision to facilitate prompt enforcement actions against those who violated the law? Did the adviser produce a thorough and probing written report detailing the findings of its review? Did the adviser voluntarily disclose information the SEC staff did not directly request and otherwise might not have uncovered? Did the adviser ask its employees to cooperate with SEC staff and make all reasonable efforts to secure that cooperation?

(12) What assurances are there that the conduct is unlikely to recur? Did the adviser adopt and ensure enforcement of new and more effective internal controls and procedures designed to prevent a recurrence of the misconduct? Did the adviser provide the SEC staff with sufficient information for it to evaluate the adviser's measures to correct the situation and ensure that the conduct does not recur?

(13) Is the adviser the same company in which the misconduct occurred, or has it changed through a merger or bankruptcy reorganization?

The full report can be viewed at *www.sec.gov/ litigation/investreport/34–44969.htm.*

§ 56. PENALTIES

When an adviser has violated the provisions of the Advisers Act, a wide array of penalties, from mild to severe, can be imposed to discourage the non-compliant adviser from engaging in that activity again.

A. Non–Monetary Sanctions

Advisers Act Section 203(e) outlines the situations (detailed above in Nutshell Section 55A) where the SEC can impose severe non-monetary sanctions on an adviser's operations, potentially having a great impact on its ability to do business. These sanctions can include limiting the adviser's activities and operations, suspending the adviser's operations for up to twelve months or revoking the adviser's registration.

Advisers Act Section 203(f) outlines the situations where a person may have severe sanctions imposed on him or her as an individual. An individual may suffer the same types of sanctions imposed on an entity adviser. Thus, the SEC may place limitations on the activities of the individual, suspend the individual for up to twelve months or bar the individual from associating with an investment adviser. The

SEC may impose these sanctions when the individual has committed any violation outlined in subsection (1), (5), (6) or (8) of Advisers Act Section 203(e) or has been convicted within the previous ten years of any offense outlined in subsection (2) of that same Section. See Nutshell Section 55.

B. Monetary Sanctions

Advisers Act Section 203(i) outlines the situations where the SEC may impose civil penalties against a person (whether natural or not), the maximum monetary penalties that it may impose against a person, and the factors it may take into consideration in determining the appropriate level of monetary penalties.

The SEC may impose a civil penalty against a person if it finds that the penalty is in the "public interest" and the person has:

(1) willfully violated any provision of the Securities Act, the Exchange Act, the Company Act, or the Advisers Act, or the rules or regulations thereunder;

(2) willfully aided, abetted, counseled, commanded, induced, or procured a violation specified in paragraph (1) above by any other person;

(3) willfully made or caused to be made in any application for registration or report required to be filed with the SEC under the Advisers Act, or in any proceeding before the SEC with respect to registration, any statement which was, at the time and in the light of the circumstances under

which it was made, false or misleading with respect to any material fact, or has omitted to state in any such application or report any material fact which was required to be stated therein; or

(4) failed to reasonably supervise, within the meaning of Advisers Act Section 203(e)(6), with a view to preventing violations of the provisions of the Advisers Act and the rules and regulations thereunder, another person who commits such a violation, if such other person is subject to his supervision.

See Advisers Act Section 203(i)(1).

The Advisers Act sets forth a system for determining what the maximum penalties that the SEC will impose will be given a certain set of circumstances. This system is outlined in tiers which reference the actions outlined in paragraphs (1) through (4) above:

(i) *First Tier*—The maximum amount of penalty for each act or omission described in paragraphs (1) through (4) above is $5,000 for a natural person or $50,000 for any other person.

(ii) *Second Tier*—Notwithstanding paragraph (i), the maximum amount of penalty for each such act or omission shall be $50,000 for a natural person or $250,000 for any other person if the act or omission in question involved fraud, deceit, manipulation or deliberate or reckless disregard of a regulatory requirement.

(iii) *Third Tier*—Notwithstanding paragraphs (i) and (ii), the maximum amount of penalty for each such act or omission shall be $100,000 for a natural person or $500,000 for any other person if:

a.   the act or omission in question involved fraud, deceit, manipulation or deliberate or reckless disregard of a regulatory requirement; and

b.   such an act or omission directly or indirectly resulted in substantial losses or created a significant risk of substantial losses to other persons or resulted in substantial pecuniary gain to the person who committed the act or omission.

See Advisers Act Section 203(i)(2).

Since the SEC must take the "public interest" into account when determining whether to impose a monetary penalty, the Advisers Act offers guidelines to help the SEC decide what exactly would be considered in the "public interest." The SEC should consider:

(A) whether the act or omission involved fraud, deceit, manipulation or deliberate or reckless disregard of a regulatory requirement;

(B) the harm to other persons resulting either directly or indirectly from that act or omission;

(C) the extent to which any person was unjustly enriched, taking into account any restitution made to persons injured by the act or omission;

(D) (i) whether it, another appropriate regulatory agency or a self-regulatory organization has found the person in question to have violated the Federal securities laws, state securities laws, or the rules of a self-regulatory organization, (ii) whether a court of competent jurisdiction has enjoined that person from violations of those laws or rules, or (iii) whether a court of competent jurisdiction has convicted that person of violations of those laws or of any felony or misdemeanor described in Advisers Act Section 203(e)(2);

(E) the need to deter the person in question and other persons from committing that act or omission; and

(F) such other matters as justice may require.

See Advisers Act Section 203(i)(3).

C. Criminal Penalties

Advisers Act Section 217 provides that any person who willfully violates the provisions of the Advisers Act, or any rule, regulation or order promulgated by the SEC, faces a fine of not more than $10,000 and/or a maximum prison term of five years if convicted.

§ 57. ACHIEVING PROHIBITED GOALS THROUGH INDIRECT MEANS

Advisers Act Section 208(d) makes it unlawful for any person, including unregistered investment advisers, to do *indirectly* what the person is prohibited from doing *directly*. For example, Advisers Act Section 203(b)(3) exempts from registration an investment adviser who, during the course of the preceding 12 months, has had fewer than 15 clients and who neither holds itself out to the public as an investment adviser nor acts as an adviser to a registered investment company. See Nutshell Section 4C. Under Section 208(d), therefore, an investment adviser who has 13 clients is prohibited from pooling four additional clients into a limited partnership to circumvent registration under the Advisers Act, as the adviser would be deemed to have 17 clients.

In addition to prohibiting certain activities by any person who provides investment advice, the SEC has also used Section 208(d) to address complex relationships between registered and unregistered investment advisers that are affiliated with each other. In Richard Ellis, SEC No–Action Letter, 1981 WL 25241 (avail. Sept. 17, 1981), the SEC allowed an unregistered U.K. partnership to establish a registered affiliate to provide investment advice to U.S. persons without violating Section 208(d) so long as the registered subsidiary had a separate existence from the foreign parent. Registration of the U.K. partnership was unnecessary so long as the investment advisory subsidiary: (1) was adequately capitalized; (2) had a buffer, such as a board of directors with a majority of directors independent of the parent, between the subsidiary's personnel and the parent; (3) had officers, directors and employees who, if engaged in providing advice in the day-to-day business of the subsidiary entity, were not otherwise engaged in the investment advisory business of the parent; (4) itself made the decisions as to what investment advice is to be communicated to, or used on behalf of, its clients and used sources of investment information not limited to its parent; and (5) kept its investment advice confidential until communicated to its clients. The SEC has also applied the *Ellis* standard to situations involving registered investment advisers and unregistered domestic affiliates. Since *Ellis,* in certain cases, including situations that involve complex relationships between registered investment advisers and their unregistered affiliates, the SEC has relaxed the *Ellis* factors. See Thomson Advisory Group L.P., SEC No–Action Letter, 1995 WL 611553 (avail. Sept. 26, 1995); SEC Div. of Investment Mgt., Protecting Investors: A Half Century of Investment Company Regulation (May 1992).

While Advisers Act Section 208(d) is designed to prohibit certain conduct, it is not intended to expand the scope of the Advisers Act to apply to all investment advice or investment advisory services related to the purchase and sale of U.S. securities. For example, under Advisers Act Section 205(a)(1) an unregistered investment adviser that is not exempt from registration under Advisers Act Section 203(b) is prohibited from using the mails or any means of interstate commerce ("jurisdictional means") to enter into or to perform any advisory contract whereby the adviser receives compensation based upon the capital gains of a fund. See Nutshell

Section 24C(1)c. This provision does not apply to unregistered investment advisers who use jurisdictional means to effect the purchase and sale of U.S. securities and receive compensation for their advisory services that they provide to non-U.S. persons or foreign investment companies. In one no-action letter, the SEC took the position that an owner of an unregistered investment adviser to a foreign investment company did not violate Sections 208(d) or Section 205(a)(1) because of its ownership of a registered investment adviser. See Forty Four Mgt., Ltd., SEC No–Action Letter, 1983 WL 30741 (avail. Jan. 31, 1983).

§ 58.   CONSULTATION WITH FEDERAL BANKING AUTHORITIES

Advisers Act Section 210A mandates cooperation and information sharing between the SEC and any appropriate Federal banking agency with respect to the investment advisory activities of (a) any bank holding company or savings and loan holding company, (b) bank or (c) separately identifiable department or division of a bank or bank holding company or savings and loan holding company that is registered as an adviser under the Advisers Act.

XIV. LIMITED PRIVATE RIGHT OF ACTION

§ 59. NO EXPRESS PROVISION

The Advisers Act contains no provision that expressly sets forth a private right of action for investment adviser misconduct. In *Transamerica Mortgage Advisors, Inc. v. Lewis*, 444 U.S. 11 (1979), the Supreme Court held that the Advisers Act only provides a limited *implied* private right of action. Clients can sue to void an investment advisory contract and for damages based on rescission (the recovery of fees paid, less any value conferred by the adviser). However, the client cannot sue for diminution of value of his assets under management.

§ 60. LIMITED PRIVATE RIGHT OF ACTION

The respondent in *Transamerica Mortgage* was a shareholder of the Mortgage Trust of America (the "Trust"), while the petitioners were the Trust, several individual trustees of the Trust, the Trust's investment adviser (TAMA), and two affiliated corporations (Land Capital and Transamerica Corp.).

The respondent made three primary allegations against the petitioners. First, the respondent alleged that the advisory contract between TAMA and the Trust was unlawful because TAMA was not registered under the Advisers Act and the compensation contained therein was "excessive." Second, the respondent alleged that TAMA breached its fiduciary duty when it caused the Trust to buy inferior securities from Land Capital, an affiliate of TAMA. Finally, the respondent alleged that TAMA had misappropriated profitable investment opportunities for the benefit of other companies affiliated with Transamerica. The respondent sought rescission of the advisory contract, restitution of fees and other consideration paid by the Trust, an accounting of illegal profits, and an award of damages.

The main issue that the Supreme Court addressed was whether there were implied private causes of action in the Advisers Act, as there were no express private causes of action. The respondent argued that clients of investment advisers were the intended beneficiaries of the Advisers Act and, therefore, the courts should imply a private cause of action. In particular, the respondent argued that private causes of actions could be inferred from Advisers Act Sections 206 and 215.

Advisers Act Section 206 proscribes fraudulent practices by investment advisers and, in many ways, is similar to Exchange Act Rule 10b–5. However, the Court disagreed with the respondent, holding instead that Section 206 only proscribed certain conduct and did not create or alter any civil liabilities. The Court based its decision on the fact that Congress provided specific judicial and administrative (SEC) means to enforce compliance with Section 206. Therefore, the Court thought it would be imprudent to imply a private remedy, especially since Congressional intent weighed against such a remedy.

Advisers Act Section 215 states that any contracts whose formation or performance would violate the Advisers Act "shall be void . . . as regards the rights of" the violator and knowing successors in interest. The Court agreed with the respondent that Section 215 did, indeed, provide an implied private cause of action. However, the Court held that the private cause of action was limited. Pursuant to it, a client may sue to void an investment advisory contract. She may also sue for damages based on rescission. However, these damages are limited to the recovery of fees paid, less any value conferred by the adviser. Importantly, the Court held that a client may not sue an investment adviser for any diminution of value of her assets under management, which is inevitably what the client desires.

§ 61. OTHER ACTIONS POSSIBLE

An investment adviser may still be named as a defendant in a private lawsuit alleging fraudulent investment activity under Exchange Act Section 10(b) and Rule 10b–5 promulgated thereunder or under the Racketeer Influenced and Corrupt Organizations Act ("RICO").

XV. PURCHASE AND SALE OF INVESTMENT ADVISERS

§ 62. GENERALLY

The purchase and sale of investment advisers occur frequently in the investment management industry. Among the many reasons for purchase and sale transactions are the retirement of the founders of an investment adviser and the desire of advisers to increase their assets under management or expand their staff of portfolio managers. Investment advisers are typically sold at prices equivalent to three to five times annual advisory fees or ten to twelve times earnings before income, taxes, depreciation and amortization ("EBITDA").

The sale of an adviser can be structured as a transfer of assets or stock, or as a merger. If the transaction is structured as an asset sale, the buyer may be able to avoid assuming some or all of the liabilities of the seller. If the transaction is structured as a sale of stock, the selling adviser's legal entity, typically a limited liability company, remains intact which may enhance business continuity and name recognition. If the transaction is a merger, the selling adviser becomes part of the buyer, and the shareholders of both the seller and the buyer may be required by state law to approve the merger.

When an unregistered entity acquires a registered adviser, Advisers Act Section 203(g) deems the buyer to be registered with the SEC if within 30 days from the date of the transaction the buyer files a Form ADV with the SEC. However, as a practical matter, most buyers will be registered prior to the closing of the acquisition in order to assure operational, administrative and investment continuity for their clients.

§ 63. ASSIGNMENT OF ADVISORY CONTRACTS

Under Advisers Act Section 205(a)(2), an investment adviser that is not exempt from registration under Advisers Act Section 203(b) generally may not enter into, extend, renew or perform any investment advisory contract *unless* the contract prohibits assignment by the adviser without the client's consent. See Nutshell Section 24C(2). Congress in 1940 wanted to put an end to the unsavory business practice of "trafficking in investment advisory contracts," whereby advisory clients had no idea who their investment adviser was or who controlled their investment adviser because of multiple sales of advisers about which advisory clients were not notified.

Section 205(a)(2)'s prohibition applies to both SEC- and state-registered advisers. Assignments of advisory contracts with registered investment companies are subject to more stringent regulation under the Company Act. Specifically, Company Act Section 15(a)(4) requires the automatic termination of such contracts in the event of their assignment.

An "assignment" is defined in Advisers Act Section 202(a)(1) as the transfer of a controlling block of the adviser's outstanding voting securities. Advisers Act Rule 202(a)(1)–1 adds that unless the transfer results "in a change of actual control or management of the adviser," there is no assignment which requires consent of the adviser's clients. Therefore, some transactions involving the sale of advisers are not "assignments" under Section 205(a) and Rule 202(a)(1)–1 because the transactions do not involve a change of actual control or management, as in some corporate reorganizations. See The Equitable Life Assurance Society, SEC No–Action Letter, 1984 WL 47223 (avail. Jan. 11, 1984); Dean Witter, Discover & Co., SEC No–Action Letter, 1997 WL 192125 (avail. Apr. 18, 1997); Nikko Int'l Capital Mgt. Co., SEC No–Action Letter, 1987 WL 108059 (avail. June 1, 1987).

Most sales of advisers, however, involve a change of actual control or management of the adviser and, therefore, require obtaining all clients' consents. Advisers typically send a letter to their clients that describes the transaction and who the buyer is and requests the client to sign a consent to the transaction and return it to the adviser. The logistical difficulties of obtaining potentially thousands of client consents has been recognized by the staff of the SEC. Indeed, the staff permits the use of "negative consents" that allow the selling adviser to notify its clients in a letter that the pending sale will be consummated within 45 to 60 days unless the client objects in writing to the pending sale. If the client does not reply, the client is deemed to have given her tacit consent to the sale of the adviser. The use of negative consents has become a standard industry practice. See Templeton Inv. Counsel Ltd., SEC No–Action Letter, 1986 WL 67662 (avail. Jan. 2, 1986); Jennison Associates Capital Corp., SEC No–Action Letter, 1985 WL 55687 (avail. Dec. 2, 1985); Scudder, Stevens & Clark, SEC No–Action Letter, 1985 WL 54004 (avail. Mar. 18, 1985).

When an adviser to a mutual fund (or any other registered investment company) is sold, Company Act Section 15(a)(4) adds addition requirements before the sale transaction may be consummated. For instance, the board of directors of the mutual fund must approve the new advisory contract and the mutual fund shareholders must also approve the new advisory contract pursuant to a proxy vote and shareholder meeting. In addition, Company Act Section 15(f) requires that: (1) for a period of three years after the transaction, at least 75% of the mutual fund's board of directors be comprised of independent directors (directors that are not affiliated with the buyer or seller of the adviser); and (2) the transaction not impose an "unfair burden" on the mutual fund, meaning that for two years after the transaction, the adviser must not receive compensation from the mutual fund other than advisory and other bona fide service fees.

Advisers that are Dual Registrants and manage money market mutual funds may use "negative consents" to transfer the money market mutual funds to a buyer without obtaining fund shareholder approval. See NASD Conduct Rule 2510(d)(2). These "bulk exchanges" require the "negative consent" letters to be accompanied by a prospectus for the buyer's money market fund, along with a comparative description of the investment objectives of each fund and a tabular comparison of the nature and amount of the fees charged by each fund. The money market mutual fund shareholders have 30 days in which to redeem from their selling mutual fund if they do not want to be invested in the buying fund.

On July 30, 2007, FINRA was created through the consolidation of the NASD and the member regulation, enforcement and arbitration operations of the NYSE. Accordingly, readers should be aware that a FINRA analog to NASD Conduct Rule 2510 will likely replace that NASD rule in the near future.

§ 64. EMPLOYMENT CONTRACTS AND NON–COMPETE/NON-SOLICIT AGREEMENTS

Employment contracts with key portfolio managers and senior management are a vital part of an adviser's business. When an adviser is sold, employment contracts must be in place to retain the portfolio managers and senior management who are critical to the success and continuity of the adviser's on-going business. Typically, buyers require "lock-up" agreements that keep the portfolio managers and senior management working for the new owner of the adviser for between five to 10 years. These agreements motivate the portfolio managers and senior management with equity participations, bonus pools and other inducements to decrease the risk of their departure.

Non-competition and non-solicitation provisions are typically included in employment agreements in order to punish wayward portfolio managers and senior management who leave prior to the end of the term of their employment contracts. Non-competition provisions generally prohibit key advisory personnel from competing with the adviser in any investment services capacity after their departure from the adviser. Non-solicitation provisions prohibit key advisory personnel from soliciting any advisory clients of the adviser and prohibit them from hiring any personnel of the adviser.

State contract law governs the terms of employment agreements, including the non-competition and non-solicitation provisions. An adviser must obtain expert advice to ensure the enforceability of these contracts and provisions, particularly since the enforceability of some contract provisions may vary from state to state.

XVI. SPECIAL ISSUES RELATING TO THE ADVISORY BUSINESS

§ 65. HOLDING COMPANIES OF INVESTMENT ADVISERS

Holding companies that buy a controlling interest in multiple public and private investment advisers are increasing in number in the investment management business. Typically, the holding company buys 80% of the equity of the adviser and leaves the remaining 20% for the portfolio managers and senior management of the adviser as a retention and incentive mechanism. The holding company is usually a publicly traded company with access to capital that it, in turn, can use to purchase additional advisers and to help fund the growth of the advisers' businesses.

These holding companies can achieve significant economies of scale by eliminating duplicative administrative, operational, accounting and legal expenses between and among the advisers it controls.

Because all the advisers have a common parent, they are all affiliates of the parent. Thus, they must implement procedures so that any securities transactions between and among the affiliated advisers are compliant with Advisers Act Section 206. See Nutshell Section 31.

§ 66. TAKING AN INVESTMENT ADVISER PUBLIC

In 2007 there was a spate of initial public offerings ("IPOs") by very large investment advisers, including Fortress, Blackstone, Och–Ziff and Pzena, among others. For the most part, these advisers "went public" to richly reward their founders and senior managers for years of very high, consistent growth as private equity and hedge fund managers.

Before selling securities to the public, the adviser must register those securities with the SEC on Registration Statement Form S–1 under the Securities Act. This registration is in addition to the adviser's registration on Form ADV under the Advisers Act. Before "going public," a given adviser must comply with the Sarbanes–Oxley Act of 2002 ("SOX"). Because most advisers are not SOX compliant, a detailed review of the adviser's governance, financial statements, audit committee, governing board, SEC filings, shareholder agreements and compliance procedures is necessary.

Many of the advisers that have gone public are structured as publicly traded partnerships in order to eliminate corporate taxation. Another highly favorable tax advantage for these advisers is that the incentive payments they receive, so called "carried interest," is taxed at capital gains rates, currently

15%, instead of as ordinary income for services, taxed at 35%.

Interestingly, since the advisers are structured as partnerships, the NYSE listing requirements do not require the securities that were issued to the public in the IPOs to be voting securities. As a consequence, these public investment advisers do not have shareholder meetings and their senior management is not subject to a shareholder vote at any time.

§ 67. "PAY–TO–PLAY" RULES RELATING TO POLITICAL CONTRIBUTIONS

In response to growing concerns that investment advisers and hedge fund managers have made campaign or other political contributions to government officials in return for investments from government employee pension plans, some states and governmental entities have adopted "pay-to-play" rules that disqualify an investment adviser or hedge fund manager from entering into an advisory contract with a governmental pension plan if the investment adviser makes contributions to a governmental official or entity. Contributions from investment advisers are prohibited in about 22 states. Other states set limits on the amount of contributions. However, in most states with "pay-to-play" laws, investment advisers are allowed to sponsor and solicit funds for a political action committee ("PAC"), but are prohibited from making contributions, compelling their employees and officers to make contributions, or augmenting their employees salaries to encourage contributions to PACs. Any contributions from an investment adviser could trigger a state's "pay-to-play" laws.

The scope and the applicability of "pay-to-play" rules vary greatly from state to state. Many states model their laws after the Municipal Securities Rule Making Board's ("MSRB") Rule G–37, a "pay-to-play" rule that applies to firms that engage in underwriting municipal bond issues. Thus, many state laws prohibit or limit contributions from any adviser for two years before and after the date of the advisory contract with a governmental entity. MSRB Rule G–37 is available at *www.msrb.org/msrb1/rules/ruleg37.htm*.

Some "pay-to-play" laws, however, follow a technical approach and restrict their applicability to specific types of investment advisory services, such as the issuance of municipal bonds used to finance highway projects, or prohibit investment advisers from making contributions to specific state officials, such as a state's treasurer or other governmental officials responsible for the state's finances. Prior to making any political or campaign contribution, an investment adviser should obtain expert advice about "pay-to-play" and Federal campaign finance rules in the relevant jurisdictions.

In 1999, the SEC proposed its own "pay-to-play" rule for investment advisers that was also modeled after MSRB Rule G–37. See Notice of Proposed

Rulemaking, Political Contributions by Certain Investment Advisers, Advisers Act Rel. 1812, 1999 WL 593615 (Aug. 10, 1999). The SEC, however, did not adopt its proposed "pay-to-play" rule.

§ 68. PAYMENTS TO LABOR ORGANIZATIONS

An investment adviser that is considering making a payment to a labor organization must comply with the disclosure procedure adopted by the U.S. Department of Labor ("DOL"). Pursuant to the Labor–Management Reporting and Disclosure Act of 1959, payments to labor organizations in excess of $250 in a fiscal year must be reported to the DOL by filing an "Employer Report" on Form LM–10 with the Secretary of Labor. Form LM–10 is available at *www.dol.gov/esa/regs/compliance/olms/ GPEA_Forms/lm–10p.pdf*.

An adviser must file the report within 90 days of the end of the adviser's fiscal year. The report must contain the following information: the date of such payment or expenditure and the amount of each transaction; the name, address and position of the person with whom the agreement or transaction was made; and a full explanation of the circumstances of all such payments, including the terms of any oral agreement or understanding pursuant to which they were made. Such expenditures include, without limitation, meals, gifts, tickets to theater and sporting events, social events, fees to attend union-sponsored events, and products or services.

*

ANNEX A

INVESTMENT ADVISERS ACT OF 1940

(Current as of January 1, 2008)

Section 201. Findings

Upon the basis of facts disclosed by the record and report of the Securities and Exchange Commission made pursuant to Section 30 of the Public Utility Holding Company Act of 1935, and facts otherwise disclosed and ascertained, it is found that investment advisers are of national concern, in that, among other things—

(1) their advice, counsel, publications, writings, analyses, and reports are furnished and distributed, and their contracts, subscription agreements, and other arrangements with clients are negotiated and performed, by the use of the mails and means and instrumentalities of interstate commerce;

(2) their advice, counsel, publications, writings, analyses, and reports customarily relate to the purchase and sale of securities traded on national securities exchanges and in interstate over-the-counter markets, securities issued by companies engaged in business in interstate commerce, and

securities issued by national banks and member banks of the Federal Reserve System; and

(3) the foregoing transactions occur in such volume as substantially to affect interstate commerce, national securities exchanges, and other securities markets, the national banking system and the national economy.

Section 202. Definitions

(a) When used in this title, unless the context otherwise requires, the following definitions apply:

(1) "Assignment" includes any direct or indirect transfer or hypothecation of an investment advisory contract by the assignor or of a controlling block of the assignor's outstanding voting securities by a security holder of the assignor; but if the investment adviser is a partnership, no assignment of an investment advisory contract shall be deemed to result from the death or withdrawal of a minority of the members of the investment adviser having only a minority interest in the business of the investment adviser, or from the admission to the investment adviser of one or more members who, after such admission, shall be only a minority of the members and shall have only a minority interest in the business.

(2) "Bank" means (A) a banking institution organized under the laws of the United States or a Federal savings association, as defined in Section 2(5) of the Home Owners' Loan Act, (B) a member bank of the Federal Reserve System, (C) any other banking institution, savings association, as defined in Section 2(4) of the Home Owners' Loan Act, or trust company, whether incorporated or not, doing business under the laws of any State or of the United States, a substantial portion of the business of which consists of receiving deposits or exercising fiduciary powers similar to those permitted to national banks under the authority of the Comptroller of the Currency, and which is supervised and examined by State or Federal authority having supervision over banks or savings associations, and which is not operated for the purpose of evading the provisions of this title, and (D) a receiver, conservator, or other liquidating agent of any institution or firm included in clauses (A), (B), or (C) of this paragraph.

(3) The term "broker" has the same meaning as given in Section 3 of the Securities Exchange Act of 1934.

(4) "Commission" means the Securities and Exchange Commission.

(5) "Company" means a corporation, a partnership, an association, a joint-stock company, a trust, or any organized group of persons, whether incorporated or not; or any receiver, trustee in a case under Title 11 of the United States Code, or similar official, or any liquidating agent for any of the foregoing, in his capacity as such.

(6) "Convicted" includes a verdict, judgment, or plea of guilty, or a finding of guilt on a plea of nolo contendere, if such verdict, judgment, plea, or finding has not been reversed, set aside, or withdrawn, whether or not sentence has been imposed.

(7) The term "dealer" has the same meaning as given in Section 3 of the Securities Exchange Act of 1934, but does not include an insurance company or investment company.

(8) "Director" means any director of a corporation or any person performing similar functions with respect to any organization, whether incorporated or unincorporated.

(9) "Exchange" means any organization, association, or group of persons, whether incorporated or unincorporated, which constitutes, maintains, or provides a market place or facilities for bringing together purchasers and sellers of securities or for otherwise performing with respect to securities the functions commonly performed by a stock exchange as that term is generally understood, and includes the market place and the market facilities maintained by such exchange.

(10) "Interstate commerce" means trade, commerce, transportation, or communication among the several States, or between any foreign country and any State, or between any State and any place or ship outside thereof.

(11) "Investment adviser" means any person who, for compensation, engages in the business of advising others, either directly or through publications or writings, as to the value of securities or as to the advisability of investing in, purchasing, or selling securities, or who, for compensation and as part of a regular business, issues or promulgates analyses or reports concerning securities; but does not include (A) a bank, or any bank holding company as defined in the Bank Holding Company Act of 1956 which is not an investment company, except that the term "investment adviser" includes any bank or bank holding company to the extent that such bank or bank holding company serves or acts as an investment adviser to a registered investment company, but if, in the case of a bank, such services or actions are performed through a separately identifiable department or division, the department or division, and not the bank itself, shall be deemed to be the investment adviser; (B) any lawyer, accountant, engineer, or teacher whose performance of such services is solely incidental to the practice of his profession; (C) any broker or dealer whose performance of such services is solely incidental to the conduct of his business as a broker or dealer and who receives no special compensation therefor; (D) the publisher of any bona fide newspaper, news magazine or business or financial publication of general and regular circulation; (E) any person whose advice, analyses, or reports relate to no securities other than securities which are direct obligations of or obligations guaranteed as to principal or interest by the United States, or securities issued or guaranteed by corporations in which the United States has a direct or indirect interest which shall have been designated by the Secretary of the Treasury, pursuant to Section

3(a)(12) of the Securities Exchange Act of 1934, as exempted securities for the purposes of that Act; (F) any nationally recognized statistical rating organization, as that term is defined in Section 3(a)(62) of the Securities Exchange Act of 1934, unless such organization engages in issuing recommendations as to purchasing, selling, or holding securities or in managing assets, consisting in whole or in part of securities, on behalf of others; or (G) such other persons not within the intent of this paragraph, as the Commission may designate by rules and regulations or order.

(12) "Investment company", "affiliated person", and "insurance company" have the same meanings as in the Investment Company Act of 1940. "Control" means the power to exercise a controlling influence over the management or policies of a company, unless such power is solely the result of an official position with such company.

(13) "Investment supervisory services" means the giving of continuous advice as to the investment of funds on the basis of the individual needs of each client.

(14) "Means or instrumentality of interstate commerce" includes any facility of a national securities exchange.

(15) "National securities exchange" means an exchange registered under Section 6 of the Securities Exchange Act of 1934.

(16) "Person" means a natural person or a company.

(17) The term "person associated with an investment adviser" means any partner, officer, or director of such investment adviser (or any person performing similar functions), or any person directly or indirectly controlling or controlled by such investment adviser, including any employee of such investment adviser, except that for the purposes of Section 203 of this title (other than subsection (f) thereof), persons associated with an investment adviser whose functions are clerical or ministerial shall not be included in the meaning of such term. The Commission may by rules and regulations classify, for the purposes of any portion or portions of this, persons, including employees controlled by an investment adviser.

(18) "Security" means any note, stock, treasury stock, security future, bond, debenture, evidence of indebtedness, certificate of interest or participation in any profit-sharing agreement, collateral-trust certificate, preorganization certificate or subscription, transferable share, investment contract, voting-trust certificate, certificate of deposit for a security, fractional undivided interest in oil, gas, or other mineral rights, any put, call, straddle, option, or privilege on any security (including a certificate of deposit) or on any group or index of securities (including any interest therein or based on the value thereof), or any put, call, straddle, option, or privilege entered into on a national securities exchange relating to foreign currency, or, in general, any interest or instrument commonly known as a "security", or any certificate of interest or participation in, temporary or interim certificate for, receipt for, guaranty of, or warrant or right to subscribe to or purchase any of the foregoing.

(19) "State" means any State of the United States, the District of Columbia, Puerto Rico, the Virgin Islands, or any other possession of the United States.

(20) "Underwriter" means any person who has purchased from an issuer with a view to, or sells for an issuer in connection with, the distribution of any security, or participates or has a direct or indirect participation in any such undertaking, or participates or has a participation in the direct or indirect underwriting of any such undertaking; but such term shall not include a person whose interest is limited to a commission from an underwriter or dealer not in excess of the usual and customary distributor's or seller's commission. As used in this paragraph the term "issuer" shall include in addition to an issuer, any person directly or indirectly controlling or controlled by the issuer, or any person under direct or indirect common control with the issuer.

(21) "Securities Act of 1933", "Securities Exchange Act of 1934", "Public Utility Holding Company Act of 1935", and "Trust Indenture Act of 1939'', mean those Acts, respectively, as heretofore or hereafter amended.

(22) ''Business development company'' means any company which is a business development company as defined in Section 2(a)(48) of Title I of this Act and which complies with Section 55 of Title I of this Act, except that—

(A) the 70 per centum of the value of the total assets condition referred to in Sections 2(a)(48) and 55 of Title I shall be 60 per centum for purposes of determining compliance therewith;

(B) such company need not be a closed-end company and need not elect to be subject to the provisions of Sections 55 through 65 of Title I of this Act; and

(C) the securities which may be purchased pursuant to Section 55(a) of Title I of this Act may be purchased from any person.

For purposes of this paragraph, all terms in Sections 2(a)(48) and 55 of Title I of this Act shall have the same meaning set forth in such title as if such company were a registered closed-end investment company, except that the value of the assets of a business development company which is not subject to the provisions of Sections 55 through 65 of Title I of this Act shall be determined as of the date of the most recent financial statements which it furnished to all holders of its securities, and shall be determined no less frequently than annually.

(23) "Foreign securities authority" means any foreign government, or any governmental body or regulatory organization empowered by a foreign government to administer or enforce its laws as they relate to securities matters.

(24) "Foreign financial regulatory authority" means any (A) foreign securities authority, (B) other governmental body or foreign equivalent of a self-regulatory organization empowered by a foreign government to administer or enforce its laws relating to the regulation of fiduciaries, trusts, commercial lending, insurance, trading in contracts of sale of a commodity for future delivery, or other instruments traded on or subject to the rules of a contract market, board of trade or foreign equivalent, or other financial activities, or (C) membership organization a function of which is to regulate the participation of its members in activities listed above.

(25) "Supervised person" means any partner, officer, director (or other person occupying a similar status or performing similar functions), or employee of an investment adviser, or other person who provides investment advice on behalf of the investment adviser and is subject to the supervision and control of the investment adviser.

(26) The term "separately identifiable department or division" of a bank means a unit—

(A) that is under the direct supervision of an officer or officers designated by the board of directors of the bank as responsible for the day-to-day conduct of the bank's investment adviser activities for one or more investment companies, including the supervision of all bank employees engaged in the performance of such activities; and

(B) for which all of the records relating to its investment adviser activities are separately maintained in or extractable from such unit's own facilities or the facilities of the bank, and such records are so maintained or otherwise accessible as to permit independent examination and enforcement by the Commission of this Act or the Investment Company Act of 1940 and rules and regulations promulgated under this Act or the Investment Company Act of 1940.

(27) The terms "security future" and "narrow-based security index" have the same meanings as provided in Section 3(a)(55) of the Securities Exchange Act of 1934.

(28) The term "credit rating agency" has the same meaning as in Section 3 of the Securities Exchange Act of 1934.

(b) No provision in this title shall apply to, or be deemed to include, the United States, a State, or any political subdivision of a State, or any agency, authority, or instrumentality of any one or more of the foregoing, or any corporation which is wholly owned directly or indirectly by any one or more of the foregoing, or any officer, agent, or employee of any of the foregoing acting as such in the course of his official duty, unless such provision makes specific reference thereto.

(c) Consideration of Promotion of Efficiency, Competition, and Capital Formation

Whenever pursuant to this title the Commission is engaged in rulemaking and is required to consider or determine whether an action is necessary or appropriate in the public interest, the Commission shall also consider, in addition to the protection of investors, whether the action will promote efficiency, competition, and capital formation.

Section 203. Registration of Investment Advisers

(a) Necessity of Registration

Except as provided in subsection (b) of this section and Section 203A, it shall be unlawful for any investment adviser, unless registered under this section, to make use of the mails or any means or instrumentality of interstate commerce in connection with his or its business as an investment adviser.

(b) Investment Advisers Who Need Not Be Registered

The provisions of subsection (a) of this section shall not apply to—

(1) any investment adviser all of whose clients are residents of the State within which such investment adviser maintains his or its principal office and place of business, and who does not furnish advice or issue analyses or reports with respect to securities listed or admitted to unlisted trading privileges on any national securities exchange;

(2) any investment adviser whose only clients are insurance companies;

(3) any investment adviser who during the course of the preceding twelve months has had fewer than fifteen clients and who neither holds himself out generally to the public as an investment adviser nor acts an investment adviser to any investment company registered under Title I of this Act, or a company which has elected to be a business development company pursuant to Section 54 of Title I of this Act and has not withdrawn its election. For purposes of determining the number of clients of an investment adviser under this paragraph, no shareholder, partner, or beneficial owner of a business development company, as defined in this title, shall be deemed to be a client of such investment adviser unless such person is a client of such investment adviser separate and apart from his status as a shareholder, partner, or beneficial owner;

(4) any investment adviser that is a charitable organization, as defined in Section 3(c)(10)(D) of the Investment Company Act of 1940, or is a trustee, director, officer, employee, or volunteer of such a charitable organization acting within the scope of such person's employment or duties with such organization, whose advice, analyses, or reports are provided only to one or more of the following:

(A) any such charitable organization;

(B) a fund that is excluded from the definition of an investment company under Section 3(c)(10)(B) of the Investment Company Act of 1940; or

(C) a trust or other donative instrument described in Section 3(c)(10)(B) of the Investment Company Act of 1940, or the trustees, administrators, settlors (or potential settlors), or beneficiaries of any such trust or other instrument;

(5) any plan described in Section 414(e) of the Internal Revenue Code of 1986, any person or entity eligible to establish and maintain such a plan under the Internal Revenue Code of 1986, or any trustee, director, officer, or employee of or volunteer for any such plan or person, if such person or entity, acting in such capacity, provides investment advice exclusively to, or with respect to, any plan, person, or entity or any company, account, or fund that is excluded from the definition of an investment company under Section 3(c)(14) of the Investment Company Act of 1940; or

(6) any investment adviser that is registered with the Commodity Futures Trading Commission as a commodity trading advisor whose business does not consist primarily of acting as an investment adviser, as defined in Section

202(a)(11) of this title, and that does not act as an investment adviser to—

(A) an investment company registered under title I of this Act; or

(B) a company which has elected to be a business development company pursuant to Section 54 of title I of this Act and has not withdrawn its election.

(c) Procedure for Registration; Filing of Application; Effective Date of Registration; Amendment of Registration

(1) An investment adviser, or any person who presently contemplates becoming an investment adviser, may be registered by filing with the Commission an application for registration in such form and containing such of the following information and documents as the Commission, by rule, may prescribe as necessary or appropriate in the public interest or for the protection of investors:

(A) the name and form of organization under which the investment adviser engages or intends to engage in business; the name of the State or other sovereign power under which such investment adviser is organized; the location of his or its principal business office and branch offices, if any; the names and addresses of his or its partners, officers, directors, and persons performing similar functions or, if such an investment adviser be an individual, of such individual; and the number of his or its employees;

(B) the education, the business affiliations for the past ten years, and the present business affiliations of such investment adviser and of his or its partners, officers, directors, and persons performing similar functions and of any controlling person thereof;

(C) the nature of the business of such investment adviser, including the manner of giving advice and rendering analyses or reports;

(D) a balance sheet certified by an independent public accountant and other financial statements (which shall, as the Commission specifies, be certified);

(E) the nature and scope of the authority of such investment adviser with respect to clients' funds and accounts;

(F) the basis or bases upon which such investment adviser is compensated;

(G) whether such investment adviser, or any person associated with such investment adviser, is subject to any disqualification which would be a basis for denial, suspension, or revocation of registration of such investment adviser under the provisions of subsection (e) of this section; and

(H) a statement as to whether the principal business of such investment adviser consists or is to consist of acting as investment adviser and a statement as to whether a substantial part of the business of such investment adviser, consists or is to consist of rendering investment supervisory services.

(2) Within forty-five days of the date of the filing of such application (or within such longer period as to which the applicant consents) the Commission shall—

(A) by order grant such registration; or

(B) institute proceedings to determine whether registration should be denied. Such proceedings shall include notice of the grounds for denial under consideration and opportunity for hearing and shall be concluded within one hundred twenty days of the date of the filing of the application for registration. At the conclusion of such proceedings the Commission, by order, shall grant or deny such registration. The Commission may extend the time for conclusion of such proceedings for up to ninety days if it finds good cause for such extension and publishes its reasons for so finding or for such longer period as to which the applicant consents.

The Commission shall grant such registration if the Commission finds that the requirements of this section are satisfied and that the applicant is not prohibited from registering as an investment advisor under Section 203A. The Commission shall deny such registration if it does not make such a finding or if it finds that if the applicant were so registered, its registration would be subject to suspension or revocation under subsection (e) of this section.

(d) OTHER ACTS PROHIBITED BY SUBCHAPTER

Any provision of this title (other than subsection (a) of this section) which prohibits any act, practice, or course of business if the mails or any means or instrumentality of interstate commerce are used in connection therewith shall also prohibit any such act, practice, or course of business by any investment adviser registered pursuant to this section or any person acting on behalf of such an investment adviser, irrespective of any use of the mails or any means or instrumentality of interstate commerce in connection therewith.

(e) CENSURE, DENIAL, OR SUSPENSION OF REGISTRATION; NOTICE AND HEARING

The Commission, by order, shall censure, place limitations on the activities, functions, or operations of, suspend for a period not exceeding twelve months, or revoke the registration of any investment adviser if it finds, on the record after notice and opportunity for hearing, that such censure, placing of limitations, suspension, or revocation is in the public interest and that such investment adviser, or any person associated with such investment adviser, whether prior to or subsequent to becoming so associated—

(1) has willfully made or caused to be made in any application for registration or report required to be filed with the Commission under this title, or in any proceeding before the Commission with respect to registration, any statement which was at the time and in the light of the circumstances under which it was made false or misleading with respect to any material fact, or has omitted to state in any such application or report any material fact which is required to be stated therein.

(2) has been convicted within ten years preceding the filing of any application for registration or at any time thereafter of any felony or misdemeanor or of a substantially equivalent crime by a foreign court of competent jurisdiction which the Commission finds—

(A) involves the purchase or sale of any security, the taking of a false oath, the making of a false report, bribery, perjury, burglary, any substantially equivalent activity however denominated by the laws of the relevant foreign government, or conspiracy to commit any such offense;

(B) arises out of the conduct of the business of a broker, dealer, municipal securities dealer, investment adviser, bank, insurance company, government securities broker, government securities dealer, fiduciary, transfer agent, credit rating agency, foreign person performing a function substantially equivalent to any of the above, or entity or person required to be registered under the Commodity Exchange Act or any substantially equivalent statute or regulation;

(C) involves the larceny, theft, robbery, extortion, forgery, counterfeiting, fraudulent concealment, embezzlement, fraudulent conversion, or misappropriation of funds or securities or substantially equivalent activity however denominated by the laws of the relevant foreign government; or

(D) involves the violation of Section 152, 1341, 1342, or 1343 or Chapter 25 or 47 of Title 18, United States Code, or a violation of [any] substantially equivalent foreign statute.

(3) has been convicted during the 10–year period preceding the date of filing of any application for registration, or at any time thereafter, of—

(A) any crime that is punishable by imprisonment for 1 or more years, and that is not described in paragraph (2); or

(B) a substantially equivalent crime by a foreign court of competent jurisdiction.

(4) is permanently or temporarily enjoined by order, judgment, or decree of any court of competent jurisdiction, including any foreign court of competent jurisdiction, from acting as an investment adviser, underwriter, broker, dealer, municipal securities dealer, government securities broker, government securities dealer, transfer agent, credit rating agency, foreign person performing a function substantially equivalent to any of the above, or entity or person required to be registered under the Commodity Exchange Act or any substantially equivalent statute or regulation, or as an affiliated person or employee of any investment company, bank, insurance company, foreign entity substantially equivalent to any of the above, or entity or person required to be registered under the Commodity Exchange Act or any substantially equivalent statute or regulation, or from engaging in or continuing any conduct or practice in connection with any such activity, or in connection with the purchase or sale of any security.

(5) has willfully violated any provision of the Securities Act of 1933, the Securities Exchange Act of 1934, the Investment Company Act of 1940, this title, the Commodity Exchange Act, or the rules or regulations under any such statutes or any rule of the Municipal Securities Rulemaking Board, or is unable to comply with any such provision.

(6) has willfully aided, abetted, counseled, commanded, induced, or procured the violation by any other person of any provision of the Securities Act of 1933, the Securities Exchange Act of 1934, the Investment Company Act of 1940, this title, the Commodity Exchange Act, the rules or regulations under any of such statutes, or the rules of the Municipal Securities Rulemaking Board, or has failed reasonably to supervise, with a view to preventing violations of the provisions of such statutes, rules, and regulations, another person who commits such a violation, if such other person is subject to his supervision. For the purposes of this paragraph no person shall be deemed to have failed reasonably to supervise any person, if—

(A) there have been established procedures, and a system for applying such procedures, which would reasonably be expected to prevent and detect, insofar as practicable, any such violation by such other person, and

(B) such person has reasonably discharged the duties and obligations incumbent upon him by reason of such procedures and system without reasonable cause to believe that such procedures and system were not being complied with.

(7) is subject to any order of the Commission barring or suspending the right of the person to be associated with an investment adviser;

(8) has been found by a foreign financial regulatory authority to have—

(A) made or caused to be made in any application for registration or report required to be filed with a foreign securities authority, or in any proceeding before a foreign securities authority with respect to registration, any statement that was at the time and in light of the circumstances under which it was made false or misleading with respect to any material fact, or has omitted to state in any application or report to a foreign securities authority any material fact that is required to be stated therein;

(B) violated any foreign statute or regulation regarding transactions in securities or contracts of sale of a commodity for future delivery traded on or subject to the rules of a contract market or any board of trade; or

(C) aided, abetted, counseled, commanded, induced, or procured the violation by any other person of any foreign statute or regulation regarding transactions in securities or contracts of sale of a commodity for future delivery traded on or subject to the rules of a contract market or any board of trade, or has been found, by the foreign financial regulatory authority, to have failed reasonably to supervise, with a view to preventing violations of statutory provisions, and rules and regulations promulgated thereunder, another person who commits such a violation, if such other person is subject to his supervision; or

(9) is subject to any final order of a State securities commission (or any agency or officer performing like functions), State authority that supervises or examines banks, savings associations, or credit unions, State insurance commission (or any agency or office performing like functions), an appropriate Federal banking agency (as defined in Section 3 of the Federal Deposit Insurance Act (12 U.S.C. 1813(q))), or the National Credit Union Administration, that—

(A) bars such person from association with an entity regulated by such commission, authority, agency, or officer, or from engaging in the business of securities, insurance, banking, savings association activities, or credit union activities; or

(B) constitutes a final order based on violations of any laws or regulations that prohibit fraudulent, manipulative, or deceptive conduct.

(f) BAR OR SUSPENSION FROM ASSOCIATION WITH INVESTMENT ADVISER; NOTICE AND HEARING

The Commission, by order, shall censure or place limitations on the activities of any person associated, seeking to become associated, or, at the time of the alleged misconduct, associated or seeking to become associated with an investment adviser, or suspend for a period not exceeding twelve months or bar any such person from being associated with an investment adviser, if the Commission finds, on the record after notice and opportunity for hearing, that such censure, placing of limitations, suspension, or bar is in the public interest and that such person has committed or omitted any act or omission enumerated in paragraph (1), (5), (6), (8), or (9) of subsection (e) of this section or has been convicted of any offense specified in paragraph (2) or (3) of subsection (e) within ten years of the commencement of the proceedings under this subsection, or is enjoined from any action, conduct, or practice specified in paragraph (4) of subsection (e) It shall be unlawful for any person as to whom such an order suspending or barring him from being associated with an investment adviser is in effect willfully to become, or to be, associated with an investment adviser without the consent of the Commission, and it shall be unlawful for any investment adviser to permit such a person to become, or remain, a person associated with him without the consent of the Commission, if such investment adviser knew, or in the exercise of reasonable care, should have known, of such order.

(g) REGISTRATION OF SUCCESSOR TO BUSINESS OF INVESTMENT ADVISER

Any successor to the business of an investment adviser registered under this section shall be deemed likewise registered hereunder, if within thirty days from its succession to such business it shall file an application for registration under this section, unless and until the Commission, pursuant to subsection (c) or subsection (e) of this section, shall deny registration to or revoke or suspend the registration of such successor.

(h) WITHDRAWAL OF REGISTRATION

Any person registered under this section may, upon such terms and conditions as the Commission finds necessary in the public interest or for the protection of investors, withdraw from registration by filing a written notice of withdrawal with the Commission. If the Commission finds that any person registered under this section, or who has pending an application for registration filed under this section, is no longer in existence, is not engaged in business as an investment adviser or is prohibited from registering as an investment adviser under Section 203A, the Commission shall by order cancel the registration of such person.

(i) MONEY PENALTIES IN ADMINISTRATIVE PROCEEDINGS

(1) AUTHORITY OF COMMISSION

In any proceeding instituted pursuant to subsection (e) or (f) against any person, the Commission may impose a civil penalty if it finds, on the record after notice and opportunity for hearing, that such person—

(A) has willfully violated any provision of the Securities Act of 1933, the Securities Exchange Act of 1934, the Investment Company Act of 1940, or this title, or the rules or regulations thereunder;

(B) has willfully aided, abetted, counseled, commanded, induced, or procured such a violation by any other person;

(C) has willfully made or caused to be made in any application for registration or report required to be filed with the Commission under this title, or in any proceeding before the Commission with respect to registration, any statement which was, at the time and in the light of the circumstances under which it was made, false or misleading with respect to any material fact, or has omitted to state in any such application or report any material fact which was required to be stated therein; or

(D) has failed reasonably to supervise, within the meaning of subsection (e)(6) with a view to preventing violations of the provisions of this title and the rules and regulations thereunder, another person who commits such a violation, if such other person is subject to his supervision;

and that such penalty is in the public interest.

(2) MAXIMUM AMOUNT OF PENALTY

(A) FIRST TIER

The maximum amount of penalty for each act or omission described in paragraph (1) shall be $5,000 for a natural person or $50,000 for any other person.

(B) SECOND TIER

Notwithstanding subparagraph (A), the maximum amount of penalty for each such act or omission shall be $50,000 for a natural person or $250,000 for any other person if the act or omission described in paragraph (1) involved fraud, deceit, manipulation, or deliberate or reckless disregard of a regulatory requirement.

(C) THIRD TIER

Notwithstanding subparagraphs (A) and (B), the maximum amount of penalty for each such act or omission shall be $100,000 for a natural person or $500,000 for any other person if—

(i) the act or omission described in paragraph (1) involved fraud, deceit, manipulation, or deliberate or reckless disregard of a regulatory requirement; and

(ii) such act or omission directly or indirectly resulted in substantial losses or created a significant risk of substantial losses to other persons or resulted in substantial pecuniary gain to the person who committed the act or omission.

(3) DETERMINATION OF PUBLIC INTEREST

In considering under this section whether a penalty is in the public interest, the Commission may consider—

(A) whether the act or omission for which such penalty is assessed involved fraud, deceit, manipulation, or deliberate or reckless disregard of a regulatory requirement;

(B) the harm to other persons resulting either directly or indirectly from such act or omission;

(C) the extent to which any person was unjustly enriched, taking into account any restitution made to persons injured by such behavior;

(D) whether such person previously has been found by the Commission, another appropriate regulatory agency, or a self-regulatory organization to have violated the Federal securities laws, State securities laws, or the rules of a self-regulatory organization, has been enjoined by a court of competent jurisdiction from violations of such laws or rules, or has been convicted by a court of competent jurisdiction of violations of such laws or of any felony or misdemeanor described in Section 203(e)(2) of this title;

(E) the need to deter such person and other persons from committing such acts or omissions; and

(F) such other matters as justice may require.

(4) EVIDENCE CONCERNING ABILITY TO PAY

In any proceeding in which the Commission may impose a penalty under this section, a respondent may present evidence of the respondent's ability to pay such penalty. The Commission may, in its discretion, consider such evidence in determining whether such penalty is in the public interest. Such evidence may relate to the extent of such person's ability to continue in business and the collectability of a penalty, taking into account any other claims of the United States or third parties upon such person's assets and the amount of such person's assets.

(j) AUTHORITY TO ENTER ORDER REQUIRING ACCOUNTING AND DISGORGEMENT

In any proceeding in which the Commission may impose a penalty under this section, the Commission may enter an order requiring accounting and disgorgement, including reasonable interest. The Commission is authorized to adopt rules, regulations, and orders concerning payments to investors, rates of interest, periods of accrual, and such other matters as it deems appropriate to implement this subsection.

(k) CEASE-AND-DESIST PROCEEDINGS

(1) AUTHORITY OF THE COMMISSION

If the Commission finds, after notice and opportunity for hearing, that any person is violating, has violated, or is about to violate any provision of this title, or any rule or regulation thereunder, the Commission may publish its findings and enter an order requiring such person, and any other person that is, was, or would be a cause of the violation, due to an act or omission the person knew or should have known would contribute to such violation, to cease and desist from committing or causing such violation and any future violation of the same provision, rule, or regulation. Such order may, in addition to requiring a person to cease and desist from committing or causing a violation, require such person to comply, or to take steps to effect compliance, with such provision, rule, or regulation, upon such terms and conditions and within such time as the Commission may specify in such order. Any such order may, as the Commission deems appropriate, require future compliance or steps to effect future compliance, either permanently or for such period of time as the Commission may specify, with such provision, rule, or regulation with respect to any security, any issuer, or any other person.

(2) HEARING

The notice instituting proceedings pursuant to paragraph (1) shall fix a hearing date not earlier than 30 days nor later than 60 days after service of the notice unless an earlier or a later date is set by the Commission with the consent of any respondent so served.

(3) TEMPORARY ORDER

(A) IN GENERAL

Whenever the Commission determines that the alleged violation or threatened violation specified in the notice instituting proceedings pursuant to paragraph (1), or the continuation thereof, is likely to result in significant dissipation or conversion of assets, significant harm to investors, or substantial harm to the public interest, including, but not limited to, losses to the Securities Investor Protection Corporation, prior to the completion of the proceedings, the Commission may enter a temporary order requiring the respondent to cease and desist from the violation or threatened violation and to take such action to prevent the violation or threatened violation and to prevent dissipation or conversion of assets, significant harm to investors, or substantial harm to the public interest as the Commission deems appropriate pending completion of such proceedings. Such an order shall be entered only after notice and opportunity for a hearing, unless the Commission, notwithstanding Section 211(c) of this title, determines that notice and hearing prior to entry would be impracticable or contrary to the public interest. A temporary order shall become effective upon service upon the respondent and, unless set aside, limited, or suspended by the Commission or a court of competent jurisdiction, shall remain effective and enforceable pending the completion of the proceedings.

(B) APPLICABILITY

This paragraph shall apply only to a respondent that acts, or, at the time of the alleged misconduct acted, as a broker, dealer, investment adviser, investment company, municipal securities dealer, government securities broker, government securities dealer, or transfer agent, or is, or was at the time of the alleged misconduct, an associated person of, or a person seeking to become associated with, any of the foregoing.

(4) REVIEW OF TEMPORARY ORDERS

(A) COMMISSION REVIEW

At any time after the respondent has been served with a temporary cease-and-desist order pursuant to paragraph (3), the respondent may apply to the Commission to have the order set aside, limited, or suspended. If the respondent has been served with a temporary cease-and-desist order entered without a prior Commission hearing, the respondent may, within 10 days after the date on which the order was served, request a hearing on such application and the Commission shall hold a hearing and render a decision on such application at the earliest possible time.

(B) Judicial Review

Within—

(i) 10 days after the date the respondent was served with a temporary cease-and-desist order entered with a prior Commission hearing, or

(ii) 10 days after the Commission renders a decision on an application and hearing under subparagraph (A), with respect to any temporary cease-and-desist order entered without a prior Commission hearing,

the respondent may apply to the United States district court for the district in which the respondent resides or has its principal place of business, or for the District of Columbia, for an order setting aside, limiting, or suspending the effectiveness or enforcement of the order, and the court shall have jurisdiction to enter such an order. A respondent served with a temporary cease-and-desist order entered without a prior Commission hearing may not apply to the court except after hearing and decision by the Commission on the respondent's application under subparagraph (A) of this paragraph.

(C) No Automatic Stay of Temporary Order

The commencement of proceedings under subparagraph (B) of this paragraph shall not, unless specifically ordered by the court, operate as a stay of the Commission's order.

(D) EXCLUSIVE REVIEW

Section 213 of this title shall not apply to a temporary order entered pursuant to this section.

(5) AUTHORITY TO ENTER ORDER REQUIRING ACCOUNTING AND DISGORGEMENT

In any cease-and-desist proceeding under paragraph (1), the Commission may enter an order requiring accounting and disgorgement, including reasonable interest. The Commission is authorized to adopt rules, regulations, and orders concerning payments to investors, rates of interest, periods of accrual, and such other matters as it deems appropriate to implement this subsection.

Section 203A. State and Federal Responsibilities

(a) ADVISERS SUBJECT TO STATE AUTHORITIES

(1) IN GENERAL

No investment adviser that is regulated or required to be regulated as an investment adviser in the State in which it maintains its principal office and place of business shall register under Section 203, unless the investment adviser—

(A) has assets under management of not less than $25,000,000, or such higher amount as the Commission may, by rule, deem appropriate in accordance with the purposes of this title; or

(B) is an adviser to an investment company registered under Title I of this Act.

(2) DEFINITION

For purposes of this subsection, the term "assets under management" means the securities portfolios with respect to which an investment adviser provides continuous and regular supervisory or management services.

(b) ADVISERS SUBJECT TO COMMISSION AUTHORITY

(1) IN GENERAL

No law of any State or political subdivision thereof requiring the registration, licensing, or qualification as an investment adviser or supervised person of an investment adviser shall apply to any person—

(A) that is registered under Section 203 as an investment adviser, or that is a supervised person of such person, except that a State may license, register, or otherwise qualify any investment adviser representative who has a place of business located within that State; or

(B) that is not registered under Section 203 because that person is excepted from the definition of an investment adviser under Section 202(a)(11).

(2) LIMITATION

Nothing in this subsection shall prohibit the securities commission (or any agency or office performing like functions) of any State from investigating and bringing enforcement actions with respect to fraud or deceit against an investment adviser or person associated with an investment adviser.

(c) EXEMPTIONS

Notwithstanding subsection (a) the Commission, by rule or regulation upon its own motion, or by order upon application, may permit the registration with the Commission of any person or class of persons to which the application of subsection (a) would be unfair, a burden on interstate commerce, or otherwise inconsistent with the purposes of this section.

(d) STATE ASSISTANCE

Upon request of the securities commissioner (or any agency or officer performing like functions) of any State, the Commission may provide such training, technical assistance, or other reasonable assistance in connection with the regulation of investment advisers by the State.

Section 204. Reports by Investment Advisers

(a) IN GENERAL

Every investment adviser who makes use of the mails or of any means or instrumentality of interstate commerce in connection with his or its business as an investment adviser (other than one specifically exempted from registration pursuant to Section 203(b) of this title), shall make and keep for prescribed periods such records (as defined in Section 3(a)(37) of the Securities Exchange Act of 1934), furnish such copies thereof, and make and disseminate such reports as the Commission, by rule, may prescribe as necessary or appropriate in the public interest or for the protection of investors. All records (as so defined) of such investment advisers are subject at any time, or from time to time, to such reasonable periodic, special, or other examinations by representatives of the Commission as the Commission deems necessary or appropriate in the public interest or for the protection of investors.

(b) FILING DEPOSITORIES

The Commission may, by rule, require an investment adviser—

(1) to file with the Commission any fee, application, report, or notice required to be filed by this title or the rules issued under this title through any entity designated by the Commission for that purpose; and

(2) to pay the reasonable costs associated with such filing and the establishment and maintenance of the systems required by subsection (c).

(c) ACCESS TO DISCIPLINARY AND OTHER INFORMATION

(1) MAINTENANCE OF SYSTEM TO RESPOND TO INQUIRIES

(A) IN GENERAL

The Commission shall require the entity designated by the Commission under subsection (b)(1) to establish and maintain a toll-free telephone listing, or a readily accessible electronic or other process, to receive and promptly respond to inquiries regarding registration information (including disciplinary actions, regulatory, judicial, and arbitration proceedings, and other information required by law or rule to be reported) involving investment advisers and persons associated with investment advisers.

(B) APPLICABILITY

This subsection shall apply to any investment adviser (and the persons associated with that adviser), whether the investment adviser is registered with the Commission under Section 203 of this title or regulated solely by a State, as described in Section 203A.

(2) RECOVERY OF COSTS

An entity designated by the Commission under subsection (b)(1) may charge persons making inquiries, other than individual investors, reasonable fees for responses to inquiries described in paragraph (1).

(3) LIMITATION ON LIABILITY

An entity designated by the Commission under subsection (b)(1) shall not have any liability to any person for any actions taken or omitted in good faith under this subsection.

Section 204A. Prevention of Misuse of Non-public Information

Every investment adviser subject to Section 204 of this title shall establish, maintain, and enforce written policies and procedures reasonably designed, taking into consideration the nature of such investment adviser's business, to prevent the misuse in violation of this chapter or the Securities Exchange

Act of 1934, or the rules or regulations thereunder, of material, nonpublic information by such investment adviser or any person associated with such investment adviser. The Commission, as it deems necessary or appropriate in the public interest or for the protection of investors, shall adopt rules or regulations to require specific policies or procedures reasonably designed to prevent misuse in violation of this chapter or the Securities Exchange Act of 1934 (or the rules or regulations thereunder) of material, nonpublic information.

Section 205. Investment Advisory Contracts

(a) COMPENSATION, ASSIGNMENT, AND PARTNERSHIP-MEMBERSHIP PROVISIONS

No investment adviser, unless exempt from registration pursuant to Section 203(b), shall make use of the mails or any means or instrumentality of interstate commerce, directly or indirectly, to enter into, extend, or renew any investment advisory contract, or in any way to perform any investment advisory contract entered into, extended, or renewed on or after November 1, 1940, if such contract—

(1) provides for compensation to the investment adviser on the basis of a share of capital gains upon or capital appreciation of the funds or any portion of the funds of the client;

(2) fails to provide, in substance, that no assignment of such contract shall be made by the in-

vestment adviser without the consent of the other party to the contract; or

(3) fails to provide, in substance, that the investment adviser, if a partnership, will notify the other party to the contract of any change in the membership of such partnership within a reasonable time after such change.

(b) Compensation Prohibition Inapplicable to Certain Compensation Computations

Paragraph (1) of subsection (a) shall not—

(1) be construed to prohibit an investment advisory contract which provides for compensation based upon the total value of a fund averaged over a definite period, or as of definite dates, or taken as of a definite date;

(2) apply to an investment advisory contract with—

(A) an investment company registered under Title I of this Act, or

(B) any other person (except a trust, governmental plan, collective trust fund, or separate account referred to in Section 203(c)(11) of title I of this Act), provided that the contract relates to the investment of assets in excess of $1 million,

if the contract provides for compensation based on the asset value of the company or fund under management averaged over a specified period and increasing and decreasing proportionately with the investment performance of the company or fund over a specified period in relation to the investment record of an appropriate index of securities prices or such other measure of investment performance as the Commission by rule, regulation, or order may specify; or

(3) apply with respect to any investment advisory contract between an investment adviser and a business development company, as defined in this title, if (A) the compensation provided for in such contract does not exceed 20 per centum of the realized capital gains upon the funds of the business development company over a specified period or as of definite dates, computed net of all realized capital losses and unrealized capital depreciation, and the condition of Section 61(a)(3)(B)(iii) of title I of this Act is satisfied, and (B) the business development company does not have outstanding any option, warrant, or right issued pursuant to Section 61(a)(3)(B) of Title I of this Act and does not have a profit-sharing plan described in Section 57(n) of Title I of this Act;

(4) apply to an investment advisory contract with a company excepted from the definition of an investment company under Section 3(c)(7) of title I of this Act; or

(5) apply to an investment advisory contract with a person who is not a resident of the United States.

(c) MEASUREMENT OF CHANGES IN COMPENSATION

For purposes of paragraph (2) of subsection (b), the point from which increases and decreases in compensation are measured shall be the fee which is paid or earned when the investment performance of such company or fund is equivalent to that of the index or other measure of performance, and an index of securities prices shall be deemed appropriate unless the Commission by order shall determine otherwise.

(d) "INVESTMENT ADVISORY CONTRACT" DEFINED

As used in paragraphs (2) and (3) of subsection (a) "investment advisory contract" means any contract or agreement whereby a person agrees to act as investment adviser to or to manage any investment or trading account of another person other than an investment company registered under Title I of this chapter.

(e) EXEMPT PERSONS AND TRANSACTIONS

The Commission, by rule or regulation, upon its own motion, or by order upon application, may conditionally or unconditionally exempt any person or transaction, or any class or classes of persons or transactions, from subsection (a)(1) if and to the extent that the exemption relates to an investment advisory contract with any person that the Commission determines does not need the protections of subsection (a)(1) on the basis of such factors as financial sophistication, net worth, knowledge of and experience in financial matters, amount of assets under management, relationship with a registered investment adviser, and such other factors as the Commission determines are consistent with this section.

Section 206. Prohibited Transactions by Investment Advisers

It shall be unlawful for any investment adviser, by use of the mails or any means or instrumentality of interstate commerce, directly or indirectly—

(1) to employ any device, scheme, or artifice to defraud any client or prospective client;

(2) to engage in any transaction, practice, or course of business which operates as a fraud or deceit upon any client or prospective client;

(3) acting as principal for his own account, knowingly to sell any security to or purchase any security from a client, or acting as broker for a person other than such client, knowingly to effect any sale or purchase of any security for the account of such client, without disclosing to such client in writing before the completion of such transaction the capacity in which he is acting and obtaining the consent of the client to such transaction. The prohibitions of this paragraph (3) shall not apply to any transaction with a customer of a broker or dealer if such broker or dealer is not acting as an investment adviser in relation to such transaction;

(4) to engage in any act, practice, or course of business which is fraudulent, deceptive, or manipulative. The Commission shall, for the purposes of this paragraph (4) by rules and regulations

define, and prescribe means reasonably designed to prevent, such acts, practices, and courses of business as are fraudulent, deceptive, or manipulative.

Section 206A. Exemptions

The Commission, by rules and regulations, upon its own motion, or by order upon application, may conditionally or unconditionally exempt any person or transaction, or any class or classes of persons, or transactions, from any provision or provisions of this subchapter or of any rule or regulation thereunder, if and to the extent that such exemption is necessary or appropriate in the public interest and consistent with the protection of investors and the purposes fairly intended by the policy and provisions of this title.

Section 207. Material Misstatements

It shall be unlawful for any person willfully to make any untrue statement of a material fact in any registration application or report filed with the Commission under Section 203 or 204, or willfully to omit to state in any such application or report any material fact which is required to be stated therein.

Section 208. General Prohibitions

(a) REPRESENTATIONS OF SPONSORSHIP BY UNITED STATES OR AGENCY THEREOF

It shall be unlawful for any person registered under Section 203 of this title to represent or imply in any manner whatsoever that such person has been sponsored, recommended, or approved, or that his abilities or qualifications have in any respect been passed upon by the United States or any agency or any officer thereof.

(b) STATEMENT OF REGISTRATION UNDER SECURITIES EXCHANGE ACT OF 1934 PROVISIONS

No provision of subsection (a) shall be construed to prohibit a statement that a person is registered under this subchapter or under the Securities Exchange Act of 1934, if such statement is true in fact and if the effect of such registration is not misrepresented.

(c) USE OF NAME "INVESTMENT COUNSEL" AS DESCRIPTIVE OF BUSINESS

It shall be unlawful for any person registered under Section 203 of this title to represent that he is an investment counsel or to use the name "investment counsel" as descriptive of his business unless (1) his or its principal business consists of acting as investment adviser, and (2) a substantial part of his or its business consists of rendering investment supervisory services.

(d) USE OF INDIRECT MEANS TO DO PROHIBITED ACT

It shall be unlawful for any person indirectly, or through or by any other person, to do any act or thing which it would be unlawful for such person to do directly under the provisions of this title or any rule or regulation thereunder.

Section 209. Enforcement of Subchapter

(a) INVESTIGATION

Whenever it shall appear to the Commission, either upon complaint or otherwise, that the provisions of this title or of any rule or regulation prescribed under the authority thereof, have been or are about to be violated by any person, it may in its discretion require, and in any event shall permit, such person to file with it a statement in writing, under oath or otherwise, as to all the facts and circumstances relevant to such violation, and may otherwise investigate all such facts and circumstances.

(b) ADMINISTRATION OF OATHS AND AFFIRMATIONS, SUBPOENA OF WITNESSES, ETC.

For the purposes of any investigation or any proceeding under this title, any member of the Commission or any officer thereof designated by it is empowered to administer oaths and affirmations, subpoena witnesses, compel their attendance, take evidence, and require the production of any books, papers, correspondence, memoranda, contracts, agreements, or other records which are relevant or material to the inquiry. Such attendance of witnesses and the production of any such records may be required from any place in any State or in any Territory or other place subject to the jurisdiction of the United States at any designated place of hearing.

(c) JURISDICTION OF COURTS OF UNITED STATES

In case of contumacy by, or refusal to obey a subpoena issued to, any person, the Commission may invoke the aid of any court of the United States within the jurisdiction of which such investigation or proceeding is carried on, or where such person resides or carries on business, in requiring the attendance and testimony of witnesses and the production of books, papers, correspondence, memoranda, contracts, agreements, and other records. And such court may issue an order requiring such person to appear before the Commission or member or officer designated by the Commission, there to produce records, if so ordered, or to give testimony touching the matter under investigation or in question; and any failure to obey such order of the court may be punished by such court as a contempt thereof. All process in any such case may be served in the judicial district whereof such person is an inhabitant or wherever he may be found. Any person who without just cause shall fail or refuse to attend and testify or to answer any lawful inquiry or to produce books, papers, correspondence, memoranda, contracts, agreements, or other records, if in his or its power so to do, in obedience to the subpoena of the Commission, shall be guilty of a misdemeanor, and upon conviction shall be subject to a fine of not more than $1,000 or to imprisonment for a term of not more than one year, or both.

(d) Action for Injunction

Whenever it shall appear to the Commission that any person has engaged, is engaged, or is about to engage in any act or practice constituting a violation of any provision of this title, or of any rule, regulation, or order hereunder, or that any person has aided, abetted, counseled, commanded, induced, or procured, is aiding, abetting, counseling, commanding, inducing, or procuring, or is about to aid, abet, counsel, command, induce, or procure such a violation, it may in its discretion bring an action in the proper district court of the United States, or the proper United States court of any Territory or other place subject to the jurisdiction of the United States, to enjoin such acts or practices and to enforce compliance with this title or any rule, regulation, or order hereunder. Upon a showing that such person has engaged, is engaged, or is about to engage in any such act or practice, or in aiding, abetting, counseling, commanding, inducing, or procuring any such act or practice, a permanent or temporary injunction or decree or restraining order shall be granted without bond. The Commission may transmit such evidence as may be available concerning any violation of the provisions of this title, or of any rule, regulation, or order thereunder, to the Attorney General, who, in his discretion, may institute the appropriate criminal proceedings under this title.

(f) Money Penalties in Civil Actions

(1) Authority of Commission

Whenever it shall appear to the Commission that any person has violated any provision of this subchapter, the rules or regulations thereunder, or a cease-and-desist order entered by the Commission pursuant to Section 203(k) of this title, the Commission may bring an action in a United States district court to seek, and the court shall have jurisdiction to impose, upon a proper showing, a civil penalty to be paid by the person who committed such violation.

(2) AMOUNT OF PENALTY

(A) FIRST TIER

The amount of the penalty shall be determined by the court in light of the facts and circumstances. For each violation, the amount of the penalty shall not exceed the greater of (i) $5,000 for a natural person or $50,000 for any other person, or (ii) the gross amount of pecuniary gain to such defendant as a result of the violation.

(B) SECOND TIER

Notwithstanding subparagraph (A), the amount of penalty for each such violation shall not exceed the greater of (i) $50,000 for a natural person or $250,000 for any other person, or (ii) the gross amount of pecuniary gain to such defendant as a result of the violation, if the violation described in paragraph (1) involved fraud, deceit, manipulation, or deliberate or reckless disregard of a regulatory requirement.

(C) THIRD TIER

Notwithstanding subparagraphs (A) and (B), the amount of penalty for each such violation shall not exceed the greater of (i) $100,000 for a natural person or $500,000 for any other person, or (ii) the gross amount of pecuniary gain to such defendant as a result of the violation, if—

(I) the violation described in paragraph (1) involved fraud, deceit, manipulation, or deliberate or reckless disregard of a regulatory requirement; and

(II) such violation directly or indirectly resulted in substantial losses or created a significant risk of substantial losses to other persons.

(3) PROCEDURES FOR COLLECTION

(A) PAYMENT OF PENALTY TO TREASURY

A penalty imposed under this section shall be payable into the Treasury of the United States, except as otherwise provided in Section 308 of the Sarbanes–Oxley Act of 2002.

(B) COLLECTION OF PENALTIES

If a person upon whom such a penalty is imposed shall fail to pay such penalty within the time prescribed in the court's order, the Commission may refer the matter to the Attorney General who shall recover such penalty by action in the appropriate United States district court.

(C) REMEDY NOT EXCLUSIVE

The actions authorized by this subsection may be brought in addition to any other action that the Commission or the Attorney General is entitled to bring.

(D) Jurisdiction and Venue

For purposes of Section 204 of this title, actions under this paragraph shall be actions to enforce a liability or a duty created by this title.

(4) Special Provisions Relating to Violation of Cease-and-Desist Order

In an action to enforce a cease-and-desist order entered by the Commission pursuant to Section 203(k), each separate violation of such order shall be a separate offense, except that in the case of a violation through a continuing failure to comply with the order, each day of the failure to comply shall be deemed a separate offense.

Section 210. Disclosure of Information by Commission

(a) Information Available to Public

The information contained in any registration application or report or amendment thereto filed with the Commission pursuant to any provision of this title shall be made available to the public, unless and except insofar as the Commission, by rules and regulations upon its own motion, or by order upon application, finds that public disclosure is neither necessary nor appropriate in the public interest or for the protection of investors. Photostatic or other copies of information contained in documents filed with the Commission under this title and made available to the public shall be furnished to any person at such reasonable charge and under such reasonable limitations as the Commission shall prescribe.

(b) DISCLOSURE OF FACT OF EXAMINATION OR INVESTIGATION; EXCEPTIONS

Subject to the provisions of subsections (c) and (d) of Section 209 of this title and Section 24(c) of the Securities Exchange Act of 1934, the Commission, or any member, officer, or employee thereof, shall not make public the fact that any examination or investigation under this subchapter is being conducted, or the results of or any facts ascertained during any such examination or investigation; and no member, officer, or employee of the Commission shall disclose to any person other than a member, officer, or employee of the Commission any information obtained as a result of any such examination or investigation except with the approval of the Commission. The provisions of this subsection shall not apply—

(1) in the case of any hearing which is public under the provisions of Section 212; or

(2) in the case of a resolution or request from either House of Congress.

(c) DISCLOSURE BY INVESTMENT ADVISER OF IDENTITY OF CLIENTS

No provision of this title shall be construed to require, or to authorize the Commission to require any investment adviser engaged in rendering investment supervisory services to disclose the identity, investments, or affairs of any client of such investment adviser, except insofar as such disclosure may be necessary or appropriate in a particular proceeding or investigation having as its object the enforcement of a provision or provisions of this title.

Section 210A. Consultation

(a) Examination Results and Other Information

(1) The appropriate Federal banking agency shall provide the Commission upon request the results of any examination, reports, records, or other information to which such agency may have access—

(A) with respect to the investment advisory activities of any—

(i) bank holding company or savings and loan holding company;

(ii) bank; or

(iii) separately identifiable department or division of a bank,

that is registered under Section 203 of this title; and

(B) in the case of a bank holding company or savings and loan holding company or bank that has a subsidiary or a separately identifiable department or division registered under that section, with respect to the investment advisory activities of such bank or bank holding company or savings and loan holding company.

(2) The Commission shall provide to the appropriate Federal banking agency upon request the results of any examination, reports, records, or other information with respect to the investment

advisory activities of any bank holding company
or savings and loan holding company, bank, or
separately identifiable department or division of a
bank, which is registered under Section 203 of
this title.

(3) Notwithstanding any other provision of law,
the Commission and the appropriate Federal
banking agencies shall not be compelled to disclose any information provided under paragraph
(1) or (2). Nothing in this paragraph shall authorize the Commission or such agencies to withhold
information from Congress, or prevent the Commission or such agencies from complying with a
request for information from any other Federal
department or agency or any self-regulatory organization requesting the information for purposes within the scope of its jurisdiction, or complying with an order of a court of the United
States in an action brought by the United States,
the Commission, or such agencies. For purposes
of Section 552 of Title 5, United States Code, this
paragraph shall be considered a statute described
in subsection (b)(3)(B) of such Section 552.

(b) EFFECT ON OTHER AUTHORITY

Nothing in this section shall limit in any respect the
authority of the appropriate Federal banking agency with respect to such bank holding company or
savings and loan holding company (or affiliates or
subsidiaries thereof), bank, or subsidiary, department, or division or a bank under any other provision of law.

(c) DEFINITION

For purposes of this section, the term "appropriate Federal banking agency" shall have the same meaning as given in Section 3 of the Federal Deposit Insurance Act.

Section 211. Rules, Regulations, and Orders of Commission

(a) POWER OF COMMISSION

The Commission shall have authority from time to time to make, issue, amend, and rescind such rules and regulations and such orders as are necessary or appropriate to the exercise of the functions and powers conferred upon the Commission elsewhere in this subchapter. For the purposes of its rules or regulations the Commission may classify persons and matters within its jurisdiction and prescribe different requirements for different classes of persons or matters.

(b) EFFECTIVE DATE OF REGULATIONS

Subject to the provisions of Chapter 15 of Title 44 and regulations prescribed under the authority thereof, the rules and regulations of the Commission under this title, and amendments thereof, shall be effective upon publication in the manner which the Commission shall prescribe, or upon such later date as may be provided in such rules and regulations.

(c) ORDERS OF COMMISSION AFTER NOTICE AND HEARING; TYPE OF NOTICE

Orders of the Commission under this title shall be issued only after appropriate notice and opportunity for hearing. Notice to the parties to a proceeding before the Commission shall be given by personal service upon each party or by registered mail or certified mail or confirmed telegraphic notice to the party's last known business address. Notice to interested persons, if any, other than parties may be given in the same manner or by publication in the Federal Register.

(d) GOOD FAITH COMPLIANCE WITH RULES AND REGULATIONS

No provision of this title imposing any liability shall apply to any act done or omitted in good faith in conformity with any rule, regulation, or order of the Commission, notwithstanding that such rule, regulation, or order may, after such act or omission, be amended or rescinded or be determined by judicial or other authority to be invalid for any reason.

Section 212. Hearings

Hearings may be public and may be held before the Commission, any member or members thereof, or any officer or officers of the Commission designated by it, and appropriate records thereof shall be kept.

Section 213. Court Review of Orders

(a) PETITION; JURISDICTION; FINDINGS OF COMMISSION; ADDITIONAL EVIDENCE; FINALITY

Any person or party aggrieved by an order issued by the Commission under this title may obtain a re-

view of such order in the United States court of
appeals within any circuit wherein such person
resides or has his principal place of business, or in
the United States Court of Appeals for the District
of Columbia, by filing in such court, within sixty
days after the entry of such order, a written petition
praying that the order of the Commission be modified or set aside in whole or in part. A copy of such
petition shall be forthwith transmitted by the clerk
of the court to any member of the Commission, or
any officer thereof designated by the Commission
for that purpose, and thereupon the Commission
shall file in the court the record upon which the
order complained of was entered, as provided in
Section 2112 of Title 28, United States Code. Upon
the filing of such petition such court shall have
jurisdiction, which upon the filing of the record
shall be exclusive, to affirm, modify, or set aside
such order, in whole or in part. No objection to the
order of the Commission shall be considered by the
court unless such objection shall have been urged
before the Commission or unless there were reasonable grounds for failure so to do. The findings of the
Commission as to the facts, if supported by substantial evidence, shall be conclusive. If application is
made to the court for leave to adduce additional
evidence, and it is shown to the satisfaction of the
court that such additional evidence is material and
that there were reasonable grounds for failure to
adduce such evidence in the proceeding before the
Commission, the court may order such additional
evidence to be taken before the Commission and to
be adduced upon the hearing in such manner and

upon such terms and conditions as to the court may seem proper. The Commission may modify its findings as to the facts by reason of the additional evidence so taken, and it shall file with the court such modified or new findings, which, if supported by substantial evidence, shall be conclusive, and its recommendation, if any, for the modification or setting aside of the original order. The judgment and decree of the court affirming, modifying, or setting aside, in whole or in part, any such order of the Commission shall be final, subject to review by the Supreme Court of the United States upon certiorari or certification as provided in Section 1254 of Title 28.

(b) STAY OF COMMISSION'S ORDER

The commencement of proceedings under subsection (a) shall not, unless specifically ordered by the court, operate as a stay of the Commission's order.

Section 214. Jurisdiction of Offenses and Suits

The district courts of the United States and the United States courts of any Territory or other place subject to the jurisdiction of the United States shall have jurisdiction of violations of this title or the rules, regulations, or orders thereunder, and, concurrently with State and Territorial courts, of all suits in equity and actions at law brought to enforce any liability or duty created by, or to enjoin any violation of this subchapter or the rules, regulations, or orders thereunder. Any criminal proceeding may be brought in the district wherein any act or transaction constituting the violation occurred. Any suit or action to enforce any liability or duty created by, or to enjoin any violation of this title or rules, regulations, or orders thereunder, may be brought in any such district or in the district wherein the defendant is an inhabitant or transacts business, and process in such cases may be served in any district of which the defendant is an inhabitant or transacts business or wherever the defendant may be found. Judgments and decrees so rendered shall be subject to review as provided in Sections 1254, 1291, 1292, and 1294 of Title 28, United States Code. No costs shall be assessed for or against the Commission in any proceeding under this title brought by or against the Commission in any court.

Section 215. Validity of Contracts

(a) WAIVER OF COMPLIANCE AS VOID

Any condition, stipulation, or provision binding any person to waive compliance with any provision of this title or with any rule, regulation, or order thereunder shall be void.

(b) RIGHTS AFFECTED BY INVALIDITY

Every contract made in violation of any provision of this title and every contract heretofore or hereafter made, the performance of which involves the violation of, or the continuance of any relationship or practice in violation of any provision of this title, or any rule, regulation, or order thereunder, shall be void (1) as regards the rights of any person who, in violation of any such provision, rule, regulation, or order, shall have made or engaged in the performance of any such contract, and (2) as regards the rights of any person who, not being a party to such contract, shall have acquired any right thereunder with actual knowledge of the facts by reason of which the making or performance of such contract was in violation of any such provision.

Section 216. Omitted

Section 217. Penalties

Any person who willfully violates any provision of this title, or any rule, regulation, or order promulgated by the Commission under authority thereof, shall, upon conviction, be fined not more than $10,000, imprisoned for not more than five years, or both.

Section 218. Hiring and Leasing Authority of Commission

The provisions of Section 4(b) of the Securities Exchange Act of 1934 shall be applicable with respect to the power of the Commission—

(1) to appoint and fix the compensation of such other employees as may be necessary for carrying out its functions under this title, and

(2) to lease and allocate such real property as may be necessary for carrying out its functions under this title.

Section 219. Separability

If any provision of this title or the application of such provision to any person or circumstances shall be held invalid, the remainder of the title and the application of such provision to persons or circumstances other than those as to which it is held invalid shall not be affected thereby.

Section 220. Short Title

This title may be cited as the "Investment Advisers Act of 1940".

Section 221. Effective Date

This title shall become effective on November 1, 1940.

Section 222. State Regulation of Investment Advisers

(a) JURISDICTION OF STATE REGULATORS

Nothing in this title shall affect the jurisdiction of the securities commissioner (or any agency or officer performing like functions) of any State over any security or any person insofar as it does not conflict with the provisions of this title or the rules and regulations thereunder.

(b) DUAL COMPLIANCE PURPOSES

No State may enforce any law or regulation that would require an investment adviser to maintain any books or records in addition to those required under the laws of the State in which it maintains its principal place of business, if the investment adviser—

(1) is registered or licensed as such in the State in which it maintains its principal place of business; and

(2) is in compliance with the applicable books and records requirements of the State in which it maintains its principal place of business.

(c) LIMITATION ON CAPITAL AND BOND REQUIREMENTS

No State may enforce any law or regulation that would require an investment adviser to maintain a higher minimum net capital or to post any bond in addition to any that is required under the laws of the State in which it maintains its principal place of business, if the investment adviser—

(1) is registered or licensed as such in the State in which it maintains its principal place of business; and

(2) is in compliance with the applicable net capital or bonding requirements of the State in which it maintains its principal place of business.

(d) NATIONAL DE MINIMIS STANDARD

No law of any State or political subdivision thereof requiring the registration, licensing, or qualification as an investment adviser shall require an investment adviser to register with the securities commissioner of the State (or any agency or officer performing like functions) or to comply with such law (other than any provision thereof prohibiting fraudulent conduct) if the investment adviser—

(1) does not have a place of business located within the State; and

(2) during the preceding 12–month period, has had fewer than 6 clients who are residents of that State.

ANNEX B

GENERAL RULES AND REGULATIONS UNDER THE INVESTMENT ADVISERS ACT OF 1940

(current as of January 1, 2008)

Rule 0–2. General Procedures for Serving Non–Residents.

(a) *General procedures for serving process, pleadings, or other papers on non-resident investment advisers, general partners and managing agents.* Under Forms ADV and ADV–NR, a person may serve process, pleadings, or other papers on a non-resident investment adviser, or on a non-resident general partner or non-resident managing agent of an investment adviser by serving any or all of its appointed agents:

(1) A person may serve a non-resident investment adviser, non-resident general partner, or non-resident managing agent by furnishing the Commission with one copy of the process, pleadings, or papers, for each named party, and one additional copy for the Commission's records.

(2) If process, pleadings, or other papers are served on the Commission as described in this Rule 0–2, the Secretary of the Commission (Secretary) will promptly forward a copy to each named

party by registered or certified mail at that party's last address filed with the Commission.

(3) If the Secretary certifies that the Commission was served with process, pleadings, or other papers pursuant to paragraph (a)(1) of this Rule 0–2 and forwarded these documents to a named party pursuant to paragraph (a)(2) of this Rule 0–2, this certification constitutes evidence of service upon that party.

(b) *Definitions*. For purposes of this Rule 0–2:

(1) Managing agent means any person, including a trustee, who directs or manages, or who participates in directing or managing, the affairs of any unincorporated organization or association other than a partnership.

(2) "Non-resident" means:

(i) An individual who resides in any place not subject to the jurisdiction of the United States;

(ii) A corporation that is incorporated in or that has its principal office and place of business in any place not subject to the jurisdiction of the United States; and

(iii) A partnership or other unincorporated organization or association that has its principal office and place of business in any place not subject to the jurisdiction of the United States.

(3) "Principal office and place of business" has the same meaning as in Investment Advisers Act Rule 203A–3(c) of this chapter.

Rule 0–3. References to Rules and Regulations.

The term "rules and regulations" refers to all rules and regulations adopted by the Commission pursuant to the Act, including the forms for registration and reports and the accompanying instructions thereto.

Rule 0–4. General Requirements of Papers and Applications.

(a) *Filings*.

(1) All papers required to be filed with the Commission shall, unless otherwise provided by the rules and regulations, be delivered through the mails or otherwise to the Securities and Exchange Commission, Washington, DC 20549. Except as otherwise provided by the rules and regulations, such papers shall be deemed to have been filed with the Commission on the date when they are actually received by it.

(2) All filings required to be made electronically with the Investment Adviser Registration Depository ("IARD") shall, unless otherwise provided by the rules and regulations in this part, be deemed to have been filed with the Commission upon acceptance by the IARD. Filings required to be made through the IARD on a day that the IARD is closed shall be considered timely filed with the Commission if filed with the IARD no later than the following business day.

(3) Filings required to be made through the IARD during the period in December of each year that the IARD is not available for submission of filings shall be considered timely filed with the Commission if filed with the IARD no later than the following January 7.

(b) *Formal Specifications Respecting Applications.* Every application for an order under any provision of the Act, for which a form with instructions is not specifically prescribed, and every amendment to such application, shall be filed in quintuplicate. One copy shall be signed by the applicant, but the other four copies may have facsimile or typed signatures. Such applications shall be on paper no larger than 8 1/2 x 11 inches in size. To the extent that the reduction of larger documents would render them illegible, those documents may be filed on paper larger than 8 1/2 x 11 inches in size. The left margin should be at least 1 1/2 inches wide and, if the application is bound, it should be bound on the left side. All typewritten or printed matter (including deficits in financial statements) should be set forth in black so as to permit photocopying and microfilming.

(c) *Authorization Respecting Applications.*

(1) Every application for an order under any provision of the Act, for which a form with instructions is not specifically prescribed and which is executed by a corporation, partnership, or other company and filed with the Commission, shall contain a concise statement of the applicable pro-

visions of the articles of incorporation, bylaws, or similar documents, relating to the right of the person signing and filing such application to take such action on behalf of the applicant, and a statement that all such requirements have been complied with and that the person signing and filing the same is fully authorized to do so. If such authorization is dependent on resolutions of stockholders, directors, or other bodies, such resolutions shall be attached as an exhibit to, or the pertinent provisions thereof shall be quoted in, the application.

(2) If an amendment to any such application shall be filed, such amendment shall contain a similar statement or, in lieu thereof, shall state that the authorization described in the original application is applicable to the individual who signs such amendment and that such authorization still remains in effect.

(3) When any such application or amendment is signed by an agent or attorney, the power of attorney evidencing his authority to sign shall contain similar statements and shall be filed with the Commission.

(d) *Verification of Applications and Statements of Fact.* Every application for an order under any provision of the Act, for which a form with instructions is not specifically prescribed and every amendment to such application, and every statement of fact formally filed in support of, or in opposition to, any application or declaration shall be verified by

the person executing the same. An instrument executed on behalf of a corporation shall be verified in
substantially the following form, but suitable
changes may be made in such form for other kinds
of companies and for individuals:

State of _____

County of _____, ss:

The undersigned being duly sworn deposes and says
that he has duly executed the attached ___ dated
___, 2___, for and on behalf of _____ (Name of
Company); that he is the _____ (Title of Officer)
of such company; and that all action by stockholders, directors, and other bodies necessary to authorize deponent to execute and file such instrument
has been taken. Deponent further says that he is
familiar with such instrument, and the contents
thereof, and that the facts therein set forth are true
to the best of his knowledge, information and belief.

_____

(Signature)

_____

(Type or Print Name
Beneath)

Subscribed and sworn to before me a _____ (Title
of Officer) this _____ day of _____, 2___.

(Official Seal) _____

My commission expires _____

(e) *Statement of Grounds for Application.* Each application should contain a brief statement of the reasons why the applicant is deemed to be entitled to the action requested with a reference to the provisions of the Act and of the rules and regulations under which application is made.

(f) *Name and Address.* Every application shall contain the name and address of each applicant and the name and address of any person to whom any applicant wishes any question regarding the application to be directed.

(g) *Proposed Notice.* A proposed notice of the proceeding initiated by the filing of the application shall accompany each application as an exhibit thereto and, if necessary, shall be modified to reflect any amendments to such application.

(h) *Definition of Application.* For purposes of this rule, an "application" means any application for an order of the Commission under the Act other than an application for registration as an investment adviser.

(i) The manually signed original (or in the case of duplicate original) one duplicate originals of all registrations, applications, statements, reports, or other documents filed under the Investment Advisers Act of 1940, as amended, shall be numbered sequentially (in addition to any internal numbering which otherwise may be present) by handwritten, typed, printed, or other legible form of notation from the facing page of the document through the last page of that document and any exhibits or attachments thereto. Further, the total number of pages contained in a numbered original shall be set forth on the first page of the document.

Rule 0–5. Procedure With Respect to Applications And Other Matters.

The procedure herein below set forth will be followed with respect to any proceeding initiated by the filing of an application, or upon the Commission's own motion, pursuant to any section of the Act or any rule or regulation thereunder, unless in the particular case a different procedure is provided:

(a) Notice of the initiation of the proceeding will be published in the Federal Register and will indicate the earliest date upon which an order disposing of the matter may be entered. The notice will also provide that any interested person may, within the period of time specified therein, submit to the Commission in writing any facts bearing upon the desirability of a hearing on the matter and may request that a hearing be held, stating his reasons therefor and the nature of his interest in the matter.

(b) An order disposing of the matter will be issued as of course following the expiration of the period of time referred to in paragraph (a) unless the Commission thereafter orders a hearing on the matter.

(c) The Commission will order a hearing on the matter, if it appears that a hearing is necessary or appropriate in the public interest or for the protection of investors: (1) upon the request of any interested person or (2) upon its own motion.

(d) *Definition of Application.* For purposes of this rule, an "application" means any application for an order of the Commission under the Act other than an application for registration as an investment adviser.

Rule 0–6. Incorporation by Reference in Applications.

(a) A person filing an application may, subject to the limitations of Regulation S–B Item 10(f) and Regulation S–K Item 10 (d), incorporate by reference as an exhibit to such application any document or part thereof, including any financial statement or part thereof, previously or concurrently filed with the Commission pursuant to any act administered by the Commission. The incorporation may be made whether the matter incorporated was filed by such applicant or any other person. If any modification has occurred in the text of any such document since the filing thereof, the applicant shall file with the reference a statement containing the text of any such modification and the date thereof. If the number of copies of any document previously or concurrently filed with the Commission is less than the number required to be filed with the application which incorporates such document, the applicant shall file therewith as many additional copies of the document as may be necessary to meet the requirements of the application.

(b) Notwithstanding paragraph (a) of this rule, a certificate of an independent public accountant or accountants previously or concurrently filed may not be incorporated by reference in any application unless the written consent of the accountant or accountants to such incorporation is filed with the application.

(c) In each case of incorporation by reference, the matter incorporated shall be clearly identified in the reference. An express statement shall be made to the effect that the specified matter is incorporated in the application at the particular place where the information is required.

(d) Notwithstanding paragraph (a) of this rule, no application shall incorporate by reference any exhibit or financial statement which: (1) has been withdrawn, or (2) was filed under any act administered by the Commission in connection with a registration which has ceased to be effective, or (3) is contained in an application for registration, registration statement, or report subject, at the time of the incorporation by reference, to pending proceedings under Section 8(b) or 8(d) of the Securities Act of 1933, Section 8(e) of the Investment Company Act of 1940, Section 15(b)(4)(A) of the Securities Exchange Act of 1934, Section 203(e)(1) of the Investment Advisers Act of 1940 or to an order entered under any of those sections.

(e) Notwithstanding paragraph (a) of this rule, the Commission may refuse to permit incorporation by reference in any case in which in its judgment such incorporation would render an application incomplete, unclear, or confusing.

(f) *Definition of Application.* For purposes of this rule, an application means any application for an order of the Commission under the Act other than an application for registration as an investment adviser.

Rule 0–7. Small Entities Under the Investment Advisers Act for Purposes of the Regulatory Flexibility Act.

(a) For purposes of Commission rulemaking in accordance with the provisions of Chapter Six of the Administrative Procedure Act and unless otherwise defined for purposes of a particular rulemaking proceeding, the term small business or "small organization" for purposes of the Investment Advisers Act of 1940 means an investment adviser that:

(1) Has assets under management, as defined under Section 203A(a)(2) of the Investment Advisers Act and reported on its annual updating amendment to Form ADV, of less than $25 million, or such higher amount as the Commission may by rule deem appropriate under Section 203A(a)(1)(A) of the Investment Advisers Act;

(2) Did not have total assets of $5 million or more on the last day of the most recent fiscal year; and

(3) Does not control, is not controlled by, and is not under common control with another investment adviser that has assets under management

of $25 million or more (or such higher amount as the Commission may deem appropriate), or any person (other than a natural person) that had total assets of $5 million or more on the last day of the most recent fiscal year.

(b) For purposes of this Rule 0–7:

(1) "Control" means the power, directly or indirectly, to direct the management or policies of a person, whether through ownership of securities, by contract, or otherwise.

(i) A person is presumed to control a corporation if the person:

(A) Directly or indirectly has the right to vote 25 percent or more of a class of the corporation's voting securities; or

(B) Has the power to sell or direct the sale of 25 percent or more of a class of the corporation's voting securities.

(ii) A person is presumed to control a partnership if the person has the right to receive upon dissolution, or has contributed, 25 percent or more of the capital of the partnership.

(iii) A person is presumed to control a limited liability company (LLC) if the person:

(A) Directly or indirectly has the right to vote 25 percent or more of a class of the interests of the LLC;

(B) Has the right to receive upon dissolution, or has contributed, 25 percent or more of the capital of the LLC; or

(C) Is an elected manager of the LLC.

(iv) A person is presumed to control a trust if the person is a trustee or managing agent of the trust.

(2) *Total assets* means the total assets as shown on the balance sheet of the investment adviser or other person described above under paragraph (a)(3) of this Rule 0–7, or the balance sheet of the investment adviser or such other person with its subsidiaries consolidated, whichever is larger.

Rule 202(a)(1)–1. Certain Transactions Not Deemed Assignments.

A transaction which does not result in a change of actual control or management of an investment adviser is not an assignment for purposes of Section 205(a)(2) of the Act.

Rule 202(a)(11)–1. Certain Broker–Dealers. [*VACATED BY COURT ORDER*]

(a) *Special Compensation*. A broker or dealer registered with the Commission under Section 15 of the Securities Exchange Act of 1934 (15 U.S.C. 78o) (the "Exchange Act"):

(1) Will not be deemed to be an investment adviser based solely on its receipt of special compensation (except as provided in paragraph (b)(1) of this section), provided that:

(i) Any investment advice provided by the broker or dealer with respect to accounts from which it receives special compensation is solely incidental to the brokerage services provided to those accounts (including, in particular, that the broker or dealer does not exercise investment discretion as provided in paragraphs (b)(3) and (d) of this section); and

(ii) Advertisements for, and contracts, agreements, applications and other forms governing, accounts for which the broker or dealer receives special compensation include a prominent statement that: "Your account is a brokerage account and not an advisory account. Our interests may not always be the same as yours. Please ask us questions to make sure you understand your rights and our obligations to you, including the extent of our obligations to disclose conflicts of interest and to act in your best interest. We are paid both by you and, sometimes, by people who compensate us based on what you buy. Therefore, our profits, and our salespersons' compensation, may vary by product and over time." The prominent statement also must identify an appropriate person at the firm with whom the customer can discuss the differences.

(2) Will not be deemed to have received special compensation solely because the broker or dealer charges a commission, mark-up, mark-down or similar fee for brokerage services that is greater than or less than one it charges another customer.

(b) *Solely Incidental to.* A broker or dealer provides advice that is not solely incidental to the conduct of its business as a broker or dealer within the meaning of Section 202(a)(11)(C) of the Advisers Act or to the brokerage services provided to accounts from which it receives special compensation within the meaning of paragraph (a)(1)(i) of this section if the broker or dealer (among other things, and without limitation):

(1) Charges a separate fee, or separately contracts, for advisory services;

(2) Provides advice as part of a financial plan or in connection with providing financial planning services and:

(i) Holds itself out generally to the public as a financial planner or as providing financial planning services;

(ii) Delivers to the customer a financial plan; or

(iii) Represents to the customer that the advice is provided as part of a financial plan or in connection with financial planning services; or

(3) Exercises investment discretion, as that term is defined in paragraph (d) of this section, over any customer accounts.

(c) *Special Rule.* A broker or dealer registered with the Commission under Section 15 of the Exchange Act is an investment adviser solely with respect to those accounts for which it provides services or receives compensation that subject the broker or dealer to the Advisers Act.

(d) *Investment Discretion.* For purpose of this section, the term investment discretion has the same meaning as given in Section 3(a)(35) of the Securities Exchange Act of 1934 (15 U.S.C. 78c(a)(35)), except that it does not include investment discretion granted by a customer on a temporary or limited basis.

Rule 203–1. Application for Investment Adviser Registration.

(a) *Form ADV*. To apply for registration with the Commission as an investment adviser, you must complete and file Form ADV by following the instructions in the Form.

(b) *Electronic Filing*.

(1) If you apply for registration after January 1, 2001, you must file electronically with the Investment Adviser Registration Depository (IARD), unless you have received a hardship exemption under Rule 203–3.

(2) You are not required to file with the Commission a copy of Part II of Form ADV if you maintain a copy of your Part II (and any brochure you deliver to clients) in your files. The copy maintained in your files is considered filed with the Commission.

(c) *When Filed*. Each Form ADV is considered filed with the Commission upon acceptance by the IARD.

(d) *Filing Fees*. You must pay NASD (the operator of the IARD) a filing fee. The Commission has approved the amount of the filing fee. No portion of the filing fee is refundable. Your completed application for registration will not be accepted by NASD, and thus will not be considered filed with the Commission, until you have paid the filing fee.

Rule 203–2. Withdrawal from Investment Adviser Registration.

(a) *Form ADV–W.* You must file Form ADV–W to withdraw from investment adviser registration with the Commission (or to withdraw a pending registration application).

(b) *Electronic Filing.* Once you have filed your Form ADV (or any amendments to Form ADV) electronically with the Investment Adviser Registration Depository (IARD), any Form ADV–W you file must be filed with the IARD, unless you have received a hardship exemption under Investment Advisers Act Rule 203–3.

(c) *Effective Date—Upon Filing.* Each Form ADV–W filed under this Rule 203–2 is effective upon acceptance by the IARD, provided however that your investment adviser registration will continue for a period of sixty days after acceptance solely for the purpose of commencing a proceeding under Section 203(e) of the Investment Advisers Act.

(d) *Filing Fees.* You do not have to pay a fee to file Form ADV–W through the IARD.

(e) *Form ADV–W Is a Report.* Each Form ADV–W required to be filed under this section is a report within the meaning of Sections 204 and 207 of the Investment Advisers Act.

Rule 203–3. Hardship Exemptions.

This Rule 203–3 provides two "hardship exemptions" from the requirement to make Advisers Act filings electronically with the Investment Adviser Registration Depository (IARD).

(a) *Temporary Hardship Exemption—*

(1) *Eligibility for Exemption.* If you are registered or are registering with the Commission as an investment adviser and submit electronic filings on the Investment Adviser Registration Depository (IARD) system, but have unanticipated technical difficulties that prevent you from submitting a filing to the IARD system, you may request a temporary hardship exemption from the requirements of this chapter to file electronically.

(2) *Application Procedures.* To request a temporary hardship exemption, you must:

(i) File Form ADV–H in paper format with no later than one business day after the filing that is the subject of the ADV–H was due; and

(ii) Submit the filing that is the subject of the Form ADV–H in electronic format with the IARD no later than seven business days after the filing was due.

(3) *Effective Date—Upon Filing.* The temporary hardship exemption will be granted when you file a completed Form ADV–H.

(b) *Continuing Hardship Exemption—*

(1) *Eligibility for Exemption.* If you are a "small business" (as described in paragraph (b)(5) of this Rule 203–3), you may apply for a continuing

hardship exemption. The period of the exemption may be no longer than one year after the date on which you apply for the exemption.

(2) *Application Procedures.* To apply for a continuing hardship exemption, you must file Form ADV–H at least ten business days before a filing is due. The Commission will grant or deny your application within ten business days after you file Form ADV–H.

(3) *Effective Date—Upon Filing.* You are not exempt from the electronic filing requirements until and unless the Commission approves your application. If the Commission approves your application, you may submit your filings to NASD in paper format for the period of time for which the exemption is granted.

(4) *Criteria for Exemption.* Your application will be granted only if you are able to demonstrate that the electronic filing requirements of this chapter are prohibitively burdensome or expensive.

(5) *Small Business.* You are a "small business" for purposes of this Rule 203–3 if you are required to answer Item 12 of Form ADV and checked no to each question in Item 12 that you were required to answer.

Rule 203(b)(3)–1. Definition of Client of an Investment Adviser.

(a) *General.* You may deem the following to be a single client for purposes of Section 203(b)(3) of the Act (15 U.S.C. 80b–3(b)(3)):

(1) A natural person, and:

   (i) Any minor child of the natural person;

   (ii) Any relative, spouse, or relative of the spouse of the natural person who has the same principal residence;

   (iii) All accounts of which the natural person and/or the persons referred to in this paragraph (a)(1) are the only primary beneficiaries; and

   (iv) All trusts of which the natural person and/or the persons referred to in this paragraph (a)(1) are the only primary beneficiaries;

(2) (i) A corporation, general partnership, limited partnership, limited liability company, trust (other than a trust referred to in paragraph (a)(1)(iv) of this section), or other "legal organization" (any of which are referred to hereinafter as a legal organization) to which you provide investment advice based on its investment objectives rather than the individual investment objectives of its shareholders, partners, limited partners, members, or beneficiaries (any of which are referred to hereinafter as an "owner"); and

   (ii) Two or more legal organizations referred to in paragraph (a)(2)(i) of this section that have identical owners.

(b) *Special Rules.* For purposes of this section:

   (1) You must count an owner as a client if you provide investment advisory services to the owner separate and apart from the investment advisory

services you provide to the legal organization, *provided, however*, that the determination that an owner is a client will not affect the applicability of this section with regard to any other owner;

(2) You are not required to count an owner as a client solely because you, on behalf of the legal organization, offer, promote, or sell interests in the legal organization to the owner, or report periodically to the owners as a group solely with respect to the performance of or plans for the legal organization's assets or similar matters;

(3) A limited partnership or limited liability company is a client of any general partner, managing member or other person acting as investment adviser to the partnership or limited liability company;

(4) You are not required to count as a client any person for whom you provide investment advisory services without compensation;

(5) If you have your principal office and place of business outside the United States, you are not required to count clients that are not United States residents, but if your principal office and place of business is in the United States, you must count all clients;

(6) You may not rely on paragraph (a)(2)(i) of this section with respect to any private fund as defined in paragraph (d) of this section; and

(7) For purposes of paragraph (b)(5) of this section, a client who is an owner of a private fund is

a resident of the place at which the client resides at the time of the client's investment in the fund.

(c) *Holding Out*. If you are relying on this section, you shall not be deemed to be holding yourself out generally to the public as an investment adviser, within the meaning of Section 203(b)(3) of the Act, solely because you participate in a non-public offering of interests in a limited partnership under the Securities Act of 1933.

(d) *Private Fund*.

(1) A private fund is a company:

(i) That would be an investment company under Section 3(a) of the Investment Company Act of 1940 but for the exception provided from that definition by either Section 3(c)(1) or Section 3(c)(7) of such Act;

(ii) That permits its owners to redeem any portion of their ownership interests within two years of the purchase of such interests; and

(iii) Interests in which are or have been offered based on the investment advisory skills, ability or expertise of the investment adviser.

(2) Notwithstanding paragraph (d)(1) of this section, a company is not a private fund if it permits its owners to redeem their ownership interests within two years of the purchase of such interests only in the case of:

(i) Events you find after reasonable inquiry to be extraordinary; and

(ii) Interests acquired through reinvestment of distributed capital gains or income.

(3) Notwithstanding paragraph (d)(1) of this section, a company is not a private fund if it has its principal office and place of business outside the United States, makes a public offering of its securities in a country other than the United States, and is regulated as a public investment company under the laws of the country other than the United States.

Rule 203(b)(3)–2. Methods for Counting Clients in Certain Private Funds. [*VACATED BY COURT ORDER*]

(a) For purposes of Section 203(b)(3) of the Act, you must count as clients the shareholders, limited partners, members, or beneficiaries (any of which are referred to hereinafter as an "owner") of a private fund as defined in paragraph (d) of Rule 203(b)(3)–1, unless such owner is your advisory firm or a person described in paragraph (d)(1)(iii) of Rule 205–3.

(b) If you provide investment advisory services to a private fund in which an investment company registered under the Investment Company Act of 1940 is, directly or indirectly, an owner, you must count the owners of that investment company as clients for purposes of Section 203(b)(3) of the Act.

(c) If you have your principal office and place of business outside the United States, you may treat a private fund that is organized or incorporated under the laws of a country other than the United States as your client for all purposes under the Act, other than Sections 203, 204, 206(1) and 206(2).

Rule 203A–1. Eligibility for SEC Registration; Switching to or from SEC Registration.

(a) *Eligibility for SEC Registration—*

(1) *Threshold for SEC Registration—$30 Million of Assets Under Management.* If the State where you maintain your principal office and place of business has enacted an investment adviser statute, you are not required to register with the Commission, unless:

(i) You have assets under management of at least $30,000,000, as reported on your Form ADV; or

(ii) You are an investment adviser to an investment company registered under the Investment Company Act of 1940.

(2) *Exemption for Investment Advisers Having Between $25 And $30 Million Of Assets Under Management.* If the State where you maintain your principal office and place of business has enacted an investment adviser statute, you may register with the Commission if you have assets under management of at least $25,000,000 but less than $30,000,000, as reported on your Form ADV. This paragraph (a)(2) shall not apply if:

(i) You are an investment adviser to an investment company registered under the Investment Company Act of 1940; or

(ii) You are eligible for an exemption described in Investment Advisers Rule 203A–2 of this chapter.

(b) *Switching to or From SEC Registration—*

(1) *State–Registered Advisers—*Switching to SEC Registration. If you are registered with a State securities authority, you must apply for registration with the Commission within 90 days of filing an annual updating amendment to your Form ADV reporting that you have at least $30 million of assets under management.

(2) *SEC–Registered Advisers—*Switching to State Registration. If you are registered with the Commission and file an annual updating amendment to your Form ADV reporting that you no longer have $25 million of assets under management (or are not otherwise eligible for SEC registration), you must file Form ADV–W to withdraw your SEC registration within 180 days of your fiscal year end (unless you then have at least $25 million of assets under management or are otherwise eligible for SEC registration). During this period while you are registered with both the Commission and one or more State securities authorities, the Investment Advisers Act of 1940 and applicable State law will apply to your advisory activities.

Rule 203A–2. Exemptions from Prohibition on SEC Registration.

The prohibition of Section 203A(a) of the Act does not apply to:

(a) *Nationally Recognized Statistical Rating Organizations.* An investment adviser that is a nationally recognized statistical rating organization, as that term is used in paragraphs (c)(2)(vi)(E), (F), and (H) of § 240.15c3–1 of this chapter.

(b) *Pension Consultants.*

(1) An investment adviser that is a "pension consultant", as defined in this Rule 203A–2, with respect to assets of plans having an aggregate value of at least $50,000,000.

(2) An investment adviser is a pension consultant, for purposes of paragraph (b) of this rule, if the investment adviser provides investment advice to:

(i) Any employee benefit plan described in Section 3(3) of the Employee Retirement Income Security Act of 1974 ("ERISA");

(ii) Any governmental plan described in Section 3(32) of ERISA; or

(iii) Any church plan described in Section 3(33) of ERISA.

(3) In determining the aggregate value of assets of plans, include only that portion of a plan's assets for which the investment adviser provided investment advice (including any advice with respect to the selection of an investment adviser to manage such assets). Determine the aggregate value of assets by cumulating the value of assets of plans with respect to which the investment adviser was last employed or retained by contract

to provide investment advice during a 12–month period ended within 90 days of filing an annual updating amendment to Form ADV.

(c) *Investment Advisers Controlling, Controlled by, or Under Common Control With an Investment Adviser Registered With the Commission.* An investment adviser that controls, is controlled by, or is under common control with, an investment adviser eligible to register, and registered with, the Commission ("registered adviser"), provided that the principal office and place of business of the investment adviser is the same as that of the registered adviser. For purposes of this paragraph, control means the power to direct or cause the direction of the management or policies of an investment adviser, whether through ownership of securities, by contract, or otherwise. Any person that directly or indirectly has the right to vote 25 percent or more of the voting securities, or is entitled to 25 percent or more of the profits, of an investment adviser is presumed to control that investment adviser.

(d) *Investment Advisers Expecting to be Eligible for Commission Registration Within 120 days.* An investment adviser that:

(1) Immediately before it registers with the Commission, is not registered or required to be registered with the Commission or a securities commissioner (or any agency or officer performing like functions) of any State and has a reasonable expectation that it would be eligible to register with the Commission within 120 days after the

date the investment adviser's registration with the Commission becomes effective;

(2) Indicates on Schedule D of its Form ADV that it will withdraw from registration with the Commission if, on the 120th day after the date the investment adviser's registration with the Commission becomes effective, the investment adviser would be prohibited by Section 203A(a) of the Investment Advisers Act from registering with the Commission; and

(3) Notwithstanding § 275.203A–1(b)(2) of this chapter, files a completed Form ADV–W withdrawing from registration with the Commission within 120 days after the date the investment adviser's registration with the Commission becomes effective.

(e) *Multi-State Investment Advisers.* An investment adviser that:

(1) Upon submission of its application for registration with the Commission, is required by the laws of 30 or more States to register as an investment adviser with the securities commissioners (or any agencies or officers performing like functions) in the respective States, and thereafter would, but for this Rule 203A–2, be required by the laws of at least 25 States to register as an investment adviser with the securities commissioners (or any agencies or officers performing like functions) in the respective States;

(2) Indicates on Schedule D of its Form ADV that the investment adviser has reviewed the applica-

ble State and federal laws and has concluded that, in the case of an application for registration with the Commission, it is required by the laws of 30 or more States to register as an investment adviser with the State securities authorities in the respective States or, in the case of an amendment to Form ADV, it would be required by the laws of at least 25 States to register as an investment adviser with the State securities authorities in the respective States, within 90 days prior to the date of filing Form ADV;

(3) Undertakes on Schedule D of its Form ADV to withdraw from registration with the Commission if the adviser indicates on an annual updating amendment to Form ADV that the investment adviser would be required by the laws of fewer than 25 States to register as an investment adviser with the securities commissioners (or any agencies or officers performing like functions) in the respective States, and that the investment adviser would be prohibited by Section 203A(a) of the Investment Advisers Act from registering with the Commission, by filing a completed Form ADV–W within 180 days of the adviser's fiscal year end (unless the adviser then has at least $25 million of assets under management or is otherwise eligible for SEC registration); and

(4) Maintains in an easily accessible place a record of the States in which the investment adviser has determined it would, but for the exemption, be required to register for a period of not less than five years from the filing of a Form ADV

that includes a representation that is based on such record.

(f) Internet Investment Advisers.

(1) An investment adviser that:

(i) Provides investment advice to all of its clients exclusively through an interactive website, except that the investment adviser may provide investment advice to fewer than 15 clients through other means during the preceding twelve months;

(ii) Maintains, in an easily accessible place, for a period of not less than five years from the filing of a Form ADV that includes a representation that the adviser is eligible to register with the Commission under paragraph (f) of this Rule 203A–2, a record demonstrating that it provides investment advice to its clients exclusively through an interactive website in accordance with the limits in paragraph (f)(1)(i) of this Rule 203A–2; and

(iii) Does not control, is not controlled by, and is not under common control with, another investment adviser that registers with the Commission under paragraph (c) of this section solely in reliance on the adviser registered under paragraph (f) of this Rule 203A–2 as its *registered adviser*.

(2) For purposes of paragraph (f) of this Rule 203 A–2, *interactive website* means a website in which computer software-based models or applications

provide investment advice to clients based on personal information each client supplies through the website.

(3) An investment adviser may rely on the definition of *client* in § 275.203(b)(3)–1 in determining whether it provides investment advice to fewer than 15 clients under paragraph (f)(1)(i) of this section.

Rule 203A–3. Definitions.

For purposes of Section 203A of the Act and the rules thereunder:

(a)(1) *Investment adviser representative*. "Investment adviser representative" of an investment adviser means a supervised person of the investment adviser:

(i) Who has more than five clients who are natural persons (other than excepted persons described in paragraph (a)(3)(i) of this section); and

(ii) More than ten percent of whose clients are natural persons (other than excepted persons described in paragraph (a)(3)(i) of this section).

(2) Notwithstanding paragraph (a)(1) of this section, a supervised person is not an investment adviser representative if the supervised person:

(i) Does not on a regular basis solicit, meet with, or otherwise communicate with clients of the investment adviser; or

(ii) Provides only impersonal investment advice.

(3) For purposes of this section:

(i) "Excepted person" means a natural person who is a qualified client as described in Investment Advisers Act Rule 205–3(d)(1).

(ii) "Impersonal investment" advice means investment advisory services provided by means of written material or oral statements that do not purport to meet the objectives or needs of specific individuals or accounts.

(4) Supervised persons may rely on the definition of "client" in Section 275.203(b)(3)–1, without giving regard to paragraph (b)(6) of that section, to identify clients for purposes of paragraph (a)(1) of this section, except that supervised persons need not count clients that are not residents of the United States.

(b) *Place of Business.* "Place of business" of an investment adviser representative means:

(1) An office at which the investment adviser representative regularly provides investment advisory services, solicits, meets with, or otherwise communicates with clients; and

(2) Any other location that is held out to the general public as a location at which the investment adviser representative provides investment advisory services, solicits, meets with, or otherwise communicates with clients.

(c) *Principal Office and Place of Business.* "Principal office and place of business" of an investment adviser means the executive office of the investment adviser from which the officers, partners, or managers of the investment adviser direct, control, and coordinate the activities of the investment adviser.

Rule 203A–4. Investment Advisers Registered With a State Securities Commission.

The Commission shall not assert a violation of Section 203 of the Act (or any provision of the Act) to which an investment adviser becomes subject upon registration under Section 203 of the Act for the failure of an investment adviser registered with the securities commission (or any agency or office performing like functions) in the State in which it has its principal office and place of business to register with the Commission if the investment adviser reasonably believes that it does not have assets under management of at least $30,000,000 and is therefore not required to register with the Commission.

Rule 203A–5. [Reserved]

Rule 203A–6. [Reserved]

Rule 204–1. Amendments to Application for Registration.

(a) *When Amendment is Required.* You must amend your Form ADV:

(1) At least annually, within 90 days of the end of your fiscal year; and

(2) More frequently, if required by the instructions to Form ADV.

(b) *Electronic Filing of Amendments.*

(1) You must file all amendments to Part 1A of your Form ADV electronically with the IARD, unless you have received a continuing hardship exemption under § 275.203–3.

(2) If you have received a continuing hardship exemption under § 275.203–3, you must, when you are required to amend your Form ADV, file a completed Part 1A of Form ADV on paper with the SEC by mailing it to the NASD.

(c) *Special Rule for Part II.* You are not required to file with the Commission a copy of Part II of Form ADV if you maintain a copy of your Part II (and any brochure you deliver to clients) in your files. The copy maintained in your files is considered filed with the Commission.

(d) *Filing Fees.* You must pay the NASD (the operator of the IARD) an initial filing fee when you first electronically file Part 1A of Form ADV. After you pay the initial filing fee, you must pay an annual filing fee each time you file your annual updating amendment. No portion of either fee is refundable. The Commission has approved the filing fees. Your amended Form ADV will not be accepted by NASD, and thus will not be considered filed with the Commission, until you have paid the filing fee.

(e) *Amendments to Form ADV Are Reports.* Each amendment required to be filed under this Rule

204–1 is a "report" within the meaning of Sections 204 and 207 of the Investment Advisers Act.

Rule 204–2. Books and Records to be Maintained by Investment Advisers.

(a) Every investment adviser registered or required to be registered under Section 203 of the Act shall make and keep true, accurate and current the following books and records relating to its investment advisory business:

(1) A journal or journals, including cash receipts and disbursements, records, and any other records of original entry forming the basis of entries in any ledger.

(2) General and auxiliary ledgers (or other comparable records) reflecting asset, liability, reserve, capital, income and expense accounts.

(3) A memorandum of each order given by the investment adviser for the purchase or sale of any security, of any instruction received by the investment adviser concerning the purchase, sale, receipt or delivery of a particular security, and of any modification or cancellation of any such order or instruction. Such memoranda shall show the terms and conditions of the order, instruction, modification or cancellation; shall identify the person connected with the investment adviser who recommended the transaction to the client and the person who placed such order; and shall show the account for which entered, the date of entry, and the bank, broker or dealer by or

through whom executed where appropriate. Orders entered pursuant to the exercise of discretionary power shall be so designated.

(4) All check books, bank statements, cancelled checks and cash reconciliations of the investment adviser.

(5) All bills or statements (or copies thereof), paid or unpaid, relating to the business of the investment adviser as such.

(6) All trial balances, financial statements, and internal audit working papers relating to the business of such investment adviser.

(7) Originals of all written communications received and copies of all written communications sent by such investment adviser relating to (i) any recommendation made or proposed to be made and any advice given or proposed to be given, (ii) any receipt, disbursement or delivery of funds or securities, or (iii) the placing or execution of any order to purchase or sell any security; *provided, however*: (a) That the investment adviser shall not be required to keep any unsolicited market letters and other similar communications of general public distribution not prepared by or for the investment adviser, and (b) that if the investment adviser sends any notice, circular or other advertisement offering any report, analysis, publication or other investment advisory service to more than 10 persons, the investment adviser shall not be required to keep a record of the names and addresses of the persons to whom it

was sent; except that if such notice, circular or advertisement is distributed to persons named on any list, the investment adviser shall retain with the copy of such notice, circular or advertisement a memorandum describing the list and the source thereof.

(8) A list or other record of all accounts in which the investment adviser is vested with any discretionary power with respect to the funds, securities or transactions of any client.

(9) All powers of attorney and other evidences of the granting of any discretionary authority by any client to the investment adviser, or copies thereof.

(10) All written agreements (or copies thereof) entered into by the investment adviser with any client or otherwise relating to the business of such investment adviser as such.

(11) A copy of each notice, circular, advertisement, newspaper article, investment letter, bulletin or other communication that the investment adviser circulates or distributes, directly or indirectly, to 10 or more persons (other than persons connected with such investment adviser), and if such notice, circular, advertisement, newspaper article, investment letter, bulletin or other communication recommends the purchase or sale of a specific security and does not state the reasons for such recommendation, a memorandum of the investment adviser indicating the reasons therefor.

(12) (i) A copy of the investment adviser's code of ethics adopted and implemented pursuant to § 275.204A–1 that is in effect, or at any time within the past five years was in effect;

(ii) A record of any violation of the code of ethics, and of any action taken as a result of the violation; and

(iii) A record of all written acknowledgments as required by § 275.204A–1(a)(5) for each person who is currently, or within the past five years was, a supervised person of the investment adviser.

(13) (i) A record of each report made by an access person as required by § 275.204A–1(b), including any information provided under paragraph (b)(3)(iii) of that section in lieu of such reports;

(ii) A record of the names of persons who are currently, or within the past five years were, access persons of the investment adviser; and

(iii) A record of any decision, and the reasons supporting the decision, to approve the acquisition of securities by access persons under § 275.204A–1(c), for at least five years after the end of the fiscal year in which the approval is granted.

(14) A copy of each written statement and each amendment or revision thereof, given or sent to any client or prospective client of such investment adviser in accordance with the provisions of Rule 204–3 under the Act, and a record of the

dates that each written statement, and each amendment or revision thereof, was given, or offered to be given, to any client or prospective client who subsequently becomes a client.

(15) All written acknowledgments of receipt obtained from clients pursuant to § 275.206(4)–3(a)(2)(iii)(B) and copies of the disclosure documents delivered to clients by solicitors pursuant to § 275.206(4)–3.

(16) All accounts, books, internal working papers, and any other records or documents that are necessary to form the basis for or demonstrate the calculation of the performance or rate of return of any or all managed accounts or securities recommendations in any notice, circular, advertisement, newspaper article, investment letter, bulletin or other communication that the investment adviser circulates or distributes, directly or indirectly, to 10 or more persons (other than persons connected with such investment adviser); *provided, however*, that, with respect to the performance of managed accounts, the retention of all account statements, if they reflect all debits, credits, and other transactions in a client's account for the period of the statement, and all worksheets necessary to demonstrate the calculation of the performance or rate of return of all managed accounts shall be deemed to satisfy the requirements of this paragraph.

(17)(i) A copy of the investment adviser's policies and procedures formulated pursuant to

§ 275.206(4)–7(a) of this chapter that are in effect, or at any time within the past five years were in effect, and

(ii) Any records documenting the investment adviser's annual review of those policies and procedures conducted pursuant to § 275.206(4)–7(b) of this chapter.

(b) If an investment adviser subject to paragraph (a) of this rule has custody or possession of securities or funds of any client, the records required to be made and kept under paragraph (a) above shall include:

(1) A journal or other record showing all purchases, sales, receipts and deliveries of securities (including certificate numbers) for such accounts and all other debits and credits to such accounts.

(2) A separate ledger account for each such client showing all purchases, sales, receipts and deliveries of securities, the date and price of each purchase and sale, and all debits and credits.

(3) Copies of confirmations of all transactions effected by or for the account of any such client.

(4) A record for each security in which any such client has a position, which record shall show the name of each such client having any interest in such security, the amount or interest of each such client, and the location of each such security.

(c)(1) Every investment adviser subject to paragraph (a) of this rule who renders any investment supervisory or management service to any client shall, with respect to the portfolio being supervised or managed and to the extent that the information is reasonably available to or obtainable by the investment adviser, make and keep true, accurate and current:

(i) Records showing separately for each such client the securities purchased and sold, and the date, amount and price of each such purchase and sale.

(ii) For each security in which any such client has a current position, information from which the investment adviser can promptly furnish the name of each such client, and the current amount or interest of such client.

(2) Every investment adviser subject to paragraph (a) of this Rule that exercises voting authority with respect to client securities shall, with respect to those clients, make and retain the following:

(i) Copies of all policies and procedures required by Rule 206(4)–6.

(ii) A copy of each proxy statement that the investment adviser receives regarding client securities. An investment adviser may satisfy this requirement by relying on a third party to make and retain, on the investment adviser's behalf, a copy of a proxy statement (provided that the adviser has obtained an undertaking from the third party to provide a copy of the proxy statement promptly upon request) or may rely on obtaining a copy of a proxy statement from the Commission's Electronic Data Gathering, Analysis, and Retrieval (EDGAR) system.

(iii) A record of each vote cast by the investment adviser on behalf of a client. An investment adviser may satisfy this requirement by relying on a third party to make and retain, on the investment adviser's behalf, a record of the vote cast (provided that the adviser has obtained an undertaking from the third party to provide a copy of the record promptly upon request).

(iv) A copy of any document created by the adviser that was material to making a decision how to vote proxies on behalf of a client or that memorializes the basis for that decision.

(v) A copy of each written client request for information on how the adviser voted proxies on behalf of the client, and a copy of any written response by the investment adviser to any (written or oral) client request for information on how the adviser voted proxies on behalf of the requesting client.

(d) Any books or records required by this section may be maintained by the investment adviser in such manner that the identity of any client to whom such investment adviser renders investment supervisory services is indicated by numerical or alphabetical code or some similar designation.

(e)(1) All books and records required to be made under the provisions of paragraphs (a) to (c)(1)(i), inclusive, and (c)(2) of this section (except for books and records required to be made under the provisions of paragraphs (a)(11), (a)(12)(i), (a)(12)(iii), (a)(13)(ii), (a)(13)(iii), (a)(16), and (a)(17)(i) of this section), shall be maintained and preserved in an easily accessible place for a period of not less than five years from the end of the fiscal year during which the last entry was made on such record, the first two years in an appropriate office of the investment adviser.

(2) Partnership articles and any amendments thereto, articles of incorporation, charters, minute books, and stock certificate books of the investment adviser and of any predecessor, shall be maintained in the principal office of the investment adviser and preserved until at least three years after termination of the enterprise.

(3)(i) Books and records required to be made under the provisions of paragraphs (a)(11) and (a)(16) of this rule shall be maintained and preserved in an easily accessible place for a period of not less than five years, the first two years in an appropriate office of the investment adviser, from the end of the fiscal year during which the investment adviser last published or otherwise disseminated, directly or indirectly, the notice, circular, advertisement, newspaper article, investment letter, bulletin or other communication.

(ii) *Transition Rule.* If you are an investment adviser to a private fund as that term is defined in § 275.203(b)(3)–1, and you were exempt from registration under Section 203(b)(3) of the Act prior to February 10, 2005, paragraph (e)(3)(i) of this section does not require you to maintain or preserve books and records that would otherwise be required to be maintained or preserved under the provisions of paragraph (a)(16) of this section to the extent those books and records pertain to the performance or rate of return of such private fund or other account you advise for any period ended prior to February 10, 2005, provided that you were not registered with the Commission as an investment adviser during such period, and provided further that you continue to preserve any books and records in your possession that pertain to the performance or rate of return of such private fund or other account for such period.

(f) An investment adviser subject to paragraph (a) of this rule, before ceasing to conduct or discontinuing business as an investment adviser shall arrange for and be responsible for the preservation of the books and records required to be maintained and preserved under this section for the remainder of the period specified in this section, and shall notify the Commission in writing, at its principal office, Washington, D.C. 20549, of the exact address where such books and records will be maintained during such period.

(g) Micrographic and Electronic Storage Permitted.

(1) *General.* The records required to be maintained and preserved pursuant to this part may be maintained and preserved for the required time by an investment adviser on:

(i) Micrographic media, including microfilm, microfiche, or any similar medium; or

(ii) Electronic storage media, including any digital storage medium or system that meets the terms of this Rule 204–2.

(2) *General Requirements.* The investment adviser must:

(i) Arrange and index the records in a way that permits easy location, access, and retrieval of any particular record;

(ii) Provide promptly any of the following that the Commission (by its examiners or other representatives) may request:

(A) A legible, true, and complete copy of the record in the medium and format in which it is stored;

(B) A legible, true, and complete printout of the record; and

(C) Means to access, view, and print the records; and

(iii) Separately store, for the time required for preservation of the original record, a duplicate copy of the record on any medium allowed by this Rule 204–2.

(3) *Special Requirements for Electronic Storage Media*. In the case of records on electronic storage media, the investment adviser must establish and maintain procedures:

(i) To maintain and preserve the records, so as to reasonably safeguard them from loss, alteration, or destruction;

(ii) To limit access to the records to properly authorized personnel and the Commission (including its examiners and other representatives); and

(iii) To reasonably ensure that any reproduction of a non-electronic original record on electronic storage media is complete, true, and legible when retrieved.

(h)(1) Any book or other record made, kept, maintained and preserved in compliance with Rules 17a–3 and 17a–4 under the Securities Exchange Act of 1934, which is substantially the same as the book or other record re-quired to be made, kept, maintained and preserved under this rule, shall be deemed to be made, kept maintained and preserved in compliance with this rule.

(2) A record made and kept pursuant to any provision of paragraph (a) of this rule, which contains all the information required under any other provision of paragraph (a) of this section, need not be maintained in duplicate in order to meet the requirements of the other provision of paragraph (a) of this rule.

(i) As used in this rule the term "discretionary power" shall not include discretion as to the price at which or the time when a transaction is or is to be effected, if, before the order is given by the investment adviser, the client has directed or approved the purchase or sale of a definite amount of the particular security.

(j)(1) Except as provided in paragraph (j)(3) hereof, each non-resident investment adviser registered or applying for registration pursuant to Section 203 of the Act shall keep, maintain and preserve, at a place within the United States designated in a notice from him as provided in paragraph (j)(2) hereof, true, correct,complete and current copies of books and records which he is required to make, keep current, maintain or preserve pursuant to any provision of any rule or regulation of the Commission adopted under the Act.

(2) Except as provided in paragraph (j)(3) hereof, each nonresident investment adviser subject to this paragraph (j) shall furnish to the Commission a written notice specifying the address of the place within the United States where the copies of the books and records required to be kept and preserved by him pursuant to paragraph (j)(1) hereof are located. Each non-resident investment adviser registered or applying for registration when this paragraph becomes effective shall file such notice within 30 days after such rule becomes effective. Each non-resident investment adviser who files an application for registration af-

ter this paragraph becomes effective shall file such notice with such application for registration.

(3) Notwithstanding the provisions of paragraphs (j)(1) and (j)(2) hereof, a non-resident investment adviser need not keep or preserve within the United States copies of the books and records referred to in said paragraphs (j)(1) and (j)(2), if:

(i) Such non-resident investment adviser files with the Commission, at the time or within the period provided by paragraph (j)(2) hereof, a written undertaking, in form acceptable to the Commission and signed by a duly authorized person, to furnish to the Commission, upon demand, at its principal office in Washington, D.C., or at any Regional or District Office of the Commission designated in such demand, true, correct, complete and current copies of any or all of the books and records which he is required to make, keep current, maintain or preserve pursuant to any provision of any rule or regulation of the Commission adopted under the Act, or any part of such books and records which may be specified in such demand. Such undertaking shall be in substantially the following form:

"The undersigned hereby undertakes to furnish at its own expense to the Securities and Exchange Commission at its principal office in Washington, D.C. or at any Regional or District Office of said Commission specified in a demand for copies of books and records made by or on behalf of said Commission, true, correct, complete and current copies of any or all, or any part, of the books and records which the undersigned is required to make, keep current or preserve pursuant to any provision of any rule or regulation of the Securities and Exchange Commission under the Investment Advisers Act of 1940. This undertaking shall be suspended during any period when the undersigned is making, keeping current, and preserving copies of all of said books and records at a place within the United States in compliance with Rule 204–2(j) under the Investment Advisers Act of 1940. This undertaking shall be binding upon the undersigned and the heirs, successors and assigns of the undersigned, and the written irrevocable consents and powers of attorney of the undersigned, its general partners and managing agents filed with the Securities and Exchange Commission shall extend to and cover any action to enforce same."

and

(ii) Such non-resident investment adviser furnishes to the Commission, at his own expense 14 days after written demand therefor forwarded to him by registered mail at his last address of record filed with the Commission and signed by the Secretary of the Commission or such person as the Commission may authorize to act in its behalf, true, correct, complete and current copies of any or all books and records which such investment adviser is required to make, keep current or preserve pursuant to any provision of any rule or regulation of the Commission adopted under the Act, or any part of such books and records which may be specified in said written demand. Such copies shall be furnished to the Commission at its principal office in Washington, D.C., or at any Regional Office of the Commission which may be specified in said written demand.

(4) For purposes of this rule the term "nonresident investment adviser" shall have the meaning set out in Rule 0–2(d)(3) under the Act. [Note: Rule 0–2(d)(3) no longer exists. "Nonresident investment adviser" is now found in Rule 0–2(b)(2).]

(k) Every investment adviser that registers under Section 203 of the Act after July 8, 1997 shall be required to preserve in accordance with this section the books and records the investment adviser had been required to maintain by the State in which the investment adviser had its principal office and place of business prior to registering with the Commission.

(l) *Records of Private Funds.* If an investment adviser subject to paragraph (a) of this section advises a private fund (as defined in § 275.203(b)(3)-1), and the adviser or any related person (as defined in Form ADV) of the adviser acts as the private fund's general partner, managing member, or in a comparable capacity, the books and records of the private fund are records of the adviser for purposes of Section 204 of the Act.

Rule 204–3. Written Disclosure Statements.

(a) *General requirement.* Unless otherwise provided in this rule, an investment adviser, registered or required to be registered pursuant to Section 203 of the Act shall, in accordance with the provisions of this section, furnish each advisory client and prospective advisory client with a written disclosure statement which may be either a copy of Part II of its form ADV which complies with Rule 204–1(b) under the Act or a written document containing at least the information then so required by Part II of Form ADV.

(b) *Delivery.*

(1) An investment adviser, except as provided in paragraph (2), shall deliver the statement required by this rule to an advisory client or prospective advisory client (i) not less than 48 hours prior to entering into any written or oral investment advisory contract with such client or prospective client, or (ii) at the time of entering into any such contract, if the advisory client has a right to terminate the contract without penalty within five business days after entering into the contract.

(2) Delivery of the statement required by paragraph (1) need not be made in connection with entering into (i) an investment company contract or (ii) a contract for impersonal advisory services.

(c) *Offer to Deliver*.

(1) An investment adviser, except as provided in paragraph (2), annually shall, without charge, deliver or offer in writing to deliver upon written request to each of its advisory clients the statement required by this rule.

(2) The delivery or offer required by paragraph (c)(1) of this rule need not be made to advisory clients receiving advisory services solely pursuant to (i) an investment company contract or (ii) a contract for impersonal advisory services requiring a payment of less than $200.

(3) With respect to an advisory client entering into a contract or receiving advisory services pursuant to a contract for impersonal advisory services which requires a payment of $200 or more, an offer of the type specified in paragraph (1) shall also be made at the time of entering into an advisory contract.

(4) Any statement requested in writing by an advisory client pursuant to an offer required by this paragraph must be mailed or delivered within seven days of the receipt of the request.

(d) *Omission of Inapplicable Information*. If an investment adviser renders substantially different types of investment advisory services to different advisory clients, any information required by Part II of Form ADV may be omitted from the statement furnished to an advisory client or prospective advisory client if such information is applicable only to a type of investment advisory service or fee which is not rendered or charged, or proposed to be rendered or charged, to that client or prospective client.

(e) *Other Disclosures.* Nothing in this rule shall relieve any investment adviser from any obligation pursuant to any provision of the Act or the rules and regulations thereunder or other federal or state law to disclose any information to its advisory clients or prospective advisory clients not specifically required by this rule.

(f) *Sponsors of Wrap Fee Programs.*—

(1) An investment adviser, registered or required to be registered pursuant to Section 203 of the Act, that is compensated under a wrap fee program for sponsoring, organizing, or administering the program, or for selecting, or providing advice to clients regarding the selection of, other investment advisers in the program, shall, in lieu of the written disclosure statement required by paragraph (a) of this section and in accordance with the other provisions of this section, furnish each client and prospective client of the wrap fee program with a written disclosure statement containing at least the information required by Schedule H of Form ADV. Any additional information included in such disclosure statement should be limited to information concerning wrap fee programs sponsored by the investment adviser.

(2) If an investment adviser is required under this paragraph (f) to furnish disclosure statements to clients or prospective clients of more than one wrap fee program, the investment advis-

er may omit from the disclosure statement furnished to clients and prospective clients of a wrap fee program or programs any information required by Schedule H that is not applicable to clients or prospective clients of that wrap fee program or programs.

(3) An investment adviser need not furnish the written disclosure statement required by paragraph (f)(1) of this section to clients and prospective clients of a wrap fee program if another investment adviser is required to furnish and does furnish the written disclosure statement to all clients and prospective clients of the wrap fee program.

(4) An investment adviser that is required under this paragraph (f) to furnish a disclosure statement to clients of a wrap fee program shall furnish the disclosure statement to each client of the wrap fee program (including clients that have previously been furnished the brochure required under paragraph (a) of this section) no later than October 1, 1994.

(g) *Definitions*. For the purpose of this rule:

(1) "Contract for impersonal advisory services" means any contract relating solely to the provision of investment advisory services (i) by means of written material or oral statements which do not purport to meet the objectives or needs of specific individuals or accounts; (ii) through the issuance of statistical information containing no expression of opinion as to the investment merits

of a particular security; or (iii) any combination of the foregoing services.

(2) "Entering into," in reference to an investment advisory contract, does not include an extension or renewal without material change of any such contract which is in effect immediately prior to such extension or renewal.

(3) "Investment company contract" means a contract with an investment company registered under the Investment Company Act of 1940 which meets the requirements of Section 15(c) of that Act.

(4) "Wrap fee program" means a program under which any client is charged a specified fee or fees not based directly upon transactions in a client's account for investment advisory services (which may include portfolio management or advice concerning the selection of other investment advisers) and execution of client transactions.

Rule 204–4. [Reserved]

Rule 204–5. [Reserved]

Rule 204A–1. Investment Adviser Codes of Ethics.

(a) *Adoption of Code of Ethics.* If you are an investment adviser registered or required to be registered under Section 203 of the Act, you must establish, maintain and enforce a written code of ethics that, at a minimum, includes:

(1) A standard (or standards) of business conduct that you require of your supervised persons, which standard must reflect your fiduciary obligations and those of your supervised persons;

(2) Provisions requiring your supervised persons to comply with applicable Federal securities laws;

(3) Provisions that require all of your access persons to report, and you to review, their personal securities transactions and holdings periodically as provided below;

(4) Provisions requiring supervised persons to report any violations of your code of ethics promptly to your chief compliance officer or, provided your chief compliance officer also receives reports of all violations, to other persons you designate in your code of ethics; and

(5) Provisions requiring you to provide each of your supervised persons with a copy of your code of ethics and any amendments, and requiring your supervised persons to provide you with a written acknowledgment of their receipt of the code and any amendments.

(b) *Reporting Requirements.*

(1) *Holdings Reports.* The code of ethics must require your access persons to submit to your chief compliance officer or other persons you designate in your code of ethics a report of the access person's current securities holdings that meets the following requirements:

(i) *Content of Holdings Reports.* Each holdings report must contain, at a minimum:

(A) The title and type of security, and as applicable the exchange ticker symbol or CUSIP number, number of shares, and principal amount of each reportable security in which the access person has any direct or indirect beneficial ownership;

(B) The name of any broker, dealer or bank with which the access person maintains an account in which any securities are held for the access person's direct or indirect benefit; and

(C) The date the access person submits the report.

(ii) *Timing of Holdings Reports.* Your access persons must each submit a holdings report:

(A) No later than 10 days after the person becomes an access person, and the information must be current as of a date no more than 45 days prior to the date the person becomes an access person.

(B) At least once each 12–month period thereafter on a date you select, and the information must be current as of a date no more than 45 days prior to the date the report was submitted.

(2) *Transaction Reports.* The code of ethics must require access persons to submit to your chief compliance officer or other persons you designate

in your code of ethics quarterly securities transactions reports that meet the following requirements:

(i) *Content of Transaction Reports*. Each transaction report must contain, at a minimum, the following information about each transaction involving a reportable security in which the access person had, or as a result of the transaction acquired, any direct or indirect beneficial ownership:

(A) The date of the transaction, the title, and as applicable the exchange ticker symbol or CUSIP number, interest rate and maturity date, number of shares, and principal amount of each reportable security involved;

(B) The nature of the transaction (*i.e.*, purchase, sale or any other type of acquisition or disposition);

(C) The price of the security at which the transaction was effected;

(D) The name of the broker, dealer or bank with or through which the transaction was effected; and

(E) The date the access person submits the report.

(ii) *Timing of Transaction Reports*. Each access person must submit a transaction report no later than 30 days after the end of each calendar quarter, which report must cover, at a minimum, all transactions during the quarter.

(3) *Exceptions from Reporting Requirements.* Your code of ethics need not require an access person to submit:

(i) Any report with respect to securities held in accounts over which the access person had no direct or indirect influence or control;

(ii) A transaction report with respect to transactions effected pursuant to an automatic investment plan;

(iii) A transaction report if the report would duplicate information contained in broker trade confirmations or account statements that you hold in your records so long as you receive the confirmations or statements no later than 30 days after the end of the applicable calendar quarter.

(c) *Pre-approval of Certain Investments.* Your code of ethics must require your access persons to obtain your approval before they directly or indirectly acquire beneficial ownership in any security in an initial public offering or in a limited offering.

(d) *Small Advisers.* If you have only one access person (*i.e.*, yourself), you are not required to submit reports to yourself or to obtain your own approval for investments in any security in an initial public offering or in a limited offering, if you maintain records of all of your holdings and transactions that this section would otherwise require you to report.

(e) *Definitions.* For the purpose of this section:

(1) *Access person* means:

   (i) Any of your supervised persons:

      (A) Who has access to nonpublic information regarding any clients' purchase or sale of securities, or nonpublic information regarding the portfolio holdings of any reportable fund, or

      (B) Who is involved in making securities recommendations to clients, or who has access to such recommendations that are nonpublic.

   (ii) If providing investment advice is your primary business, all of your directors, officers and partners are presumed to be access persons.

(2) *Automatic investment plan* means a program in which regular periodic purchases (or withdrawals) are made automatically in (or from) investment accounts in accordance with a predetermined schedule and allocation. An automatic investment plan includes a dividend reinvestment plan.

(3) *Beneficial ownership* is interpreted in the same manner as it would be under § 240.16a–1(a)(2) of this chapter in determining whether a person has beneficial ownership of a security for purposes of Section 16 of the Securities Exchange Act of 1934 and the rules and regulations thereunder. Any report required by paragraph (b) of this section may contain a statement that the report will not be construed as an admission that

the person making the report has any direct or indirect beneficial ownership in the security to which the report relates.

(4) *Federal securities laws* means the Securities Act of 1933 (15 U.S.C. 77a-aa), the Securities Exchange Act of 1934 (15 U.S.C. 78a-mm), the Sarbanes–Oxley Act of 2002 (Pub.L. 107–204, 116 Stat. 745 (2002)), the Investment Company Act of 1940 (15 U.S.C. 80a), the Investment Advisers Act of 1940 (15 U.S.C. 80b), title V of the Gramm–Leach–Bliley Act (Pub.L. 106–102, 113 Stat. 1338 (1999)), any rules adopted by the Commission under any of these statutes, the Bank Secrecy Act (31 U.S.C. 5311–5314; 5316–5332) as it applies to funds and investment advisers, and any rules adopted thereunder by the Commission or the Department of the Treasury.

(5) *Fund* means an investment company registered under the Investment Company Act.

(6) *Initial public offering* means an offering of securities registered under the Securities Act of 1933, the issuer of which, immediately before the registration, was not subject to the reporting requirements of Sections 13 or 15(d) of the Securities Exchange Act of 1934.

(7) *Limited offering* means an offering that is exempt from registration under the Securities Act of 1933 pursuant to Section 4(2) or Section 4(6) or pursuant to §§ 230.504, 230.505, or 230.506 of this chapter.

(8) *Purchase or sale* of a security includes, among other things, the writing of an option to purchase or sell a security.

(9) *Reportable fund* means:

(i) Any fund for which you serve as an investment adviser as defined in Section 2(a)(20) of the Investment Company Act of 1940 (*i.e.*, in most cases you must be approved by the fund's board of directors before you can serve); or

(ii) Any fund whose investment adviser or principal underwriter controls you, is controlled by you, or is under common control with you. For purposes of this section, *control* has the same meaning as it does in Section 2(a)(9) of the Investment Company Act of 1940.

(10) *Reportable security* means a security as defined in Section 202(a)(18) of the Act, except that it does not include:

(i) Direct obligations of the Government of the United States;

(ii) Bankers' acceptances, bank certificates of deposit, commercial paper and high quality short-term debt instruments, including repurchase agreements;

(iii) Shares issued by money market funds;

(iv) Shares issued by open-end funds other than reportable funds; and

(v) Shares issued by unit investment trusts that are invested exclusively in one or more open-end funds, none of which are reportable funds.

Rule 205–1. Definition of Investment Performance of an Investment Company and Investment Record of an Appropriate Index of Securities Prices.

(a) "Investment Performance" of an investment company for any period shall mean the sum of:

(1) The change in its net asset value per share during such period;

(2) The value of its cash distributions per share accumulated to the end of such period; and

(3) The value of capital gains taxes per share paid or payable on undistributed realized long-term capital gains accumulated to the end of such period; expressed as a percentage of its net asset value per share at the beginning of such period. For this purpose, the value of distributions per share of realized capital gains, of dividends per share paid from investment income and of capital gains taxes per share paid or payable on undistributed realized long-term capital gains shall be treated as reinvested in shares of the investment company at the net asset value per share in effect at the close of business on the record date for the payment of such distributions and dividends and the date on which provision is made for such taxes, after giving effect to such distributions, dividends and taxes.

(b) "Investment record" of an appropriate index of securities prices for any period shall mean the sum of:

(1) The change in the level of the index during such period; and

(2) The value, computed consistently with the index, of cash distributions made by companies whose securities comprise the index accumulated to the end of such period; expressed as a percentage of the index level at the beginning of such period. For this purpose cash distributions on the securities which comprise the index shall be treated as reinvested in the index at least as frequently as the end of each calendar quarter following the payment of the dividend.

Rule 205–2. Definition of Specified Period Over Which the Asset Value of the Company or Fund Under Management is Averaged.

(a) For purposes of this rule:

(1) "Fulcrum fee" shall mean the fee which is paid or earned when the investment company's performance is equivalent to that of the index or other measure of performance.

(2) "Rolling period" shall mean a period consisting of a specified number of subperiods of definite length in which the most recent subperiod is substituted for the earliest subperiod as time passes.

(b) The specified period over which the asset value of the company or fund under management is averaged shall mean the period over which the investment performance of the company or fund and the investment record of an appropriate index of securities prices or such other measure of investment performance are computed.

(c) Notwithstanding paragraph (b) the specified period over which the asset value of the company or fund is averaged for the purpose of computing the fulcrum fee may differ from the period over which the asset value is averaged for computing the performance related portion of the fee, only if:

(1) The performance related portion of the fee is computed over a rolling period and the total fee is payable at the end of each subperiod of the rolling period; and

(2) The fulcrum fee is computed on the basis of the asset value averaged over the most recent subperiod or subperiods of the rolling period.

Rule 205–3. Exemption From the Compensation Prohibition of Section 205(a)(1) for Investment Advisers.

(a) *General.* The provisions of Section 205(a)(1) of the Act will not be deemed to prohibit an investment adviser from entering into, performing, renewing or extending an investment advisory contract that provides for compensation to the investment adviser on the basis of a share of the capital gains upon, or the capital appreciation of, the funds, or any portion of the funds, of a client, *provided*, that the client entering into the contract subject to this section is a qualified client, as defined in paragraph (d)(1) of this Rule 205–3.

(b) *Identification of the Client.* In the case of a private investment company, as defined in paragraph (d)(3) of this Rule 205–3, an investment company registered under the Investment Company Act of 1940, or a business development company, as defined in Section 202(a)(22) of the Act, each equity owner of any such company (except for the investment adviser entering into the contract and any other equity owners not charged a fee on the basis of a share of capital gains or capital appreciation) will be considered a client for purposes of paragraph (a) of this Rule 205–3.

(c)(1) *Transition Rule.* An investment adviser that entered into a contract before August 20, 1998 and satisfied the conditions of this section as in effect on the date that the contract was entered into will be considered to satisfy the conditions of this section; *provided*, however, that this Rule 205–3 will apply with respect to any natural person or company who is not a party to the contract prior to and becomes a party to the contract after August 20, 1998.

(2) *Advisers to Private Funds with Non–Qualified Investors.* If you are an investment adviser to a private investment company that is a private fund as that term is defined in § 275.203(b)(3)–1, and you were exempt from registration under

Section 203(b)(3) of the Act prior to February 10, 2005, paragraph (b) of this section will not apply to the existing account of any equity owner of a private investment company who was an equity owner of that company prior to February 10, 2005.

(3) *Advisers to Private Funds with Non–Qualified Clients.* If you are an investment adviser to a private investment company that is a private fund as that term is defined in § 275.203(b)(3)–1, and you were exempt from registration under Section 203(b)(3) of the Act prior to February 10, 2005, Section 205(a)(1) of the Act will not apply to any investment advisory contract you entered into prior to February 10, 2005, provided, however, that this paragraph will not apply with respect to any contract to which a private investment company is a party, and provided further that Section 205(a)(1) of the Act will apply with respect to any natural person or company who is not a party to the contract prior to and becomes a party to the contract on or after February 10, 2005.

(d) *Definitions.* For the purposes of this Rule 205–3:

(1) The term ''qualified client'' means:

(i) A natural person who or a company that immediately after entering into the contract has at least $750,000 under the management of the investment adviser;

(ii) A natural person who or a company that the investment adviser entering into the contract (and any person acting on his behalf) reasonably believes, immediately prior to entering into the contract, either:

(A) Has a net worth (together, in the case of a natural person, with assets held jointly with a spouse) of more than $1,500,000 at the time the contract is entered into; or

(B) Is a qualified purchaser as defined in Section 2(a)(51)(A) of the Investment Company Act of 1940 at the time the contract is entered into; or

(iii) A natural person who immediately prior to entering into the contract is:

(A) An executive officer, director, trustee, general partner, or person serving in a similar capacity, of the investment adviser; or

(B) An employee of the investment adviser (other than an employee performing solely clerical, secretarial or administrative functions with regard to the investment adviser) who, in connection with his or her regular functions or duties, participates in the investment activities of such investment adviser, provided that such employee has been performing such functions and duties for or on behalf of the investment adviser, or substantially similar functions or duties for or on behalf of another company for at least 12 months.

(2) The term "company" has the same meaning as in Section 202(a)(5) of the Investment Advisers Act, but does not include a company that is required to be registered under the Investment Company Act of 1940 but is not registered.

(3) The term "private investment company" means a company that would be defined as an investment company under Section 3(a) of the Investment Company Act of 1940 but for the exception provided from that definition by Section 3(c)(1) of such Act.

(4) The term "executive officer" means the president, any vice president in charge of a principal business unit, division or function (such as sales, administration or finance), any other officer who performs a policy-making function, or any other person who performs similar policy-making functions, for the investment adviser.

Rule 206(3)–1. Exemption of Investment Advisers Registered as Broker–Dealers In Connection With The Provision Of Certain Investment Advisory Services.

(a) An investment adviser which is a broker or dealer registered pursuant to Section 15 of the Securities Exchange Act of 1934 shall be exempt from Section 206(3) in connection with any transaction in relation to which such broker or dealer is acting as an investment adviser solely (1) by means of publicly distributed written materials or publicly made oral statements; (2) by means of written materials or oral statements which do not purport to meet the objectives or needs of specific individuals or accounts; (3) through the issuance of statistical information containing no expressions of opinion as to the investment merits of a particular security; or (4) any combination of the foregoing services: *provided, however,* that such materials and oral statements include a statement that if the purchaser of the advisory communication uses the services of the adviser in connection with a sale or purchase of a security which is a subject of such communication, the adviser may act as principal for its own account or as agent for another person.

(b) For the purpose of this rule, publicly distributed written materials are those which are distributed to 35 or more persons who pay for such materials, and publicly made oral statements are those made simultaneously to 35 or more persons who pay for access to such statements.

Rule 206(3)–2. Agency Cross Transactions For Advisory Clients.

(a) An investment adviser, or a person registered as a broker-dealer under Section 15 of the Securities Exchange Act of 1934 and controlling, controlled by, or under common control with an investment adviser, shall be deemed in compliance with the provisions of Sections 206(3) of the Act in effecting an agency cross transaction for an advisory client, if:

(1) The advisory client has executed a written consent prospectively authorizing the investment adviser, or any other person relying on this rule, to effect agency cross-transactions for such advi-

sory client, provided that such written consent is obtained after full written disclosure that with respect to agency cross transactions the investment adviser or such other person will act as broker for, receive commissions from, and have a potentially conflicting division of loyalties and responsibilities regarding, both parties to such transactions;

(2) The investment adviser, or any other person relying on this rule, sends to each such client a written confirmation at or before the completion of each such transaction, which confirmation includes (i) a statement of the nature of such transaction, (ii) the date such transaction took place, (iii) an offer to furnish upon request, the time when such transaction took place, and (iv) the source and amount of any other remuneration received or to be received by the investment adviser and any other person relying on this rule in connection with the transaction, *provided, however*, that if, in the case of a purchase, neither the investment adviser nor any other person relying on this rule was participating in a distribution, or in the case of a sale, neither the investment adviser nor any other person relying on this rule was participating in a tender offer, the written confirmation may state whether any other remuneration has been or will be received and that the source and amount of such other remuneration will be furnished upon written request of such customer;

(3) The investment adviser, or any other person relying in this rule, sends to each such client, at least annually, and with or as part of any written statement or summary of such account from the investment adviser or such other person, a written disclosure statement identifying the total number of such transactions during the period since the date of the last such statement or summary, and the total amount of all commissions or other remuneration received or to be received by the investment adviser or any other person relying on this rule in connection with such transactions during such period;

(4) Each written disclosure statement and confirmation required by this rule includes a conspicuous statement that the written consent referred to in paragraph (a)(i) of this rule may be revoked at any time by written notice to the investment adviser, or to any other person relying on this rule, from the advisory client; and

(5) No such transaction is effected in which the same investment adviser or an investment adviser and any person controlling, controlled by or under common control with such investment adviser recommended the transaction to both any seller and any purchaser.

(b) For purposes of this rule the term "agency cross-transaction for an advisory client" shall mean a transaction in which a person acts as an investment adviser in relation to a transaction in which such investment adviser, or any person controlling, controlled by, or under common control with such investment adviser, acts as broker for both such advisory client and for another person on the other side of the transaction.

(c) This rule shall not be construed as relieving in any way the investment adviser or another person relying on this rule from acting in the best interests of the advisory client, including fulfilling the duty with respect to the best price and execution for the particular transaction for the advisory client; nor shall it relieve such person or persons from any disclosure obligation which may be imposed by sub-paragraphs (1) or (2) of Section 206 of the Act or by other applicable provisions of the federal securities laws.

Rule 206(3)–3T. Temporary Rule for Principal Trades with Certain Advisory Clients.

(a) An investment adviser shall be deemed in compliance with the provisions of Section 206(3) of the Advisers Act when the adviser directly or indirectly, acting as principal for its own account, sells to or purchases from an advisor client any security if:

(1) The investment adviser exercises no "investment discretion" (as such term is defined in Section 3(a)(35) of the Securities Exchange Act of 1934 ("Exchange Act")), except investment discretion granted by the advisory client on a temporary or limited basis, with respect to the client's account;

(2) Neither the investment adviser nor any person controlling, controlled by, or under common control with the investment adviser is the issuer of, or, at the time of the sale, an underwriter (as defined in Section 202(a)(20) of the Advisers Act of, the security; *except that* the investment adviser or a person controlling, controlled by, or under common control with the investment adviser may be an underwriter of an investment grade debt security (as defined in paragraph (c) of this section));

(3) The advisory client has executed a written, revocable consent prospectively authorizing the investment adviser directly or indirectly to act as principal for its own account in selling any security to or purchasing any security from the advisory client, so long as such written consent is obtained after written disclosure to the advisory client explaining:

(i) The circumstances under which the investment adviser directly or indirectly may engage in principal transactions;

(ii) The nature and significance of conflicts with its client's interests as a result of the transactions; and

(iii) How the investment adviser addresses those conflicts;

(4) The investment adviser, prior to the execution of each principal transaction:

(i) Informs the advisory client, orally or in writing, of the capacity in which it may act with respect to such transaction; and

(ii) Obtains consent from the advisory client, orally or in writing, to act as principal for its own account with respect to such transaction;

(5) The investment adviser sends a written confirmation at or before completion of each such transaction that includes, in addition to the information required by 17 CFR 240.10b–10, a conspicuous, plain English statement informing the advisory client that the investment adviser:

(i) Disclosed to the client prior to the execution of the transaction that the adviser may be acting in a principal capacity in connection with the transaction and the client authorized the transaction; and

(ii) Sold the security to, or bought the security from, the client for its own account;

(6) The investment adviser sends to the client, no less frequently than annually, written disclosure containing a list of all transactions that were executed in the client's account in reliance upon this section, and the date and price of such transactions;

(7) The investment adviser is a broker-dealer registered under Section 15 of the Exchange Act and each account for which the investment adviser relies on this section is a brokerage account subject to the Exchange Act, and the rules thereun-

der, and the rules of the self-regulatory organization(s) of which it is a member; and

(8) Each written disclosure required by this section includes a conspicuous, plain English statement that the client may revoke the written consent referred to in paragraph (a)(3) of this section without penalty at any time by written notice to the investment adviser.

(b) This section shall not be construed as relieving in any way an investment adviser from acting in the best interests of an advisory client, including fulfilling the duty with respect to the best price and execution for the particular transaction for the advisory client; nor shall it relieve such person or persons from any obligation that may be imposed by sections 206(1) or (2) of the Advisers Act or by other applicable provisions of the federal securities laws.

(c) For purposes of paragraph (a)(2) of this section, an investment grade debt security means a nonconvertible debt security that, at the time of sale, is rated in one of the four highest rating categories of at least two nationally recognized statistical rating organizations (as defined in Section 3(a)(62) of the Exchange Act).

(d) This section will expire and no longer be effective on December 31, 2009.

Rule 206(4)–1. Advertisements by Investment Advisers.

(a) It shall constitute a fraudulent, deceptive, or manipulative act, practice, or course of business within the meaning of Section 206(4) of the Act for any investment adviser registered or required to be registered under Section 203 of the Act, directly or indirectly, to publish, circulate, or distribute any advertisement:

(1) Which refers, directly or indirectly, to any testimonial of any kind concerning the investment adviser or concerning any advice, analysis, report or other service rendered by such investment adviser; or

(2) Which refers, directly or indirectly, to past specific recommendations of such investment adviser which were or would have been profitable to any person: *provided, however*, that this shall not prohibit an advertisement which sets out or offers to furnish a list of all recommendations made by such investment adviser within the immediately preceding period of not less than one year if such advertisement, and such list if it is furnished separately:

(A) State the name of each such security recommended, the date and nature of each such recommendation (e.g., whether to buy, sell or hold), the market price at that time, the price at which the recommendation was to be acted upon, and the market price of each such security as of the most recent practicable date, and

(B) contain the following cautionary legend on the first page thereof in print or type as large as the largest print or type used in the body or text thereof:

"It should not be assumed that recommendations made in the future will be profitable or will equal the performance of the securities in this list";

or

(3) Which represents, directly or indirectly, that any graph, chart, formula or other device being offered can in and of itself be used to determine which securities to buy or sell, or when to buy or sell them; or which represents directly or indirectly, that any graph, chart, formula or other device being offered will assist any person in making his own decisions as to which securities to buy, sell, or when to buy or sell them, without prominently disclosing in such advertisement the limitations thereof and the difficulties with respect to its use; or

(4) Which contains any statement to the effect that any report, analysis, or other service will be furnished free or without charge, unless such report, analysis or other service actually is or will be furnished entirely free and without any condition or obligation, directly or indirectly; or

(5) Which contains any untrue statement of a material fact, or which is otherwise false or misleading.

(b) For the purposes of this rule the term "advertisement" shall include any notice, circular, letter or other written communication addressed to more than one person, or any notice or other announcement in any publication or by radio or television, which offers (1) any analysis, report, or publication concerning securities, or which is to be used in making any determination as to when to buy or sell any security, or which security to buy or sell, or (2) any graph, chart, formula, or other device to be used in making any determination as to when to buy or sell any security, or which security to buy or sell, or (3) any other investment advisory service with regard to securities.

Rule 206(4)–2. Custody of Funds or Securities of Clients by Investment Advisers.

(a) *Safekeeping Required.* If you are an investment adviser registered or required to be registered under Section 203 of the Act, it is a fraudulent, deceptive, or manipulative act, practice or course of business within the meaning of Section 206(4) of the Act for you to have custody of client funds or securities unless:

(1) *Qualified Custodian.* A qualified custodian maintains those funds and securities:

(i) In a separate account for each client under that client's name; or

(ii) In accounts that contain only your clients' funds and securities, under your name as agent or trustee for the clients.

(2) *Notice to Clients.* If you open an account with a qualified custodian on your client's behalf, either under the client's name or under your name as agent, you notify the client in writing of the qualified custodian's name, address, and the man-

ner in which the funds or securities are maintained, promptly when the account is opened and following any changes to this information.

(3) *Account Statements to Clients.—*

(i) *By Qualified Custodian.* You have a reasonable basis for believing that the qualified custodian sends an account statement, at least quarterly, to each your clients for which it maintains funds or securities, identifying the amount of funds and of each security in the account at the end of the period and setting forth all transactions in the account during that period; or

(ii) *By Adviser.*

(A) You send a quarterly account statement to each of your clients for whom you have custody of funds or securities, identifying the amount of funds and of each security of which you have custody at the end of the period and setting forth all transactions during that period;

(B) An independent public accountant verifies all of those funds and securities by actual examination at least once during each calendar year at a time that is chosen by the accountant without prior notice or announcement to you and that is irregular from year to year, and files a certificate on Form ADV–E with the Commission within 30 days after the completion of the examination, stating that it has examined the funds and securities and describing the nature and extent of the examination; and

(C) The independent public accountant, upon finding any material discrepancies during the course of the examination, notifies the Commission within one business day of the finding, by means of a facsimile transmission or electronic mail, followed by first class mail, directed to the attention of the Director of the Office of Compliance Inspections and Examinations; and

(iii) *Special Rule* for *Limited Partnerships and Limited Liability Companies.* If you are a general partner of a limited partnership (or managing member of a limited liability company, or hold a comparable position for another type of pooled investment vehicle), the account statements required under paragraphs (a)(3)(i) or (a)(3)(ii) of this section must be sent to each limited partner (or member or other beneficial owner).

(4) *Independent Representatives.* A client may designate an independent representative to receive, on his behalf, notices and account statements as required under paragraphs (a)(2) and (a)(3) of this section.

(b) *Exceptions.*—

(1) *Shares of Mutual Funds.* With respect to shares of an open-end company as defined in Section 5(a)(1) of the Investment Company Act of 1940 ("mutual fund"), you may use the mutual

fund's transfer agent in lieu of a qualified custodian for purposes of complying with paragraph (a) of this section;

(2) *Certain Privately Offered Securities.*

(i) You are not required to comply with this section with respect to securities that are:

(A) Acquired from the issuer in a transaction or chain of transactions not involving any public offering;

(B) Uncertificated, and ownership thereof is recorded only on books of the issuer or its transfer agent in the name of the client; and

(C) Transferable only with prior consent of the issuer or holders of the outstanding securities of the issuer.

(ii) Notwithstanding paragraph (b)(2)(i) of this section, the provisions of this paragraph (b)(2) are available with respect to securities held for the account of a limited partnership (or limited liability company, or other type of pooled investment vehicle) only if the limited partnership is audited, and the audited financial statements are distributed, as described in paragraph (b)(3) of this section.

(3) *Limited Partnerships Subject to Annual Audit.* You are not required to comply with paragraph (a)(3) of this section with respect to the account of a limited partnership (or limited liability company, or another type of pooled investment vehicle) that is subject to audit (as defined

in Section 2(d) of Article 1 of Regulation S–X) at least annually and distributes its audited financial statements prepared in accordance with generally accepted accounting principles to all limited partners (or members or other beneficial owners) within 120 days of the end of its fiscal year, or in the case of a fund of funds within 180 days of the end of its fiscal year; and

(4) *Registered Investment Companies.* You are not required to comply with this section with respect to the account of an investment company registered under the Investment Company Act of 1940.

(c) *Definitions.* For the purposes of this section:

(1) "Custody" means holding, directly or indirectly, client funds or securities, or having any authority to obtain possession of them. Custody includes:

(i) Possession of client funds or securities, (but not of checks drawn by clients and made payable to third parties,) unless you receive them inadvertently and you return them to the sender promptly but in any case within three business days of receiving them;

(ii) Any arrangement (including a general power of attorney) under which you are authorized or permitted to withdraw client funds or securities maintained with a custodian upon your instruction to the custodian; and

(iii) Any capacity (such as general partner of a limited partnership, managing member of a limited liability company or a comparable position for another type of pooled investment vehicle, or trustee of a trust) that gives you or your supervised person legal ownership of or access to client funds or securities.

(2) "Independent representative" means a person that:

(i) Acts as agent for an advisory client, including in the case of a pooled investment vehicle, for limited partners of a limited partnership (or members of a limited liability company, or other beneficial owners of another type of pooled investment vehicle) and by law or contract is obliged to act in the best interest of the advisory client or the limited partners (or members, or other beneficial owners);

(ii) Does not control, is not controlled by, and is not under common control with you; and

(iii) Does not have, and has not had within the past two years, a material business relationship with you.

(3) "Qualified custodian" means:

(i) A bank as defined in Section 202(a)(2) of the Advisers Act or a savings association as defined in Section 3(b)(1) of the Federal Deposit Insurance Act that has deposits insured by the Federal Deposit Insurance Corporation under the Federal Deposit Insurance Act;

(ii) A broker-dealer registered under Section 15(b)(1) of the Securities Exchange Act of 1934, holding the client assets in customer accounts;

(iii) A futures commission merchant registered under Section 4f(a) of the Commodity Exchange Act, holding the client assets in customer accounts, but only with respect to clients' funds and security futures, or other securities incidental to transactions in contracts for the purchase or sale of a commodity for future delivery and options thereon; and

(iv) A foreign financial institution that customarily holds financial assets for its customers, provided that the foreign financial institution keeps the advisory clients' assets in customer accounts segregated from its proprietary assets.

(4) *Fund of funds* means a limited partnership (or limited liability company, or another type of pooled investment vehicle) that invests 10 percent or more of its total assets in other pooled investment vehicles that are not, and are not advised by, a related person (as defined in Form ADV), of the limited partnership, its general partner, or its adviser.

Rule 206(4)–3. Cash Payments for Client Solicitations.

(a) It shall be unlawful for any investment adviser required to be registered pursuant to Section 203 of the Act to pay a cash fee, directly or indirectly, to a solicitor with respect to solicitation activities unless:

(1)(i) The investment adviser is registered under the Act;

(ii) The solicitor is not a person (A) subject to a Commission order issued under Section 203(f)of the Act, or (B) convicted within the previous ten years of any felony or misdemeanor in-volving conduct described in Section 203(e)(2)(A) through (D) of the Act, or (C) who has been found by the Commission to have engaged, or has been convicted of engaging, in any of the conduct specified in paragraphs (1), (5) or (6) of Section 203(e) of the Act, or (D) is subject to an order, judgment or decree described in Section 203(e)(4) of the Act; and

(iii) Such cash fee is paid pursuant to a written agreement to which the adviser is a party; and

(2) Such cash fee is paid to a solicitor:

(i) With respect to solicitation activities for the provision of impersonal advisory services only; or

(ii) Who is (A) a partner, officer, director or employee of such investment adviser or (B) a partner, officer, director or employee of a per-son which controls, is controlled by, or is under common control with such investment adviser: *provided*, That the status of such solicitor as a partner, officer, director or employee of such investment adviser or other person, and any affiliation between the investment adviser and such other person, is disclosed to the client at the time of the solicitation or referral; or

(iii) Other than a solicitor specified in paragraph (a)(2)(i) or (ii) above if all of the following conditions are met:

(A) The written agreement required by paragraph (a)(1)(iii) of this rule: (1) Describes the solicitation activities to be engaged in by the solicitor on behalf of the investment adviser and the compensation to be received therefor; (2) contains an undertaking by the solicitor to perform his duties under the agreement in a manner consistent with the instructions of the investment adviser and the provisions of the Act and the rules thereunder; (3) requires that the solicitor, at the time of any solicitation activities for which compensation is paid or to be paid by the investment adviser, provide the client with a current copy of the investment adviser's written disclosure statement required by Rule 204–3 ("brochure rule") and a separate written disclosure document described in paragraph (b) of this rule.

(B) The investment adviser receives from the client, prior to, or at the time of, entering into any written or oral investment advisory contract with such client, a signed and dated acknowledgment of receipt of the investment adviser's written disclosure statement and the solicitor's written disclosure document.

(C) The investment adviser makes a *bona fide* effort to ascertain whether the solicitor has complied with the agreement, and has a reasonable basis for believing that the solicitor has so complied.

(b) The separate written disclosure document required to be furnished by the solicitor to the client pursuant to this section shall contain the following information:

(1) The name of the solicitor;

(2) The name of the investment adviser;

(3) The nature of the relationship, including any affiliation, between the solicitor and the investment adviser;

(4) A statement that the solicitor will be compensated for his solicitation services by the investment adviser;

(5) The terms of such compensation arrangement, including a description of the compensation paid or to be paid to the solicitor; and

(6) The amount, if any, for the cost of obtaining his account the client will be charged in addition to the advisory fee, and the differential, if any, among clients with respect to the amount or level of advisory fees charged by the investment adviser if such differential is attributable to the existence of any arrangement pursuant to which the investment adviser has agreed to compensate the solicitor for soliciting clients for, or referring clients to, the investment adviser.

(c) Nothing in this rule shall be deemed to relieve any person of any fiduciary or other obligation to which such person may be subject under any law.

(d) For purposes of this rule,

(1) "Solicitor" means any person who, directly or indirectly, solicits any client for, or refers any client to, an investment adviser.

(2) "Client" includes any prospective client.

(3) "Impersonal advisory services" means investment advisory services provided solely by means of (i) written materials or oral statements which do not purport to meet the objectives or needs of the specific client, (ii) statistical information containing no expressions of opinions as to the investment merits of particular securities, or (iii) any combination of the foregoing services.

Rule 206(4)–4. Financial and Disciplinary Information That Investment Advisers Must Disclose To Clients.

(a) It shall constitute a fraudulent, deceptive, or manipulative act, practice, or course of business within the meaning of Section 206(4) of the Act for any investment adviser registered or required to be registered under Section 203 of the Act to fail to disclose to any client or prospective client all material facts with respect to:

(1) A financial condition of the adviser that is reasonably likely to impair the ability of the adviser to meet contractual commitments to clients, if the adviser has discretionary authority (express or implied) or custody over such client's funds or securities, or requires prepayment of advisory

fees of more than $500 from such client, six months or more in advance; or

(2) A legal or disciplinary event that is material to an evaluation of the adviser's integrity or ability to meet contractual commitments to clients.

(b) It shall constitute a rebuttable presumption that the following legal or disciplinary events involving the adviser or a management person of the adviser (any of the foregoing being referred to hereafter as "person") that were not resolved in the person's favor or subsequently reversed, suspended, or vacated are material within the meaning of paragraph (a)(2) of the rule for a period of 10 years from the time of the event:

(1) A criminal or civil action in a court of competent jurisdiction in which the person—

(i) Was convicted, pleaded guilty or *nolo contendere* (no contest) to a felony or misdemeanor, or is the named subject of a pending criminal proceeding (any of the foregoing referred to hereafter as "action"), and such action involved: an investment-related business; fraud, false statements, or omissions; wrongful taking of property; or bribery, forgery, counterfeiting, or extortion;

(ii) Was found to have been involved in a violation of an investment-related statute or regulation; or

(iii) Was the subject of any order, judgment, or decree permanently or temporarily enjoining the person from, or otherwise limiting the person from, engaging in any investment-related activity.

(2) Administrative proceedings before the Securities and Exchange Commission, and other federal regulatory agency or any state agency (any of the foregoing being referred to hereafter as "agency") in which the person—

(i) Was found to have caused an investment-related business to lose its authorization to do business; or

(ii) Was found to have been involved in a violation of an investment-related statute or regulation and was the subject of an order by the agency denying, suspending, or revoking the authorization of the person to act in, or barring or suspending the person's association with, an investment-related business; or otherwise significantly limiting the person's investment-related activities.

(3) Self–Regulatory Organization (SRO) proceedings in which the person—

(i) Was found to have caused an investment-related business to lose its authorization to do business; or

(ii) Was found to have been involved in a violation of the SRO's rules and was the subject of an order by the SRO barring or suspending the person from membership or from association with other members, or expelling the person from membership; fining the person more than $2,500; or otherwise significantly limiting the person's investment-related activities.

(c) The information required to be disclosed by paragraph (a) shall be disclosed to clients promptly, and to prospective clients not less than 48 hours prior to entering into any written or oral investment advisory contract, or no later than the time of entering into such contract if the client has the right to terminate the contract without penalty within five business days after entering into the contract.

(d) For purposes of this rule:

(1) "Management person" means a person with power to exercise, directly or indirectly, a controlling influence over the management or policies of an adviser which is a company or to determine the general investment advice given to clients.

(2) "Found" means determined or ascertained by adjudication or consent in a final SRO proceeding, administrative proceeding, or court action.

(3) "Investment-related" means pertaining to securities commodities, banking, insurance, or real estate (including, but not limited to, action as or being associated with a broker, dealer, investment company, investment adviser, government securities broker or dealer, municipal securities dealer, bank, savings and loan association, entity or person required to be registered under the Commodity Exchange Act, or fiduciary).

(4) "Involved" means acting or aiding, abetting, causing, counseling, commanding, inducing, conspiring with or failing reasonably to supervise another in doing an act.

(5) "Self–Regulatory Organization" or "SRO" means any national securities or commodities exchange, registered association, or registered clearing agency.

(e) For purposes of calculating the 10–year period during which events are presumed to be material under paragraph (b), the date of a reportable event shall be the date on which the final order, judgment, or decree was entered, or the date on which any rights of appeal from preliminary orders, judgments, or decrees lapsed.

(f) Compliance with paragraph (b) shall not relieve any investment adviser from the disclosure obligations of paragraph (a): compliance with paragraph (a) shall not relieve any investment adviser from any other disclosure requirement under the Act, the rules and regulations thereunder, or under any other federal or state law.

Rule 206(4)–6. Proxy Voting.

If you are an investment adviser registered or required to be registered under Section 203 of the Act, it is a fraudulent, deceptive, or manipulative act, practice or course of business within the meaning of Section 206(4) of the Act, for you to exercise voting authority with respect to client securities, unless you:

(a) Adopt and implement written policies and procedures that are reasonably designed to ensure that you vote client securities in the best interest of clients, which procedures must include how you address material conflicts that may arise between your interests and those of your clients;

(b) Disclose to clients how they may obtain information from you about how you voted with respect to their securities; and

(c) Describe to clients your proxy voting policies and procedures and, upon request, furnish a copy of the policies and procedures to the requesting client.

Rule 206(4)–7. Compliance Procedures and Practices.

If you are an investment adviser registered or required to be registered under Section 203 of the Investment Advisers Act of 1940, it shall be unlawful within the meaning of Section 206 of the Act for you to provide investment advice to clients unless you:

(a) *Policies and Procedures.* Adopt and implement written policies and procedures reasonably designed to prevent violation, by you and your supervised persons, of the Act and the rules that the Commission has adopted under the Act;

(b) *Annual Review.* Review, no less frequently than annually, the adequacy of the policies and procedures established pursuant to this section and the effectiveness of their implementation; and

(c) *Chief Compliance Officer*. Designate an individual (who is a supervised person) responsible for administering the policies and procedures that you adopt under paragraph (a) of this section.

Rule 206(4)–8. Pooled Investment Vehicles.

(a) *Prohibition*. It shall constitute a fraudulent, deceptive, or manipulative act, practice, or course of business within the meaning of Section 206(4) of the Act for any investment adviser to a pooled investment vehicle to:

(1) Make any untrue statement of a material fact or to omit to state a material fact necessary to make the statements made, in the light of the circumstances under which they were made, not misleading, to any investor or prospective investor in the pooled investment vehicle; or

(2) Otherwise engage in any act, practice, or course of business that is fraudulent, deceptive, or manipulative with respect to any investor or prospective investor in the pooled investment vehicle.

(b) *Definition*. For purposes of this section "pooled investment vehicle" means any investment company as defined in Section 3(a) of the Investment Company Act of 1940 or any company that would be an investment company under Section 3(a) of that Act but for the exclusion provided from that definition by either Section 3(c)(1) or Section 3(c)(7) of that Act.

Rule 222–1. Definitions.

For purposes of Section 222 of the Act:

(a) *Place of Business.* "Place of business" of an investment adviser means:

(1) An office at which the investment adviser regularly provides investment advisory services, solicits, meets with, or otherwise communicates with clients; and

(2) Any other location that is held out to the general public as a location at which the investment adviser provides investment advisory services, solicits, meets with, or otherwise communicates with clients.

(b) *Principal Place of Business.* "Principal place of business" of an investment adviser means the executive office of the investment adviser from which the officers, partners, or managers of the investment adviser direct, control, and coordinate the activities of the investment adviser.

Rule 222–2. Definition of "Client" For Purposes of the National de Minimis Standard.

For purposes of Section 222(d)(2) of the Act (15 U.S.C. 80b–18a(d)(2)), an investment adviser may rely upon the definition of "client" provided by section 275.203(b)(3)–1 without giving regard to paragraph (b)(6) of that section.

INDEX

References are to Pages

ACCESS PERSON (see Code of Ethics)

ACCOUNTING
Accountants (as Investment Advisers) (see Investment Advisers)
Recordkeeping (see Recordkeeping Requirements)

ADVERTISING (by Investment Advisers)
    Generally, 128–151, 332, 334–335, 338, 345
Advertising Rule (Advisers Act Rule 206(4)–1), 129–138, 149
Association for Investment Management and Research (AIMR), 147
Definition of an "advertisement", 129–130
One-on-one presentation, 146–147
Performance information/results, 78, 128, 138–149
Portability of performance information, 147–151
Special Restrictions
    Charts, graphs and formulae, 135–136
    Free services, 136
    Past specific recommendations, 132–135
    Testimonials, 131–132
    Websites, 129

ADVERTISING RULE (see Advertising (by Investment Advisers))

ADVISERS ACT (see Investment Advisers Act of 1940)

ADVISORY AGREEMENTS (Contracts)
    Generally, 180–202
Arbitration provisions, 201–202

541

ADVISORY AGREEMENTS (Contracts)—Cont'd
Assignment of advisory contracts, 126, 182, 196–198, 372–375
Disclaimer of liability/indemnification provisions, 198–201
General contractual provisions, 181–182
Necessity of a writing, 180–181
Notification of change in partnership, 198
Prohibited provisions, 182–198
Termination, 202

ADVISORY SERVICES
Impersonalized, 36–39, 156, 159, 161–162
Personalized, 38–41, 156, 159–160, 162–164

AFFILIATED BROKERAGE (see Trading)

AGENCY CROSS TRANSACTIONS (see Trading)

AGGREGATION OF CLIENT ORDERS (see Trading)

AIMR (Association for Investment Management and Research)
(see Advertising (by Investment Advisers))

ALLOCATION OF SECURITIES AMONG CLIENTS (see Trading)

**ASSOCIATION FOR INVESTMENT MANAGEMENT AND RE-
SEARCH (AIMR)** (see Advertising (by Investment Advisers))

ANNUAL REPORT ON FORM N–PX (see Proxy Voting)

ASSET-BASED FEES (see Fees)

ASSETS UNDER MANAGEMENT, 5, 55–56, 58–62, 66–67, 70, 77,
81, 106, 108, 137, 184, 188, 194, 223, 277, 285, 331, 342, 368,
370–371

ASSIGNMENT (of Advisory Contract) (see Advisory Agreement
(Contracts))

BALANCE SHEET (Provision of), 116

**BANKS AND BANK HOLDING COMPANIES (as Investment
Advisers)** (see Investment Advisers)

BEST EXECUTION
Generally, 234–237
Conflicts of interest, 236
Continuing duties, 236–237
What constitutes best execution?, 235–236

BROCHURE (see Disclosure (to Clients))

BROCHURE RULE (Advisers Act Rule 204–3) (see Disclosure (to Clients))

BROKER-DEALER SAFE HARBOR (former Advisers Act Rule 202(a)(11)–1) (see Brokers and Dealers)

BROKERS AND DEALERS
Affiliated brokerage (see Brokerage Arrangements below)
As investment advisers
      Generally, 17, 21–35
    Definitional exclusion, 21–29
    Dual Registrants, 35, 196, 202, 233, 238–240, 247, 280, 374
    Exchange Act registration, 22
    Foreign broker-dealers, 29–30
    Other exclusions, 32–35
    Registered representative of a broker-dealer, 30–32
    "Solely incidental" requirement, 23–26
    "Special compensation" requirement, 26–29
Brokerage Arrangements
    Adviser benefitting from brokerage, 276–280
    Affiliated brokerage, 280–282
    Directed brokerage (by clients), 274–276
    Soft dollars (see Soft Dollars)
Broker–Dealer Safe Harbor (former Advisers Act Rule 202(a)(11)–1), 22–23, 25, 27, 29, 31–34, 43
Churning, 281, 286
Reverse churning, 286

BUSINESS DEVELOPMENT COMPANY, 46, 51–53, 95, 192–193, 195

CASH SOLICITATION RULE (Advisers Act Rule 206(4)–3) (see Solicitation and Referral Arrangements)

CARRIED INTEREST (see Fees)

CDOs (see Collateralized Debt Obligations)

CFMA (see Commodity Futures Modernization Act of 2000) (see Commodities)

CFTC (see Commodity Futures Trading Commission) (see Commodities)

CHIEF COMPLIANCE OFFICER
    Generally, 297, 300–301, 303, 325–339, 344
CCOutreach program (SEC's), 325
Code of ethics (see Code of Ethics)

CHIEF COMPLIANCE OFFICER—Cont'd
ComplianceAlert online newsletters (SEC's), 326
Compliance manual, 338–339
Necessity, 325–326
Role, 326–338

CHURNING (see Brokers and Dealers)

CLAIMS AGAINST THIRD PARTIES (Pursuing), 231–232

CODE OF ETHICS
Generally, 296–307, 309, 316–317, 330, 332, 335
Analogous rules for advisers with mutual fund clients, 306–307
Chief compliance officer (see Chief Compliance Officer)
Distinction between a "supervised person" and an "access person", 298–300
Ethics Code Rule (Advisers Act Rule 204A–1), 296–298, 300, 302, 304, 316–317
Pre-approval of certain investments, 304–306
Recordkeeping (see Recordkeeping Requirements)
Reporting requirements
Holdings reports, 301–303
Transaction reports, 303–304

COLLATERALIZED DEBT OBLIGATIONS (CDOs), 46, 67, 75, 93, 101–103

COMMODITIES
CFTC regulations affecting investment advisers, 71–74
Commodity Exchange Act (CEA), 71–73
Commodity Futures Modernization Act of 2000 (CFMA), 54
Commodity Futures Trading Commission (CFTC), 54, 71–74
Commodity pool operator, 73
Commodity trading adviser, 45, 53–54, 71–74, 107, 114
Exemption from registering as a commodity pool operator, 73–74
Exemption from registering as a commodity trading adviser, 71–73
National Futures Association, 73–74

COMMODITY FUTURES MODERNIZATION ACT OF 2000 (CFMA) (see Commodities)

COMMODITY FUTURES TRADING COMMISSION (CFTC) (see Commodities)

COMPANY ACT (see Investment Company Act of 1940)

COMPLIANCE, INSPECTION AND ENFORCEMENT
Generally, 340–367
Compliance, 109–110, 121, 155, 169–171, 176, 200, 237, 254, 267–268, 288, 290, 297, 325–327, 330–349, 351, 357, 370, 378
Compliance manual (see Chief Compliance Officer)
Culture of compliance, 332–333, 339, 342, 349
Enforcement
Generally, 62, 64–65, 94, 128, 137, 179, 213, 232, 246, 340–341, 343, 346, 351, 353–360
Adviser "cooperation", 356–360
Division of Enforcement (SEC's), 341, 347, 351, 353
Failure to supervise, 6, 327, 355–356
Policing advisers under Advisers Act Sections 203(e) & (f), 353–355
Inspection phases
Generally, 347–352
On-site inspection phase, 350–351
Post-inspection phase, 351–352
Pre-inspection phase, 348–350
Office of Compliance Inspections and Examinations (OCIE) (SEC's), 325, 342, 344–348, 350
Penalties
Generally, 360–364
Criminal penalties, 364
Monetary sanctions, 361–364
Non-monetary sanctions, 360–361
SEC inspections
Generally, 341–347
Cause inspections, 347
Examination results, 346–347
Inspection process, 344–346
Routine inspections, 342–347
Sweep inspections, 347

COMPLIANCE MANUAL (see Chief Compliance Officer)

CUSTODY AND POSSESSION (of Securities)
Generally, 58, 65, 108, 111, 116, 120, 121, 126, 175, 203, 217, 223–228, 264–265, 268–269, 309, 320–321, 338, 342, 345
Custody Rule (Advisers Act Rule 206(4)–2), 223–226
Exceptions to the Custody Rule, 227–228
Recordkeeping (see Recordkeeping Requirements)

DEPARTMENT OF LABOR (U.S.) (see ERISA)

DIRECTED BROKERAGE (by Clients) (see Brokers and Dealers)

DISCLOSURE (to Clients)
    Generally, 3, 7, 65, 75–76, 84, 104–105, 112, 117, 141–144,
        155–156, 158, 160–164, 169–180, 182, 218, 220–221,
        240–243, 275, 285, 290–294, 315, 328, 337, 345
Adverse financial conditions and disciplinary events
        Generally, 174–177
    Legal or disciplinary events presumptively subject to disclo-
        sure, 177–178
    Timing and delivery of disclosure, 178–180
Brochure Rule (Advisers Act Rule 204–3)
        Generally, 104, 111, 116–117, 160, 163, 169–173, 180, 203,
            284–285, 290–291, 313, 315, 328
    Contents of brochure, 111–117, 172–173
    Hedge fund advisers, 173–174
    Timing of delivery, 171–172
Form ADV (see Form ADV)
Solicitor disclosure document (see Solicitation and Referral
    Agreements)
Wrap fee brochure (see Wrap Fee Programs)
Wrap fee program (see Wrap Fee Programs)

DISCLOSURE REPORTING PAGE (DRP) (see Form ADV)

DRP (Disclosure Reporting Page) (see Form ADV)

DUAL REGISTRANT (see Brokers and Dealers)

**EARNINGS BEFORE INCOME, TAXES, DEPRECIATION AND
    AMORTIZATION (EBITDA),** 371

EBITDA (see Earnings Before Income, Taxes, Depreciation and
    Amortization)

EDGAR (see Electronic, Data, Gathering, Analysis, and Retrieval
    system)

EFFECTIVENESS OF FORM ADV (see Form ADV)

**ELECTRONIC, DATA, GATHERING, ANALYSIS, AND RETRIEV-
    AL SYSTEM (EDGAR) (SEC's),** 321

**EMPLOYEE RETIREMENT INCOME SECURITY ACT OF 1974
    (ERISA)**
    Generally, 57, 67–70, 181, 217, 222, 233, 254
Bonding requirements, 69–70
Department of Labor (U.S.), 68–70, 381

EMPLOYEE RETIREMENT INCOME SECURITY ACT OF 1974 (ERISA)—Cont'd
"Handling" retirement plan assets, 69–70
Investment manager, 68
Qualified professional asset manager (QPAM), 68–69

ENFORCEMENT PROCEEDINGS (see Compliance, Inspection and Enforcement)

ENGINEERS (as Investment Advisers) (see Investment Advisers)

ERISA (see Employee Retirement Income Security Act of 1974)

ETHICS CODE RULE (Advisers Act Rule 204A–1) (see Code of Ethics)

EXCHANGE ACT (see Securities Exchange Act of 1934)

FAIR CREDIT REPORTING ACT, 209

FEES
    Generally, 5, 10, 16, 24, 27–28, 33, 40, 44, 60–61, 64–65, 77–78, 88–89, 100, 111–112, 116–117, 137, 141–144, 146, 163, 168, 172–173, 175, 181–196, 202, 243–244, 246–247, 272, 277, 329, 331, 337, 338, 343, 368–371, 375
Abusive fee arrangements, 184–187
Asset-based fees, 188, 246–247
Performance Fees
    Carried interest, 78, 84, 378
    Exceptions to performance fee prohibition
        Generally, 187–188
      Asset-based fees, 188, 246–247
      Business development companies, 192–193
      Fulcrum fees
        Generally, 188–190
        Choosing an appropriate index, 190–191
        Making the comparison, 191–192
      Hedge fund advisers, 195–196
      NASD Conduct Rule 2330(f), 196
      Non–U.S. resident clients, 193–194
      "Qualified Clients", 194–195
      Section 3(c)(7) funds, 193
    General prohibition, 10, 44, 65, 88–89, 168, 182–196
Wrap fees (see Wrap Fee Programs)

FIDUCIARY OBLIGATIONS (of Investment Advisers)
　　Generally, 3, 33, 90–91, 155, 169, 181, 185, 187, 200, 202, 215,
　　　　217–232, 234, 240, 242, 244–245, 249, 252–254, 278,
　　　　281, 283, 295–297, 300, 304, 316, 329, 369
Care, 222
Disclosure, 218–221, 244, 278
Loyalty and fairness, 221–222

FINANCIAL INDUSTRY REGULATORY AUTHORITY (FINRA), 21,
　　118, 138, 196, 229, 234, 248, 264, 280, 353, 375

FINRA (see Financial Industry Regulatory Authority)

FORM ADV
　　Generally, 59–61, 66–67, 104–127, 146, 164, 170, 172–173,
　　　　175, 181, 222, 225–226, 236, 243, 276, 281, 284–285,
　　　　290–292, 313, 328, 337–338, 342, 344, 372, 378
Amendments, 119–122, 337
Brochure (see Disclosure (to Clients))
Disclosing conflicts of interest, 218–221, 244, 278
Disclosure Reporting Page (DRP), 109
Disclosure Schedule, 109
Effectiveness, 122–124
Filing, 117–119
Filing fee, 118–119, 127
Fraud, 124–125
Information concerning affiliated persons, 108–110
Part 1A, 105–109
Part 1B, 109–111
Part II, 111–117
Qualification
　　Advisers, 122–125
　　Associated persons, 125
State notice filings, 126–127
Suspension and revocation, 124–125
Withdrawal, 66–67, 98, 125–126

FORM ADV–E, 226

FORM ADV–H, 119

FORM ADV–W, 66–67, 98, 126

FORM N–PX (see Proxy Voting)

FRONT RUNNING (Practice of), 218, 295

FULCRUM FEES (see Fees)

GAAP (see generally accepted accounting principles)

GENERALLY ACCEPTED ACCOUNTING PRINCIPLES (GAAP), 227

GLASS-STEAGALL BANKING ACT OF 1933 (GSA), 6

GLBA (see Gramm–Leach–Bliley Financial Modernization Act of 1999)

GOVERNMENT ENTITIES (as Investment Advisers) (see Investment Advisers)

GOVERNMENTAL SECURITIES ADVISERS (as Investment Advisers) (see Investment Advisers)

GRAMM-LEACH–BLILEY FINANCIAL MODERNIZATION ACT OF 1999 (GLBA), 6, 203–204, 297

GSA (see Glass–Steagall Banking Act of 1933)

HEDGE FUND ADVISERS
  Generally, 4, 7, 46, 48–49, 51, 67, 75–103, 173–174, 183, 195–196, 207, 220, 378–379
  Exemption from Advisers Act registration, 46–53, 82–83, 173–174
  Former hedge fund adviser registration provisions
    Generally, 7, 83–92
    Counting "clients" under the former provisions, 86–88
    Definition of a "private fund", 85–86
    Demise of the former provisions, 89–98
    Withdrawing previous registration, 98–100
  Private equity advisers, 270, 378

HEDGE FUNDS
  Generally, 6–7, 46, 48–49, 51, 61, 75–103, 173, 196, 207, 227, 253, 283, 343
  Definition, 77–78
  Exemptions from Company Act registration
    Section 3(c)(1) of the Company Act, 78–80, 82
    Section 3(c)(7) of the Company Act, 78, 80–82
  Private equity funds, 4, 46, 82, 86, 93, 97, 207, 283
  Retailization of hedge funds, 89, 95–96

IAR (see Investment Adviser Representative)

IARD (see Investment Adviser Registration Depository)

INITIAL PUBLIC OFFERING (IPO), 246–247, 305, 317, 334, 378–379

INSIDER TRADING (see Code of Ethics)

INSPECTIONS (SEC) (see Compliance, Inspection and Enforcement)

INTERNAL CROSS TRANSACTIONS (see Trading)

INTERNAL REVENUE CODE OF 1986 (IRC), 53, 217

INVESTMENT ADVISER
Accountants (as investment advisers), 17, 19–20
Advertising (see Advertising (by Investment Advisers))
Banks and bank holding companies (as investment advisers), 17–18
Brokers and dealers (as investment advisers) (see Brokers and Dealers)
Compensation (see also Fees), 15–16
Definition, 9–16
Definitional exclusions, 16–44
Disqualification of advisers, 124–126
Engineers (as investment advisers), 17, 19–21
Fiduciary duties (see Fiduciary Obligations (of Investment Advisers))
Government securities advisers (as investment advisers), 17, 42
Governmental entities (as investment advisers), 44
"In the business" (of being an investment adviser), 13–15
Lawyers (as investment advisers), 17, 19–21
Nationally Recognized Statistical Rating Organizations (NRSROs) (as investment advisers), 42–43
Providing advice concerning securities, 11–13
Publishers (as investment advisers), 17, 35–42
Purchase of investment adviser (see Purchase and Sale (of Investment Advisers))
Qualification of advisers, 122–124
Recordkeeping requirements (see Recordkeeping Requirements)
Registration (see Registration of Investment Advisers)
Sale of investment adviser (see Purchase and Sale (of Investment Advisers))
Savings associations (as investment advisers), 17–18
Teachers (as investment advisers), 17, 19–21

INVESTMENT ADVISER REGISTRATION DEPOSITORY (IARD), 98, 117–118, 122, 126–127

INVESTMENT ADVISER REPRESENTATIVE (IAR), 63–64, 127, 167–168

INVESTMENT ADVISERS ACT OF 1940 (Advisers Act)
Evolution, 3–8
Historical overview, 1–8
Rules cited (see Table of Statutes and Rules in front portion of book)
Sections cited (see Table of Statutes and Rules in front portion of book)

INVESTMENT ADVISERS SUPERVISION COORDINATION ACT, 55

INVESTMENT COMPANY ACT OF 1940 (Company Act)
IPO (see Initial Public Offering)
Rules cited (see Table of Statutes and Rules in front portion of book)
Sections cited (see Table of Statutes and Rules in front portion of book)

IRC (see Internal Revenue Code of 1986)

LAWYERS (as Investment Advisers) (see Investment Advisers)

LEVERAGE, 71, 76

LIABILITIES, 68, 199, 369, 371

LIMITED OFFERING, 97, 305, 317

NASD (see National Association of Securities Dealers, Inc.)

NATIONAL ASSOCIATION OF SECURITIES DEALERS, INC. (NASD), 21, 118–119, 138, 196, 229, 233–234, 247–248, 264, 278, 280, 375

NATIONAL FUTURES ASSOCIATION (see Commodities)

NATIONALLY RECOGNIZED STATISTICAL RATING ORGANI-ZATION (NRSRO), 8, 17, 42–43, 57

NATIONAL SECURITIES MARKETS IMPROVEMENT ACT OF 1996 (NSMIA), 5, 55, 167, 340

NEGATIVE CONSENT SOLICITATION (see Purchase and Sale (of Investment Advisers))

NEW YORK STOCK EXCHANGE, INC. (NYSE), 21, 196, 229, 234, 248, 251, 264, 280, 375, 379

NOTICE FILINGS (with States) (see Form ADV)

NRSRO (see Nationally Recognized Statistical Rating Organization)

NSMIA (see National Securities Markets Improvement Act of 1996)

NYSE (see New York Stock Exchange, Inc.)

OCIE (SEC's Office of Compliance Inspections and Examinations) (see Compliance, Inspection and Enforcement)

OFFICE OF COMPLIANCE INSPECTIONS AND EXAMINATIONS (OCIE) (SEC's) (see Compliance, Inspection and Enforcement)

OTC (Over-the-Counter), 239

PERFORMANCE FEES (see Fees)

PHILANTHROPY PROTECTION ACT OF 1995, 52

PRINCIPAL TRANSACTIONS (see Trading)

PRIVACY (of Consumer Financial Information) (Regulation S–P)
Generally, 203–216
Clients covered, 206–207
Information covered, 205–206
Investment advisers covered, 207
Notice requirements, 207–210
Opt out options
    Generally, 210–215
  Exceptions
      Generally, 212–213
    Joint marketing, 213
    Other exceptions, 214–215
    Processing and servicing transactions, 214
    Service providers, 213
Procedural safeguards, 215–216
Relationship to state laws, 216

PRIVATE ADVISER REGISTRATION EXEMPTION (Advisers Act Section 203(b)(3)) (See Private Investment Advisers)

PRIVATE EQUITY ADVISERS (see Hedge Fund Advisers)

PRIVATE EQUITY FUNDS (see Hedge Funds)

PRIVATE INVESTMENT ADVISERS
Generally, 45–47, 49–51, 82–83, 85–87, 90–91, 98–99, 101–102, 173, 183, 195, 207, 220, 377
Private Adviser Registration Exemption (Advisers Act Section 203(b)(3))
Generally, 46–51, 49–51, 82–83, 85–87, 90–91, 98–99, 101–102, 173, 195, 207, 220
Business development companies, 51–52
"Fewer than 15 clients", 47–50
General rules on counting clients, 47–49
"Holding itself out" as an investment adviser generally to the public, 50–51
Registered investment companies, 51–52
Special rules on counting clients, 47, 49–50

PRIVATE RIGHT OF ACTION
Limited implied private right of action, 368–370
No express private right of action, 368
Other actions possible, 370
Under Advisers Act Rule 206(4)–8, 94

PROPRIETARY TRADING (see Code of Ethics)

PROXY VOTING
Generally, 228–231, 329, 374
Annual Report on Form N–PX, 231
Proxy Voting Rule (Advisers Act Rule 206(4)–6), 230, 321
Proxy voting under the Advisers Act, 229–231
Proxy voting under the Company Act, 231
Recordkeeping (see Recordkeeping Requirements)

PUBLISHERS (as Investment Advisers) (see Investment Advisers)

PURCHASE AND SALE (of Investment Advisers)
Generally, 371–376
Assignment of advisory contracts (see Advisory Agreements (Contracts))
Employment contracts, 375–376
Negative consent solicitation, 197–198, 373–375

RACKETEER INFLUENCED AND CORRUPT ORGANIZATIONS ACT (RICO), 370

RECORDKEEPING REQUIREMENTS
Generally, 7, 10, 44, 75–76, 229, 267, 295, 300, 308–324, 332
Foreign advisers, 323–324

RECORDKEEPING REQUIREMENTS—Cont'd

Means of storage, 322–323

Recordkeeping Rule (Advisers Act Rule 204–2), 100, 126, 130, 139, 150–151, 158, 164, 170, 226, 230, 298, 300, 302–303, 306, 308–315, 318, 320–323, 331

Required books and records

    Generally, 308–322

    Accounting and related records, 310–311

    Adviser formation, governance and ownership documents, 310

    Client relationship records, 311–313

    Code of ethics, 316–317

    Custody records, 320–321

    Marketing and performance information, 313–315

    Personal and proprietary trading information, 316–317

    Portfolio management and trading records, 317–320

    Proxy related records, 321–322

    Solicitor records, 315–316

RECORDKEEPING RULE (Advisers Act Rule 204–2) (see Recordkeeping Requirements)

REFERRAL ARRANGEMENTS (see Solicitation and Referral Arrangements)

REGISTRATION OF INVESTMENT ADVISERS

Generally, 4, 6–10, 17, 31, 36, 44–56, 58–59, 61–62, 66–67, 75–127, 156–157, 165–169, 173, 182–183, 187, 195–196, 198, 207, 220, 287–289, 305, 328, 337, 340, 353–354, 360–361, 365–366, 372, 378

Exemption from registration

    Generally, 44–54

    Advisers to insurance companies only, 45–46

    Charitable organizations, 45, 52–53

    Church plans, 45, 53

    Commodities trading advisers, 45, 53–54

    Intrastate advisers, 45–46

    Private investment advisers (see Private Investment Advisers)

Federal (SEC) registration

    Generally, 55–62

    "Assets under management", 60–61

    Disclosure (see Disclosure (to Clients))

    Mandatory Federal registration, 56–58

    Optional Federal registration, 58–60

    State authority over SEC-registered investment advisers, 61–62

REGISTRATION OF INVESTMENT ADVISERS—Cont'd
Form ADV (see Form ADV)
National De Minimus Standard, 63
State registration
      Generally, 55–56, 62–66
   SEC authority over state-registered investment advisers,
      64–66
Transitioning from Federal (SEC) registration to state registra-
    tion, 66–67
Transitioning from state registration to Federal (SEC) registra-
    tion, 66

REGISTRATION STATEMENT (see Form ADV)

REGULATION A (Securities Act) (see Table of Statutes and
    Rules in front portion of book)

REGULATION D (Securities Act) (see Table of Statutes and
    Rules in front portion of book)

REGULATION S (Securities Act) (see Table of Statutes and
    Rules in front portion of book)

RELATED PERSON, 107–108, 114–116, 228

RETAILIZATION OF HEDGE FUNDS (see Hedge Funds)

REVERSE CHURNING (see Brokers and Dealers)

RICO (see Racketeer Influenced and Corrupt Organizations Act)

SARBANES-OXLEY ACT OF 2002 (SOX), 297, 378

SAVINGS ASSOCIATIONS (as Investment Advisers) (see In-
    vestment Advisers)

SCALPING (Practice of), 40, 218, 295

SEC (see Securities and Exchange Commission)

SECTION 3(C)(1) FUND, 78–82, 195

SECTION 3(C)(7) FUND, 80–81, 187, 193, 195

SECURITIES
Custody and possession (see Custody and Possession (of Securi-
    ties))
Definition, 12–13

SECURITIES ACT (see Securities Act of 1933)

SECURITIES ACT OF 1933 (Securities Act)
Rules cited (see Table of Statutes and Rules in front portion of book)
Sections cited (see Table of Statutes and Rules in front portion of book)

SECURITIES AND EXCHANGE COMMISSION (SEC)
Enforcement (see Compliance, Inspection & Enforcement)
Inspection (see Compliance, Inspection & Enforcement)

SECURITIES EXCHANGE ACT OF 1934 (Exchange Act)
Rules cited (see Table of Statutes and Rules in front portion of book)
Sections cited (see Table of Statutes and Rules in front portion of book)

SELF-REGULATORY ORGANIZATION (SRO), 110, 121, 178, 196, 202, 264–265, 273, 353, 364

SMALL BUSINESS INVESTMENT INCENTIVE ACT OF 1980, 52, 192

SOFT DOLLARS
Generally, 70, 251–274, 283
"Give ups", 271–272
Historical background, 251–252
Safe Harbor (Exchange Act Section 28(e))
　　　Generally, 252–254
　　Compliance, 254–274
　　Eligibility criteria for "brokerage"
　　　　Generally, 264–269
　　　Custody, 268–269
　　　Ineligible overhead, 267–268
　　　Temporal standard, 265–267
　　"Lawful and appropriate assistance", 263–264
　　Linkage between "provided by" and "effecting", 271–274
　　"Mixed-use" items, 255, 261, 269–270
　　"Reasonableness" determination, 270–271
　　"Research services"
　　　　Generally, 256–257
　　　Data, 262–263
　　　Inherently tangible products and services, 259–260
　　　Market research, 260–261
　　　Mass-marketed publications, 258–259
　　　Proxy services, 263
　　　"Section 28(e) arrangements", 272
　　　Third-party research, 261–262

SOLICITATION AND REFERRAL ARRANGEMENTS
Generally, 152–169
Affiliated solicitors, 156, 158–159, 161, 165, 168
Cash compensation generally, 152–153
Cash Solicitation Rule (Advisers Act Rule 206(4)–3)
Disclosure requirements, 160–164
Investment adviser requirements, 156–157
Solicitor requirements, 157–158
Supervisory requirements, 164
Written solicitation agreement, 158–160, 329, 338
Definition of "solicitor", 154–155
Non-cash compensation, 153, 164–166, 276
Recordkeeping (see Recordkeeping Requirements)
Referral fee, 152, 154–156, 158, 276
Registration status of solicitors
Solicitor for an SEC-registered investment adviser, 165–168
Solicitor for a state-registered investment adviser, 168–169
Unaffiliated solicitors
Promotion of impersonal advisory services, 156, 159, 161–162
Promotion of personalized advisory services, 156, 159–160, 162–164

SOLICITORS (see Solicitation and Referral Arrangements)

SOX (see Sarbanes–Oxley Act of 2002)

SRO (see Self–Regulatory Organization)

STATE NOTICE FILINGS (see Form ADV)

STOCK MARKET CRASH OF 1929, 1

SUITABILITY
Generally, 232–234, 337–338
Dual Registrants, 233–234
Proposed Advisers Act Suitability Rule (Abandoned), 232–233

TEACHERS (as Investment Advisers) (see Investment Advisers)

TIA (see Trust Indenture Act of 1939)

TOUTING (Practice of), 40

TRADING
Affiliated brokerage (see Brokerage Arrangements)
Aggregation of client orders, 248–251, 320
Allocation of securities among clients
Generally, 245–248

TRADING—Cont'd
Allocation of securities among clients—Cont'd
    Allocation statement, 250, 319
    NASD Conduct Rule 2790, 247–248
Best execution (see Best Execution)
Directed brokerage (by clients) (see Brokers and Dealers)
Investments in investment companies, 244–245
Principal and cross transactions
        Generally, 103, 237–244
    Agency cross transactions, 65, 103, 217, 237, 240–243, 281
    Internal cross transactions, 242–244
    Principal transactions, 217, 237–240, 281
    Riskless principal transactions, 253, 281
Soft dollars (see Soft Dollars)
Trading errors, 268, 282–283, 334

TRUST INDENTURE ACT OF 1939 (TIA), 1

VENTURE CAPITAL FUND, 52, 86, 93, 95, 192

WRAP FEE PROGRAMS
    Generally, 284–294
Negotiability, 285–286
Program structures, 286–287
Registration requirements, 287–290
Reverse churning (see Brokers and Dealers)
Wrap fee brochure (disclosure)
        Generally, 290–294
    Contents, 292–293
    Delivery, 293
    Updating, 293–294

†